An Introduction to
Ray Tracing

An Introduction to Ray Tracing

Edited by
ANDREW S. GLASSNER

Xerox PARC
3333 Coyote Hill Road
Palo Alto CA 94304
USA

ACADEMIC PRESS
Harcourt Brace & Company Publishers
London · San Diego · New York · Boston
Sydney · Tokyo · Toronto

ACADEMIC PRESS LIMITED
24/28 Oval Road, London NW1 7DX

United States Edition Published by
ACADEMIC PRESS INC.
San Diego, CA 92101

British Library Cataloguing in Publication Data

An Introduction to ray tracing.
 1. Computer systems. Graphic displays. Three-dimensional images.
 I. Glassner, Andrew
 006.6

ISBN 0-12-286160-4

Typeset by Mathematical Composition Setters Ltd, Salisbury
Printed in Great Britain at the University Press, Cambridge

Contributors

James Arvo, Apollo Computer Inc., 330 Billerica Road, Chelmsford, MA 01824, USA.

Robert L. Cook, Pixar, 3240 Kerner Blvd, San Rafael, CA 94901, USA.

Andrew S. Glassner, Xerox PARC, 3333 Coyote Hill Road, Palo Alto CA 94304, USA.

Eric Haines, 3D/Eye Inc., 2359 North Triphammer Road, Ithaca, NY 14850, USA.

Pat Hanrahan, Pixar, 3240 Kerner Blvd., San Rafael, CA 94901, USA

Paul S. Heckbert, 508-7 Evans Hall, UC Berkeley, Berkeley, CA 94720, USA.

David Kirk, Apollo Computer Inc., 330 Billerica Road, Chelmsford, MA 01824, USA. (Current address: California Institute of Technology, Computer Science 256-80, Pasadena, CA 91125, USA.)

Contents

Preface

This is a book about computer graphics, and the creation of realistic images. By 'realistic' we mean an image that is indistinguishable from a photograph of a real, three-dimensional scene. Of the many computer techniques that have been developed to create images, perhaps the algorithm called 'ray tracing' is now the most popular for many applications. Part of the beauty of ray tracing is its extreme simplicity — once you know the necessary background, the whole thing can be summed up in a paragraph.

This book begins with an introduction to the technique of ray tracing, describing how and why it works. Following chapters describe many of the theoretical and practical details of the complete algorithm.

I'd like to say something about how ray tracing came about in computer graphics, and how this book in particular came to be. Then I'll briefly summarize the various chapters.

A BIT OF HISTORY

Finding a way to create 'photorealistic' images has been a goal of computer graphics for many years. Generally, graphics researchers make progress by first examining the world around them, and then looking at the best computer-generated images made to date. If the computer image doesn't look as good (and even now, it usually doesn't), one asks, 'What's missing from the computer picture?' In the beginning, many features of real scenes were rapidly included in computer-generated images. Some of these improvements were made by noting that opaque objects hide objects behind them, shiny objects have highlights, and many surfaces have a surface texture, such as a wooden grain. Methods were developed to include these effects into computer-generated scenes, and so those images looked better and better.

One of the first of these successful image synthesis methods started with an idea from the physics literature. When designing lenses, physicists tradition-ally plotted on paper the path taken by rays of light starting at a light source, then passing through the lens and slightly beyond. This process of following the light rays was called 'ray tracing'.

Several computer graphics researchers thought that this simulation of light physics would be a good way to create a synthetic image. This was a good idea, but unfortunately in the early 1960s computers were too slow to make images that looked better than those made with other, cheaper image synthesis methods. Ray tracing fell out of favor, and not much attention was paid to it for several years.

As time went by, a flurry of other algorithms were developed to handle all kinds of interesting aspects of real photographs: reflections, shadows, motion blur of fast-moving objects, and so on. But most of these algorithms only worked in special cases, and they usually didn't work very well with each other. Thus you would find a picture with shadows, but no transparency, or another image with reflection, but no motion blur.

As computers became more powerful, it seemed increasingly attractive to go back and simulate the real physics. The ray tracing algorithm was extended and improved, giving it the power to handle many different kinds of optical effects.

Today ray tracing is one of the most popular and powerful techniques in the image synthesis repertoire: it is simple, elegant, and easily implemented. There are some aspects of the real world that ray tracing doesn't handle very well (or at all!) as of this writing. Perhaps the most important omissions are diffuse inter-reflections (e.g. the 'bleeding' of colored light from a dull red file cabinet onto a white carpet, giving the carpet a pink tint), and caustics (focused light, like the shimmering waves at the bottom of a swimming pool). Ray tracing may one day be able to create images indistinguishable from photographs of real scenes — or perhaps some other, more powerful algorithm will be developed to take its place. Nevertheless, right now many people feel that ray tracing is one of the best overall image synthesis techniques we've got, and as work continues it will become even more efficient and realistic.

HOW THIS BOOK CAME TO BE

This book is a revised and edited version of reference material prepared for an intensive one-day course on ray tracing. Since this book grew out of the organization and goals of the course. I'd like to describe how the course came about, and what we were trying to do with this material.

In late 1986, I felt that there was a need to have an introductory course on ray tracing at the annual meeting of SIGGRAPH (the Special Interest Group on Computer Graphics, which is part of the ACM, the society of computer professionals). Each year SIGGRAPH mounts a very large conference, covering many aspects of computer graphics. An important part of each SIGGRAPH conference is the presentation of one-day courses. There have been several courses at recent SIGGRAPHs reviewing developments in ray tracing for experts, but I felt that ray tracing had become popular enough that there should be an introductory course.

I made some phone calls, and gathered together a group of internationally-recognized researchers in the field to present our new course. Our goal from the beginning was to teach to a 'typical' SIGGRAPH audience: artists, managers, scientists, programmers, and anyone else who was interested!

Most SIGGRAPH courses include some kind of 'course notes' handed out to attendees. Since part of the reason we were teaching the course was that there was no introductory material available, we decided to write our own. As chairman of the course, I decided to ask everyone to write original, high-quality material for our course notes, and happily most of the speakers had the time and energy to do so.

The course's name was An Introduction To Ray Tracing. It was a great success at SIGGRAPH '87 in Anaheim — it was one of the two most heavily-attended courses. The response in 1987 was very good, so we decided to give the course again. With a slightly different cast we repeated the course at SIGGRAPH '88 in Atlanta. We took the opportunity to revise and improve the notes.

This book is essentially the notes from SIGGRAPH '88, edited and improved. It includes a few things we couldn't get into the notes, or that didn't come across well: color plates, good black-and-white images, a bibliography, and a glossary.

A QUICK LOOK AT THE CONTENTS

As you look over the book, remember that the level of the material varies considerably from chapter to chapter. Some chapters are very basic and assume little background, while others expect you to have some mathematical experience. The more complex chapters are for more advanced study: you can get quite far with just the less mathematical chapters.

The book begins with 'An Overview of Ray Tracing'. This opening chapter assumes little background from the reader. We tell how a synthetic image is produced, and how ray tracing works to create an image. When you're done reading this, you won't be in a position to write a program, but you should be able to understand ray tracing discussions, including most of the other chapters.

We then discuss 'Essential Ray Tracing Algorithms'. The fundamental operation in any ray tracing program is the intersection of a ray with an object. Because it's such an important step, it is important to understand it clearly. We show how to find the intersection of a ray with several important shapes, and how to write the necessary computer procedures.

More complicated kinds of objects are discussed in 'A Survey of Ray–Object Intersection Algorithms'. Because more complex shapes have more complex mathematical descriptions, the math in this section is necessarily more involved. You don't need to understand everything in this chapter to get started in ray tracing: it's more of a springboard to help you move on to more advanced topics, once you've got some momentum.

To properly compute how rays interact with surfaces, we discuss 'Surface Physics for Ray Tracing'. This chapter gives a lot of basic information that you'll need to actually get your programs running, including color descriptions, laws of optics, and surface coloring.

If you're not careful, computer-generated pictures will contain lots of ugly artifacts that don't belong in a picture, due to the nature of digital computers and the ray tracing process itself. We discuss those artifacts and how to avoid them in 'Stochastic Sampling and Distributed Ray Tracing'. The material in this chapter will help your pictures avoid nasty artifacts that don't belong in a 'realistic' picture.

'A Survey of Ray Tracing Acceleration Techniques' addresses the issue of speed. The basic ray tracing algorithm is extremely simple, but also extremely slow. It's like saying, 'To build a sand dune, pick up a grain of sand, and carry it over to where you're building the dune: do this over and over again'. The instructions are correct, but painfully slow. Lots of research has gone into ways to make ray tracing programs run faster. The bad news is that most of these techniques greatly complicated the basically simple and elegant ray tracing algorithm. The good news is that by using these methods you can make a picture much faster than with straightforward techniques.

By the time you reach the end of the book, you'll be ready for hints on 'Writing A Ray Tracer'. Writing a program is usually greatly simplified if you have a plan of attack, or a structure for building the various pieces and describing their interconnections. In this chapter we give a good organization for a ray-tracing program that is both simple to build and easy to extend. The concepts are illustrated with sample code in the C programming language.

Where can you go for more information? Well, each chapter in the book comes with its own bibliography, keyed to the material in that chapter. If you want more, then you can consult the 'Ray Tracing Bibliography'.

If you forget the meaning of a word, you can probably find it in 'A Ray Tracing Glossary'. Here we give definitions for most of the important terms used in this book, plus some other terms that you might find in the literature. Some of the entries are illustrated, since after all this is a book on graphics!

ACKNOWLEDGEMENTS

The SIGGRAPH course and this book represent the combined efforts of many people. Thanks to Mike and Cheri Bailey, who together administered the

SIGGRAPH courses in 1987 and 1988. Thanks also to the A/V squad and student volunteers at both conferences, who helped keep the courses running smoothly.

While putting together both courses and then this book, I was a graduate student in Computer Science at the University of North Carolina at Chapel Hill. My department generously made available to me its resources to help manage these projects. I thank my advisors Dr Frederick P. Brooks, Jr. and Dr Henry Fuchs, for their support.

I know that we have enjoyed writing this book. I hope some of our excitement about ray tracing and image synthesis comes through, and before too long you'll be making pictures of your own. Good luck!

Andrew S. Glassner
Palo Alto, California

1 An Overview of Ray Tracing

ANDREW S. GLASSNER

1 IMAGE SYNTHESIS

1.1 Introduction

Ray tracing is a technique for *image synthesis*: creating a 2-D picture of a 3-D world.

In this article we assume you have some familiarity with basic computer graphics concepts, such as the idea of a *frame buffer*, a *pixel*, and an *image plane*. We will use the term pixel in this article to describe three different, related concepts: a small region of a monitor, an addressable location in a frame buffer, and a small region on the image plane in the 3-D virtual world. Typically, these three devices (monitor, frame buffer, and image plane) are closely related, and the region covered by a pixel on one has a direct correspondence to the others. We will find it convenient to sometimes blur the distinction between these different devices and refer to the image plane as 'the screen.'

Most computer graphics are created for viewing on a flat screen or piece of paper. A common goal is to give the viewer the impression of looking at a photograph (or movie) of some three-dimensional scene. Our first step in simulating such an image will be to understand how a camera records a physical scene onto film, since this is the action we want to simulate.

After that we'll look at how the ray tracing algorithm simulates this physical process in a computer's virtual world. We'll then consider the issues that arise when we actually implement ray tracing on a real computer.

1.2 The Pinhole Camera Model

Perhaps the simplest camera model around is the *pinhole camera*, illustrated in *Figure 1*. A flat piece of photographic film is placed at the back of a light-proof

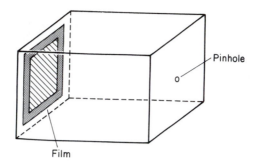

Fig. 1.   The pinhole camera model.

box. A pin is used to pierce a single hole in the front of the box, which is then covered with a piece of opaque tape. When you wish to take a picture, you hold the camera steady and remove the tape for a while. Light will enter the pinhole and strike the film, causing a chemical change in the emulsion. When you're done with the exposure you replace the tape over the hole. Despite its simplicity, this pinhole camera is quite practical for taking real pictures.

The pinhole is a necessary part of the camera. If we removed the box and the pinhole and simply exposed the entire sheet of film to the scene, light from all directions would strike all points on the film, saturating the entire surface. We'd get a blank (white) image when we developed this very overexposed film. The pinhole eliminates this problem by allowing only a very small number of light rays to pass from the scene to the film, as shown in *Figure 2*. In particular, each point on the film can receive light only along the line joining that piece of film and the pinhole. As the pinhole gets bigger, each bit of the film receives more light rays from the world, and the image gets brighter and more blurry.

Although more complicated camera models have been used in computer graphics, the pinhole camera model is still popular because of its simplicity and wide range of application. For convenience in programming and

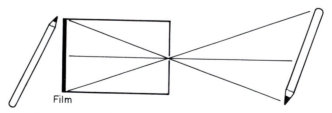

Fig. 2.   The pinhole only allows particular rays of light to strike the film.

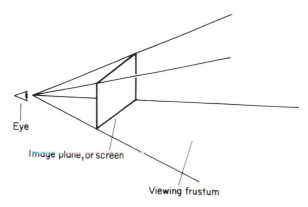

Eye

Image plune, or screen

Viewing frustum

Fig. 3.   The modified pinhole camera model as commonly used in computer graphics.

modeling, the classic computer graphics version of the pinhole camera moves the plane of the film out in *front* of the pinhole, and renames the pinhole as the *eye*, as shown in *Figure 3*. If we built a real camera this way it wouldn't work well at all, but it's fine for a computer simulation. Although we've moved things around, note that each component of the pinhole camera is accounted for in *Figure 3*. In particular, the requirement that all light rays pass through the pinhole is translated into the requirement that all light rays pass through the eyepoint. For the rest of our discussion we will use this form of the pinhole camera model.

You may want to think of the model in *Figure 3* as a Cyclopean viewer looking through a rectangular window. The image he sees on the window is determined by where his eye is placed and in what direction he is looking.

In *Figure 3* we've drawn lines from the eye to the corners of the screen and then beyond. You can think of these lines as the edges of walls that include the eye and screen. The only objects which the eye can directly see (and thus the film directly image) are those which lie within all four of the walls formed by these bounds. We also arbitrarily say that the only objects that can show up on the image plane are those in *front* of the image plane, i.e. those on the other side of the plane than the eye. This makes it easy to avoid the pitfall of having our whole image obscured by some large, nearby object. The eye also cannot directly see any objects behind itself.

All these conditions mean that the world that finally appears on the screen lies within an infinite pyramid with the top cut off (such a point-less pyramid is called a *frustum*). The three-dimensional volume that is visible to the eye, and may thus show up on the screen, is called the *viewing frustum*. The walls that form the frustum are called *clipping planes*. The plane of the screen is called the *image plane*. The location of the eye itself is simply referred to as the *eye position*.

1.3 Pixels and Rays

When we generate an image we're basically determining what color to place in each pixel. One way to think of this is to imagine each pixel as a small, independent window onto the scene. If only one color can be chosen to represent everything visible through this window, what would be the correct color? Much of the work of 3-D computer graphics is devoted to answering that question.

One way to think about the question is within the context of the pinhole camera model. If we can associate a region of film with a given pixel, then we can study what would happen to that region of the film in an actual physical situation and use that as a guide to determine what should happen to its corresponding pixel in the computer's virtual world. If we use the computer graphics pinhole camera of *Figure 3*, this correspondence is easy.

In *Figure 4*, one pixel in particular and its corresponding bit of film have been isolated. A small distribution of light rays can arrive from the scene, pass through the pinhole, and strike the film. After the exposure has completed and the pinhole is covered, that small region of film has absorbed many different rays of light. If we wish to describe the entire pixel with a 'single' color, a good first approximation might be to simply average together all the colors of all the light that struck it.

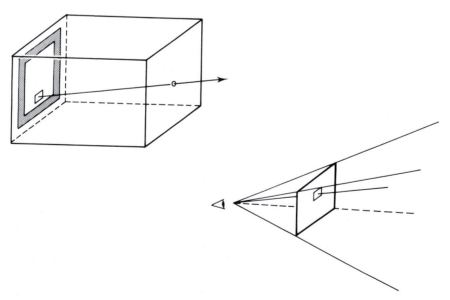

Fig. 4. Every pixel on the screen in the computer graphics camera model corresponds directly to a region of film in the pinhole camera.

This 'averaging' of the light in a pixel is in fact the way we eventually determine a single color for the pixel. The mathematics of the averaging may get somewhat sophisticated (as we'll see in later chapters), but we'll always be looking at lots of light rays and somehow combining their colors.

From this discussion we can see that the eventual goal is to fill in every pixel with the right color, and the way to find this color is to examine all the light rays that strike that pixel and average them together somehow. From now on, when we refer to the 'pinhole camera model,' or even just 'the camera,' we'll be referring to the computer graphics version of *Figure 3*.

2 TRACING RAYS

2.1 Forward Ray Tracing

We saw in the last section that one critical issue in image synthesis is the determination of the correct color for each pixel, and that one way to find that color is to average together the colors of the light rays that strike that pixel in the pinhole camera model. But how do we find those rays, and what colors are they? Indeed, just what do we mean by the 'color' of a light ray?

The color of a ray is not hard to define. We can think of a light ray as the straight path followed by a light particle (called a *photon*) as it travels through space. In the physical world, a photon carries energy, and when a photon enters our eye that energy is transferred from the photon itself to the receptor cells on our retina. The color we perceive from that photon is related to its energy. Different colors are thus carried to our retina by photons of different energies.

One way to talk of a photon's energy is as energy of vibration. Although photons don't actually 'vibrate' in any physical sense, vibration makes a useful mathematical and intuitive model for describing a photon's energy. In a vibrating photon model, different speeds of vibration are related to different energies, and thus different colors. For this reason we often speak of a given color as having a certain *frequency*. Another way to describe the rate of vibration is with the closely related concept of *wavelength*. For example, we can speak of frequency and say that our eyes respond to light between about 360 and 830 terahertz (abbreviated THz; 1 THz = 10^{12} cycles per second). Alternatively, we can speak of wavelength and describe the same range as 360–830 nanometers (1 nm = 1 billionth of a meter). In mathematical formulae, it is typical to use the symbol f to represent the frequency of a photon, and λ to represent its wavelength.

Generally speaking, each unique frequency has an associated energy, and thus will cause us to see an associated color. But colors can add both on film and in the eye; for example, if a red photon and a green photon both arrive at our eye simultaneously, we will perceive the sum of the colors: yellow.

Consider a particular pixel in the image plane. Which of the photons in a three-dimensional scene actually contribute to that pixel?

Figure 5 shows a living room, consisting of a couch, a mirror, a lamp, and a table. There's also a camera, showing the position of the eye and the screen.

Photons must begin at a light source. After all, exposing a piece of film in a completely dark room doesn't cause anything to happen to the film; no light hits it. If the lamp in the living room is off, then the room is completely dark and our picture will be all black. So imagine that the light is on. The lamp contains a single, everyday white light bulb. The job of the bulb is to create photons at all the visible frequencies and send them out in all directions. In order to get a feel for how the photons eventually contribute to the photograph, let's follow a few photons in particular.

We will not consider all the subtleties and complexities that actually occur when light bounces around in a three-dimensional scene; that discussion could fill several books! Instead, we'll stick to the most important concepts.

Let's say photon A is colored blue (that is, if the photon struck our eye we would say that we were looking at blue light). It leaves the light source in the direction of the wall, and then strikes the wall. Some complicated things can happen when the photon hits the wall's surface, which we'll talk about later in

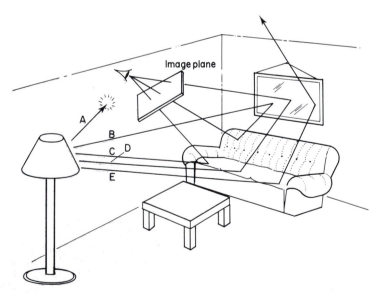

Fig. 5.   Some light rays (like A and E) never reach the image plane at all. Others follow simple or complicated routes.

the Surface Physics section. For now, we'll say that the light hits the wall, and is mostly absorbed. So photon A stops here, and doesn't contribute to the picture.

Photon C is also blue. It leaves the light and strikes the couch. At the couch, the photon is somewhat absorbed before being reflected. Nevertheless, a (somewhat weaker) blue photon leaves the couch and eventually passes through the screen and into our eye. So that's why we get to actually see the couch: light from the light source strikes the couch and gets reflected to our eye through the screen.

The reflection can get more complex. Photon B is reflected off the mirror before it hits the couch; its path is light, mirror, couch, film. Alternatively, photon D leaves the light source, strikes the couch, and then strikes the mirror to be reflected onto the film. Photon E follows a very similar path, but it never strikes the film at all. Other photons may follow much more complicated paths during their travels.

So in general, photons leave the light source and bounce around the scene. Usually, the light gets a little dimmer on each bounce, so after a couple of bounces the light is so dim you can't seen it anymore. Only photons that eventually hit the screen and then pass into our eye (when they're still bright) actually contribute to the image. You might want to look around yourself right now, identify some light source, and imagine the paths of some photons as they leave that light, bounce around the objects near you, and eventually reach your eye. Notice that if you're looking into a mirror, you can probably see some objects in the mirror that you can't see directly. The photons are leaving the light source, hitting those objects, then hitting the mirror, and eventually finding your eyes.

We've just been *ray tracing*. We followed (or traced) the path of a photon (or ray of light) as it bounced around the scene. More specifically, we've been *forward ray tracing*; that is, we followed photons from their origin at the light and into the scene, tracing their path in a forward direction, just as the photons themselves would have travelled it.

2.2 Forward Ray Tracing and Backward Ray Tracing

The technique of forward ray tracing described above is a first approximation to how the real world works. You might think that simulating this process directly would be a good way to make pictures, and you would be pretty much correct. But there is a problem with such a direct simulation, and that's the amount of time it would take to produce an image. Consider that each light source in a scene is generating possibly millions of photons every second, where each photon is vibrating at a slightly different frequency, going in a slightly different direction. Many of these photons hit objects that you would never see at all, even indirectly. Other just pass right out of the scene, for example by flying out through à window. If we were to try to create a picture by actually following photons from their source, we would find a depressingly small number of them ever hit the screen with any appreciable intensity. It might take years just to make one dim picture!

The essential problem is not that forward ray tracing is no good, but rather that many of the photons from the light source play no role in a given image. Computationally, it's just too expensive to follow useless photons.

The key insight for computational efficiency is to reverse the problem, by following the photons backwards instead of forwards. We start by asking ourselves, "Which photons *certainly* contribute to the image?" The answer is those photons that actually strike the image plane and then pass into the eye. Each of those photons travelled along some path before it hit the screen; some may have come directly from a light source, but most probably bounced around first.

Let's consider a particular point on the image plane. We can easily find the path followed by a photon that hit that point on the screen and then our eye: it's the line joining our eye and that point on the film, as shown in *Figure 6*. We know that the path of the photon is a line bounded at one end (where it strikes our eye), but the photon could have started anywhere along the line. The formal term for a line that has one endpoint fixed is a *ray*.

So if some photon actually did contribute to our view of the image at that point, it came along the ray joining our eye and that point on the film. But what object did that photon come from? If we extend the ray into the world, we can look for the nearest object along the path of the ray. The photon must have come from this object.

Consider the ray in *Figure 7*, which shows a light ray joining a sphere and the eye, passing through the image plane. It is the *possible* path of a photon; we don't know if any photon actually took that path. But if any photon hit that piece of the screen and then our eye, it had to come along that line from the sphere to our eye. So our new plan will be to ask if any photons actually did come along that path.

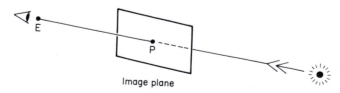

Fig. 6.   A photon bringing light to the eye (at E) arrives by passing through point P on the image plane. The photon's path is along the straight line joining E and P.

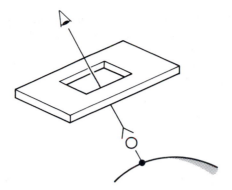

Fig. 7.   A photon leaving the sphere could fly through a pixel and into the eye.

In this approach we're following rays not forward, from the light source to objects to the eye, but *backward*, from the eye to objects to the light source. This is a critical observation because it allows us to restrict our attention to rays that we know will be useful to our image—the ones that enter our eye!

Now that we've found the object a photon may have left to strike our eye, we must find out if any photon really did travel that path, and if so what its color is. We will address those topics below.

Because forward ray tracing is so expensive, the term 'ray tracing' in computer graphics has come to mean almost exclusively backward ray tracing. Unfortunately, some of the notions of backward ray tracing have led to some possibly confusing notation. Recall that we follow a ray backwards to find out where it may have begun. Nevertheless, we often carry out that search in a program by following the path of the light ray backwards, imagining ourselves to be riding along a path taken by a photon, looking for the first object along our path; this is the object from which the ray began. So we sometimes speak of looking for the "first object hit by the ray," or the "first object on the ray's path". What we're actually referring to is the object that may have radiated the photon that eventually travelled along this ray. This backwards point of view is prevalent in ray tracing literature and algorithms, so it may be best to think things through now and not get confused later. In summary, the "first object hit by a ray" means "the object which might have emitted that ray."

2.3   Ray Combination

When we want to find the color of a light ray, we need to find all the different light that originally contributed to it. For example, if a red light ray and a green light ray find themselves on exactly the same path at the same time, we might as well say that together they form a single yellow ray (red light and green light arriving at your eye simultaneously give the impression of yellow). So in *Figure 7*, where the light at a given pixel came from a sphere, we need to find a complete description of *all* the light leaving that point of the sphere in the direction of our eye. We'll see that we can rig our examination of the point so that we're only studying the light that will actually contribute to the pixel.

To aid in our discussion, we'll conceptually divide light rays into four classes: *pixel rays* or *eye rays* which carry light directly to the eye through a pixel on the screen, *illumination rays* or *shadow rays* which carry light from a light source directly to an object surface, *reflection rays* which carry light reflected by an object, and *transparency rays* which carry light passing through an object. Mathematically, these are all just rays, but it's computationally convenient to deal with these classes.

The pixel rays are the ones we've just studied; they're the rays that carry photons that end at the eye after passing through the screen (or in backwards ray tracing, they're rays that start at the eye and pass through the screen). Let's look at the other three types of rays individually.

The whole idea is to find out what light is arriving at a particular point on a surface, and then proceeding onward to our eye. Our discussion may be broken into two pieces: the illumination at a point on the object (which describes the incoming light), and the radiation of light from that point in a particular direction. We can determine the radiated light at a point by first finding the illumination at that point, and then considering how that surface passes that light on in a given direction (of course, if the object is a light source it could add some additional light of its own).

Knowing the illumination and surface physics at a point on a surface, we can determine the properties of the light leaving that point. We broke up rays into the three classes of shadow, reflection, and transparency because they're the three principle ways that light arrives at (and then leaves from) a surface. Some light comes directly from the light source and is then re-radiated away; the properties of this incoming light are determined by the shadows rays. Some light may strike the object and then be reflected; the reflection rays model this light. Lastly, some light comes from behind the object and may pass through; this light is modeled by the transparency rays.

2.4 Shadow and Illumination Rays

Imagine yourself on the surface of an object, such as point P in *Figure 8*. Is any light coming to you from the light sources? One way to answer that question is to simply look at each light. If you can see the light source, then there's a clear path between you and the light, and at least some photons will certainly travel along this path. If any opaque objects are in your way, then no light is coming directly from the light into your eye, and you are in shadow with respect to that light.

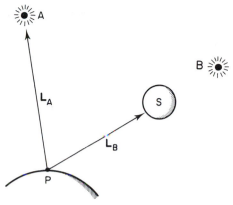

Fig. 8.   To determine the illumination at a point P, we ask if photons could possibly travel from each light source to P. We answer this by sending shadow ray **L**_A towards light source A. It arrives at A, so P **L**_A is actually an illumination ray from P to A. But ray **L**_B is blocked from light source B by sphere S, so no light arrives at P from B.

We can simulate this operation of standing on the object and looking towards the light source with a light ray called a *shadow ray*. In practice, a shadow ray is like any other ray, except that we use it to 'feel around' for shadows; thus this kind of ray is sometimes also called a *shadow feeler*. Basically we start a ray at the object and send it to the light source (remember, we're following the paths of photons backwards). If this backwards ray reaches the light source without hitting any object along the way, then certainly some photons will come forwards along this ray from the light to illuminate the object. But if any opaque objects are in our way, then the light can't get through the intervening object to us; we would then be in shadow relative to that light source. *Figure 8* shows two shadow rays leaving a surface, ray **L**_A going to light source A, and ray **L**_B going to light source B. Ray **L**_A gets to its light source without interruption, but ray **L**_B hits an opaque object along the way. Thus we deduce that light can (and will!) arrive from light A, but not from light B.

When a shadow ray is able to reach a light source without interruption, we stop thinking of it as a 'shadow feeler' and turn it around, thinking of it as an *illumination ray*, which carries light to us from the light source.

In summary, the first class of illumination rays that contribute to the color of the light leaving an object are the light rays coming directly from the light source, illuminating the object. We determine whether there actually are any photons coming from a given light by sending out a shadow ray to each light source. If the ray doesn't encounter any opaque objects along the way to the light, that's our signal that photons will arrive from that light to the object. If instead there is an opaque object in the way, then no photons arrive and the object is in shadow relative to that light source.

Throughout this discussion we've only discussed what happens when the shadow ray hits a matte, opaque object. When it hits a reflective or transparent object the situation is much more complicated. For many years, people used a variety of ad hoc tricks to handle situations where shadow rays hit reflective or transparent surfaces. We now know some better ways to handle this situation; these will be discussed later in the book when we cover stochastic ray tracing.

2.5 Propagated Light

Recall that our overall goal is to find the color of the light leaving a particular point of a surface in a particular direction. We said that the first step was to find out which light was striking the object; some of that light would perhaps continue on in our direction of interest.

In the spirit of backward ray tracing, we'll look only for the incoming light that will make a difference to the radiated light in the direction we care about. After all, if some light strikes the surface but then proceeds away in a direction we don't care about, there's no need to really know much about that incoming light.

We will use the term *propagated light* to describe the illuminating light about which we care. Of all light that is striking a surface, which light is propagated just in our direction of interest? In ray tracing, we assume that most light interaction can be accounted for with four mechanisms of light transport (more about this in the Surface Physics chapter). For now, we'll concentrate exclusively on the two mechanisms called specular reflection and specular· transmission—and since they're our only topics at the moment, well often leave off the adjective 'specular' in this section.

The general idea is that any illumination that falls on a surface and then is sent into our direction of interest either bounced off the surface like a basketball bouncing off a hardwood floor (reflection), or passed through the surface after arriving on the other side like a car driving through a tunnel (transmission). In the case of perfect (specular) reflection and transmission for a perfectly flat, shiny surface, there is exactly one direction from which light can arrive in order to be (specularly) reflected or transmitted into our eye.

When we are trying to determine the illumination at a point, recall that we originally found that point by following a ray to the object. Since we followed that ray backwards to the object, it is called the *incident ray*. Thus, our goal is to find the color of the light leaving the object in the direction opposite to the incident ray.

2.6   Reflection Rays

If we look at a perfectly flat, shiny table, we will see reflections of other objects in the tabletop. We see those reflections because light is arriving at the tabletop from the other objects, bouncing off of the tabletop, and then arriving in our eye. For a fixed eyepoint, each position on the table has exactly one direction from which light can come that will be bounced back into our eye.

For example, *Figure 9* shows a photon of light bouncing around a scene, ending up finally passing through the screen and into the eye. On its last bounce, the photon hit point P and then went into the eye. Photon B also hit point P, but it was bounced (or reflected) into a direction that didn't end up going into our eye. So for that eyepoint and that object, only a photon travelling along the path marked A could have been reflected into our direction of interest.

When we wish to find what light is reflected from a particular point into the direction of the incident ray, we find the *reflected ray* (or *reflection ray*) for that point and direction; this is the ray that can carry light to the surface that will be perfectly reflected into the direction of the incident ray. To find the color of the reflected ray, we follow it backwards to find from which object it began. The color of the light leaving that object along the line of the reflected ray is the color of that reflected ray. When we know the reflected ray's color, we can contribute it to any other light leaving the original surface struck by the incident ray.

Note the peculiar terminology of backward ray tracing: light arrives along the reflected ray and departs along the incident ray.

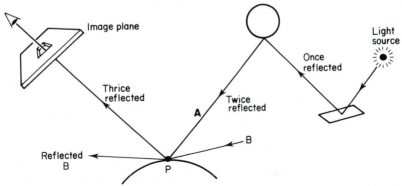

Fig. 9. The color of perfectly reflected light is dependent on the color of the object and the color of the incoming light that bounces off in the direction we care about. For example, at point P we want to know the color of the light coming in on ray **A**, since that light is then bounced into the eye.

Once we know the color of the light coming to the surface from the light sources, the reflected ray, and the transparency ray, we combine them according to the properties of the surface, and thus determine the total color leaving the surface in the direction of the incident ray.

We will see later in the book that more subtle effects can be accounted for if we use more than one transparency or reflected ray, sending them in a variety of (carefully chosen) directions and then weighting their results.

The subject of determining the way light behaves at a surface is called *surface physics*. This topic covers the geometry of light rays at a surface as well as what color changes happen to the light itself. We'll have an entire section of the course devoted to surface physics later on.

2.7   Transparency Rays

Just as there was a single direction from which light can be perfectly reflected into the direction of the incident ray, so is there a single direction from which light can be transmitted into the direction of the incident ray. The ray we create to determine the color of this light is called the *transmitted ray* or *transmitted ray*. *Figure 10* shows a possible path of a transmitted ray. Notice the bending, or *refraction*, of the light as it passes from one medium to another.

We follow the transmitted ray backwards to find which object might have radiated it, and then determine the color radiated by that object in the direction of the transmitted ray. When we know that color, we know the color of the transmitted ray, which (by construction) will be perfectly bent into the direction of the incident ray.

3   RECURSIVE VISIBILITY

The previous sections have discussed finding the color of light leaving a surface as a combination of different kinds of light arriving at the surface. In essence, the color of the radiated light is a function of the combined light from the light sources, light the object reflects, and light the object transmits. We found the colors of the reflected and transmitted light by finding the objects from which they started. But what was the color leaving this previous object? It was a combination of the light reaching it, which can be found with the same analysis.

This observation suggests a recursive algorithm, and indeed the whole ray tracing technique fits into that view very nicely.

The ray tracing process begins with a ray that starts at the eye; this is an *eye ray* or *pixel ray*. *Figure 11* shows one viewing set-up and a particular eye ray, labelled E.

Fig. 10.   Transmitted light arrives from behind a surface and passes through.

3.1 Surface Physics

We've mentioned above for reflection and transparency rays that we first find the direction they might have come from, and then look backwards along that path for a possible object at their source. The technique of determining these directions may be as simple or complicated as you like; we're approximating physical reality here, and physical reality is often complex in its details. The more accuracy you want from your model, the more detailed it will have to be. Happily, even fairly simple models seem to work very well for today's typical images.

The next step is the one that we'll repeat over and over again. We simply ask, "which object does this ray hit?" Remember that we're doing backwards ray tracing, so this question is really a confused form of the question, "given that a photon travelled along this ray to the eye, from which object did it start?"

In *Figure 11*, the eye ray hits plane 3, which we'll say is both somewhat transparent and reflective. We have two light sources, so we'll begin by sending out a shadow ray from plane 3 to each light: we'll call these rays S_1 and S_2. Since ray S_1 reaches light A without interruption, we know that plane 3 is receiving light from light A. But ray S_2 hits sphere 4 before it hits light B, so no illumination comes in along this path. Because plane 3 is both transparent and reflective, we also have to find the colors of the light it transmits and reflects; such light arrived along rays T_1 and R_1.

Following ray T_1, we see that it hits sphere 6, which we'll say is a bit reflective. We send out two shadow rays S_3 and S_4 to determine the light hitting sphere 6, and create reflection ray R_2 to see what color is reflected. Both S_3 and S_4 reach their respective light sources. Ray R_2 leaves the scene entirely, so we'll say that it hits the surrounding world, which is some constant background color. That completes ray T_1 from our original intersection with the primary ray E.

Let's now go back and follow reflected ray R_1. It strikes plane 9, which is a bit reflective and transparent. So we'll send out two shadow rays as always (S_5 and S_6), and reflected and transmitted rays T_2 and R_3. We'll then follow each of T_2 and R_3 in turn, generating new shadow and secondary rays at each intersection.

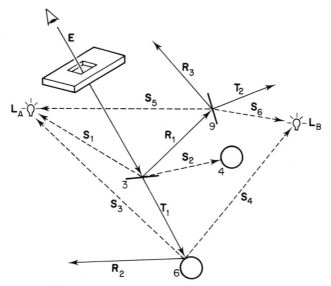

Fig. 11. An eye ray **E** propagated through a scene. Many of the intersections spawn reflected, transmitted, and shadow rays.

Figure 12 shows this whole process in a schematic form, called a *ray tree.* What ever causes the ray tree to stop? Like the non-opaque shadow ray question, the answers to this question are not easy. One ad hoc technique that usually works pretty well is to stop following rays either when they leave the scene, or their *contribution* gets too small. The former condition is handled by saying that if a ray leaves our world, then it just takes on the color of the surrounding background. The second condition is a bit harder.

How much contribution does ray **E** make to our picture? If it's the only ray at that pixel, then we'll use 100% of **E**; if the color **E** brings back is pure red, then that pixel will be pure red. But how about rays T_1 and R_1? Their contributions must be less than that of **E** since **E** is formed by adding them together. Let's arbitrarily say that plane 3 passes 40% of its transmitted light, and 20% of its reflected light (i.e. plane 3 is 40% transparent and 20% reflective).

Now recall that T_1 is composed of the light radiated by sphere 6, given by S_3, S_4, and R_2. Let's again be arbitrary, and say that object 6 is 30% transparent; thus R_2 contributes 30% to T_1. Since T_1 contributes 40% to **E**, and R_2 contributes 30% to T_1, then R_2 contributes only 12% to the final color of **E**. The farther down the ray tree we go, the less each ray will contribute to the color we really care about, the color of **E**.

So we can see that as we proceed down the ray tree, the contribution of

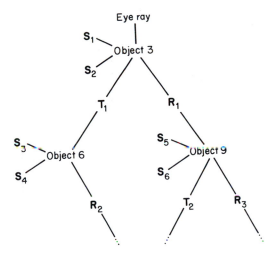

Fig. 12.　The ray tree in schematic form.

individual rays to the final image becomes less and less. As a practical matter, we usually set a threshold of some kind to stop the process of following rays. It is interesting to note that although this technique, called *adaptive tree-depth control*, sounds plausible, and in fact works pretty well in practice, there are theoretical arguments that show that it can be arbitrarily wrong.

4　ALIASING

Synthesizing an image with a digital computer is very different from exposing a piece of film to a real scene. The differences are endless, although much of computer graphics research is directed to making the differences as small as possible. But there's a fundamental problem that we're stuck with: the modern digital computer cannot represent a continuous signal.

Consider using a standard tape recorder to record a trumpet. Playing the trumpet causes the air to vibrate. The vibrating air enters a microphone, where it is changed into a continually changing electrical signal. This signal is applied to the tape head, which creates a continually changing magnetic field. This field is recorded onto a piece of magnetic tape that is passing over the head.

Now let's consider the same situation on a digital computer. The music enters the microphone, and is changed into a continuous electrical signal. But the computer cannot record that signal directly; it must first turn it into a series of numbers. In formal terms, it *samples* the *signal* so that it can store it digitally. So our continuous musical tone has been replaced with a sequence of numbers. If we take enough samples, and they are of sufficiently high precision, then when we turn those numbers back into sound it will sound like the original music.

It turns out that these notions of 'enough samples' and 'sufficiently high precision' are critically important. They have been studied in detail in a branch of engineering mathematics called *signal processing*, from which computer graphics has borrowed many important results.

Let's look at a typical sampling problem by analogy. Imagine that you're at a county fair, standing by the carousel. This carousel has six horses, numbered 1 to 6, and it's spinning so that the horses appear to be galloping to the right. Now let's say that someone tells you that the carousel is making one complete rotation every 60 seconds, so a new horse passes by every 10 seconds. You decide to confirm this claimed speed of revolution.

Now just as you're watching horse 3 pass in front of you, someone calls your name. You turn and look for the caller, but you can't find anyone. It took you 10 seconds to look around. When you turn back to the carousel, you see that now horse 4 is in front of you. You might sensibly assume that the carousel has spun one horse to the right during your absence.

Say this happens again and again; you look away for 10 seconds, and then return. Each time you turn back you see the next-numbered horse directly in front of you. You could conclude that the carousel is spinning 1/6 of the way around every 10 seconds, so it takes 60 seconds to complete a revolution. Thus the claim appears true.

Now let's say that a friend comes back the next day to double-check your observations. As soon as she reaches the carousel (looking at horse 3) she hears someone calling her name. She looks around, but although you looked only for 10 seconds, your friend searches the crowd for 70 seconds. When she turns back to the carousel, she sees exactly what you saw yesterday; horse 4 is in front of her. If this happened again and again, she could conclude that the carousel is spinning 1/6 of the way around every 70 seconds. Thus she could reasonably state that the claim is false.

We know from your observations that it is certainly going faster than that, but there's no way for your friend to know that she's wrong if she only takes one look every 70 seconds.

In fact someone's measurements in such a situation can be arbitrarily wrong. Because as long as you regularly look at the carousel, look away, and look back, you have no idea what went on when you were looking away: I can always claim that it went around any number of full turns when you weren't looking!

The computer is prone to exactly the same problem. If it samples some signal too infrequently, the information that gets recorded can be wrong, just as our determination of the carousel's speed was wrong. The problem is that one signal (1/6 revolution every 10 seconds) is masquerading as another signal (1/6 revolution every 70 seconds); they're different signals, but after sampling we can't tell them apart. This problem is given the general term *aliasing*, to remind us that one signal is looking like another.

The problem of aliasing thoroughly permeates computer graphics. It shows up in countless ways, and almost always looks noticeably bad. The problem is that, if one is not careful, aliasing will almost always occur somewhere, simply due to the nature of digital computers and the nature of the ray tracing algorithm itself. Luckily, there are techniques to avoid aliasing, known collectively as *anti-aliasing* techniques. They are the weapons we employ to solve or reduce the aliasing problem.

We'll first look at some of the symptoms of aliasing, and then look briefly at some of the ways to avoid these problems.

4.1 Spatial Aliasing

When we get aliasing because of the uniform nature of the pixel grid, we often call that *spatial aliasing*. *Figure 13* shows a quadrilateral displayed at a variety of screen resolutions. Notice the chunky edges; this effect is colloquially called

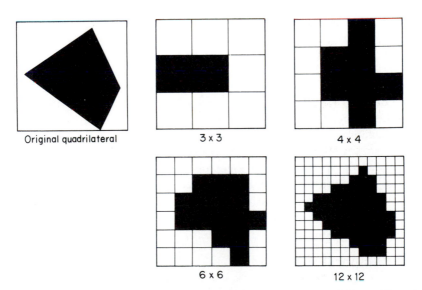

Original quadrilateral   3 x 3   4 x 4

6 x 6   12 x 12

Fig. 13. A quadrilateral shown on grids of four different resolutions. Note that the smooth edges turn into stairsteps—commonly called 'jaggies.' No matter how high we increase the resolution, the jaggies will not disappear; they will only get smaller. Thus the strategy 'use more pixels' will never cure the jaggies!

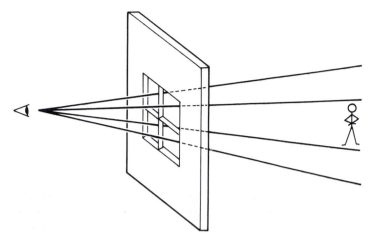

Fig. 14. No matter how closely the rays are packed, they can always miss a small object or a large object far enough away.

the jaggies, to draw attention to the jagged edge that should be smooth. Notice that the jaggies seem to become less noticeable at higher resolution. You might think that with enough pixels you could eliminate the jaggies altogether, but that won't work. Suppose you find that on your monitor can't see the jaggies at a resolution of 512 by 512. If you then take your 512-by-512 image to a movie theater and display it on a giant silver screen, each pixel would be huge, and the tiny jaggies would then be very obvious. This is one of those situations where you can't win; you can only suppress the problem to a certain extent.

Another aspect of the same problem is shown in *Figure 14*. Here a small object is falling between rays. Again, using more rays or pixels may diminish the problem, but it can never be cured that way. No matter how many rays you use, or how closely you space them together, I can always create an object that you'll miss entirely. You might think that if an object is that small, then it doesn't matter if it makes it into the image or not. Unfortunately, that's not true, and some good examples come from looking at temporal (or time) aliasing.

4.2 Temporal Aliasing

We often use computer graphics to make animated sequences. Of course, an animation is nothing more than many still frames shown one after another. It's tempting to imagine that if each still frame was very good, the animation would be very good as well. This is true to some extent, but it turns out that

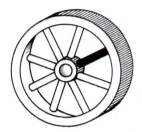

Fig. 15.　A wheel with one black spoke.

when a frame is part of an animation (as opposed to just a single still, such as a slide), the notion of 'very good' changes. Indeed, new problems occur exactly because the stills are shown in an animated sequence: these problems fall under the class of *temporal aliasing* (temporal comes from the Latin *tempus*, meaning time).

Our example of the rotating carousel above was an example of this type of aliasing. Another, classical example of temporal aliasing is a spinning wheel. You may have noticed on television or in the movies that as a wagon wheel accelerates it seems to go faster and faster, and then it seems to slow down and start going backwards! When the wheel is going slowly, the camera can faithfully record its samples of the image on film (usually about 24 or 30 samples per second).

Figure 15 shows a wheel, with one spoke painted black. We're going to sample this clockwise-spinning wheel at 6 frames per second.

Figure 16(a) shows our samples when the wheel is spinning at 1 revolution per second; no problem, watching this film we would perceive a wheel slowly spinning clockwise. *Figure 16(b)* shows the same wheel at 3 revolutions per second: now we can't tell at all which way the thing is spinning. Finally, *Figure 16(c)* shows the same wheel at 5 revolutions per second; watching this film, we would believe that the wheel was spinning slowly backwards. This 'slowly backwards motion' is aliasing for the proper, forwards motion of the wheel.

The critical notion here is that things are happening too fast for us to record accurately.

Another problem occurs with the small objects mentioned in the previous section. As a very small object moves across the screen, it will sometimes be hit by a ray (and will thus appear in the picture), and sometimes it won't be hit by any rays. Thus, as the object moves across the screen it will blink on and off, or *pop*. Even for very small objects this can be extremely distracting, especially if they happen to contrast strongly with the background (like white stars in black space).

Another bad problem is what happens to some edges. *Figure 17* shows a horizontal edge moving slowly up the screen. Every few frames, it rises from

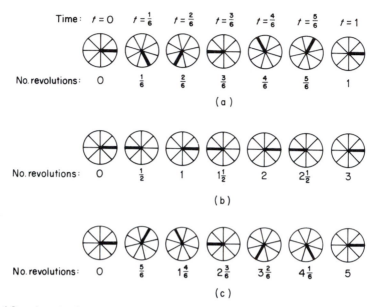

Fig. 16.   A spinning wheel sampled at a constant 6 samples per second. In row (a) the wheel is spinning at 1 revolution per second and is correctly sampled. In row (b) the wheel is spinning at 3 revolutions per second; after sampling, we cannot tell in which direction the wheel is spinning! In row (c) the wheel is spinning at 5 revolutions per second, but appears to be spinning backwards at 1 revolution per second. Thus the very fast speed is aliasing as a slower speed after sampling.

one row of pixels to the next. This is another aspect of popping: the smoothly moving edge appears to jump from one line to the next in a very distracting manner.

Techniques that solve temporal aliasing problems usually create still frames that look blurry where things are moving fast. It's easy to see that this is just what happens when we use a camera to take a picture of quickly moving objects. Imagine taking a picture of a speeding race car as it whizzes past. Even though the shutter is open for a very brief moment, the car still moves fast enough to leave a streak, or blur, behind it on the film. Because of this characteristic of the frames, solutions to the problem of temporal aliasing are sometimes referred to as techniques for including *motion blur*.

4.3   Anti-aliasing

Aliasing effects can always be tracked down to the fundamental natures of digital computers and the point-sampling nature of ray tracing. The essential

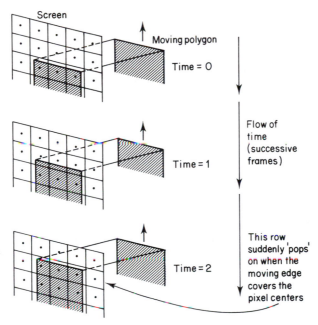

Fig. 17. A moving edge suddenly 'pops' when a new row of pixels is covered.

problem is that we're trying to represent continuous phenomena with discrete samples. Other aliasing effects abound in computer graphics; for example, frequency aliasing is very common but rarely handled correctly.

We will now consider several of the popular approaches to anti-aliasing. We'll focus on the problems of spatial aliasing, since they're easier to show on the written page than temporal aliasing. Nevertheless, many of these techniques apply to solving aliasing problems throughout computer graphics, and can be applied to advanced topics related to aliasing such as motion blur, correct texture filtering, and diffuse inter-reflections.

4.4 Supersampling

The easiest way to alleviate the effects of spatial aliasing is to use lots of rays to generate our image, and then find the color at each individual pixel by averaging the colors of all the rays within that pixel. This technique is called *supersampling*. For example, we might send nine rays through every pixel, and let each ray contribute one-ninth to the final color of the pixel.

Supersampling can help reduce the effects of aliasing, because it's a means for getting a better idea of what's seen by a pixel. If we send out nine rays in a given pixel, and six of the rays hit a green ball, and the other three hit a blue ball, the composite color in that pixel will be two-thirds green and one-third blue: a more 'accurate' color than either pure green or pure blue.

As we mentioned above, this technique cannot really *solve* aliasing problems, it just reduces them. Another problem with supersampling is that it's very expensive; our example will take nine times longer to create a picture than if we used just a single ray per pixel. But supersampling is a good starting point for better techniques.

4.5   Adaptive Supersampling

Rather than blindly firing off some arbitrary, fixed number of rays per pixel, let's try to concentrate extra rays where they'll do the most good. One way to go is to start by using five rays per pixel, one through each corner and one through the center, as in *Figure 18*. If each of the five rays is about the same color, we'll assume that they all probably hit the same object, and we'll just use their average color for this pixel.

If the rays have sufficiently different colors, then we'll subdivide the pixel into smaller regions. Then we'll treat each smaller region just as we did the whole pixel: we'll find the rays through the corners and center, and look at the resulting colors. If any given set of five rays are about the same color, then we'll average them together and use that as the color of the region; if the colors are sufficiently different, we'll subdivide again. The idea is that we'll send more rays through the pixel where there's interesting stuff happening, and in the boring regions where we just see flat fields of color we'll do no more additional work. Because this technique subdivides where the colors change, it

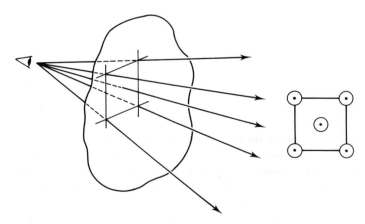

Fig. 18.   Adaptive supersampling begins at each pixel by tracing the four corner rays and the center ray.

adapts to the image in a pixel, and is thus called *adaptive supersampling*. A detailed example of the process is shown in *Figure 19*.

This approach is easy, not too slow, and often works fairly well. But its fundamental assumption is weak. It's just not fair to assume that if some fixed number of rays are about the same color, that we have then sampled the pixel well enough. One problem that persists is the issue of small objects: little objects can slip through the initial five rays, and we'll still get popping as they travel across the screen in an animated sequence.

The central problems of adaptive supersampling are that it uses a fixed, arbitrary number of rays per pixel when starting off, and that it still uses a fixed, regular grid for sampling (although that grid gets smaller and smaller as we subdivide). Often this technique is fine when you need to quickly crank out a picture that just needs to look okay, but it can leave a variety of aliasing artifacts in your pictures. Happily, there are other approaches that solve aliasing problems better.

4.6 Stochastic Ray Tracing

As we saw above, adaptive supersampling still ends up sending out rays on a regular grid, even though this grid is somewhat more finely subdivided in some places than in others. Thus, we can still get popping edges, jaggies, and all the other aliasing problems that regular grids give us, although they will usually be somewhat reduced. Let's get rid of the fixed grid, but continue to say that each pixel will initially be sampled by a fixed number of rays—we'll use nine. The difference will be that we'll scatter these rays evenly across the pixel. *Figure 20(a)* shows a pixel with nine rays plunked down more or less at random, except that they cover the pixel pretty evenly.

If each pixel gets covered with its nine rays in a different pattern, then we've successfully eliminated any regular grid. *Figure 20(b)* shows a small chunk of pixels, each sampled by nine rays, each of which is indicated by a dot. Now that we've gotten rid of the regular sampling grid, we've also gotten rid of the regular aliasing artifacts the grid gave us. Because we're randomly (or stochastically) distributing the rays across the space we want to sample, this technique is called *stochastic ray tracing*. The particular distribution that we use is important, so sometimes this technique is called *distributed ray tracing*.

Let's consider another problem with the ray tracing algorithms described in preceding sections. Consider an incident ray which will carry light away from a somewhat bumpy surface. We'll see later in the course that when we consider diffuse reflection, there are many incoming rays that will send some of their energy away from the surface along the direction of the incident ray. There's no one 'correct' ray; they all contribute. One might ask which of these incoming rays should be followed? The answer that stochastic ray tracing

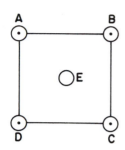

When we start a pixel, we trace rays through the four corners and the center. We then compare the colors of rays **AE**, **BE**, **CE**, and **DE**. Suppose **A** and **E** are similar and so are **D** and **E**, but both **BE** and **CE** are too different.

We'll start by looking more closely at the region bounded by **B** and **E**. We fire new rays **F, G, H** to find all four corners and the center of this region. We now compare **FG, BG, HG**, and **EG**. Suppose each pair is very similar, except **G** and **E**. So we look more closely at the region bounded by **G** and **E**.

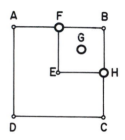

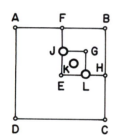

So now we fill in the square region bounded by **BE** with the three new rays **J**, **K**, and **L**. Let's suppose they're all sufficiently similar.

Now we return to the pair **CE** which we identified earlier. Since we already have **H**, we trace the new rays **M** and **N**. We compare the colors between **EM, HM, CM**, and **NM**. Suppose they are all similar except **CM**.

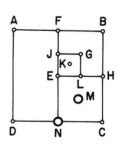

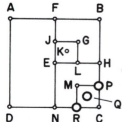

To complete the region we trace the new rays **P, Q**, and **R**. We compare **MQ, PQ**, **CQ**, and **RQ**. At this point we'll assume they're all sufficiently similar. These are no pairs of colors left to examine, so we're now done.

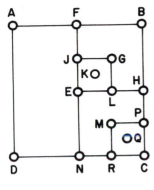

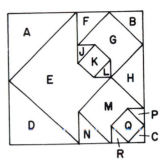

So now its time to determine the final color. The rays on the left will end up with relative weights indicated by the diagram on the right. Basically, for each quadrant we average its four subquadrants recursively. The final formula for this example could then be expressed as:

$$\frac{1}{4}\left(\frac{A+E}{2}+\frac{D+E}{2}+\frac{1}{4}\left[\frac{F+G}{2}+\frac{B+G}{2}+\frac{H+G}{2}+\frac{1}{4}\left\{\frac{J+K}{2}+\frac{G+K}{2}+\frac{L+K}{2}+\frac{E+K}{2}\right\}\right]\right.$$

$$\left.+\frac{1}{4}\left[\frac{E+M}{2}+\frac{H+M}{2}+\frac{N+M}{2}+\frac{1}{4}\left\{\frac{M+Q}{2}+\frac{P+Q}{2}+\frac{C+Q}{2}+\frac{R+Q}{2}\right\}\right]\right)$$

Fig. 19. Adaptive supersampling.

provides is that there is no single best incoming ray direction. Instead, choose a random ray direction. The next time you hit a surface and need to spawn new rays, choose a new random direction. The trick is to bias your random number selection in such a way that you send lots of rays in directions where it's likely a lot of light is arriving, and relatively few rays in directions where the incoming light is sparse.

We can describe this problem mathematically as an integration problem, where we want to find the total light arriving at a given point. But because we can't solve the integration equation directly, we sample it randomly and hope that after enough random samples we'll start getting an idea of the answer. In

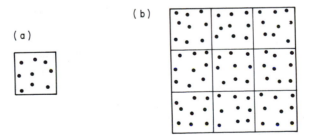

(a)

(b)

Fig. 20. We can use stochastic sample points within each pixel to help reduce spatial aliasing.

fact, our random selections can be carefully guided to help us obtain a good answer with a small number of samples.

The techniques of stochastic ray tracing lead to a variety of new effects that the deterministic ray tracing algorithms described above don't handle well or at all. For example, stochastic ray tracing helps us get *motion blur, depth of field*, and soft edges on our shadows (known as the *penumbra* region).

But although stochastic ray tracing solves many of the problems of regular ray tracing, we've picked up something new: *noise*. Since we're getting a better average with this technique, every pixel comes out more or less correct, but it's usually not quite right. This error isn't correlated to a regular grid like many of the other aliasing problems we've discussed, but instead it spreads out over the picture like static in a bad TV signal. It turns out that the human visual system is much more forgiving of this form of random noise than regular aliasing problems like the jaggies, so in this way stochastic ray tracing is a good solution to aliasing problems.

But we're still using all those rays for every pixel, even where we don't need them. Sometimes we do need them: consider a pixel that's looking out on a patchwork quilt, where one pixel sees just one red square. Then just one or two rays certainly give us the correct color in this pixel. On the other hand, consider a pixel that can see 16 differently colored squares of material. We'll need at least 16 rays, just to get one of each color. It's not clear from the above discussion how to detect when we need more samples, nor how to go about getting them.

4.7 Statistical Supersampling

One way to try getting just the right number of rays per pixel is to watch the rays as they come in. Imagine a pixel which has had four rays sent through it, distributed uniformly across the pixel. We can stop sampling if those four rays are a 'good enough' estimate of what's really out there.

We can draw upon the vast body of statistical analysis to measure the quality of our estimate and see whether some set of samples are 'good enough.' We'll look at the colors of the rays we've sent through the pixel so far, and perform some statistical tests on them. The results of these tests are a measure of how likely it is that these rays give us a good estimate of the actual color that pixel can see. If the statistics say that the estimate is probably poor, we'll send in more rays and run the statistics again. As soon as the color estimate is 'good enough,' then we'll accept that color for that pixel and move on. This is called *statistical supersampling*.

The important thing here is to determine how good is 'good enough.' In general, you can specify just how confident you'd like to be about each pixel. For example, you might tell your program to continue sending rays through pixels until the statistics say that it's 90% likely that the color you have so far is the 'true,' or correct, color. If you want the picture to finish faster, you might drop that requirement to 40%, but the quality will probably degrade.

4.8   The Rendering Equation

We can express how light bounces around in a scene mathematically, with a formula called *the rendering equation*. A solution to the rendering equation tells us just how light is falling on each of the objects in our scene. If one of those objects is an image plane, then the solution to the rendering equation is also a solution to the problem of computer graphics: what light is falling on that image plane?

The rendering equation is useful for several reasons. In one respect, it acts as a scaffolding upon which we can hang most of what we know about how light behaves when it bounces off a surface. In another respect, it tells us how light 'settles down' when a light source has been turned on in a scene and left on for a while. In this sense the rendering equation can help us use the power of *radiosity* techniques to model diffuse inter-reflections. The rendering equation also provides a nice synopsis of most of what we know about the behavior of light for image synthesis, and may provide for some new effects, such as caustics.

We mention the rendering equation here because one powerful way to solve it is by ray tracing. Specifically, an enhanced version of stochastic ray tracing (using techniques called *importance sampling* and *path tracing*) can help us find solutions to the rendering equation.

ANNOTATED BIBLIOGRAPHY

Key

[AA] Anti-aliasing; [AN] animation; [EF] efficiency; [OI] object intersections; [RT] ray tracing technique; [SH] shading; [VI] visibility.

Siggraph '77: *Comput. Graph.* **11**(2), July 1977.
Siggraph '78: *Comput. Graph.* **12**(3), August 1978.
Siggraph '79: *Comput. Graph.* **13**(2), August 1979.
Siggraph '80: *Comput. Graph.* **14**(3), July 1980.
Siggraph '81: *Comput. Graph.* **15**(3), August 1981.
Siggraph '82: *Comput. Graph.* **16**(3), July 1982.
Siggraph '83: *Comput. Graph.* **17**(3), July 1983.
Siggraph '84: *Comput. Graph.* **18**(3), July 1984.
Siggraph '85: *Comput. Graph.* **19**(3), July 1985.
Siggraph '86: *Comput. Graph.* **20**(4), August 1986.

1. Amanatides, J., Ray tracing with cones. Siggraph '84 [AA].
2. Barr, A.H., Ray tracing deformed surface. Siggraph '86 [OI].
3. Blinn, J.F., Models of light reflection for computer synthesized pictures. Siggraph '77 [SH].
4. Bouville, C., Bounding ellipsoids for ray–fractal intersection. Siggraph '85 [EF].
5. Bronsvoort, W.F. and Klok, F. Ray tracing generalized cylinders. *ACM Trans. Graph.* **4**(4), October 1985 [OI].
6. Bui-Tuong Phong, Illumination for computer generated pictures. *Commun. ACM* **18**(6), June 1975 [SH].
7. Clark, J.H., Hierarchical geometric models for visible surface algorithms. *Commun. ACM* **19**(10), October 1976 [EF].
8. Cook, R.L. and Torrance, K.E., A reflectance model for computer graphics. *ACM Trans. Graph.* **1**(1), January 1982 [SH].
9. Cook, R.L., Porter, T. and Carpenter, L., Distributed ray tracing. Siggraph '84 [RT].
10. Crow, F.C., 'The aliasing problem in computer-generated shaded images.' *Commun. ACM* **20**(11), November 1977 [AA].
11. Dippé, M.A.Z. and Wold, E.H., Antialiasing through stochastic sampling. Siggraph '85 [AA].
12. Fujimoto, A., Tanaka, T. and Iwata, K., ARTS: Accelerated Ray Tracing System. *IEEE Comput. Graph. Appl.* **6**(4), April 1986 [EF].
13. Glassner, A.S., Fast ray tracing by space subdivision. *IEEE Comput. Graph. Appl.* **4**(10), October 1984 [EF].
14. Glassner, A.S., Spacetime ray tracing for animation. *IEEE Comput. Graph. Appl.* **8**(2), March 1988 [EF, RT, AN].
15. Hall, R.A. and Greenberg D.P., A testbed for realistic image synthesis. *IEEE Comput. Graph. Appl.* **3**(8), November 1983 [SH].
16. Hanrahan, P., Ray tracing algebraic surface. Siggraph '83 [OI].
17. Heckbert, P.S. and Hanrahan, P., Beam tracing polygonal objects. Siggraph '84 [RT].
18. Joy, K.I. and Bhetanobhotla, M.N., Ray tracing parametric surface patches utilizing numerical techniques and ray coherence. Siggraph '86 [OI].
19. Kajiya, J.T., Ray tracing parametric patches. Siggraph '82 [OI].
20. Kajiya, J.T., New techniques for ray tracing procedurally defined objects. Siggraph '83 [OI].
21. Kajiya, J.T. and Von Herzen, B., Ray tracing volume densities, Siggraph '84 [OI].
22. Kajiya, J.T., The rendering equation. Siggraph '86 [RT].
23. Kay, D.S., Transparency, Refraction, and Ray Tracing for Computer Synthesized Images. M.S. Thesis, Cornell University, January 1979 [RT].
24. Kay, T.L. and Kajiya J., Ray tracing complex scenes. Siggraph '86 [EF].
25. Lee, M.E., Redner, R.A. and Uselton, S.P., Statistically optimized sampling for distributed ray tracing. Siggraph '85 [RT].
26. Newman, W. and Sproull R.F., *Principles of Interactive Computer Graphics*, 2nd Edition. McGraw-Hill, New York, 1979 [VI].
27. Potmesil, M. and Chakravarty, I., Synthetic image generation with a lens and aperture camera model. *ACM Trans. Graph.* **1**(2), April 1982 [VI].
28. Roth, S., Ray casting for modelling solids. *Comput. Graph. Image Process.* **18**, 1982 [RT].

29. Rubin, S.M. and Whitted T., A 3-dimensional representation for fast rendering of complex scenes. Siggraph '80 [EF].
30. Sederberg, T., Ray tracing steiner patches. Siggraph '84 [OI].
31. Speer, R., DeRose T.D., and Barsky B.A., A theoretical and empirical analysis of coherent ray tracing. *Proceedings of Graphics Interface 85*, May 1985 [EF].
32. Sweeney, M.A.J. and Bartels R.H., Ray tracing free-form B-spline surfaces. *IEEE Comput. Graph. Appl.* **6**(2), February 1986 [OI].
33. Toth, D.L., On ray tracing parametric surfaces. Siggraph '85 [OI].
34. Weghorst, H., Hooper G. and Greenberg D.P., Improved computational methods for ray tracing, *ACM Trans. Graph.* **3**(1), January 1984 [EF].
35. Wijk, J.J. Van, Ray tracing objects defined by sweeping planar cubic splines. *ACM Trans. Graph.* **3**(3), July 1984 [OI].
36. Wijk, J.J. Van, Ray tracing objects defined by sweeping a sphere. In *Proceedings of the Eurographics '84 Conference*, North-Holland, Amsterdam, 1984 [OI].
37. Whitted. T., An improved illumination model for shaded display. *Commun. ACM* **23**(6), June 1980 [RT].

2 Essential Ray Tracing Algorithms

ERIC HAINES

1 INTRODUCTION

The heart of any ray tracing package is the set of ray intersection routines. No matter what lighting models, texture mappings, space subdivision techniques, anti-aliasing schemes, or other elaborations of the ray tracing algorithm are desired, there is always the need to find the intersection point of a ray and an object.

When a ray is sent out into the modelled environment there are a few different kinds of questions to answer about the ray. What information is needed depends on the ray's purpose. For a ray spawned from the eye, an object intersector must return (at least) the closest intersection point and the surface's normal at this point. For a ray sent towards a light (a.k.a. a shadow feeler), all that is needed is whether the intersection point is closer than the light—if so, it blocks or filters the light. Further information may be desired for filtering, depending on the shading model. For any ray tested against a bounding volume, a simple hit/not hit determination is sometimes all that is required. However, more efficient ray tracers will take advantage of the distance along the ray (e.g. [9]).

Another piece of information that is useful in ray tracing is the intersection point's location relative to some reference frame for the surface. This location is typically used in texture mapping to find the surface properties at that point. See [7] for a good overview of texture mapping.

For anyone wishing to write a ray tracer, the ray/object algorithms are usually derived and coded from scratch. As educational as this process can be, many programmers simply do not care to go through it. Also, making these algorithms efficient is often an evolutionary procedure, as mathematically elegant solutions often make for slow algorithms. This document outlines the basic algorithms used to perform a variety of ray intersection tests and retrieve the essential data. Rather than presenting abstract equations, derivations are shown in a nuts and bolts fashion, with an example of use following each algorithm. The overarching philosophy is to present an efficient algorithmic approach.

This document covers only objects whose ray/object intersection can be found by using simple algebra. This effectively limits the discussion to quadric surfaces, of which the plane and the sphere are special cases. As the sphere is one of the simplest and most popular primitive objects, it will be discussed first. Planes are then covered, along with the additional algorithms needed for polygons. Bounding box intersection is then presented. Finally, intersection of quadric surfaces is explained. Interspersed are relevant inverse mapping techniques and other topics.

Note that the focus of this presentation is the study of algorithms used in ray tracing, though there are also uses for these methods in other rendering schemes and in other interactive graphical processes, such as hit-testing (a.k.a. picking).

Ray tracing shadows of transmitters, CSG (constructive solid geometry) trees, and some other applications [13] requires that all intersection points for the ray be found. To extend the algorithms explained in this document is fairly straightforward, and so normally will not be discussed. Another subset of ray tracing which is not addressed is ray tracing finite length rays. Such rays have uses for activities such as shadow testing, where the ray's length cannot exceed the distance to the light.

1.1 Notes on Notation

The following conventions will be used:

    * means 'multiply'
    · means 'dot product'
    ⊗ means 'cross product'
    ≡ means 'is equivalent to', and is used to show notation equivalences
    ± means 'plus/minus,' signifying that two values are produced

abs(y) means 'absolute value of y'
arccos (y) means 'inverse cosine of y'
x mod y means 'the remainder of x/y'
sin(y) means 'sine of y'
sqrt(y) means 'square root of y'

π stands for 3.1415926...
All angle calculations are in radians

V denotes a vector
M denotes a matrix
Capital letters normally denote parameters; lower case, variables

Examples

T_a, where T is a scalar with subscript 'a.'
$\mathbf{B}_0 = [1\ 2\ 4\ 8]$, where **B** is a four element vector with subscript '0.'
$\mathbf{Q}_{r1}$ is a matrix **Q** with subscript 'r1.'

2   RAY/SPHERE INTERSECTION AND MAPPING

The sphere is one of the mostly commonly used primitives in ray tracing. Also, its ease of testing for intersection with a ray makes it useful as a bounding volume. As such, an in-depth look at the solutions to this problem is made. First the straightforward algebraic solution is derived. Then the special conditions of the problem are examined and a more efficient geometric solution is presented. A comparison of the results of the analysis shows the underlying equivalence of the two algorithms.

A study of a common bug found in ray tracing is made and some solutions are presented.

The algorithm for the most common inverse mapping of a sphere concludes the section.

2.1   Intersection of the Sphere—Algebraic Solution

Define a ray as:

$$\mathbf{R}_{\text{origin}} \equiv \mathbf{R}_0 \equiv [X_0\ Y_0\ Z_0]$$
$$\mathbf{R}_{\text{direction}} \equiv \mathbf{R}_d \equiv [X_d\ Y_d\ Z_d]$$
$$\text{where } X_d^2 + Y_d^2 + Z_d^2 = 1 \text{ (i.e. normalized)}$$

which defines a ray as:

$$\text{set of points on line } \mathbf{R}(t) = \mathbf{R}_0 + \mathbf{R}_d * t, \text{ where } t > 0. \qquad \text{(A1)}$$

Points on the line where $t < 0$ are behind the ray's origin. Why $t = 0$ is not included as a point on the ray is explained in the 'Precision Problems' section. Note that the ray direction does not have to be normalized for these calculations. However, such normalization is recommended, otherwise t will represent the distance in terms of the length of the direction vector. Normalizing the direction vector once for the ray before intersection testing ensures that t will equal the distance from the ray's origin in terms of world coordinates.

Equation (A1) is the *parametric* or *explicit* form of the ray equation. This means that all the points on the ray can be generated directly by varying the value of t.

The sphere is defined by:

$$\begin{aligned}
&\text{Sphere's center} \equiv \mathbf{S_c} \equiv [X_c\ Y_c\ Z_c]\\
&\text{Sphere's radius} \equiv S_r\\
&\text{Sphere's surface is the set of points } [X_s\ Y_s\ Z_s]\\
&\text{where } (X_s - X_c)^2 + (Y_s - Y_c)^2 + (Z_s - Z_c)^2 = S_r^2.
\end{aligned} \tag{A2}$$

The sphere's surface is expressed as an *implicit* equation. In this form points on the surface cannot be directly generated. Instead, each point $[X_s\ Y_s\ Z_s]$ can be tested by the implicit equation; if it fulfills the equation's conditions, the point is on the surface.

To solve the intersection problem, the ray equation is substituted into the sphere equation and the result is solved for t. This is done by expressing the ray equation (A1) as a set of equations for the set of points $[X\ Y\ Z]$ in terms of t:

$$\begin{aligned}
X &= X_0 + X_d * t\\
Y &= Y_0 + Y_d * t\\
Z &= Z_0 + Z_d * t.
\end{aligned} \tag{A3}$$

Substituting this set of equations into the sphere equation's variables $[X_s\ Y_s\ Z_s]$, we obtain:

$$\begin{aligned}
&(X_0 + X_d * t - X_c)^2 +\\
&(Y_0 + Y_d * t - Y_c)^2 +\\
&(Z_0 + Z_d * t - Z_c)^2 = S_r^2.
\end{aligned} \tag{A4}$$

In terms of t, this simplifies to:

$$A * t^2 + B * t + C = 0 \tag{A5}$$

where

$$\begin{aligned}
A &= X_d^2 + Y_d^2 + Z_d^2 = 1\\
B &= 2 * (X_d * (X_0 - X_c) + Y_d * (Y_0 - Y_c) + Z_d * (Z_0 - Z_c))\\
C &= (X_0 - X_c)^2 + (Y_0 - Y_c)^2 + (Z_0 - Z_c)^2 - S_r^2.
\end{aligned}$$

Note that coefficient A is always equal to 1, as the ray direction is normalized.

Also note that S_r^2 could be pre-computed for the sphere. This equation is quadratic, and the solution for t is (with $A = 1$):

$$t_0 = \frac{-B - \sqrt{(B^2 - 4 * C)}}{2}$$

$$t_1 = \frac{-B + \sqrt{(B^2 - 4 * C)}}{2}.$$

$$(A6)$$

When the discriminant (the part in the sqrt() function) is negative, the line misses the sphere. A more accurate formulation for the solution of t_0 and t_1 is found in Section 5.5 of [11].

Since $t > 0$ is part of the ray definition, the roots t_0 and t_1 are examined. The smaller, positive real root is the closest intersection distance on the ray. If no such root exists, then the ray misses the sphere. Some calculation can be avoided by calculating t_0, checking if it is greater than 0, then calculating t_1 if it is not.

Once the distance t is found, the actual intersection point is:

$$\mathbf{r}_{intersect} \equiv \mathbf{r}_i = [x_i \ y_i \ z_i] = [X_0 + X_d * t \ \ Y_0 + Y_d * t \ \ Z_0 + Z_d * t]. \quad (A7)$$

The unit vector normal at the surface is then simply:

$$\mathbf{r}_{normal} \equiv \mathbf{r}_n = \left[\frac{(x_i - X_c)}{S_r} \ \frac{(y_i - Y_c)}{S_r} \ \frac{(z_i - Z_c)}{S_r} \right]. \quad (A8)$$

If the ray originates inside the sphere (and so hits the inside), $\mathbf{r}_n$ should be negated so that it points back towards the ray.

Note that it may be more profitable to pre-calculate the multiplicative inverse of the radius and multiply by this in (A8), since division often takes a fair bit longer than multiplication.

To summarize, the steps in the algorithm are:

Step 1: calculation of A, B, and C of the quadratic.
Step 2: calculation of discriminant.
Step 3: calculation of t_0 and comparison.
Step 4: possible calculation of t_1 and comparison.
Step 5: intersection point calculation.
Step 6: calculation of normal at point.

Assuming the most is made out of pre-calculated constants (such as S_r^2) and intermediate results, the calculations associated with each step are:

Step 1: 8 additions/subtractions and 7 multiplies.
Step 2: 1 subtraction, 2 multiplies, and 1 compare.
Step 3: 1 subtraction, 1 multiply, 1 square root, and 1 compare.

Step 4: 1 subtraction, 1 multiply, and 1 compare.
Step 5: 3 additions, 3 multiplies.
Step 6: 3 subtractions, 3 multiplies.

For the worst case this gives a total of 17 additions/subtractions, 17 multiplies, 1 square root, and 3 compares.

Example

Given a ray with an origin at $[1 \ -2 \ -1]$ and a direction vector of $[1 \ 2 \ 4]$, find the nearest intersection point with a sphere of radius $S_r = 3$ centered at $[3 \ 0 \ 5]$.

First normalize the direction vector, which yields:

$$\text{direction vector magnitude} = \sqrt{(1 * 1 + 2 * 2 + 4 * 4)} = \sqrt{21}$$
$$\mathbf{R_d} = [1/\sqrt{21} \quad 2/\sqrt{21} \quad 4/\sqrt{21}]$$
$$= [0.218 \ 0.436 \ 0.873].$$

Now find A, B, and C, using equation (A5):

$$A = 1 \text{ (because the ray direction is normalized)}$$
$$B = 2 * (0.218 * (1 - 3) + 0.436 * (-2 - 0) + 0.873 * (-1 - 5))$$
$$= -13.092$$
$$C = (1 - 3)^2 + (-2 - 0)^2 + (-1 - 5)^2 - 3^2$$
$$= 35.$$

We now check if the discriminant is positive (A6):

$$\text{Is } B^2 - 4 * C > 0?$$
$$\text{Substituting: is } -13.092^2 - 4 * 35 > 0?$$
$$\text{Yes, } 31.400 > 0.$$

This means the ray intersects the sphere. From this we can calculate t_0 from (A6):

$$t_0 = \frac{-B - \sqrt{(B^2 - 4 * C)}}{2}$$

$$= \frac{13.092 - \sqrt{(31.400)}}{2}$$

$$= 3.744$$

Since t_0 is positive, we don't have to calculate t_1. The actual intersection point is, by (A7):

$$r_i = [X_0 + X_d * t \quad Y_0 + Y_d * t \quad Z_0 + Z_d * t]$$
$$= [1 + 0.218 * 3.744 \quad -2 + 0.436 * 3.744 \quad -1 + 0.873 * 3.744]$$
$$= [1.816 \quad -0.368 \quad 2.269].$$

The unit vector normal is, by (A8):

$$r_n = \left[\frac{(x_i - X_c)}{S_r} \quad \frac{(y_i - Y_c)}{S_r} \quad \frac{(z_i - Z_c)}{S_r} \right]$$
$$= [\ (1.816 - 3)/3 \quad (-0.368 - 0)/3 \quad (2.269 - 5)/3]$$
$$= [-0.395 \quad -0.123 \quad -0.910].$$

2.2   Intersection of the Sphere—Geometric Solution

Now that a simple sphere intersection routine has been outlined, the next question is, "How can we make it run faster?" Some basic ideas about computing efficiency are useful here.

One observation which generally holds is that using the square root function should be avoided when possible. Check timings on the machine used: often the sqrt() function takes 15–30 times as long as a multiply. Similarly, divisions usually take longer than multiplications, so it is often worthwhile to use the multiplicative inverse to avoid division. For clarity these substitutions are not made within this text, and most should be obvious to the implementer.

Another observation is that calculations can often be cut short. In the case of a sphere, there are a number of tests which can be made to check whether an intersection takes place. The purpose of these tests is to avoid calculations until they are needed.

By studying the geometry of the situation, other properties of the problem become apparent. For example, often the ray points away from the sphere and so does not intersect it. By studying such possibilities, another strategy for testing the intersection of the ray and the sphere was discovered:

(1) Find if the ray's origin is outside the sphere.
(2) Find the closest approach of the ray to the sphere's center.
(3) If the ray is outside and points away from the sphere, the ray must miss the sphere.
(4) Else, find the squared distance from the closest approach to the sphere surface.
(5) If the value is negative, the ray misses the sphere.

(6) Else, from the above, find the ray/surface distance.
(7) Calculate the $[x_i \ y_i \ z_i]$ intersection coordinates.
(8) Calculate the normal at the intersection point.

This strategy essentially breaks up the equations (A5) and (A6) into shorter expressions, which are evaluated as needed. Conditions (3) and (5) detect when the ray misses the sphere, allowing an early halt to calculations.

The above strategy will now be fleshed out and explained. Begin with the original ray (A1) and sphere (A2) equations. To start, find whether the ray's origin is inside the sphere by calculating:

$$\text{origin to center vector} \equiv \mathbf{OC} = \mathbf{S_c} - \mathbf{R_0}$$
$$\text{length squared of } \mathbf{OC} \equiv L_{2oc} = \mathbf{OC} \cdot \mathbf{OC}. \tag{A9}$$

If $L_{2oc} < S_r^2$ then the ray origin is inside the sphere. If $L_{2oc} \geq S_r^2$ then the origin is on or outside the sphere, and the ray may not hit the sphere. Examples for these two cases are shown in *Figure 1*. For the sake of efficiency, S_r^2 could be pre-computed and stored.

Note that a ray originating on a sphere is considered not to hit the sphere at the ray's origin. This is standard in ray tracing, where reflected and refracted rays originate on a surface previously intersected. The problem of avoiding these intersections at the origin is discussed in the 'Precision Problems' section.

In either case, the next step is to calculate the distance from the origin to the point on the ray closest to the sphere's center. This is equivalent to finding the intersection of the ray with the plane perpendicular to it which passes through

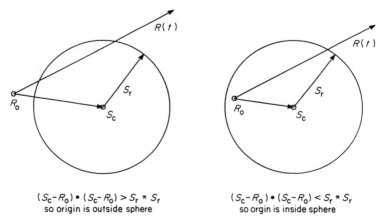

$(S_c-R_0) \bullet (S_c-R_0) > S_r * S_r$
so origin is outside sphere

$(S_c-R_0) \bullet (S_c-R_0) < S_r * S_r$
so orgin is inside sphere

Fig. 1.   The ray origin with respect to sphere location.

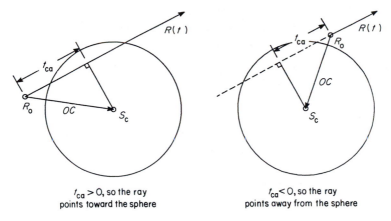

$t_{ca} > 0$, so the ray
points toward the sphere

$t_{ca} < 0$, so the ray
points away from the sphere

Fig. 2.   Ray/sphere pointing directions.

the center of the sphere. This calculation is:

$$\text{closest approach along ray} \equiv t_{ca} = \mathbf{OC} \cdot \mathbf{R_d}. \qquad (A10)$$

If $t_{ca} < 0$ then the center of the sphere lies behind the origin. This is not all that important for rays originating inside the sphere, since these must intersect. For rays originating outside this means that the ray cannot hit the sphere and testing is completed. Another way of saying this is that if $t_{ca} < 0$, the ray points away from the center of the sphere. Examples of these cases are shown in *Figure 2*.

Once the closest approach distance is calculated, the distance from this point to the sphere's surface is determined. This distance is:

$$\text{half chord distance squared} \equiv t_{hc}^2 \equiv t_{2hc} = S_r^2 - D^2 \qquad (A11)$$

where D is the distance from the ray's closest approach to the sphere's center. Calculate D by the Pythagorean theorem:

$$D^2 = L_{oc}^2 - t_{ca}^2. \qquad (A12)$$

Substituting this into (A11):

$$t_{2hc} = S_r^2 - L_{2oc} + t_{ca}^2. \qquad (A13)$$

The geometric meaning of these equations is shown in *Figure 3*. This calculation leads to another test as to whether the ray hits the sphere. If

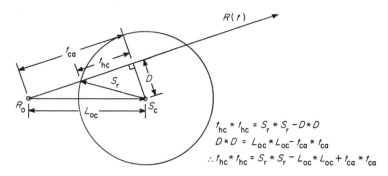

$$t_{hc} * t_{hc} = S_r * S_r - D*D$$
$$D*D = L_{oc}*L_{oc} - t_{ca}*t_{ca}$$
$$\therefore t_{hc}*t_{hc} = S_r * S_r - L_{oc}*L_{oc} + t_{ca}*t_{ca}$$

Fig. 3. Geometry of sphere intersection.

$t_{2hc} < 0$, then the ray misses the sphere. This can happen, of course, only when the ray originates outside the sphere.

At this point all factors have been calculated to determine the actual intersection point's distance along the ray. It is:

$$t = t_{ca} - \sqrt{t_{2hc}} \text{ for rays originating outside the sphere,}$$
$$t = t_{ca} + \sqrt{t_{2hc}} \text{ for rays originating inside or on the sphere.} \qquad \text{(A14)}$$

The difference in these formulae is simply that different intersection points along the rays' lines are needed in different cases. Rays which hit (and are not tangent) have two distinct intersection points along the ray's line. When the ray originates outside the sphere, the smaller distance along the ray is desired. If inside, the smaller distance is negative (behind the ray), so the larger distance is used.

Use equations (A7) and (A8) as before to calculate the intersection point and normal.

To summarize, the steps in the algorithm are:

Step 1: find distance squared between ray origin and center.
Step 2: calculate ray distance which is closest to center.
Step 3: test if ray is outside and points away from sphere.
Step 4: find square of half chord intersection distance.
Step 5: test if square is negative.
Step 6: calculate intersection distance.
Step 7: find intersection point.
Step 8: calculate normal at point.

Assuming the most is made out of pre-calculated constants and intermediate results, the calculations associated with each step are:

Step 1: 5 additions/subtractions and 3 multiplies.
Step 2: 2 additions and 3 multiplies.
Step 3: 2 compares (1 if origin inside sphere).
Step 4: 2 additions/subtractions and 1 multiply.
Step 5: 1 compare (none if origin inside sphere).
Step 6: 1 addition/subtraction and 1 square root.
Step 7: 3 additions, 3 multiplies.
Step 8: 3 subtractions, 3 multiplies.

At worst this gives a total of 16 additions/subtractions, 13 multiplies, 1 square root, and 3 compares. Note that this is less than our original method, and that a determination of when the ray misses the sphere can take place after fewer calculations.

Example

Given a ray with an origin at $[1 \ -2 \ -1]$ and a direction vector of $[1 \ 2 \ 4]$, find the intersection point with a sphere of radius $S_r = 3$ centered at $[3 \ 0 \ 5]$.

As before, first normalize the direction vector, which yields:

$$\text{direction vector magnitude} = \sqrt{(1 * 1 + 2 * 2 + 4 * 4)} = \sqrt{21}$$
$$\mathbf{R_d} = [1/\sqrt{21} \quad 2/\sqrt{21} \quad 4/\sqrt{21}]$$
$$= [0.218 \ 0.436 \ 0.873].$$

First find the ray to the center and its length squared (A9):

$$\mathbf{OC} = [3 \ 0 \ 5] - [1 \ -2 \ -1]$$
$$= [2 \ 2 \ 6]$$
$$L_{2oc} = [2 \ 2 \ 6] \cdot [2 \ 2 \ 6]$$
$$= 44.$$

Checking if $L_{2oc} \geq S_r^2$, it is found that the ray originates outside the sphere. Now calculate the closest approach along the ray to the sphere's center (A10):

$$t_{ca} = [2 \ 2 \ 6] \cdot [0.218 \ 0.436 \ 0.873]$$
$$= 6.546.$$

Checking if $t_{ca} < 0$, it is found that the center of the sphere lies in front of the origin, so calculation must continue. Calculate the half chord distance squared (A13):

$$t_{2hc} = 3 * 3 - 44 + 6.546 * 6.546$$
$$= 7.850.$$

$t_{2hc} > 0$, so the ray must hit the sphere. The intersection distance is then, by (A14):

$$t = 6.546 - \sqrt{7.850}$$
$$= 3.744$$

This is the same answer calculated for t_0 in the earlier algebraic example. As before, the intersection point is, by (A7):

$$\mathbf{r_i} = [X_0 + X_d * t \ \ Y_0 + Y_d * t \ \ Z_0 + Z_d * t]$$
$$= [1 + 0.218 * 3.744 \ \ \ -2 + 0.436 * 3.744 \ \ \ -1 + 0.873 * 3.744]$$
$$= [1.816 \ \ \ -0.368 \ \ \ 2.269]$$

The unit vector normal is, by (A8):

$$\mathbf{r_n} = \left[\frac{(x_i - X_c)}{S_r} \ \ \frac{(y_i - Y_c)}{S_r} \ \ \frac{(z_i - Z_c)}{S_r} \right]$$
$$= [(1.816 - 3)/3 \ \ \ (-0.368 - 0)/3 \ \ \ (2.269 - 5)/3]$$
$$= [-0.395 \ \ \ -0.123 \ \ \ -0.910]$$

2.3 Comparison of Algebraic and Geometric Solutions

The algebraic solution is certainly valid, and is fairly close to the geometric solution in number of operations. The strength of the geometric solution lies in its timely use of comparisons. The first geometric test is to find whether the ray is outside and pointing away from the sphere. This test is pretty worthwhile, considering that a randomly placed ray will face away from a sphere half of the time. The original algebraic algorithm does not include this test.

The question arises of why these two solutions should be different at all. The explanation is simple enough: the algebraic algorithm is just inefficient. Compare the operations to calculate $A, B,$ and C in equation (A5) with the geometric calculations of (A9) through (A13). The following relationships can be identified:

$$B = -2 * t_{ca}$$
$$C = L^2_{oc} - S^2_r. \tag{A15}$$

With these in hand, equation (A14) becomes:

$$t = t_{ca} \pm \sqrt{t_{2hc}}$$

$$= -B/2 \pm \sqrt{((-B/2)^2 - C)}$$

$$= \frac{-B \pm \sqrt{(B^2 - 4 * C)}}{2}.$$

This is the algebraic solution (A6). However, the algebraic solution is still more complicated than the geometric, as there is still a negation, a multiplication by 4 and a division by 2. Looking at equation (A5), we see that B is calculated by a multiplication by 2. Instead, calculate NB, which is set to $-B/2$. Substituting $-2 * NB$ for B in (A6) and simplifying:

$$t = \frac{-(-2 * NB) \pm \sqrt{((-2 * NB)^2 - 4 * C)}}{2}$$

$$= \frac{-(-2 * NB) \pm 2 * \sqrt{(NB^2 - C)}}{2} \qquad \text{(A16)}$$

$$= NB \pm \sqrt{(NB^2 - C)}.$$

These equations are almost as clean as geometric equation (A14), except for the ' $\pm$ ' operation. From substituting $-2 * NB$ for B in (A5), NB is simply:

$$NB = X_d * (X_c - X_0) + Y_d * (Y_c - Y_0) + Z_d * (Z_c - Z_0).$$

Note that NB is equivalent to t_{ca} (equation (A10)).

To eliminate the ' $\pm$ ' problem, where two values t_0 and t_1 must be calculated for the sphere and the smaller positive value accepted, we need to look deeper. A flaw in the algebraic solution was a lack of a way to cut the processing short. By the equivalences in (A15) we can tell the ray origin lies outside the sphere only if $C > 0$. This eliminates the need for calculating t_0 and t_1, as the criterion of (A14) can be used to know whether to subtract or add the discriminant from NB.

Similarly, the ray must point away from the sphere's center if $NB < 0$. This fact gives a complete equivalence of the two algorithms. The algebraic solution originally did not have a number of useful features. Using insight into the geometry of the situation, a better algorithm was found. Looking back on the algebraic solution, the efficiencies inherent in the situation became clear.

The point here is that studying the nature of the problem can yield algorithmic speed-ups. The algebraic solution was straightforward, but it was aimed at solving the general problem of finding the intersection points of a line and a sphere. The geometric approach homed in on the special characteristics of the ray (i.e. that a ray defines only part of a line) and the requirements of the problem (i.e. that only the closest intersection point is required).

2.4   Precision Problems

Doing floating-point calculations is like moving piles of sand around. Every time you move a pile you lose a little sand and pick up a little dirt [5]. Imprecision can cause a number of errors which must be addressed. A discussion of general numerical problems in computer graphics appears in [5]. What follows is a brief discussion of a common problem to all ray tracing intersection routines.

In ray tracing often the origin of the ray $\mathbf{R}_0$ is a point on the sphere itself. Theoretically, $t = 0$ for these points, which are ignored by testing for this condition. However, in practice, calculational imprecision will creep in and throw these tests off. This imprecision will cause rays shot from the surface to hit the surface itself. Computationally what occurs is that t's are found which are very close to, but not necessarily equal to, zero. If uncorrected, those larger than zero will be considered valid intersections. The result is the nonsensical situation in which a small surface area is shadowed by itself. This problem is shown in *Figure 4*. The practical effect of this imprecision is a case of 'surface acne.' The surface will sometimes shadow itself, causing blotches and spots to appear. Some method of coping with this imprecision is necessary to clean up this problem. The discussion below also applies to any other primitive intersected, as all surfaces have this potential problem.

One method to avoid imprecision is to pass a flag telling whether the origin

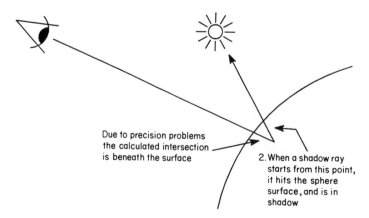

Due to precision problems the calculated intersection is beneath the surface

2. When a shadow ray starts from this point, it hits the sphere surface, and is in shadow

Fig. 4.   Problem in surface intersection.

is actually on the sphere. In ray tracing, the last intersection point is known, so the procedure can be informed that the ray starts on the surface. However, if the sphere is a transmitter some testing must be done to allow refraction rays to pass through the sphere and hit its other side. The same problem arises with reflections from the inside of the sphere. In these cases the t_1 solution is the valid answer.

A simple solution is to check if t is within some tolerance. For example, if $abs(t) < 0.00001$, then that t describes the origin as being on the sphere. Scaling this tolerance to the size of the environment is advisable. For example, if the spheres were atoms and the radii were expressed in meters, 0.00001 meters would be much larger than any atom. Choosing these tolerances can be done empirically or, more accurately, by numerical methods for error analysis. For example, the tolerance could also be based on the radius of the sphere intersected.

Root polishing methods may also be useful in solving imprecision problems. For example, say a ray is traced and the t of the closest object (i.e. the object the ray first hits) is found. Find this intersection point (equation (A7)) and use this as the origin of a new ray which uses the same direction. By intersecting the sphere with this new ray and accepting the solution for t closest to zero (even if t is negative), a more accurate intersection point can be found. While t is greater than some given tolerance this procedure is repeated. This method does not eliminate the need for a tolerance factor, but it does allow the programmer to be confident that the intersection point is within a certain distance of the surface.

A fourth solution is to move the intersection point outside or inside the sphere as needed. That is, when the intersection point is found and new rays are spawned, assure that the new origins are on the proper sides of the surface. This can be done by moving each new ray's origin along the normal until it is found to be on the proper side of the sphere. This involves testing if the point is inside or outside by substituting the intersection point into the sphere equation and checking on which side of the surface the point lies (which is done by checking the sign of the surface expression). If not on the desired side, the point is moved by some tolerance along the normal, then tested again. Note that reflection and shadow rays will always move positively along the normal, refraction rays negatively. This method assures that the origin of the spawned ray will be on the correct side of the sphere, so that the ray will not intersect the sphere.

All of the above methods will work to varying degrees. If possible, the first method should be implemented as it is practically foolproof (almost tangent rays can sometimes have problems; however, these are rare). For spheres and other quadrics this is possible. If not, then some design decisions have to be made to choose the solution proper to the application.

2.5   Spherical Inverse Mapping

Once an intersection point and normal are found on a sphere, further operations may be desired. A common shading trick is texture mapping, in which the position of the intersection point on the sphere's surface is used to vary the surface characteristics [2]. For example, say a globe is to be rendered, and there is a map of the world stored in the computer. Each time the sphere is intersected the proper color is found on the map and used to color that pixel.

The problem is simply to convert the intersection point into a longitude and latitude. The derivation is fairly straightforward, though it involves some time-consuming trigonometric operations.

The input to this process is the normal $\mathbf{S_n}$ (A8) at the point of intersection $\mathbf{R_i}$ (A7) and the following description of the sphere and its axes:

$$\mathbf{S_{pole}} \equiv \mathbf{S_p} \equiv [X_p \ Y_p \ Z_p]$$
$$\mathbf{S_{equator}} \equiv \mathbf{S_e} \equiv [X_e \ Y_e \ Z_e] \tag{B1}$$
$$\text{by definition, } \mathbf{S_p} \cdot \mathbf{S_e} = 0 \text{ (i.e. are perpendicular).}$$

$\mathbf{S_p}$ is a unit vector which points from the sphere's center to the north pole of the sphere. $\mathbf{S_e}$ is a unit vector which points to a reference point on the equator. The parameter u varies along the equator from zero to one. It is traced in the standard direction of the coordinate system used (e.g. if the right hand coordinate system is used, then it varies counterclockwise around the equator). At the poles, define u to be zero. The parameter v varies from zero to one from the south pole to the north (technically speaking, $-\mathbf{S_p}$ to $+\mathbf{S_p}$). This mapping is shown in *Figure 5*.

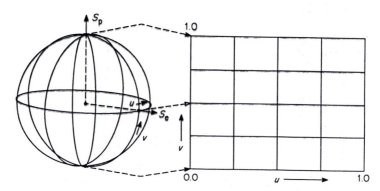

Fig. 5.   Inverse mapping for a sphere.

The point of intersection's normal $\mathbf{r_n}$ is the same as the unit vector formed by the center and the intersection point.

From these definitions, first obtain the latitudinal parameter. This is equal to the arccosine of the dot product between the intersection's normal and the north pole:

$$\phi = \arccos\left(-\mathbf{S_n} \cdot \mathbf{S_p}\right)$$
$$v = \phi/\pi. \tag{B2}$$

Note the division by π can be changed into a multiplication for extra speed. If v is equal to zero or one, then u is defined to be equal to zero. Otherwise calculate the longitudinal parameter:

$$\theta = \frac{\arccos\left((\mathbf{S_e} \cdot \mathbf{S_n})/\sin(\phi)\right)}{2 * \pi}. \tag{B3}$$

Now take the cross product of the two sphere axes defining angles and compare this direction with the direction of the normal:

$$\text{if } ((\mathbf{S_p} \otimes \mathbf{S_e}) \cdot \mathbf{S_n}) > 0 \tag{B4}$$
$$\text{then } u = \theta;$$
$$\text{else } u = 1 - \theta.$$

Note that the cross product can be pre-calculated once in advance. The effect of this test is to determine which side of the $\mathbf{S_e}$ vector the intersection point lies upon.

Example

Begin with an intersection point normal $\mathbf{S_n} = [0.577 \ -0.577 \ 0.577]$ on a sphere whose axes are:

$$\mathbf{S_p} = [0\ 0\ 1]$$
$$\mathbf{S_e} = [1\ 0\ 0].$$

From these first find the latitudinal parameter (B2):

$$\phi = \arccos\left(-[0\ 0\ 1] \cdot [0.577\ -0.577\ 0.577]\right) = 2.186$$
$$v = 2.186/3.14159 = 0.696.$$

The longitudinal parameter calculations are (B3):

$$\theta = \frac{\arccos\ ([1\ 0\ 0] \cdot [0.577\ -0.577\ 0.577]/\ \sin\ (2.186))}{2 * 3.14159}$$

$$= 0.125.$$

Now test which side of the axis S_e the point is on (B4):

$$([0\ 0\ 1] \otimes [1\ 0\ 0]) \cdot [0.577\ -0.577\ 0.577]) = \ -0.577.$$

This value is less than 0, so:

$$u = 1 - 0.125 = 0.875.$$

The final answer is then $(u, v) = (0.875, 0.696)$.

3   RAY/PLANE ALGORITHMS

This section consists of algorithms which deal with intersecting a ray with a polygon. First the ray/plane intersection itself is presented. Next is an algorithm for testing whether the intersection point is inside a polygon on the plane. Mapping onto polygons is also discussed.

3.1   Ray/Plane Intersection

Define a ray in terms of its origin and a direction vector:

$$\mathbf{R}_{origin} \equiv \mathbf{R}_0 \equiv [X_0\ Y_0\ Z_0]$$
$$\mathbf{R}_{direction} \equiv \mathbf{R}_d \equiv [X_d\ Y_d\ Z_d]$$
$$\text{where } X_d^2 + Y_d^2 + Z_d^2 = 1 \text{ (i.e. normalized)}$$

which defines a ray as:

$$\text{set of points on ray } \mathbf{R}(t) = \mathbf{R}_0 + \mathbf{R}_d * t, \text{ where } t > 0. \qquad \text{(C1)}$$

The ray direction does not need to be normalized for these calculations. However, such normalization is recommended, otherwise t will represent the distance in terms of the length of the direction vector.

Define the plane in terms of $[A\ B\ C\ D]$, which defines the plane as:

$$\text{Plane} \equiv A * x + B * y + C * z + D = 0$$
$$\text{where } A^2 + B^2 + C^2 = 1.$$

(C2)

The unit vector normal of the plane is defined as:

$$\mathbf{P}_{\text{normal}} \equiv \mathbf{P}_{\text{n}} = [A\ B\ C]$$

and the distance from the coordinate system origin $[0\ 0\ 0]$ to the plane is simply D. The sign of D determines which side of the plane the system origin is located. This is the implicit formulation of the plane.

The distance from the ray's origin to the intersection with the plane P is derived by simply substituting the expansion of equation (C1) into the plane equation (C2):

$$A * (X_0 + X_{\text{d}} * t) + B * (Y_0 + Y_{\text{d}} * t) + C * (Z_0 + Z_{\text{d}} * t) + D = 0$$

and solving for t:

$$t = \frac{-(A * X_0 + B * Y_0 + C * Z_0 + D)}{A * X_{\text{d}} + B * Y_{\text{d}} + C * Z_{\text{d}}}.$$

(C3)

In vector notation, this equation is:

$$t = \frac{-(\mathbf{P}_{\text{n}} \cdot \mathbf{R}_0 + D)}{\mathbf{P}_{\text{n}} \cdot \mathbf{R}_{\text{d}}}.$$

(C4)

To use (C3) more efficiently, first calculate the dot product:

$$v_{\text{d}} = \mathbf{P}_{\text{n}} \cdot \mathbf{R}_{\text{d}} = A * X_{\text{d}} + B * Y_{\text{d}} + C * Z_{\text{d}}.$$

If $v_{\text{d}} = 0$, then the ray is parallel to the plane and no intersection occurs. Admittedly, a ray could be in the same plane, but this case is irrelevant in practice; hitting a polygon edge-on has no effect on rendering. Also, if $v_{\text{d}} > 0$, the normal of the plane is pointing away from the ray. If the modelling system uses one-sided planar objects, testing could end here, as the plane is culled. If the ray passes these tests, calculate the second dot product:

$$v_0 = -(\mathbf{P}_{\text{n}} \cdot \mathbf{R}_0 + D) = -(A * X_0 + B * Y_0 + C * Z_0 + D).$$

(C6)

Now calculate the ratio of the dot products:

$$t = v_0/v_d \qquad (C7)$$

If $t < 0$, then the line defined by the ray intersects the plane behind the ray's origin and so no actual intersection occurs. Else, calculate the intersection point:

$$\mathbf{r_i} = [x_i \; y_i \; z_i] = [X_0 + X_d * t \quad Y_0 + Y_d * t \quad Z_0 + Z_d * t]. \qquad (C8)$$

Usually, the surface normal desired is for the surface facing the ray, and so the sign of the normal vector $\mathbf{P_n}$ may be adjusted depending on its relationship with the direction vector $\mathbf{R_d}$. The sign of the normal should be reversed in order to point back toward the ray origin.

$$\text{If } \mathbf{P_n} \cdot \mathbf{R_d} < 0 \qquad (C9)$$
$$\text{(in other words, if } v_d < 0)$$
$$\text{then } \mathbf{r_n} = \mathbf{P_n};$$
$$\text{else } \mathbf{r_n} = -\mathbf{P_n}.$$

For those with memory to burn, the reversed normal could be pre-computed and saved.

To summarize, the steps in the algorithm are:

Step 1: calculate v_d and compare it to zero.
Step 2: calculate v_0 and t and compare t to zero.
Step 3: compute intersection point.
Step 4: compare v_0 to zero and reverse normal.

Assuming the most is made out of pre-calculated constants and intermediate results, the calculations associated with each step are:

Step 1: 2 additions, 3 multiplies, and 1 compare.
Step 2: 3 additions, 3 multiplies, 1 division, and 1 compare.
Step 3: 3 additions and 3 multiplies.
Step 4: 1 compare.

This gives a total of 8 additions/subtractions, 9 multiplies, 1 division and 3 compares for the worst case.

Example

Given a plane [1 0 0 – 7] (which describes a plane where $x = 7$) and a ray with an origin of [2 3 4] and a direction of [0.577 0.577 0.577], find the intersection with a plane. Assume the plane is two-sided.

First calculate v_d by (C5):

$$v_d = 1 * 0.577 + 0 * 0.577 + 0 * 0.577 = 0.577.$$

In this case, $v_d > 0$, so the plane points away from the ray. For this example the plane has two sides, so in this case there is no early termination. Calculate v_0:

$$v_0 = - (1 * 2 + 0 * 3 + 0 * 4 + (-7)) - 5.$$

Now calculate t:

$$t = 5/0.577 = 8.66.$$

Distance t is positive, so the point is not behind the ray. This value represents the distance from the ray's origin to the intersection point. The intersection point components are:

$$x_i = 2 + 0.577 * 8.66 = 7$$
$$y_i = 3 + 0.577 * 8.66 = 8$$
$$z_i = 4 + 0.577 * 8.66 = 9.$$

So $R_i = [7\ 8\ 9]$. To determine whether the plane's normal points in a direction towards the ray's origin, check if $v_d > 0$. It is, which means that the plane faces away from the ray. Simply negating the normal will give a normal which faces towards the ray, i.e. $[-1\ 0\ 0]$.

3.2   Polygon Intersection

This section deals with finding if a point on a plane is inside a polygon on that plane. The polygon is assumed to be entirely within the plane. The plane equation is assumed to be known. If the plane equation is not given, it must be derived. See Rogers' excellent book [12] for methods of deriving the normal.

Point/polygon inside/outside testing

Once the plane equation is derived, ray/polygon intersection can be performed. After calculating the ray/plane intersection, the next step is to determine if the intersection point is inside the polygon.

A number of different methods are available to solve this problem. Berlin [1] gives a good overview of some techniques. The method presented here is a modified version of the 'ray intersection' algorithm presented in [14]. This algorithm works by shooting a ray in an arbitrary direction from the intersection point and counts the number of line segments crossed. If the number of crossings is odd, the point is inside the polygon; else it is outside. This is known as the Jordan curve theorem. *Figure 6* depicts the use of this theorem. The modified algorithm presented below elegantly handles the special cases where the test ray intersects a vertex in the polygon. It is my own invention, and appears to be an optimal solution.

Define the polygon as a set of N points:

$$\text{polygon} \equiv \text{set of } \mathbf{G}_n = [X_n\ Y_n\ Z_n], \text{ where } n = (0, 1,\dots,N-1).$$

The plane defined by these points is:

$$\text{plane} \equiv A*X + B*Y + C*Z + D = 0. \tag{D1}$$

The (not necessarily normalized) normal of the plane is defined as:

$$\mathbf{P}_{normal} \equiv \mathbf{P}_n = [A\ B\ C]$$

Begin with an intersection point:

$$\mathbf{R}_i \equiv [X_i\ Y_i\ Z_i]$$

which is given as being on the plane $[A\ B\ C\ D]$.

The first step is to project the polygon onto a two-dimensional plane. In this plane all points are specified by a pair (U, V). So, all that is desired is a (U, V)

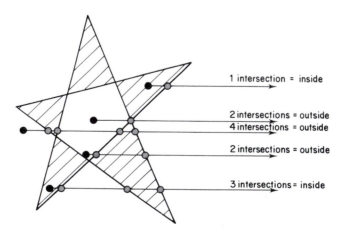

Fig. 6.   Jordan curve theorem.

pair for each [$X\,Y\,Z$] coordinate, such that the topology of the situation is unchanged.

One method would be to rotate around some axis until the normal became parallel to some other axis (say Z). After this is done, the two remaining axes (X and Y, in this case) could be used to generate the (U, V) pairs. The drawback of this scheme is that a rotation matrix must be generated and stored for each polygon, and that a matrix multiply must be performed for each coordinate.

These costs can be eliminated by simply throwing away one of the [$X\,Y\,Z$] coordinates and using the other two. This action projects the polygon onto the plane defined by the two chosen coordinates. The area of the polygon is not preserved, but the topology stays the same. Choosing which coordinate to throw away is defined as follows: throw away the coordinate whose corresponding plane equation value is of the greatest magnitude. For example, for a polygon with a $\mathbf{P_n}$ = [0 −5 3] the Y coordinates would be thrown away, with X and Z assigned to U and V (which is U and which is V is arbitrary). We'll refer to the coordinate with largest magnitude as the dominant coordinate.

Once the polygon has been projected upon a plane, the inside–outside test is fairly simple. Translate the polygon so that the intersection point is at the origin, i.e. subtract the intersection point's coordinates (U_i, V_i) from each vertex. Label these new vertices as (U', V'). Now imagine a ray starting from this origin and proceeding along the $+U'$ axis. Each edge of the polygon is tested against the ray. If the edge crosses the ray, note this fact. If the total count of crossings is odd, the point is inside the polygon. This operation is shown in *Figure 7*.

As Berlin [1] points out, vertices exactly on the ray must be dealt with as special cases. These special cases can be avoided by defining them away. The

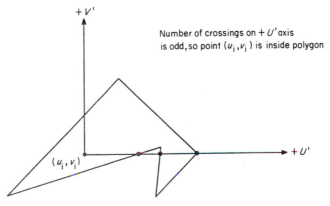

Fig. 7.   Polygon inside/outside test.

ray extending along the $+U'$ axis splits the plane into two parts. However, there are also points which are on the U' axis itself. The definition which must be added is to declare that vertices which lie on the ray (i.e. where $V' = 0$) are to be considered on the $+V'$ side of the plane. In this way no points actually lie on the ray, and the special cases disappear. The ray itself has to be redefined to be infinitesimally close to the original ray, but not to pass through any points. It is now a dividing line, instead of a family of points.

The algorithm is then:

For the NV vertices $[X_n\ Y_n\ Z_n]$, where $n = 0$ to $NV - 1$, project these onto the dominant coordinate's plane, creating a list of vertices (U_n, V_n).

Translate the (U, V) polygon so that the intersection point is the origin. Call these points

$$(U_n', V_n').$$

Set the number of crossings NC to zero.

Set the sign holder SH as a function of V_0', the V' value of the first vertex of the first edge: $\hspace{4cm}$ (D2)

$\hspace{3cm}$ Set to -1 if V_0' is negative.
$\hspace{3cm}$ Set to $+1$ if V_0' is zero or positive.

For each edge of the polygon formed by points (U_a', V_a') and (U_b', V_b'), where $a = 0$ to $NV - 1$, $b = (a + 1)$ mod NV:

Set the next sign holder NSH: $\hspace{4cm}$ (D3)

$\hspace{3cm}$ Set to -1 if V_b' is negative.
$\hspace{3cm}$ Set to $+1$ if V_b' is zero or positive.

If SH is not equal to NSH: $\hspace{4.5cm}$ (D4)

If U_a' is positive and U_b' is positive then $\hspace{1.5cm}$ (D5)
$\hspace{2cm}$ the line must cross $+U'$, so $NC = NC + 1$.

Else if either U_a' is positive or U_b' is positive then $\hspace{1cm}$ (D6)
$\hspace{2cm}$ the line might cross, so compute intersection on U' axis:

If $U_a' - V_a' * (U_b' - U_a') / (V_b' - V_a') > 0$ then $\hspace{1cm}$ (D7)
$\hspace{2cm}$ the line must cross $+U'$, so $NC = NC + 1$.

Set $SH = NSH$. $\hspace{5cm}$ (D8)

Next edge

If NC is odd, the point is inside the polygon, else it is outside. $\hspace{0.5cm}$ (D9)

The algorithm's first test (D4) checks whether the edge crosses the U' axis. If it does not, the edge can be ignored. For those edges that do cross, the vertices are checked (D5) to see if both endpoints are on the $+U'$ part of the plane. If so, the $+U'$ axis must be crossed. Else, if either of the endpoints are in the $+U'$ part (D6), then the exact U' location of where the edge hits the U' axis must be found. If (D7) this U' location is positive (i.e. on the $+U'$ axis), then the edge indeed crosses $+U'$.

This method is highly efficient because most edges can be trivially rejected or accepted. Only when the edge extends from diagonally opposite quadrants does any serious calculation have to be performed.

A minor problem with this and other inside–outside test algorithms is that intersection points exactly on an edge are arbitrarily determined to be inside or outside. There are solutions to this problem, but in practice intersection points on the edges are mostly irrelevant. This is because if an intersection point falls on an edge between two polygons, and both polygons are projected onto the same plane, the algorithm determines that the point is inside one and only one of these polygons (regardless of precision error).

Example

Given a triangle:

$$\mathbf{G}_0 = [-3 \; -3 \; 7]$$
$$\mathbf{G}_1 = [\;\; 3 \; -4 \; 3]$$
$$\mathbf{G}_2 = [\;\; 4 \; -5 \; 4]$$

and an intersection point $\mathbf{R}_i = [-2 \; -2 \; 4]$, find if the point lies within the triangle. The plane equation is:

$$\mathbf{P} = [1 \; 2 \; 1 \; -2]$$

The dominant coordinate in the plane equation is Y, so these coordinates are discarded leaving:

$$\mathbf{G}_{uv0} = [-3 \; 7]$$
$$\mathbf{G}_{uv1} = [\;\; 3 \; 3]$$
$$\mathbf{G}_{uv2} = [\;\; 4 \; 4]$$
$$\mathbf{R}_{uvi} = [-2 \; 4]$$

The situation at this point is shown in *Figure 8*.

Translating the intersection point $[-2 \; 4]$ to the coordinate system origin, the triangle is now:

$$\mathbf{G}'_{uv0} = [-1 \;\;\;\; 3]$$
$$\mathbf{G}'_{uv1} = [\;\; 5 \; -1]$$
$$\mathbf{G}'_{uv2} = [\;\; 6 \;\;\;\; 0].$$

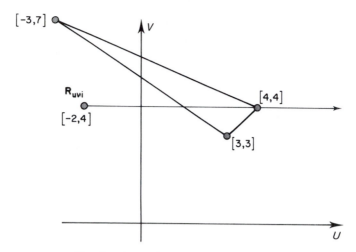

Fig. 8. Inside/outside test example.

The first edge is defined by $(U'_a, V'_a) = (-1, 3)$, $(U'_b, V'_b) = (5, -1)$. The sign holder *SH* is $+1$ since V'_a is positive.

NSH is -1 since V'_b is negative. The first edge passes (D4), since *SH* and *NSH* don't match. Since U'_a is positive and U'_b is not, (D5) fails and (D6) passes, so the true intersection point must be calculated (D7):

$$U'_a - V'_a * (U'_b - U'_a)/(V'_b - V'_a) \equiv -1 - 3 * (5 - (-1))/(-1 - 3) = 3.5.$$

This means that the intersection point is on the $+U'$ axis at 3.5. By the (D7) test, this is considered to be a crossing, and so *NC* is incremented to 1. At the end of testing *SH* is changed to -1 by being set to *NSH* (D8).

The second edge is defined by $(U'_a, V'_a) = (5, -1)$, $(U'_b, V'_b) = (6, 0)$. By (D3), *NSH* is $+1$, and since *SH* doesn't match *NSH*, (D4) is passed, so the line segment must intersect the U' axis. U'_a and U'_b are positive, so by (D5) a crossing takes place, and *NC* is incremented to 2. *SH* is set to $+1$ by *NSH* (D8).

The third edge is defined by $(U'_a, V'_a) = (6, 0)$, $(U'_b, V'_b) = (-1, 3)$. *NSH* is $+1$, and since *SH* matches *NSH*, no crossing takes place.

NC ends as 2, which is an even number, so the point is decided to be outside the polygon. Note how the vertex $(U', V') = (6, 0)$ lay on the $+U'$ axis, and how it was dealt with by considering the vertex to be consistently above the $+U'$ axis ray.

Winding number testing

In *Figure 6* the center pentagon of the star is not considered inside the star, as the number of crossings is even. An alternate definition of the polygon is to consider these points to be inside the polygon.

To perform the inside–outside test for this class of polygons requires a simple change to the previous algorithm. The change is to increment NC when the edge crossing the $+U'$ axis passes from $+V'$ to $-V'$, and decrement NC when it passes from $-V'$ to $+V'$. If NC is 0, the point is outside the polygon, else it's inside.

The number NC is called the *winding number*. Imagine the polygon is made of string, and a pencil point is put on the intersection point. If the string is pulled taut, the winding number is how many times the string goes around the point. The sign of NC is the direction of the rotation: ' + ' is clockwise, ' – ' counterclockwise.

3.3 Convex Quadrilateral Inverse Mapping

Once an intersection point has been found within a polygon, a number of other operations can be performed. If the polygon has been assigned a color pattern, the color at the intersection point must be retrieved. Similar operations must be performed for other texture mapping procedures, such as bump maps. If the polygon is a patch on a curved surface, the exact normal must be derived from the differing normals of the vertices.

This section will present the algorithm for obtaining the location of a point within a convex quadrilateral, since this shape is frequently used in a variety of applications. The parametric values (u, v) are calculated by the algorithm. This coordinate pair represents the location of the point with respect to the four edges, taken as pairs of coordinate axes ranging from 0 to 1. The problem is shown in *Figure 9*.

Note that the mapping itself can also be used as an inside–outside test. If the point is outside the quadrilateral, the (u, v) pair(s) calculated will fall outside the range $(0..1, 0..1)$.

Begin with an intersection point on the quadrilateral's plane:

$$\mathbf{R}_i = [X_i \ Y_i \ Z_i]$$

and a convex quadrilateral defined by four points:

$$\text{Quadrilateral} \equiv \text{set of } \mathbf{P}_{uv}, \text{ where } u = 0, 1 \text{ and } v = 0, 1, \text{ with} \quad (E1)$$
$$\mathbf{P}_{uv} = [X_{uv} \ Y_{uv} \ Z_{uv}]$$

The points define the axes of u and v, e.g. $(\mathbf{P}_{00}, \mathbf{P}_{10})$ defines the u axis at $v = 0$. The normal of the plane (which does not have to be normalized) is called $\mathbf{P}_n$.

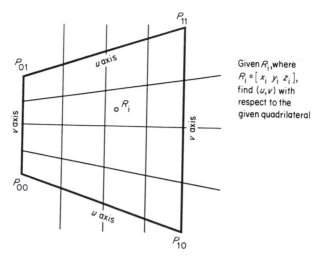

Given R_i, where
$R_i = [\ x_i\ y_i\ z_i\ ],$
find (u,v) with
respect to the
given quadrilateral

Fig. 9.   Quadrilateral inverse mapping.

The derivation is rather involved, so will not be included in this discussion. It is fully covered in [15]. A number of factors must be calculated for the interpolation. These factors divide into two classes: point-plane dependent and plane dependent. Those which are plane dependent can (and should, unless there are other limiting factors such as memory space) be calculated in advance and passed to the algorithm. These plane-dependent factors are:

$$
\begin{aligned}
D_{u0} &= \mathbf{N}_c \cdot \mathbf{P}_d \\
D_{u1} &= \mathbf{N}_a \cdot \mathbf{P}_d + \mathbf{N}_c \cdot \mathbf{P}_b \\
D_{u2} &= \mathbf{N}_a \cdot \mathbf{P}_b \\
\mathbf{N}_a &= \mathbf{P}_a \otimes \mathbf{P}_n \\
\mathbf{N}_c &= \mathbf{P}_c \otimes \mathbf{P}_n
\end{aligned} \qquad (\mathrm{E2})
$$

where:

$$
\begin{aligned}
\mathbf{P}_a &= \mathbf{P}_{00} - \mathbf{P}_{10} + \mathbf{P}_{11} - \mathbf{P}_{01} \\
\mathbf{P}_b &= \mathbf{P}_{10} - \mathbf{P}_{00} \\
\mathbf{P}_c &= \mathbf{P}_{01} - \mathbf{P}_{00} \\
\mathbf{P}_d &= \mathbf{P}_{00}.
\end{aligned}
$$

The basic idea is to define a function for u describing the distance of the perpendicular plane (defined by that u and the quadrilateral's axes) from the coordinate system origin:

$$D(u) = (\mathbf{N_c} + \mathbf{N_a} * u) \cdot (\mathbf{P_d} + \mathbf{P_b} * u). \qquad (E3)$$

The factors computed in (E2) are used to represent this plane-dependent equation. Given $\mathbf{r_i}$, the distance of the perpendicular plane containing this point is:

$$D_r(u) = (\mathbf{N_c} + \mathbf{N_a} * u) \cdot \mathbf{R_i}. \qquad (E4)$$

Setting $D(u)$ equal to $D_r(u)$, solving for u and simplifying:

$$A * u^2 + B * u + C = 0, \qquad (E5)$$

where

$$A = D_{u2}$$
$$B = D_{u1} - (\mathbf{R_i} \cdot \mathbf{N_a})$$
$$C = D_{u0} - (\mathbf{R_i} \cdot \mathbf{N_c}).$$

This is simply a quadratic equation, the solution of which is straightforward and so will not be shown. To gain further efficiency, some other factors are worth computing once for each quadrilateral and storing. Note that these can be calculated only when $D_{u2} \neq 0$. These factors are:

$$\mathbf{Q_{ux}} = \mathbf{N_a}/(2 * D_{u2})$$
$$D_{ux} = -D_{u1}/(2 * D_{u2})$$
$$\mathbf{Q_{uy}} = -\mathbf{N_c}/D_{u2} \qquad (E6)$$
$$D_{uy} = D_{u0}/D_{u2}.$$

With the nine factors from (E2) and (E6) the value of u can be calculated. The solution takes two forms, dependent upon whether the u axes are parallel. Determine whether the axes are parallel by the condition:

$$\text{If } D_{u2} = 0, \text{ then the '}u\text{' axes are parallel.} \qquad (E7)$$

If the axes are parallel, the solution is:

$$u_p = -C/B = (\mathbf{N_c} \cdot \mathbf{R_i} - D_{u0})/(D_{u1} - \mathbf{N_a} \cdot \mathbf{R_i}). \qquad (E8)$$

If not parallel, calculate the following:

$$K_a = D_{ux} + (\mathbf{Q_{ux}} \cdot \mathbf{R_i})$$
$$K_b = D_{uy} + (\mathbf{Q_{uy}} \cdot \mathbf{R_i}).$$

There are two answers:

$$u_0 = K_a - \sqrt{(K_a^2 - K_b)}$$
$$u_1 = K_a + \sqrt{(K_a^2 - K_b)}. \tag{E9}$$

At most one value of these two will lie in the range $(0..1)$, so it is the useful value. If the final u value does not lie in $(0..1)$, then the point is outside of the quadrilateral. One quick test is to test if K_a is less than the discriminant. If it is not, calculate u_0, else u_1. Then check the final u value to see if it is less than 1. Note that if both u_0 and u_1 are in the valid range, then the quadrilateral is not convex.

The value v can be calculated in a similar fashion. The corresponding factors of (E2) are:

$$D_{v0} = \mathbf{N}_b \cdot \mathbf{P}_d$$
$$D_{v1} = \mathbf{N}_a \cdot \mathbf{P}_d + \mathbf{N}_b \cdot \mathbf{P}_c$$
$$D_{v2} = \mathbf{N}_a \cdot \mathbf{P}_c \tag{E10}$$
$$\mathbf{N}_a = \mathbf{P}_a \otimes \mathbf{P}_n$$
$$\mathbf{N}_b = \mathbf{P}_b \otimes \mathbf{P}_n$$

and of (E6) are:

$$\mathbf{Q}_{vx} = \mathbf{N}_a/(2 * D_{v2})$$
$$D_{vx} = -D_{v1}/(2 * D_{v2})$$
$$\mathbf{Q}_{vy} = -\mathbf{N}_b/D_{v2} \tag{E11}$$
$$D_{vy} = D_{v0}/D_{v2}.$$

The corresponding equations for (E7) to (E9) are formed by substituting v for u and substituting $\mathbf{N}_b$ for $\mathbf{N}_c$.

The calculations needed for the point-plane-dependent process itself are, per u or v value, 8 additions/subtractions, 7 multiplies, 1 square root, and 4 compares.

Example
Given a quadrilateral:

$$\mathbf{P}_{00} = [-5 \quad 1 \quad 2]$$
$$\mathbf{P}_{10} = [-2 \quad -3 \quad 6]$$
$$\mathbf{P}_{11} = [\quad 2 \quad -1 \quad 4]$$
$$\mathbf{P}_{01} = [\quad 1 \quad 4 \quad -1]$$

and an intersection point $[-2 \ -1 \ 4]$, find the (u, v) inverse mapping. The plane equation is:

$$B + C - 3 = 0, \text{ so}$$
$$\mathbf{P}_n = [0\ 1\ 1].$$

The factors can be calculated from (E2):

$$\mathbf{P}_a = [-2\ -1\quad 1]$$
$$\mathbf{P}_b = [\quad 3\ -4\quad 4]$$
$$\mathbf{P}_c = [\quad 6\quad 3\ -3]$$
$$\mathbf{P}_d = [-5\quad 1\quad 2]$$

so:

$$\mathbf{N}_a = [-2\ -1\ 1] \otimes [0\ 1\ 1] = [-2\ 2\ -2]$$
$$\mathbf{N}_c = [6\ 3\ -3] \otimes [0\ 1\ 1] = [6\ -6\ 6]$$
$$D_{u0} = [6\ -6\ 6] \cdot [-5\ 1\ 2] = -24$$
$$D_{u1} = [-2\ 2\ -2] \cdot [-5\ 1\ 2] + [6\ -6\ 6] \cdot [3\ -4\ 4] = 74$$
$$D_{u2} = [-2\ 2\ -2] \cdot [3\ -4\ 4] = -22.$$

The other factors are, from (E6):

$$\mathbf{Q}_{ux} = [0.0455\ -0.0455\ 0.0455]$$
$$D_{ux} = 1.68$$
$$\mathbf{Q}_{uy} = [0.272\ -0.272\ 0.272]$$
$$D_{uy} = 1.09.$$

Because $D_{u2} < 0$, the u axes are not parallel. This leads to solving (E9):

$$K_a = 1.68 + [0.0455\ -0.0455\ 0.0455] \cdot [-2\ -1\ 4] = 1.82$$
$$K_b = 1.09 + [0.272\ -0.272\ 0.272] \cdot [-2\ -1\ 4] = 1.91$$

so:

$$u_0 = 1.82 - \sqrt{(1.82 * 1.82 - 1.91)} = 0.636.$$

v is calculated by:

$$\mathbf{N}_a = [-2\ 2\ -2] \text{ (from before)}$$
$$\mathbf{N}_b = [3\ -4\ 4] \otimes [0\ 1\ 1] = [-8\ -3\ 3]$$
$$D_{v0} = [-8\ -3\ 3] \cdot [-5\ 1\ 2] = 43$$
$$D_{v1} = [-2\ 2\ -2] \cdot [-5\ 1\ 2] + [-8\ -3\ 3] \cdot [6\ 3\ -3] = -58$$
$$D_{v2} = [-2\ 2\ -2] \cdot [6\ 3\ -3] = 0.$$

Since $D_{v2} = 0$, the v axes must be parallel. By analog of (E8):

$$v_p = ([-8 \ -3 \ 3] \cdot [-2 \ -1 \ 4] - 43)/(-58 - [-2 \ 2 - 2] \cdot [-2 \ -1 \ 4])$$
$$= 0.231.$$

The solution is then that the points lie at $(u, v) = (0.636, 0.231)$ within the quadrilateral.

Triangle inverse mapping

Inverse mapping can also be applied to triangles. One technique is to pass the triangle to the algorithm, doubling the last vertex in order to give the routine four points to work with. For example, if the standard routine accepts the quadrilateral's points in the order $\mathbf{P}_{00}, \mathbf{P}_{10}, \mathbf{P}_{11}, \mathbf{P}_{01}$, then the triangle's last point $\mathbf{P}_{11}$ is sent again for $\mathbf{P}_{01}$. In this case the mapping of (u, v) would appear as in *Figure 10*. Note that the u axes are defined as being parallel.

A special case occurs when the point to be mapped is at the doubled vertex. At this vertex, all values of one parameter converge. In the example, at $\mathbf{P}_{11}$ in *Figure 10* all u values are correct. Since this singularity has no valid answer, we can choose to either consider it as an invalid point which is outside the polygon, or can assign it an arbitrary value (zero is a likely candidate). Test for this special case by checking if the divisor in equation (E8) is equal to zero.

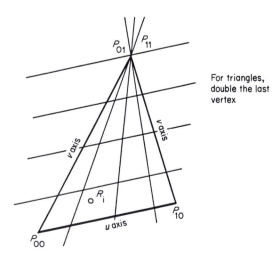

Fig. 10.   Inverse mapping for a triangle.

4   RAY/BOX INTERSECTION

A common form used within ray tracing is the rectangular box. This primitive object is used both for objects which are visible and for bounding volumes, which are used to speed the intersection testing of complex objects.

Kay and Kajiya presented a method of handling these objects based on slabs [9]. A slab is simply the space between two parallel planes. The intersection of a set of slabs defines the bounding volume. The method relies on intersection of each pair of slabs by the ray, keeping track of the near and far intersection distances. If the largest near value is greater than the smallest far value, then the ray misses the bounding volume; otherwise, it hits.

One of the simplest finite bounding volumes is the intersection of two parallel planes each aligned so that their normals are in the same direction as the X, Y, and Z axes. This configuration has a number of properties which make it efficient to test for intersection. The following algorithm uses these properties to allow quick testing of a bounding box. It is written so as to return a boolean value: TRUE if the box has hit, FALSE otherwise.

Define the orthogonal box by two coordinates:

$$\text{box's minimum extent} \equiv \mathbf{B}_l = [X_l \ Y_l \ Z_l]$$
$$\text{box's maximum extent} \equiv \mathbf{B}_h = [X_h \ Y_h \ Z_h]. \tag{F1}$$

Define a ray in terms of its origin and a direction vector:

$$\mathbf{R}_{\text{origin}} \equiv \mathbf{R}_0 = [X_0 \ Y_0 \ Z_0]$$
$$\mathbf{R}_{\text{direction}} \equiv \mathbf{R}_d = [X_d \ Y_d \ Z_d]$$

which defines a ray as:

$$\text{set of points on ray} \equiv \mathbf{R}(t) = \mathbf{R}_0 + \mathbf{R}_d * t \tag{F2}$$

where $t > 0$. We do not require the ray direction to be normalized for these calculations, though this normalization is desirable if the intersection distance is needed.

The algorithm is as follows, returning TRUE if the box is hit:

Set $t_{\text{near}} = -\infty$ and $t_{\text{far}} = \infty$ (i.e. arbitrarily large).

For each pair of planes *PP* associated with X, Y, and Z (shown here for the set of X planes):

If the direction X_d is equal to zero, then the ray is parallel to the planes, so:

If the origin X_0 is not between the slabs, i.e. $X_0 < X_l$ or $X_0 > X_h$, then return FALSE.

Else, if the ray is not parallel to the planes, then

begin:
Calculate intersection distances of planes:
$$t_1 = (X_1 - X_0)/X_d$$
$$t_2 = (X_h - X_0)/X_d$$

If $t_1 > t_2$, swap t_1 and t_2.
If $t_1 > t_{near}$, set $t_{near} = t_1$.
If $t_2 < t_{far}$, set $t_{far} = t_2$.

If $t_{near} > t_{far}$, box is missed so return FALSE.
If $t_{far} < 0$, box is behind ray so return FALSE.
end.
end of for loop.

Since the box survived all tests, return TRUE.

If the box is hit, the intersection distance is equal to t_{near}, and the ray's exit point is t_{far}. The intersection point can be calculated as shown in the 'Ray/Plane Intersection' section, equation (C8). *Figure 11* shows two cases for the intersection test. For a more efficient algorithm, unwrap the loop, expand the swap of t_1 and t_2 into two branches, and change the calculations to multiply by the inverse of the ray's direction to avoid divisions. Unwrapping the loop allows elimination of comparing t_1 and t_2 to t_{near} and t_{far} for the X planes, as t_{near} will always be set to the smaller and t_{far} the larger of t_1 and t_2.

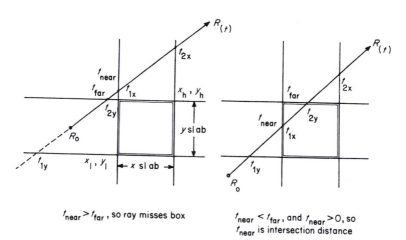

Fig. 11.   Ray/box intersection testing.

Example

Given a ray with origin [0 4 2] and direction [0.218 – 0.436 0.873] and a box with corners:

$$\mathbf{B}_1 = [-1 \ 2 \ 1]$$
$$\mathbf{B}_h = [3 \ 3 \ 3]$$

find if the ray hits the box. The algorithm begins by looking at the X slab, defined by $X = -1$ and $X = 3$. The distances to these are:

$$t_{1x} = (-1 - 0)/0.218 = -4.59$$
$$t_{2x} = (3 - 0)/0.218 = 13.8$$

and so set $t_{near} = -4.59$ and $t_{far} = 13.8$. Neither $t_{near} > t_{far}$ (impossible for the first slabs test) nor $t_{far} < 0$, so the Y slab is examined:

$$t_{1y} = (2 - 4)/-0.436 = 4.59$$
$$t_{2y} = (3 - 4)/-0.436 = 2.29.$$

Since $t_{1y} > t_{2y}$, swap these values. Update $t_{near} = 2.29$ and $t_{far} = 4.59$. Again, neither test was failed, so check the Z slab:

$$t_{1z} = (1 - 2)/0.873 = -1.15$$
$$t_{2z} = (3 - 2)/0.873 = 1.15.$$

t_{near} is not updated and so is still 2.29, and $t_{far} = 1.15$. $t_{near} > t_{far}$ at this stage, so the ray must miss the box.

5 RAY/QUADRIC INTERSECTION AND MAPPING

A general class of objects which are relatively simple to intersect with a ray are the quadrics: cylinders, cones, ellipsoids, paraboloids, hyperboloids, etc. Spheres and planes are special subclasses of this family of objects. For reasons of efficiency, such simple objects are often given their own intersection routines. For example, see [13] for a quicker cylinder intersection method. This section will cover the generalized intersection of these objects. Again, a parametric ray formulation and an implicit surface equation are used to solve the intersection problem. Standard mappings are discussed at the section's end.

5.1   Ray/Quadric Intersection

The technique for intersection is to use the ray equation:

$$\mathbf{R}_{origin} \equiv \mathbf{R}_0 \equiv [X_0 \ Y_0 \ Z_0]$$
$$\mathbf{R}_{direction} \equiv \mathbf{R}_d \equiv [X_d \ Y_d \ Z_d]$$
$$\text{where } X_d^2 + Y_d^2 + Z_d^2 = 1 \text{ (i.e. normalized)}$$

which defines a ray as:

set of points on line $\mathbf{R}(t) = \mathbf{R}_0 + \mathbf{R}_d * t$, where $t > 0$.   (G1)

Using the formulation in [4], the quadric surface equation is:

$$[X \ Y \ Z \ 1] * \begin{bmatrix} A \ B \ C \ D \\ B \ E \ F \ G \\ C \ F \ H \ I \\ D \ G \ I \ J \end{bmatrix} * \begin{bmatrix} X \\ Y \\ Z \\ 1 \end{bmatrix} = 0 \qquad (G2)$$

The matrix is labelled $\mathbf{Q}$ and is useful for performing transformations and other operations on the quadric. See [6] and [4] for further discussion of these operations. This equation is equivalent to where the function $F(X, Y, Z) = 0$:

$$F(X, Y, Z) \equiv A^* X^2 + 2^* B^* X^* Y + 2^* C^* X^* Z + 2^* D^* X +$$
$$E^* Y^2 + 2^* F^* Y^* Z + 2^* G^* Y +$$
$$H^* Z^2 + 2^* I^* Z + J$$

Substituting (G1) into (G2) and solving for t yields coefficients for the quadratic formula:

$$A_q = A^* X_d^2 + 2^* B^* X_d {}^* Y_d + 2^* C^* X_d {}^* Z_d +$$
$$E^* Y_d^2 + 2^* F^* Y_d {}^* Z_d +$$
$$H^* Z_d^2$$

$$B_q = 2^* (A^* X_0 {}^* X_d + B^* (X_0 {}^* Y_d + X_d {}^* Y_0) + C^* (X_0 {}^* Z_d + X_d {}^* Z_0) +$$
$$D^* X_d + E^* Y_0 {}^* Y_d + F^* (Y_0 {}^* Z_d + Y_d {}^* Z_0) + G^* Y_d +$$
$$H^* Z_0 {}^* Z_d + I^* Z_d)$$

$$C_q = A^* X_0^2 + 2^* B^* X_0 {}^* Y_0 + 2^* C^* X_0 {}^* Z_0 + 2^* D^* X_0 +$$
$$E^* Y_0^2 + 2^* F^* Y_0 {}^* Z_0 + 2^* G^* Y_0 +$$
$$H^* Z_0^2 + 2^* I^* Z_0 + J.$$

If $A_q \neq 0$, then check the squared discriminant. If $B_q^2 - 4^* A_q^* C_q < 0$, no intersection takes place. Otherwise calculate t_0 and possibly t_1, if needed. The smallest positive value of t is used to calculate the closest intersection point.

$$t_0 = \frac{- B_q - \sqrt{(B_q^2 - 4^* A_q^* C_q)}}{2^* A_q}$$

$$t_1 = \frac{- B_q + \sqrt{(B_q^2 - 4^* A_q^* C_q)}}{2^* A_q} \tag{G3}$$

If $A_q = 0$, then the equation to be solved is simply:

$$t = - C_q/B_q \tag{G4}$$

Once t has been computed, the intersection point $\mathbf{r_i}$ is calculated using equation (C8). The normal of a quadric surface is formed by taking partial derivatives of the function F with respect to X, Y, and Z:

$$\mathbf{r_n} \equiv [x_n\, y_n\, z_n] = [\mathrm{d}F/\mathrm{d}X \quad \mathrm{d}F/\mathrm{d}Y \quad \mathrm{d}F/\mathrm{d}Z] \tag{G5}$$

$$x_n = 2^*(A^* x_i + B^* y_i + C^* z_i + D)$$
$$y_n = 2^*(B^* x_i + E^* y_i + F^* z_i + G)$$
$$z_n = 2^*(C^* x_i + F^* y_i + H^* z_i + I).$$

Note that $\mathbf{r_n}$ is not normalized. The multiplication by 2 can be deleted, since the length of the normal is unimportant at this point. Also, the normal should be for the surface facing the ray, so the direction of this vector must be reversed depending on its relationship with the direction vector $\mathbf{R_d}$. If $\mathbf{r_n} \cdot \mathbf{R_d} > 0$, then the normal should be reversed.

Example

Given a ray with an origin at $[4\ 5\ -3]$ and a direction vector of $[0.577\ 0.577\ -0.577]$, find the intersection point with an ellipsoid at $[6\ 9\ -2]$ with the axes lengths $X_a = 12$, $Y_a = 24$, $Z_a = 8$.

From basic analytic geometry, the ellipsoid's equation is:

$$\frac{(X - 6)^2}{12^2} + \frac{(Y - 9)^2}{24^2} + \frac{(Z - (-2))^2}{8^2} = 1$$

Simplifying, the quadric function is then:

$$F(X, Y, Z) \equiv 4^* X^2 - 48^* X + Y^2 - 18^* Y + 9^* Z^2 + 36^* Z - 315 = 0.$$

The equivalent matrix (G2) is formed by finding equivalences to the parameters A through J, and is:

$$[X\ Y\ Z\ 1] * \begin{bmatrix} 4 & 0 & 0 & -24 \\ 0 & 1 & 0 & -9 \\ 0 & 0 & 9 & 18 \\ -24 & -9 & 18 & -315 \end{bmatrix} * \begin{bmatrix} X \\ Y \\ Z \\ 1 \end{bmatrix} = 0 \qquad \text{(G2)}$$

The coefficients for t are:

$$\begin{aligned} A_q = \ & 4^*0.577^*0.577 + 2^*0^*0.577^*0.577 + 2^*0^*0.577^*(-0.577) + \\ & 1^*0.577^*0.577 + 2^*0^*0.577^*(-0.577) + \\ & 9^*(-0.577)^*(-0.577) \end{aligned}$$

$$= 4.67$$

$$\begin{aligned} B_q = \ & 2^*(4^*4^*0.577 + 0^*(4^*0.577 + 0.577^*5) + 0^*(4^*(-0.577) + \\ & 0.577^*(-3)) - 24^*0.577 + \\ & 1^*5^*0.577 + 0^*(5^*(-0.577) + 0.577^*(-3)) - 9^*0.577 + \\ & 9^*(-3)^*(-0.577) + 18^*(-0.577)) \end{aligned}$$

$$= -3.46$$

$$\begin{aligned} C_q = \ & 4^*4^*4 + 2^*0^*4^*5 + 2^*0^*4^*(-3) + 2^*(-24)^*4 + \\ & 1^*5^*5 + 2^*0^*5^*(-3) + 2^*(-9)^*5 + \\ & 9^*(-3)^*(-3) + 2^*18^*(-3) - 315 \end{aligned}$$

$$= -535.$$

The expression $B_q^2 - 4^*A_q^*C_q$ is positive, so an intersection point exists. The distance t is then either t_0 or t_1. First check t_0 by (G3):

$$t_0 = \frac{-(-3.46) - \sqrt{((-3.46)^2 - 4*4.67*(-535))}}{2*4.67}$$

$$= -10.3.$$

t_0 is negative (behind the ray), so check t_1:

$$t_1 = \frac{-(-3.46) + \sqrt{((-3.46)^2 - 4*4.67*(-535))}}{2*4.67}$$

$$= 11.1.$$

t_1 is positive, so this is the intersection point distance t. Note that the origin is inside the ellipsoid because only t_1 is positive. The intersection point is then (A8):

$$\mathbf{r_i} = [4 + 0.577^*11.1 \quad 5 + 0.577^*11.1 \quad -3 + (-0.577)^*11.1]$$
$$= [10.4 \quad 11.4 \quad -9.4].$$

Calculate the normal at the surface (G5):

$$x_n = 4^*10.4 + 0^*11.4 + 0^*(-9.4) - 24 = 17.6$$
$$y_n = 0^*10.4 + 1^*11.4 + 0^*(-9.4) - 9 = 2.4$$
$$z_n = 0^*10.4 + 0^*11.4 + 9^*(-9.4) + 18 = -66.6.$$

Normalizing, we get:

$$\mathbf{r_n} = [0.255 \quad 0.0348 \quad -0.966].$$

This is a vector whose dot product with $\mathbf{R_d}$:

$$[0.255 \; 0.0348 \; -0.966] \cdot [0.577 \; 0.577 \; -0.577]$$

is 0.725, which means that the surface normal faces in the direction of the ray. This means that the direction of the normal should be reversed so as to point toward the ray's origin.

Efficiency concerns

There are quite a few techniques which can be applied to this algorithm to make it more computationally efficient. One important idea is factoring out common values in an equation. This makes for less elegant-looking formulae, but for efficiency buffs this is unimportant. For example, the formula for calculating A_q in (G3) could be rewritten:

$$A_q = X_d^{*}(Z^{*}X_d + 2^{*}B^{*}Y_d + 2^{*}C^{*}Z_d) +$$
$$Y_d^{*}(E^{*}Y_d + 2^{*}F^{*}Z_d) +$$
$$H^{*}Z_d^2$$

thereby getting rid of 3 multiplies. Another simple change is to factor all constant multiplications (i.e. '2^{*}...') into the factors given, creating new factors as needed. This is recommended only if memory constraints are not a problem. Finally, modifying the quadratic equation in a manner similar to (A16) will save a few more operations. In essence, substitute $NB_q = B_q/2$ into the equation (G3) and solve.

Kernighan and Plauger's [10] basic programming rule is "Write clearly—don't be too clever." This should be balanced against Press' comment [11], "Come the (computer) revolution, all persons found guilty of such criminal behavior [of not factoring] will be summarily executed, and their programs won't be!" A good route is to carefully comment any confusing formulae that are created for efficiency reasons.

Incorporating all of these changes leads to a modified (G3):

$$t_0 = K_a - \sqrt{(K_a^2 - K_b)}$$
$$t_1 = K_a + \sqrt{(K_a^2 - K_b)}$$

where:

$$K_a = -NB_q / A_q$$
$$K_b = C_q / A_q$$

$$A_q = X_d{}^* (A^* X_d + NB^* Y_d + NC^* Z_d) +$$
$$Y_d{}^* (E^* Y_d + NF^* Z_d) +$$
$$H^* Z_d^2$$

$$NB_q = X_d{}^* (A^* X_0 + B^* Y_0 + C^* Z_0 + D) +$$
$$Y_d{}^* (B^* X_0 + E^* Y_0 + F^* Z_0 + G) +$$
$$Z_d{}^* (C^* X_0 + F^* Y_0 + H^* Z_0 + I)$$

$$C_q = X_0{}^* (A^* X_0 + NB^* Y_0 + NC^* Z_0 + ND) +$$
$$Y_0{}^* (E^* Y_0 + NF^* Z_0 + NG) +$$
$$Z_0{}^* (H^* Z_0 + NI) + J$$

where:

$$NB = 2^* B, \ NC = 2^* C, \ ND = 2^* D, \ NF = 2^* F, \ NG = 2^* G, \ NI = 2^* I.$$

For reasons of efficiency, the normal calculation could be separate from the intersection routine [16]. Of all the surfaces tested, only one will actually be closest to the ray's origin, which means that this object would be the only one where the normal was relevant. For calculations such as shadow testing the normal is never needed. After all calculations, the normal could be computed if desired.

The problems of floating point arithmetic imprecision must again be addressed. This imprecision affects the tests for A_q and B_q almost equal to 0. The case where the origin of the ray begins on the quadric surface must also be addressed. Refer to 'Precision Problems' in the 'Ray/Sphere Intersection' section to find a discussion of the problem and its possible solutions. The quadratic formula calculation as given in section 5.5 of [11] is recommended to help avoid precision problems.

The steps of the algorithm are:

Step 1: calculate coefficients.
Step 2: if A_q is not zero, compute K_a and K_b.
Step 3: if $K_a^2 - K_b$ is less than zero, no solution exists.
Step 4: compute the intersection distance t_0 or t_1.
Step 5: compute the intersection point.
Step 6: compute the normal, without normalizing or sign change.
Step 7: redirect normal.
Step 8: normalize normal.

Assuming precomputation and following the worst case, the calculations for each step are:

Step 1: 25 additions and 30 multiplies.
Step 2: 1 subtraction, 2 divides, 1 compare.
Step 3: 1 subtraction, 1 multiply and 1 compare.
Step 4: 1 subtraction, 1 multiply, 1 square root and 1 compare.
Step 5: 3 additions and 3 multiplies.
Step 6: 9 additions and 9 multiplies.
Step 7: 2 additions, 3 multiplies, 1 compare.
Step 8: 2 additions, 6 multiplies, 1 division, 1 square root.

The total is 44 additions/subtractions, 53 multiplies, 3 divisions, 2 square roots, and 4 compares.

5.2 Standard Inverse Mappings

How to perform inverse mappings from a quadric intersection point to (u, v) parametric space is mostly a matter of choice. This is especially true for the less used quadrics, such as the hyperboloid sheets. However, there are objects used in solid modelling and other computer graphics-related fields which have standard mapping definitions. These algorithms are included here, as they can aid both graphical functions such as texture mapping and also a number of non-graphical applications. Mapping parametric coordinates to world coordinates is not covered, as this mapping is not normally needed within most ray tracing applications.

Inverse mapping for a circle

The inverse mapping of a circle is mostly just a problem of converting from Cartesian to polar coordinates. Define a circle laying on the XY plane with its

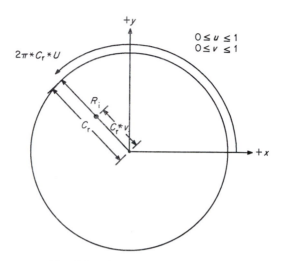

Fig. 12.   Circle inverse mapping.

center at the origin and a radius C_r:

$$X_c^2 + Y_c^2 = C_r^2 \tag{H1}$$

Obviously, in an environment a circle will have a different orientation and location than this simple definition. Assume that some transformation matrix is associated with the circle, so that the circle and related data can be made to coincide with the definition.

   Also given is an intersection point:

$$\mathbf{R_i} = [X_i \ Y_i \ Z_i]$$

which lies on the XY plane (i.e. $Z_i = 0$). The (u, v) coordinates are defined as u ranging from $(0..1)$ starting at the $+X$ axis moving towards the $+Y$ axis, and v ranging from $(0..1)$ from the origin to the edge of the circle. This mapping is shown in *Figure 12*. These parameters are calculated from $\mathbf{R_i}$ as follows:

$$v = \sqrt{((X_i^2 + Y_i^2)/C_r^2)}$$

$$u' = \frac{\arccos\ (X_i/\sqrt{(X_i^2 + Y_i^2)})}{2 * \pi} \tag{H2}$$

   if $Y_i < 0$ then set $u = 1 - u'$, else set $u = u'$.

Note that we could eliminate a multiply and a division by setting $C_r = 1$. This

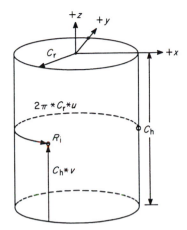

Fig. 13.   Cylindrical inverse mapping.

could be performed by concatenating a scaling matrix into the earlier transformation matrix for the object so that the circle is a unit circle.

Inverse mapping for a cylinder

Define a cylinder of radius C_r and height C_h as:

$$X_c^2 + Y_c^2 = C_r^2, \text{ with } 0 \leqslant Z_c \leqslant C_h \tag{H3}$$

and again have an intersection point $\mathbf{R}_i$ vec $|i$. The (u, v) coordinates are defined as u ranging from $(0..1)$ starting at the $+X$ axis moving towards the $+Y$ axis, and v ranging from $(0..1)$ from the base to the top of the cylinder. This mapping is shown in *Figure 13*. These parameters are calculated as follows:

$$v = Z_i / C_h \tag{H4}$$

$$u' = \frac{\arccos{(X_i / C_r)}}{2 * \pi}$$

if $Y_i < 0$ then set $u = 1 - u'$, else $u = u'$.

Inverse mapping for a cone

Define a cone of height C_h with radius C_{r0} at $Z = 0$ and C_{rh} at $Z = C_h$ as:

$$\sqrt{(X_c^2 + Y_c^2)} = C_{r0} + (C_{rh} - C_{r0}) * Z_c / C_h, \tag{H5}$$
$$\text{with } 0 \leqslant Z_c \leqslant C_h$$

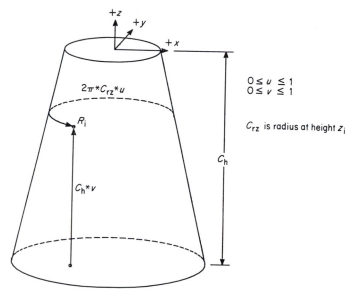

Fig. 14.   Conic inverse mapping.

and an intersection point R_i. The (u, v) coordinates are defined as u ranging from $(0..1)$ starting at the $+X$ axis moving towards the $+Y$ axis, and v ranging from $(0..1)$ from the base to the top of the cylinder. This mapping is shown in *Figure 14*. These parameters are calculated as follows:

$$v = Z_i/C_h \tag{H6}$$

$$u' = \frac{\arccos\left(X_i/(C_{r0} + (C_{rh} - C_{r0}) * Z_i/C_h)\right)}{2 * \pi}$$

if $Y_i < 0$ then set $u = 1 - u'$, else $u = u'$.

Alternatively u could be calculated as for the circle. Note that a number of the divisions could be done once for the cone and re-used. Also, note that when $C_{r0} = 0$ and $Z_i = 0$ (or $C_{rh} = 0$ and $Z_i = C_h$), division by zero will result. At this point u is undefined, and can arbitrarily be assigned any value from $(0..1)$.

BIBLIOGRAPHY AND REFERENCES

1. Berlin, E.P. Jr., 'Efficiency Considerations in Image Synthesis.' Siggraph Course Notes, Vol. 11, July 1985.

2. Blinn, J.F. and Newell, M.E., Texture and reflection in computer generated images. *Commun. ACM* **19**(10), 542–547, October 1976.
3. Blinn, J.F., A homogeneous formulation for lines in 3 space, *Comput. Graph.* **11** (2) Summer 1977.
4. Blinn, J.F., 'The Algebraic Properties of Homogenous Second Order Surface.' Siggraph Course Notes, Vol. 12, July 1984.
5. Duff, T., 'Numerical Methods for Computer Graphics'. Siggraph Course Notes, Vol. 15, July 1984.
6. Goldman, R.N., Two approaches to a computer model for quadric surfaces. *IEEE Comput. Graph. Appl.* **3**(6), 21–24, September 1983.
7. Heckbert, P.S., Survey of texture mapping *IEEE Comput. Graph Appl.* **6**(11), 56–67, November 1986.
8. Kajiya, J.T., 'Siggraph '83 Tutorial on Ray Tracing.' Siggraph '83 State of the Art in Image Synthesis Course Notes, July 1983.
9. Kay, T.L. and Kajiya, J.T., 'Ray Tracing Complex Scenes.' Siggraph '86 Proceedings, p. 269–278, August 1986.
10. Kernighan, B.W. and Plauger, P.J., *The Elements of Programming Style*, McGraw-Hill, New York, 1978.
11. Press, W.H. *et al.*, *Numerical Recipes*, Cambridge University Press, Cambridge, England, 1986.
12. Rogers, D.F., *Procedural Elements for Computer Graphics*, McGraw-Hill, New York, 1985.
13. Roth, S.D., 'Ray casting for modeling solids.' *Comput. Graph. Image Process.* **18**(2), 109–144, Feb. 1982.
14. Sedgewick, R., *Algorithms*, Addison-Wesley, Reading, Mass., pp. 315–317.
15. Ullner, M.K., Parallel Machines for Computer Graphics. PhD Thesis, California Institute of Technology, Computer Science Technical Report 5112, 1983.
16. Whitted, T., 'The Hacker's Guide to Making Pretty Pictures.' Siggraph '85 Image Rendering Tricks Course Notes, July 1985.

3 A Survey of Ray–Surface Intersection Algorithms

PAT HANRAHAN

1 INTRODUCTION

Complicated scenes will often consist of many different types of geometric primitives. In order to generate an image of such scenes, the rendering system must be able to handle this diversity. One of the major advantages of ray tracing is that it has a simple object-oriented structure. The program has a ray tracing section, which computes the optical properties by casting or tracing the appropriate rays, and an intersection section, which checks whether rays intersect different types of objects. Since the interface is so well defined, new objects can be integrated into the program if a few basic operations on them are provided. An important theme when performing these calculations is to retain the geometric primitives in their natural form and not to prematurely reduce them to other primitives. The intersection calculations are significantly speeded up by exploiting special properties, such as symmetries, knowledge about the number of potential intersections, hierarchy or coherence, which are lost if the object is converted to another representation.

In this chapter we begin with a general discussion of surface models, emphasizing similarities and differences between *implicit* versus *explicit* or *parametric* surfaces. Various types of geometric calculations are then discussed. Transformations are emphasized since they are prevalent in both viewing and modeling, and can be used to reduce the number of calculations required. Following that is a survey of different types of surfaces and how to solve for their intersection with a ray.

2   BASIC GEOMETRY

2.1   Types of Geometric Models

To model the geometry of three-space we need mathematical models of volumes, surfaces and curves. Two basic methods exist to do this, *classification* and *enumeration*.

The basic idea of the first method is that there exists a *point-membership classification* function. This is given by either a formula or a three-valued procedure, that given the coordinates of a point, returns whether the point is *inside*, *outside*, or *on* the shape. Mathematically, this can be expressed as

$$F(x, y, z) \quad \begin{cases} < 0 & \text{inside} \\ = 0 & \text{on} \\ > 0 & \text{outside.} \end{cases}$$

The locus of points where the function is 0 defines the boundary between the inside and the outside. Assuming there are no degeneracies, this boundary is a surface. Since the points on the surface are not known without performing the above test, surfaces defined in this way are called *implicit*. Surfaces can be further classified depending on the types of arithmetic operations used to calculate F. If only polynomials are used, the surface is an *algebraic surface*, and if smooth functions are used, the surface is an *analytic surface*. More generally, F can be computed with an arbitrary procedure. Two common examples are: (i) Julia and Mandelbrot sets, where F is calculated by following the path of a point and testing whether it converges to a stable position or diverges, and (ii) constructive solid geometry, where F is given by a regularized boolean equation involving primitive classification functions. Volume density arrays, such as that produced by CT or NMR scans, also can be thought of as an implicit function which naturally defines iso-density surfaces.

The second method *enumerates* the points of interest by explicitly generating them. In this case, the function is a mapping from a set of parameters to a set of points. Calling the function with a given parameter set generates a point on the shape. If the object is a curve, there is only one parameter; if it's a surface there are two parameters; and if it's a volume there are three parameters. In the case of surfaces, this can be mathematically expressed as

$$(x(u, v), y(u, v), z(u, v), w(u, v))$$

where x, y, z and w are independent functions of the parameters u and v. A surface defined in this way is often called an *explicit* or *parametric* surface. The most common example of this type of surface is a bicubic patch, which is given by the *tensor product* of two cubic polynomials, one in u and the other in v. A more common example is a sphere which is parameterized by its latitude and longitude.

A mathematical model of a shape is not unique and the two methods described above are not mutually exclusive. For many primitive shapes both types of descriptions can be used. A plane, for example, is represented implicitly with the equation

$$ax + by + cz + dw = 0$$

or parametrically as

$$
\begin{bmatrix} x \\ y \\ z \end{bmatrix} = u \begin{bmatrix} x_u \\ y_u \\ z_u \end{bmatrix} + v \begin{bmatrix} x_v \\ y_v \\ z_v \end{bmatrix} + \begin{bmatrix} x_0 \\ y_0 \\ z_0 \end{bmatrix}
$$

where (x_0, y_0, z_0) is a point in the plane, and two non-parallel vectors, (x_u, y_u, z_u) and (x_v, y_v, z_v), are contained in the plane. Motivation for having both forms for a surface is provided by the surface–surface intersection problem. The parametric equations for each coordinate from one surface can be inserted into the implicit equation for the other surface to yield an implicit equation involving only the parametric coordinates. This equation represents the curve of intersection in parametric coordinates. Another example of this is curve–surface or line–surface intersection which yields an implicit equation in a single parameter; this is discussed in great detail below.

The advantages of implicit surface over explicit surfaces are:

- Point-membership classification functions are needed for solid modeling systems based on *constructive solid geometry* (CSG).
- Ray–surface intersection calculations reduce to solving for the roots of univariate functions.
- Algebraic surfaces, in particular, have several additional advantages. Intersections of algebraic surfaces are closed; that is, a curve corresponding to the intersection of two algebraic surfaces is an algebraic curve. Algebraic parametric surfaces can be considered a subset of the general algebraic surface [61]. Parametric surfaces can always be converted to algebraic surfaces using a process of *implicitization*. The reverse process, finding the parameters given a point on the surface, is called *inversion*.

The advantages of explicit surface descriptions are:

- It's very easy to generate polygons or line segments that cover the surface.

- Bounding volumes are usually easier to compute.
- BREP-based modeling systems specify solids as surface sections joined along their curve boundaries. With a parametric surface, a subset of the surface can be specified by giving the range of its parameters.
- A surface parametrization is needed for some types of texture mapping.

2.2   Generic Operations

It must be possible to perform certain operations on geometric primitives to utilize them in a modeling or rendering system. Some of these are:

- Transformations are used to instance objects in different positions and orientations and to view objects from different viewpoints with different types of projections.
- Rectangular boxes or spheres are often used to bound the spatial extent of an object so that calculations can take advantage of spatial coherence.
- Surface normals must be computed for shading. The normal is also used in ray tracing to generate the reflected and transmitted rays.
- Point classification against primitives is needed if CSG is used to model more complicated objects.
- Surface–surface and curve–surface intersections must often be computed. For ray tracing, the ray(line)–surface calculation is critical.
- Texture mapping methods require surface parameters to be generated for any given point on the surface. Converting a point on a surface to a parameter is called *inversion*.
- Conversion to other representations. This can take many forms, converting to a print representation, converting to a database representation, converting to line segments, to polygons.

2.3   Points, Planes, Lines and Rays

In this section we briefly review vector and homogeneous representations of points, planes and lines. In projective three-space a point is represented as the four-component vector

$$\mathbf{x} = (x, y, z, w)$$

and its coordinates in Euclidean three-space are

$$\left(\frac{x}{w}, \frac{y}{w}, \frac{z}{w}\right).$$

If w equals 1, we may safely ignore the fourth component. One of the advantages of the homogeneous representation is that points and planes are duals of each other. This means that all calculations involving operations between points can be replaced by calculations involving operations between planes. The representation of a plane is

$$\mathbf{a} = (a, b, c, d).$$

A point with a homogeneous coordinate of 0 corresponds to a *point at infinity*. These points can be considered direction vectors. One advantage of the homogeneous representation is that directions and finite points can be used interchangably. This isn't always true when using vector arithmetic.

A line is all linear combinations of two points,

$$\mathbf{p} = s\mathbf{x} + t\mathbf{y},$$

or two planes,

$$\mathbf{p} = s\mathbf{a} + t\mathbf{b}$$

In the above equations, the same point or plane is generated for all parameter values which give the same ratio of s/t. The point form of the line equation is more commonly interpreted in the following way

$$\mathbf{p} = \mathbf{o} + t\mathbf{d}$$

Where $\mathbf{o}$ is a finite point (homogeneous coordinate equal to 1), and $\mathbf{d}$ is a direction (homogeneous coordinate equal to 0). If we restrict t to only positive values, the above equation represents a *ray*, where $\mathbf{o}$ is its origin and $\mathbf{d}$ is the direction in which its moving. As we'll see later, the plane form of a line is useful for intersecting lines with parametric surfaces.

2.4   Modeling and Viewing Transformations

In most computer graphics applications it's necessary to transform geometry. Linear 4×4 transformations are particularly important since they allow translation, rotation, shear and skew, scale, and projection to be performed. Non-linear local and global transformations are also a very powerful modeling tool. More details about linear transformations can be found in the standard references [22, 48, 50] and about non-linear transformation in Barr's paper [3].

Transformations exist in two forms, a point form and a plane form. Most transformations are expressed in the point form since they are easy to visualize and define in that form.

$$\mathbf{x}' = \mathbf{T}\mathbf{x}$$

where $\mathbf{T}$ is a 4×4 matrix representing the linear transformation. This equation is also used to transform directions. Since in this case $w = 0$, the translation terms have no effect which is consistent with the interpretation of the point as a direction vector. Given a point transformation, there is a dual plane transformation:

$$\mathbf{a}' = \mathbf{T}\dagger\mathbf{a}$$

where $\mathbf{T}\dagger$ is the transpose of the adjoint (the inverse can also be used) of $\mathbf{T}$. The correct way to transform a surface normal is to treat it as a tangent plane. It's not correct to treat it as a direction.

Lines are normally transformed into lines by linear transformations (lines will transform into more complicated curves under non-linear transformations).

$$\mathbf{r}' = \mathbf{T}\mathbf{r} = \mathbf{T}\mathbf{o} + t\mathbf{T}\mathbf{d}.$$

If the ray is represented as two planes, $\mathbf{T}\dagger$ is used instead.

The input to a ray tracing program is a camera position modeled as a viewing transformation and a scene consisting of a collection of objects. The viewing transformation transforms from world space to the screen or raster coordinate system. The objects are usually defined in an object coordinate system and they are positioned in world space using a modeling transformation. The outer loop of the ray tracing program generates one or more rays per pixel. Rays are defined in the screen coordinate system since that is most convenient, but then must be transformed to either world or object coordinates. If the viewing transformation involves perspective, the eye or focal point can be transformed once into world space. This can be done by applying the inverse of the point transformation from world space to screen space to the point $(0, 0, -1, 0)$. Notice that this reduces to extracting a single row from the viewing matrix. Another point on the ray is given by transforming the screen location of the pixel into world coordinates. If the viewing transformation is orthographic, the eye point is at infinity. Rays can be still generated with a single transformation by observing that all rays are parallel and hence travel in the same direction. In the viewing coordinate system this direction is $(0, 0, 1, 0)$ and can be transformed once to find the corresponding world space direction. Once again the ray is defined by transforming the screen space coordinates of the pixel into world space.

Ray tracers usually trace rays in world coordinates. One reason for this is that the reflected and transmitted rays must be generated in an orthogonal coordinate system—that is, a coordinate system such that the angle of incidence will equal the angle of reflection, etc. Modeling and viewing transformations involving skew or perspective do not preserve angles and thus can give rise to strange shading effects. Another reason for tracing rays in a fixed reference coordinate system is that many of the algorithms used to speed the search for ray intersections are based on spatial coherence. All the objects should be placed in this coordinate system so that their spatial extents can be directly compared. It's always possible to transform an object into this coordinate system but as will be seen it is often more convenient to transform a ray to the object's coordinate system to perform the intersection calculation. The advantage of transforming the object to world coordinates is that it only has to be done once per object whereas transforming the ray must be done once per ray. Unfortunately, when an object is transformed not only are its coordinates affected but it may be transformed into an object of a different type. For example, a common modeling technique is to scale a sphere into an ellipsoid. Perspective transformations can change a sphere into an arbitrary quadric surface such as a hyperboloid or paraboloid. Non-rational curves and surfaces may be transformed into rational curves and surfaces by 4×4 transformations. Because the type of surface changes under transformation, the type of ray–surface intersection calculation required also changes.

3 RAY–SURFACE INTERSECTIONS

3.1 Implicit Surfaces

General ray-implicit surface

In the remainder of the chapter the ray equation will be represented as

$$\mathbf{x} = \mathbf{x}_1 t + \mathbf{x}_0$$

or, writing each coordinate out separately,

$$x = x_1 t + x_0$$
$$y = y_1 t + y_0$$
$$z = z_1 t + z_0.$$

Given an implicit surface defined by

$$F(x, y, z) = 0,$$

the points of intersection are obtained by substituting the ray equation into the implicit surface equation, yielding a new equation in the single variable t.

$$F(x_1 t + x_0, y_1 t + y_0, z_1 t + z_0) = F^*(t) = 0$$

The solutions (sometimes called the roots or zeros) $t_0, t_1, \ldots, t_n$ of this equation give us the parameter values at which intersections occur. These can be ordered by their distance from the origin of the ray; the first positive root corresponds to the nearest intersection. The corresponding points of intersection are given by substituting these values of t into the ray equation.

$$(x_1 t_0 + x_0, y_1 t_0 + y_0, z_1 t_0 + z_0)$$
$$(x_1 t_1 + x_0, y_1 t_1 + y_0, z_1 t_1 + z_0)$$
$$\ldots$$
$$(x_1 t_n + x_0, y_1 t_n + y_0, z_1 t_n + z_0).$$

Sometimes the roots are complex numbers, in which case the points would also be complex, and can be safely ignored. There may also exist multiple solutions corresponding to the same value of t. These generally occur if either the ray has intersected a silhouette, or has intersected a singularity where the surface is self-intersecting or contains a cusp.

In the simplest ray tracers only the first root is important and the others need never be computed. Algorithms which avoid these unnecessary computations are a big win. Sometimes, however, all the roots need to be computed. The major example of this is CSG; where all the intersections of the ray with all the objects in the CSG tree may be required. In this case it is also important to consider intersections behind the ray origin. Another case of interest is when only intersections within a finite interval need be considered since the root finder can be optimized for this case. Finally, it is sometimes necessary to only test whether a ray intersection has occurred, but it is not necessary to compute the actual point of intersection. These last two situations occur when doing shadow computations. An object is in shadow only if another object intersects the ray between its origin and the light.

Algebraic surfaces

An algebraic surface is an implicit surface that can be written as a polynomial equation involving the coordinates. Common examples are planes, spheres, cones, cylinders, and toruses. A recent survey of machined parts indicates that 95% of them can be modeled with the above primitives. The general algebraic surface is given by the equation

$$P(x, y, z) = \sum_{i=0}^{l} \sum_{j=0}^{m} \sum_{k=0}^{n} a_{ijk} x^i y^j z^k.$$

The degree of the surface is equal to the maximum combined degree of the coordinates, $d = l + m + n$. The number of terms in a surface of degree d is $(n + 1)(n + 2)(n + 3)/6$. A $d = 2$ or quadric surface has 10 terms; on the other hand, an 18th-degree surface representing a bicubic patch may have 1330 terms.

For an algebraic surface a univariate polynomial is formed after substituting the ray equation

$$P^*(t) = \sum_{i=0}^{d} a_i^* t^i$$

where the a_i^* are linear combinations of the original a_i. The coefficients are polynomials in the ray coordinates. In general, performing the substitution and generating the coefficients of the univariate polynomial is a messy and error-prone procedure for all but the simplest cases. Fortunately, symbolic math systems have the capabilities to perform the above substitution and simplify to a univariate polynomial. It's also very important to simplify these equations so common subexpressions are not reevaluated [29].

Many of the equations of interest have degree less than 5. For these equations there exist analytical solutions requiring the nth root of a real number. Linear equations can be trivially solved; quadratic equations can be solved by the quadratic formula, requiring a square root. Closed-form methods for the roots of cubics and quartics are also known. These techniques are described in the standard mathematical references [72]. Unfortunately, these methods are susceptible to numerical provision problems; see [53] for a description of how to reliably solve the quadratic formula. To our knowledge no equivalent analysis has been done for the cubic and quartic formulas.

Higher order equations can be solved numerically by adapting standard techniques such as binary search, Newton's method, and *regula falsi* to polynomial root finding [16]. The most reliable technique seems to be Laquerre's method which approximates the polynomial with a second-degree curve in the neighborhood of the current estimate [54]. The convergence of the above methods depends on the accuracy of the initial approximation and whether singularities or multiple roots are present. These problems can often be avoided by using properties of polynomials to first find an interval containing a single root. Sturm's sequences can be used to find the exact number of roots in an interval, and Descartes' rule of sign can be used to detect whether an interval has 0, 1 or more roots. If all the points of intersection need to be found, the root-finding algorithm can be reapplied to the polynomial resulting after $(t - t_0)$ is factored from the original polynomial. More detail about general polynomial root finders and ray tracing can be found in [11, 29, 34, 74]. *Figure 1* shows an interesting algebraic surface, Steiner's quartic surface.

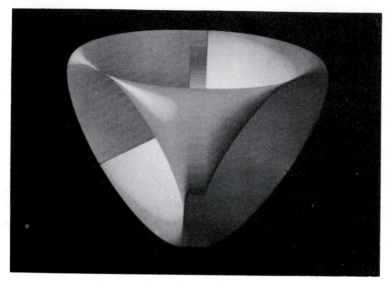

Fig. 1.   Steiner's quartic surface

Plane

A plane is given by the equation

$$ax + by + cz + dw = 0.$$

Substituting the ray equation into the above yields

$$t = -\frac{ax_0 + by_0 + cz_0 + dw_0}{ax_1 + by_1 + cz_1 + dw_1}.$$

Note that the plane equations for a stack of parallel planes differ from each other only by the value of d. In this case, the first three terms in the numerator and denominator remain the same and therefore need only be computed once [39].

Another common situation is where the plane is perpendicular to one of the coordinate axes. Assuming the plane equation is

$$z = 0$$

the solution is simply

$$t = -\frac{z_0}{z_1}.$$

This optimization is similar to that used in clipping lines to the viewing frustum [9, 66]. Since planes transform into planes there is no real advantage to performing the above calculations in one coordinate system over another unless the normal is parallel to one of the axes (of course, this can always be arranged by a suitable transformation).

Quadrics

In this section algorithms for ray tracing quadric surfaces are discussed. Because they are second-degree implicit surfaces they have the advantage that the intersection of a ray and a quadric surface can be found using the quadratic formula. Quadrics were used as the earliest ray tracers developed at MAGI [25]; more recent references include [57] and [8]. *Figure 2* shows the principal quadrics.

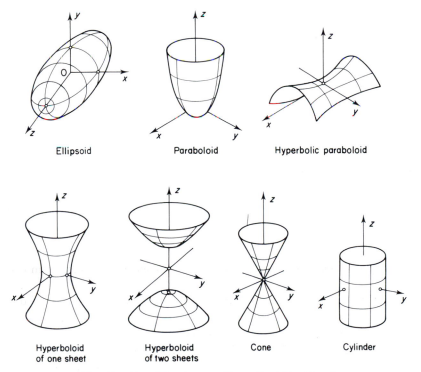

Fig. 2.   Quadric classes (from Paul Heckbert).

General quadric   The general implicit equation for a quadric surface can be written as

$$ax^2 + 2bxy + 2cxz + 2dxw + ey^2 + 2fyz + 2gyw + hz^2 + 2izw + jw^2 = 0.$$

This can be succinctly expressed with the following matrix equation

$$\mathbf{x}^t \mathbf{Q} \mathbf{x} = 0$$

where $\mathbf{Q}$ is the symmetric 4×4 matrix

$$\mathbf{Q} = \begin{bmatrix} a & b & c & d \\ b & e & f & g \\ c & f & h & i \\ d & g & i & j \end{bmatrix}$$

and $\mathbf{x}$ is a column vector and $\mathbf{x}^t$ (transpose) is a row vector. Substituting the ray equation into this equation yields

$$a_2 t^2 + a_1 t + a_0 = 0$$

where

$$a_2 = \mathbf{x}_1^t \mathbf{Q} \mathbf{x}_1$$
$$a_1 = 2\mathbf{x}_1^t \mathbf{Q} \mathbf{x}_0$$
$$a_0 = \mathbf{x}_0^t \mathbf{Q} \mathbf{x}_0.$$

This is a quadratic polynomial in t and can be solved with the quadratic equation.

Note that $\mathbf{Q}$ can be transformed into the world coordinate system to form a new quadric $\mathbf{Q}' = \mathbf{T} \mathbf{Q} \mathbf{T}$ †. As mentioned previously, quadrics transform into quadrics but the type of the quadric does not necessarily remain invariant.

Alternatively, a quadric can be transformed so that only diagonal terms remain [19, 43]. A subset of the general quadric, but which contains all but the degenerate quadrics (two planes, etc.) are the *quadrics of revolution*. These are given by the following general equation

$$x^2 + y^2 + az^2 + bz + c = 0$$

in their canonical coordinate system. Since this equation has fewer terms than the general quadric the intersection calculation can usually be done more rapidly. Spheres, cylinders and cones are sometimes referred to as the *natural quadrics* since they are the natural result of basic machining processes [26].

Sphere   The equation of a sphere in its canonical coordinate system is

$$x^2 + y^2 + z^2 - 1 = 0.$$

Substituting the ray equation into the above yields

$$t^2(x_1^2 + y_1^2 + z_1^2) + 2t(x_0x_1 + y_0y_1 + z_0z_1) + (x_0^2 + y_0^2 + z_0^2) - 1 = 0.$$

If the sphere is positioned at arbitrary location, and if it has an arbitrary radius, it's still possible to use this equation. Just translate the origin of the ray so that it is relative to the center of the sphere and use the radius squared instead of 1. Another optimization to take note of is that if the ray direction has been unitized, $x_1^2 + y_1^2 + z_1^2 = 1$.

Cylinder   The canonical equation for an infinite cylinder is

$$x^2 + y^2 - 1 = 0.$$

Substituting the ray equation into the above yields

$$t^2(x_1^2 + y_1^2) + 2t(x_0x_1 + y_0y_1) + (x_0^2 + y_0^2) - 1 = 0$$

which involves even less computation than the sphere.

Cone   The canonical equation for an infinite cone is

$$x^2 + y^2 - z^2 = 0.$$

Substituting the ray equation into the above yields

$$t^2(x_1^2 + y_1^2 - z_1^2) + 2t(x_0x_1 + y_0y_1 - z_0z_1) + (x_0^2 + y_0^2 - z_0^2) = 0.$$

Paraboloid   The canonical equation for a paraboloid is

$$x^2 + y^2 + z = 0.$$

This yields the following quadratic equation

$$t^2(x_1^2 + y_1^2) + 2t(x_0x_1 + y_0y_1 + z_1) + (x_0^2 + y_0^2 + z_0) = 0.$$

Hyperboloid   The canonical equation for a hyperboloid of two sheets is

$$x^2 + y^2 - z^2 + 1 = 0$$

and of one sheet is

$$x^2 + y^2 - z^2 - 1 = 0.$$

These give rise to the following equations for t, respectively.

$$t^2(x_1^2 + y_1^2 - z_1^2) + 2t(x_0x_1 + y_0y_1 - z_0z_1) + (x_1^2 + y_0^2 - z_0^2) + 1 = 0,$$

$$t^2(x_1^2 + y_1^2 - z_1^2) + 2t(x_0x_1 + y_0y_1 - z_0z_1) + (x_0^2 + y_0^2 - z_0^2) - 1 = 0.$$

Tori

Another common implicit surface is the torus, sometimes called an anchor-ring or doughnut. The cross section of the classic torus consists of two circles of radius b centered at $x = \pm a, z = 0$ (see *Figure 3*). The equations of two circles is given by

$$((x - a)^2 + z^2 - b^2)((x + a)^2 + z^2 - b^2) = 0.$$

This equation can be rearranged to yield the following equation

$$(x^2 + z^2 - (a^2 + b^2))^2 = 4a^2(b^2 - z^2).$$

A three-dimensional torus is formed by revolving the two circles about the z axis. This is most simply done by replacing x^2 by the radius $r^2 = x^2 + y^2$

$$(x^2 + y^2 + z^2 - (a^2 + b^2))^2 = 4a^2(b^2 - z^2).$$

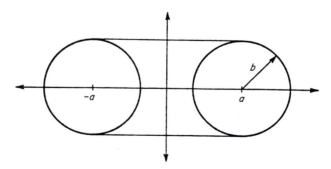

Fig. 3.   A cross section of the common circular torus.

Substituting the ray equation into this equation yields the following quartic:

$$a_4 = (x_1^2 + y_1^2 + z_1^2)^2$$
$$a_3 = 4(x_0 x_1 + y_0 y_1 + z_0 z_1)(x_1^2 + y_1^2 + z_1^2)$$
$$a_2 = 2(x_1^2 + y_1^2 + z_1^2)((x_0^2 + y_0^2 + z_0^2) - (a^2 + b^2)) + 4(x_0 x_1 + y_0 y_1$$
$$\qquad + z_0 z_1)^2 + 4a^2 z_1^2$$
$$a_1 = 4(x_0 x_1 + y_0 y_1 + z_0 z_1)((x_0^2 + y_0^2 + z_0^2) - (a^2 + b^2)) - 8a^2 z_0 z_1$$
$$a_0 = ((x_0^2 + y_0^2 + z_0^2) - (a^2 + b^2))^2 - 4a^2(b^2 - z_0^2).$$

The roots of the quartic can be found analytically.

There are several other interesting tori. The Fichter–Hunt or *fecund* torus is the surface swept out by two series-connected rotational linkages. Many other toroidal surfaces can be derived systematically from any bounded, planar quartic curve of the form $f(x^2, y) = 0$ by substituting $x^2 + y^2$ for x and z for y. Examples are the *eminscate* and *oval of cassini*. These are discussed in [28].

Other implicit surfaces

Here we briefly describe other types of algebraic surfaces that have appeared in the literature.

Blend and join surfaces

Various researchers [32, 45] have described methods for blending between two intersecting or adjoining surfaces. This method is based on the idea that most implicit surfaces can be used to generate a family of surfaces. Suppose we are given two surfaces,

$$f_1(x, y, z) = s_1$$
$$f_2(x, y, z) = s_2$$

then by varying s_1 and s_2 a series of 'concentric' surfaces is created. If we create a new surface

$$g(s_1, s_2) = g(f_1(x, y, z), f_2(x, y, z)) = 0,$$

it blends between the two other surfaces. To smoothly blend between f_1 and f_2, Hoffman and Hopcroft propose that g should have the following properties: (i) g should intersect each surface in a curve, (ii) g should be tangent to these surfaces along the curve of intersection, and (iii) g should be smooth between these curves. One choice is the following ellipse

$$g(s_1, s_2) = \frac{(s_1 - a)^2}{a^2} + \frac{(s_2 - b)^2}{b^2} - 1 = 0$$

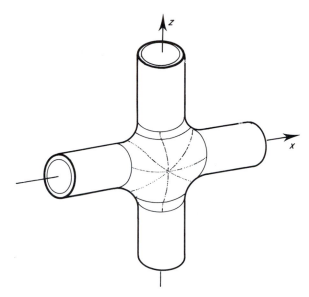

Fig. 4. A quartic blend surface between two cylinders (from Hoffmann and Hopcroft).

where a is the value of s_1 where f_1 intersects f_2 and b is the value of s_2 where f_2 intersects f_1. Using this method, the degree of the blend surface is $2\deg(f_1)$ $\deg(f_2)$ which in the case of quadric primitives yields a surface of degree 4. Other conics can also be used to give different types of blends. A quartic blend between two perpendicular cylinders is shown in *Figure 4*.

Another method for joining two surfaces is to combine them with a *homotopy*. A simple example of this method is to use z to join between f_1 at $z = 1$ to f_2 at $z = 0$.

$$g(x, y) = z^2 f_1 + (z - 1)^2 f_2 = 0.$$

If the original functions are quadrics, this again leads to a quartic surface.

Implicitization of tensor product surfaces—bilinear and bicubic patches

The parametric form of a uniform bicubic patch is

$$x = \mathbf{u}^t \mathbf{X} \mathbf{v}$$
$$y = \mathbf{u}^t \mathbf{Y} \mathbf{v}$$
$$z = \mathbf{u}^t \mathbf{Z} \mathbf{v}$$

where $\mathbf{u} = (u^3, u^2, u, 1)$ and $\mathbf{v} = (v^3, v^2, v, 1)$ and $\mathbf{X}$, $\mathbf{Y}$ and $\mathbf{Z}$ are matrices of *control points*. Similar equations can be written for bilinear, biquadratic and higher order surfaces by simply changing the highest degree of u in **u** and v in **v** to 1, 2, or n. The corresponding rational surfaces will also have a w term.

Sederberg [61–63], reviving several techniques from classical algebraic geometry, discusses several techniques for turning these surfaces into implicit surfaces. In general, the degree of the implicit surface is equal to $2\,mn$, where m and n are the degrees of the u and v polynomials, respectively. Thus, a bilinear patch leads to a surface of degree 2, a biquadratic patch to a surface of degree 8, and a bicubic patch to a surface of degree 18. This last observation means that a line can intersect a bicubic patch in as many as 18 points. Steinberg also discusses techniques for converting biquadratic and bicubic patches to implicit surfaces [65].

One problem that occurs when solving for intersections with parametric surface patches using implicitization is that intersections may occur outside the parameters which define the path. The problem of finding the parameters of a patch given a point on the patch is termed *inversion*. Fortunately, for polynomial patches it is possible to derive algebraic equations for the parameters of patch in terms of the point of intersection. The parameters will typically be the ratio of two polynomials of degree $2mn$ [61].

Methods to directly ray trace patches in their parametric forms using numerical technique or subdivision algorithms are discussed below.

Simplicial splines and Steiner patches

A disadvantage of tensor product surfaces is that not all surfaces can be covered with quadrilaterals. In these cases it's convenient to have a surface patch defined on a triangle. A simplicial spline [14], sometimes referred to as a B-net, Bezier or triangular spline, or Bernstein basis, has a similar parametric form to the tensor product surface except that only the upper diagonal of **X, Y,** and **Z** have non-zero elements. In general, implicitization of a triangular patch will yield an implicit surface of degree n^2.

An example of this is the Steiner patch, which is a biquadratic Bezier patch. This can be implicitized using an elegant construction based on its *triple point* to give a surface of degree 4 [63]. Since this is a quartic it is easy to ray trace.

Superquadrics

Barr and Edwards [20] have developed techniques for ray tracing superquadrics. Superquadrics are most easily defined as the spherical products of superconics. A spherical product surface formed from two curves, $g(u) = (g_x(u), g_y(u))$ and $h(v) = (h_x(v), h_y(v))$ is

$$x(u, v) = g_x(u)h_x(v)$$
$$y(u, v) = g_y(u)h_x(v)$$
$$z(u, v) = h_y(v)$$

The most common example of this is a sphere, where the curves $g(u) =$ $(\cos(u), \sin(u))$ and $h(v) = (\cos(v), \sin(v))$ are circles, and u is interpreted as the longitude and v as the latitude of the sphere. Other quadric surfaces can be formed by forming the spherical products of other conics, for example, ellipses and hyperbolas. The hyperboloid of one sheet is the product of a hyperbola and a circle; a hyperboloid of two sheets is the product of two hyperbolas. Superconics are similar to normal conics except the trigonometric terms are raised to arbitrary power. A superellipse is

$$x = a \cos(\theta)^{e_1}$$
$$y = b \sin(\theta)^{e_1}$$

and a superhyperbola is

$$x = a \sec(\theta)^{e_1}$$
$$y = b \tan(\theta)^{e_1}$$

The parameter e_1 controls the *roundness* of the curve. If e_1 equals 1, the curve is a conic. If it is less than 1, the curve becomes squarer and in the limit, the superellipse actually becomes a rectangle. If it is greater than 2, the ellipse becomes pinched and is concave.

Superquadric surfaces are to quadric surfaces as superconics are to conics. Superellipsoids are the spherical product of two superellipses (see *Figure 5*). Similarly, superhyperboloids of one and two sheets are the product of a superhyperbola and a superellipse and superhyperbola, respectively. A super-torus can also be formed by taking the spherical product of two superellipses, if the origin of one is translated relative to the origin of the other.

Superquadrics can all easily be converted into an implicit form. The point

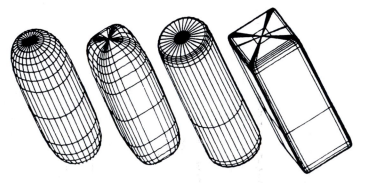

Fig. 5.   A series of superellipsoids (from Barr).

membership classification function of a superellipsoid is:

$$f(x, y, z) = \left(\left(\frac{x}{a_1} \right)^{2/e_2} + \left(\frac{y}{a_2} \right)^{2/e_2} \right)^{e_2/e_1} + \left(\frac{z}{a_3} \right)^{2/e_1} - 1 = 0.$$

Implicit equations for other superquadrics are described in [2].

Edwards' technique for solving for the intersection of a ray with a superquadric involves first isolating intervals in which only a single root occurs. Once such an interval is found the true root can be found by using binary search or *regula falsi* along the ray. Intervals containing roots can be found by first finding the intersection of the ray with the bounding box surrounding the superquadric and interior planes at 45 degrees. The planes divide the ray into intervals and the transitions between intervals can be classified with respect to the superquadric. Because of the nature of the superquadric at most one root can be contained in each interval. If the super-quadric is convex, there are at most two intersections, and the number of intervals that need to be considered is fewer than in the case where the superquadric is concave (a *pinchy*).

Blobs

A system for generating pictures of *blobs* made from superimposed exponent-ial density distributions has been described in [10]. The density distribution is

$$F(x, y, z) = \sum_{i=0}^{n} b_i e^{-d_i} - T = 0$$

where T is a threshold and

$$d_i = a_i(\mathbf{x}^t \mathbf{Q} \mathbf{x})$$

is a quadratic surface. A sum of two density functions is shown in *Figure 6*. In most cases the quadric matrix corresponds to a sphere, so that $d_i = a_i (r_i^2 - R_i^2)$, where r_i is the distance of a point from the center of the ith sphere and R_i is its radius. Because the kernel is quadratic, Blinn was able to transform the volume density into the viewing coordinate system to yield the following equation

$$d_i(x, y, z) = a(x, y)z^2 + b(x, y)z + c(x, y) = 0.$$

Alternatively, the ray equation can be directly substituted into the quadratic kernel to yield a quadratic equation in t

$$d_i(x, y, z) = A(\mathbf{x}_0, \mathbf{x}_1)t^2 + B(\mathbf{x}_0, \mathbf{x}_1)t + C(\mathbf{x}_0, \mathbf{x}_1) = 0.$$

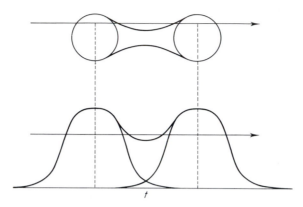

Fig. 6.   Two superimposed density distributions.

Many of the heuristic techniques described in his paper can be used to solve for the roots of this equation. It's possible to solve for the intersection with a single blob by first taking the logarithm of the density function and then solving a quadratic equation. To solve for the intersection with a group of blobs, these single-blob intersections and the centers of each individual blob can be used as the initial guesses to a numerical root finder. More details about these models are described in [10].

Omura has described a modeling primitive, a *metaball*, which is a variation of this technique [49]. Instead of using an exponential density function they use a piecewise quadratic.

$$
d_i = \left\{
\begin{array}{ll}
a_i[1 - 3r_i{}^2] & 0 \leq r_i \leq 1/3 \\
(3/2)a_i[1 - r_i^2] & 1/3 \leq r_i \leq 1 \\
0 & 1 \leq r_i
\end{array}
\right.
$$

where $r_i^2 = \mathbf{x}^t \mathbf{Q} \mathbf{x}$. Once the ray equation is substituted into the above equation, t is broken into intervals where the spheres of various radii intersect the ray. The centers of the intervals correspond to the closest point to the center of the sphere. Immediately on either side of that are intervals where $r_i \leq 1/3$, and on either side of those, an interval where $1/3 \leq r_i \leq 1$. The ray can thus be intersected with each quadratic, and if an intersection occurs the point is tested to see if it lies in the relevant interval. The neat thing about this system is that if a sum of density distributions is used these can be superimposed along the ray. The intervals for each metaball are superimposed and broken into new intervals each of which has a sum of quadratic densities associated with it. Since the sum of quadratics is still a quadratic, the points of intersection with the superimposed density distribution can be directly solved by using the quadratic formula. Unfortunately, details of this technique have not been published but the results have been widely seen in Kawaguchi's movies.

A variation of the above technique is to use a density function which is a hermite cubic whose slope is 0 at 0 and r_i, and whose value is equal to 0 and 1 at those points [77]. r_i^2 is substituted directly into this polynomial to give rise to a sixth-degree polynomial. Blobs of this type could also be ray traced, although since the degree of this polynomial is higher than with the metaball method, it would not seem to be better.

Voxel arrays and spatial subdivisions

Ray tracing has also been used to display three-dimensional arrays. Such arrays arise naturally in medical imaging and scientific simulation [41, 60, 70]. The three-dimensional array of values can be interpreted as an implicit function whose value at a point is equal to the value of the array at the corresponding lattice position. As for any implicit function, a surface is defined to be the locus of points where the implicit function has the same value. For a voxel array, the surface is formed by picking a threshold:

$$V[x][y][z] - T = 0.$$

A ray can be traced through this three-dimensional array by using an incremental line drawing algorithm such as Bresenhahm's algorithm [23]. However, instead of terminating when the endpoint is reached, the line drawing is terminated when the first interior voxel is reached. Although converting to a binary solid introduces jaggy surfaces, storing a true normal with each voxel allows reasonably smooth shading. More sophisticated shading models can also be applied to volumes [36].

The major use of voxel techniques, however, has not been to display volumetric data but to exploit spatial coherency when ray tracing many objects [26]. Each voxel contains a list of surfaces which intersect it. The ray is traced by incrementally moving through the voxel array testing only those surfaces contained in each voxel. It's also possible to trace rays through hierarchical spatial subdivisions such as octrees [24, 38, 77] or BSP-trees [46] although the methods of traversal are more complicated because it is harder to find a cell's immediate neighbors. Once again, these methods are usually used to guide intersection searches, but if an object can be modeled as spatial subdivision they could serve as geometric primitives.

3.2 Explicit Surfaces

General techniques

A very general technique for ray tracing parametric surfaces can be derived if we treat a line as the intersection of two planes. These planes can be any plane through the line.

$$a_1^t \mathbf{x} = a_1 x + b_1 y + c_1 z + d_1 w = 0$$
$$a_2^t \mathbf{x} = a_2 x + b_2 y + c_2 z + d_2 w = 0$$

(for methods to compute these planes given the point form of the ray see [67] or [51]). A vector representing all points of a parametric surface,

$$(x(u, v), y(u, v), z(u, v), w(u, v)),$$

can be inserted into the above line equations to yield two implicit equations involving the parametric coordinates u and v.

$$F_1(u, v) = a_1 x(u, v) + b_1 y(u, v) + c_1 z(u, v) + d_1 w(u, v) = 0$$
$$F_2(u, v) = a_2 x(u, v) + b_2 y(u, v) + c_2 z(u, v) + d_2 w(u, v) = 0.$$

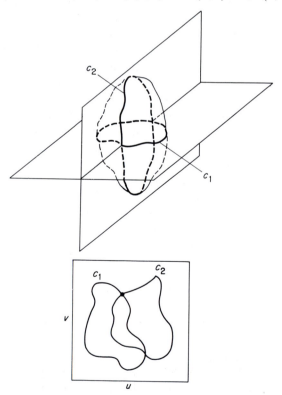

Fig. 7.   Parametric surface intersected by two planes.

Each of these equations represent a curve in parameter space which corresponds to the curve of intersection between the parametric surface and the two planes. Since the planes both contain the line, these curves intersect where the line intersects the surface (see *Figure 7*). Two basic methods have been proposed for solving these equations: if the parametric surface is a polynomial, these equations can be solved using polynomial techniques such as elimination or resultants. Alternatively, the above equations can be solved using numerical techniques.

Bicubic patches

In the case of bicubic patches, F_1 and F_2 are sixth-degree polynomials [34]. If we write these in the following form

$$F_1(u, v) = a_3(u)v^3 + a_2(u)v^2 + a_1(u)v + a_0(u) = 0$$
$$F_2(u, v) = b_3(u)v^3 + b_2(u)v^2 + b_1(u)v + b_0(u) = 0,$$

we can eliminate v from these two equations to form a single univariate equation in u which will be of sixth degree. Since each of these values of v can then be substituted in one of the above equations to yield a cubic equation in u, this cubic will have three solutions, so the total number of possible solutions is 18. Kajiya [34] discusses one method for doing this; Sederberg discuss several others [62]. If the surface patches are biquadratic polynomials, the above equations represent conics so there are at most eight solutions. When using this technique all the solutions must be generated; if only the closest point of intersection is needed this can involve extra computation.

Numerical methods

Numerical techniques for solving simultaneous implicit curve equations can be derived using two-dimensional Newton iteration. Given the two functions, F_1 and F_2, and a guess at the surface parameters corresponding to the point of intersection, (u^0, v^0), Newton's method attempts to improve on these using the following iterative equation:

$$u^{i+1} = u^i + \Delta u^{i+1}$$
$$v^{i+1} = v^i + \Delta v^{i+1},$$

where the deltas are calculated from the following equation:

$$
\begin{bmatrix} \dfrac{\partial F_1}{\partial u} & \dfrac{\partial F_1}{\partial v} \\[2ex] \dfrac{\partial F_2}{\partial u} & \dfrac{\partial F_2}{\partial v} \end{bmatrix}
\begin{bmatrix} \Delta u^{i+1} \\[1ex] \Delta v^{i+1} \end{bmatrix}
=
\begin{bmatrix} F_1(u^i, v^i) \\[1ex] F_2(u^i, v^i) \end{bmatrix}
$$

Solving this equation requires that the Jacobian always has an inverse. This is true if

$$(\mathbf{a}_1 \times \mathbf{a}_2) \left(\frac{\partial \mathbf{x}}{\partial u} \times \frac{\partial \mathbf{x}}{\partial v} \right) \neq 0$$

which has the geometric interpretation that the normal to the surface is never perpendicular to the ray.

Another approach is to formulate the ray–surface intersection problem as one of solving for

$$f(u, v, t) = 0$$

where u and v are surface parameters and t is the ray parameter [4, 69]. This can be done directly using three-dimensional multivariate Newton iteration. One iteration has the geometric interpretation of solving for the intersection of the ray with the tangent plane to the surface at the point given by (u, v). The problem with Newton iteration is that if the initial guess is not close to the final solution it will not converge. Toth describes a method, based on interval mathematics, for finding an interval in which simple Newton iteration will converge to a solution.

The problem of solving for roots can also be cast as one of minimizing the distance from a point on a ray to a point on the surface [33]. If this distance is 0, an intersection has been found. They discuss quasi-Newton methods, based on *BFGS* update of the inverse Hessian, for more rapidly iterating to the solution. They also discuss exploiting ray to ray coherence when employing numerical methods.

The above numerical methods are very general and may be applied to any parametric surface—not just bicubic patches. One example of this is an offset surface—that is, a surface which is displaced a constant amount in the direction of its normal relative to the original surface. If the original surface is a bicubic patch, the resulting surface will *not* be a bicubic. Another example of more complicated surfaces are those generated by deformations; these are discussed further below.

3.3 Procedural Surfaces

Polygons

The major complication when ray tracing polygons is that not only must the ray intersect the plane, but the point of intersection also must lie inside the polygon. Two basic methods have been used to test whether the point is actually inside the polygon: (i) transform the point to a surface coordinate system in which the test is trivial, or (ii) perform a general *point-in-polygon* test. The process of finding surface coordinates is just the inversion problem discussed previously. However, since the equation of a plane is linear in its coordinates, the problem reduces to just a linear homogeneous transformation. In most cases this transformation can be done trivially, by just using two of the three Cartesian coordinates, either xy, yz or zx in the object's coordinate system. In the general case, however, this transformation may involve a perspective term, and require a division. This transformation is analogous to the one mapping screen coordinates to texture coordinates when performing texture mapping [30]. This transformation can be concatenated with the world to object transformation, so there is no extra cost.

The extents of triangles and rectangles can be simply parameterized once in their canonical coordinate system. A triangle is given by the region in parameter space

$$u \geq 0$$
$$v \geq 0$$
$$u + v \leq 1.$$

Any triangle can be mapped to this coordinate system using a simple affine transformation (no homogeneous term). A rectangle can be mapped to the unit square and any quadrilateral can be mapped to a rectangle using a 3×3 homogeneous transformation. Note that a quadrilateral can be modeled as a bilinear patch but then the mapping to the unit square is more complicated (requiring a square root).

If the polygon has more sides, the inside test is more complicated. One method is to represent the polygon as a boolean combination of line halfspaces and evaluate the point against these halfspaces. Convex polygons are simplest since the point must be inside all the halfspaces. Once a test against a line equation fails, the point is outside the polygon [5]. Another point-in-polygon algorithm based on set operations models the polygon as the union of triangles and applies the triangle inside test described above [7, 58]. A well-known result in computational geometry is that the inside test for convex polygons can be done in $O(\log n)$ steps (with preprocessing) [44, 52]. This result also holds for arbitrary polygons [52] although it is unclear whether these algorithms are practical for polygons with a small number of sides (say less than 10). The most common way to test whether a point is inside an arbitrary polygon is to exploit the Jordan curve theorem. This theorem states the intuitively obvious result: for regions bounded by curves that are not self-intersecting, a point is inside the region if a ray from the point to infinity intersects the curve an odd number of times. (A variation of this theorem also holds in three dimensions and can be used to test whether a point is inside a polyhedron [37, 40, 42].) Details concerning algorithms for point-in-polygon tests may be found in [5, 8, 27, 59]. These algorithms are made more complicated by singularities in which case neighborhoods need to be considered [68]. Finally, if the polygons are self-intersecting, there are two methods for defining inside points: one based on the Jordan curve theorem and the other based on winding or wrapping numbers. These definitions are discussed in [47].

Parallelpiped, cube

The test for ray intersection against a cube defined as the region

$$- 1 \leq x \leq 1$$
$$- 1 \leq y \leq 1$$
$$- 1 \leq z \leq 1$$

is easily done. Since the faces exist on three sets of parallel planes and the normals to these planes are parallel to the coordinate axis, the intersection calculations can be performed more quickly than in the general case. Also, since the edges of the faces are also parallel to the coordinate axis it is very easy to test whether a ray is inside the face.

Polyhedra

Ray intersections with convex polyhedra can be performed by intersecting with each plane and then classifying the point of intersection against the polyhedra. This is done by testing whether the point is inside the halfspaces defined by all the other planes.

Kay and Kajiya describe an algorithm for intersecting a ray with a polyhedra defined by pairs of parallel planes [39]. Their algorithm is similar to the Cyrus–Beck clipping algorithm [18].

Techniques from computational geometry are also applicable to polyhedra although to our knowledge they have not been published.

Sweep surfaces

Translational sweeps: cylinders and cones

A large number of interesting objects can be modeled by translating a planar curve along a straight line to form a cylinder. A variation allows the radius of the cylinder to change to form a cone. These two types of sweeps are shown in *Figure 8*. Procedures to ray trace these shapes have been developed by MAGI [25] and [8, 35, 75].

The basic idea in these algorithms is to reduce the intersection from a 3-D line–surface problem to a 2-D line–curve intersection problem. One advantage of reducing the problem to 2-D is that now the equation of the line can be

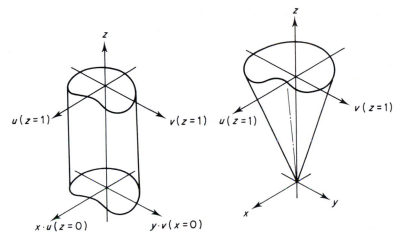

Fig. 8. Translational sweeps (from Van Wijk).

represented as an implicit equation and therefore it's easily intersected with parametric curves.

Assume the curve defining the cross section lies in the x–y plane and the sweep is along the z-axis. Projecting the ray onto the x–y plane gives rise to the following parametric equations representing the ray

$$x = x_1 t + x_0$$
$$y = y_1 t + y_0$$

which is equivalent to the 2-D line equation

$$(y_1) x - (x_1) y - (x_0 y_1 - y_0 x_1) = 0.$$

If the sweep is a cone, we need to scale the u–v coordinates of the curve to get the x–y coordinates.

$$zu = x$$
$$zv = y.$$

Substituting the ray equations into this gives

$$(z_1 t + z_0) u = x_1 t + x_0$$
$$(z_1 t + z_0) v = y_1 t + y_0.$$

This can also be turned into an implicit equation (relabeling (u, v) as (x, y))

$$(y_0 z_1 - z_0 y_1)x - (x_0 z_1 - z_0 x_1)y + (x_0 y_1 - y_0 x_1) = 0.$$

Given a parametric polynomial curve $(x(s), y(s))$, it can be inserted into the above line equation to yield an univariate polynomial in s [75]

$$(y_0 z_1 - z_0 y_1)x(s) - (x_0 z_1 - z_0 x_1)y(s) + (x_0 y_1 - y_0 x_1) = 0.$$

This equation has the same degree as the parametric curve. For the common case of a cubic curve finding intersections involves finding the roots of a cubic polynomial.

Kajiya describes how to intersect a 2-D line with a polygon containing many segments using strip trees [35].

Surfaces of revolution

Another common modeling technique is to revolve a curve around an axis. This problem can be solved by reducing it from a 3-D intersection to a 2-D intersection problem just as in translational sweep (see *Figure 9*).

The equations relating a position in the object's coordinates to the coordinates of the curve being revolved are

$$u^2 = x^2 + y^2 = (x_1 t + x_0)^2 + (y_1 t + y_0)^2$$
$$v = z = z_1 t + z_0.$$

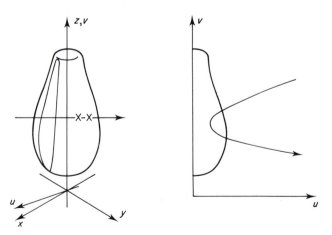

Fig. 9.   Surface of revolution and the ray–curve intersection diagram (based on Van Wijk).

Eliminating t from these two equations gives us the following implicit equation which represents the path of the ray in the (u, v) coordinate system

$$au^2 + bv^2 + cv + d = 0$$

where

$$a = -z_1^2$$
$$b = x_1^2 + y_1^2$$
$$c = 2(x_0 a + z_1(x_0 x_1 + y_0 y_1))$$
$$d = (x_0 z_1 - z_0 x_1^2) + (y_0 z_1 - z_0 y_1^2).$$

This equation is an implicit second degree equation in the curve coordinates. Substituting the curve into this equation (relabeling (u, v) as (x, y))

$$ax(s)^2 + by(s)^2 + cy(s) + d = 0.$$

If cubic polynomials are used to represent the curve being rotated, the root-finder must solve a sixth-degree equation in s.

Intersections with polygonal curves containing many vertices can be done using strip trees [35].

Another method for handling surfaces of revolution is to turn them into series of stacked cones. Each cone is bounded by the two planes where it is joined with the previous and next cone [8]. If the surface needs to be continuous in the y direction three consecutive points along the polygon can be used to define a piecewise parabola with C^1 continuity.

General swept surfaces: sweeping a sphere

There is a well-developed theory for computing the envelope of a moving part [21]. This is the region in space that the part may occupy during some part of its movement. These techniques can be modified to generate shapes which are generated by sweeping along paths. Given a surface which changes through time

$$f(x, y, z, t) = 0$$

the envelope can be computed by eliminating t from the above equation and the following equation

$$\frac{\partial f(x, y, z, t)}{\partial t} = 0.$$

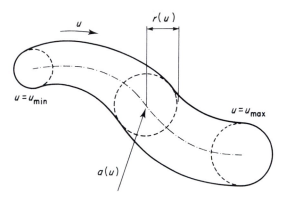

Fig. 10.   A swept sphere of varying radius (from Van Wijk).

If $f(x, y, z, t)$ is algebraic, this can always be done using elimination. A similar theory also exists for parametric surfaces.

Van Wijk has applied this method to ray tracing a sphere moving along a cubic space curve with cubically varying radius (see *Figure 10*). For this shape, f is

$$(x - a_x(u))^2 + (y - a_y(u))^2 + (z - a_z(u))^2 - r^2(u) = 0$$

where $(a_x(u), a_y(u), a_z(u))$ is the center of the sphere and $r(u)$ is the radius. In the general case, the resulting implicit equation will have degree $= 2(2d - 1)$ where d is the degree of the trajectory. Thus, for a cubic trajectory the result will be a tenth-degree equation.

Generalized cylinders

A *generalized cylinder* is the surface defined by sweeping a two-dimensional contour along a three-dimensional trajectory. To make this definition exact the position and orientation of the contour relative to the trajectory must also be specified. The most natural method to do this is to orient the contour relative to the Frenet frame of the trajectory. Methods for performing the ray intersection calculation for this primitive are described in [13].

Constructive solid geometry—CSG

One of the most popular methods to model solid objects or volumes is *constructive solid geometry*. Solids of more complicated objects are constructed from simpler objects by performing set operations, usually union or difference. A composite object can be represented as a binary tree where each node contains a set operation and two child nodes which may also be

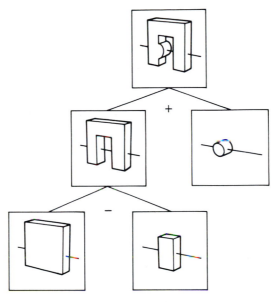

Fig. 11.   Example of a solid object formed using CSG (from Roth).

composite solids. The leaves of this tree are primitive objects such as spheres, planes, etc. This is shown in *Figure 11*. One of the advantages of this representational scheme is its completeness; another advantage is the ease with which it can be ray traced.

Evaluating set operations usually reduces to classification of geometry with respect to other geometry [55]. A curve, surface or volume is deemed to be inside, outside or on another solid. When ray tracing, it is necessary to classify a ray with respect to the solid the ray is being intersected against. This intersection path may be represented with a *Roth diagram* (see *Figure 12*) [57]. This diagram is a line from $-\infty$ to ∞ where each point represents a value of the ray parameter t. Each point on this line is either inside, on or outside the solid. The transitions from inside to outside, and vice versa, will be at intersections of the ray with the primitive volumes comprising the solid. If the solid is a primitive, it is easy to generate the Roth diagram. Each intersection of the ray with the solid is shown on the line. Ignoring singularities, any point of the line can be classified by testing an interior point (between two intersections) with respect to the primitive. Sometimes this is unnecessary since it is known *a priori* what the classification of the origin of the ray is with respect to the primitive (for example, if the ray starts at the eye and it is known that eye point is outside all the objects, or if the origin of the ray corresponds to a previous intersection which has already been classified). Once one

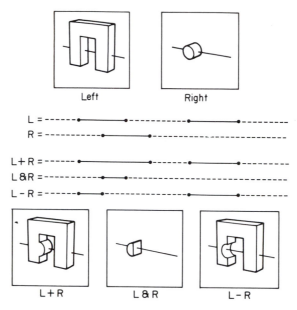

Fig. 12.   Example of a Roth diagram for analyzing CSG operations (from Roth).

interval has been classified, all other intervals are alternately classified inside or outside (assuming the surfaces of the primitives are not self-intersecting and there are no singularities). (For a discussion of how to handle the more general problem of curve–solid classification see [68] or [55].) If the surface is orientable, whether a transition is from inside to outside or vice versa can be determined directly from the surface normal at the point of intersection. Note that in order to create a Roth diagram for a solid it is necessary to find all the intersections of a ray with a primitive volume.

Roth describes a method to combine these diagrams using set operations. This allows the Roth diagram for a composite solid to be recursively computed. First the Roth diagrams of the two solids being combined are computed and then these diagrams are merged to form the diagram for the composite solid. The diagrams of two solids can be combined by using the one-dimensional set operation on the line intervals comprising the diagram. This is done in a three-step process. (1) The intersection points from the two diagrams are merged together into a single diagram (this takes time proportional to the total number of intersections). (2) The intersection points are classified depending on the classification of the original two diagrams and the set operation being performed. (3) The interval is simplified by removing intersections which do not result in a change in the classification. The rules for combining classifications are given in *Table 1* based on well-known rules of

Table 1. Rules for combining classifications.

Set operator	L	R	Composite
Union	IN	IN	IN
	IN	OUT	IN
	OUT	IN	IN
	OUT	OUT	OUT
Intersection	IN	IN	IN
	IN	OUT	OUT
	OUT	IN	OUT
	OUT	OUT	OUT
Difference	IN	IN	OUT
	IN	OUT	IN
	OUT	IN	OUT
	OUT	OUT	OUT

boolean algebra. Once again, these rules for combining intervals are only valid when there are no singularities—that is, no ON classifications. If this occurs a table does not suffice and the classification must make use of neighborhood information [68]. Fortunately, when ray tracing this is seldom a problem.

As will be mentioned below, ray tracing is significantly speeded up if the scene is arranged in a tree of bounding volumes. A CSG tree can serve as this tree (although it may not be the best choice) by combining bounding volumes of the subtrees according to the set operation. Usually, all the bounding volumes in the tree are either spheres or boxes so it is reasonably easy to form a new bounding volume from them. The union of the two bounding volumes can be formed by enclosing both of them; the intersection by enclosing the intersection of the two bounding volumes. If the operation is difference, the bounding volume of the composite is the same as the bounding volume of the object not being subtracted.

Roth also observed that the result of a set operation is sometimes known after the ray has been classified with respect to only one of the two child solids. For example, if the operator is intersection and one solid has no intersections with the ray, there is no need to intersect the ray against the other solid. A similar situation occurs when doing a difference; if the ray is outside the positive solid no intersection can possibly occur.

Hierarchical bounding volumes

Many ray tracing algorithms use a hierarchical tree of bounding volumes to either speed up the search for an intersection or to control the generation of the recursively defined surface. In the second use, a ray piercing a volume signals the surface associated with that volume to continue subdividing. Subdivision either produces a simpler primitive, such as a polygon, or terminates for some other reasons, for example, the screen space size of the bounding volume is below some threshold or the recursion limit is reached.

The straightforward application of this algorithm tests for intersections with all volumes and then sorts them to find the closest intersection [58]. Since the search is depth first and the arrangement of branches at each level is arbitrary, the order in which bounding volumes are searched is essentially random. Objects that are distant from the ray origin are just as likely to be tested as near objects. An improvement to this method is to search objects in the order in which the ray intersects their volumes, in the hope that an early intersection will avoid unnecessary intersection tests [11, 35, 39, 51, 67].

A *primitive* node of the tree is one that intersects the ray and in which the point of intersection can be computed exactly (or to the resolution needed). A *candidate* node is a node which is not a primitive and thus contains child nodes. Associated with each candidate node is also a bounding volume. If the ray intersects the bounding volume of the candidate node, the node is considered active—that is, it may potentially generate a real intersection. The following code fragment searches active nodes in ray order:

```
Initialize closest intersection point to infinity;
Initialize active node heap;
while (active node list is not empty) {
    Set node equal to top of active node heap;
    if (closest intersection point is closer than node)
        break;
    if (node is primitive) {
        Compute intersection with primitive;
        if (ray intersects primitive)
            if (intersection is closer than closest intersection point)
                Update closest intersection point;
    }
    else {
        for (each child of the node) {
            Compute intersection with bounding volume;
            if (ray intersects bounding volume)
                Insert node into active node heap;
        }
    }
}
```

Subdivision algorithms for patches

Many subdivision methods have been employed to solve for the intersection of a ray with a bicubic patch. Whitted [73] used an algorithm similar to Catmull's early patch-rendering algorithm [15]. Each patch was modeled as a hierarchy of bounding spheres which was created on demand. If a ray intersected the bounding sphere of a patch, the patch was subdivided and each subpatch was bounded by another sphere. An intersection is recorded if the ray intersects a sphere below the size of a pixel. The recursion can also be terminated when the patch has been reduced to a size where it can be approximated with another geometric primitive and the intersection can be performed directly. Various researchers have subdivided the patch into planar rectangles either based on size or flatness [58,71].

Another approach is to refine the patch until the bounding volume is reasonably small or at given level of detail and then to numerically solve for the point of intersection. Associated with each leaf node in the tree is a starting (u, v) and a valid parameter range for the numerical iteration [67], sub-divided the patch into a fixed size rectangular mesh. The bounding box of the leaf nodes was centered at the b-spline control vertices of this mesh (since these control points are closest to the patch) and extended towards the neighboring vertices. This extent, although it required a heuristic *overlap* parameter, was tighter than the bounding box surrounding the 16 control points. [51] converted the b-spline basis to a Bezier basis and then enclosed the 16 control points with a bounding box. Because some of the control points of the Bezier patch are on the patch, the bounding volumes were tighter than those based on B-splines. When using these methods it is important that the numerical iteration does not converge to parametric coordinates that lie outside the valid range. When reflected or refracted rays are generated it is also important to insure that the solution does not iterate to the origin of the ray on the surface.

Fractals

The above subdivision algorithms can also be adapted to fractal subdivision algorithms [35]. One method to generate a fractal height field is to subdivide a triangle. Each edge is split in two, and the height at the midpoint is set randomly such that the mean is given by the average of the two original vertices and its variance is proportional to the edge length raised to the fractal dimension. The height field inside a triangle can be bounded by a *cheesecake extent* or triangular prism. Since there is a chance the fractal could reach any height, there is no way to choose an absolute extent; instead the extent must be chosen such that the probability that the fractal will lie outside the extent is below some predetermined minimum (Loren Carpenter has observed that if the random numbers are generated with tables, that an absolute extent can be determined). Each time the fractal is subdivided, the original triangular prism is replaced with 4 new triangular prisms. The subdivision is terminated either when an intersection occurs with small prism or a preset maximum level of subdivision is reached. Following a suggestion of Kajiya, that the maximum possible height is greatest at the midpoint of the edge, [12] added bounding ellipsoids to the triangular prism. Elliptical extents are probably quite useful for other primitives.

Height fields

Fractals are often used to generate terrains. However, real terrain data sets are available as digital terrain or elevation models. A height field is an altitude function $z(x, y)$ defined on a rectangular mesh. Special purpose hidden line [1, 76] and hidden surface [56] are available for displaying height fields. The computational complexity of displaying height fields has also been recently addressed.

These methods benefit from two important properties of terrains: (i) the priority of individual terrain elements can be easily determined from just the direction of view, and (ii) the height field is a function and the ray–surface intersection problem is easier than the intersection problem for general surfaces. The mesh cells of the terrain which needed to be tested for intersection are those whose domains intersect the projection of the ray onto the plane $z = 0$. The cells are searched in order along the direction of the ray so that the first intersection found is the visible terrain element. The intersection test at each mesh element can often be avoided by comparing the range of heights in the terrain with the range of heights of the ray as it enters and exits that mesh element. A height of a ray can be parameterized by one of the principal directions of the terrain (without loss of generality choose x):

$$y_r = y_0 + y_1 x$$
$$z_r = z_0 + z_1 x.$$

The terrain itself is also parameterized by (x, y):

$$z_t = z(x, y).$$

The quadrilateral terrain mesh cell is usually broken into two triangles in which case the solution requires only solving linear equations, or the terrain is bilinearly interpolated from the corners of the quadrilateral in which case the solution requires solving a quadratic [17].

Ray tracing height fields defined on other topologies can use many of the same techniques. For example, a triangular irregular network (TIN) can be

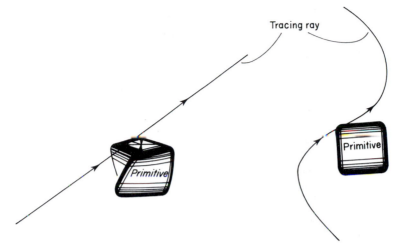

Fig. 13.   Deforming a ray rather than an object (from Barr).

traversed by following a two-dimensional ray through the two-dimensional triangulation. Each time a ray enters a triangle, that triangle is tested for surface intersection. If none is found, the ray is tested against the other edges of the triangle to find which one it exits from. If triangle–triangle adjacency is stored, the ray–surface intersection test can quickly proceed to the next triangle.

Deformed surfaces

Recently, Al Barr has shown how to use non-linear local and global transformations to deform models [3]. Examples include bending, twisting and tapering. Piecewise transformations based on trivariate Bernstein polynomials can also be used to deform volumes [64]. Numerical methods, similar in many ways to those discussed above, can be adapted to solve for the intersection of rays with deformed surfaces [4]. These methods are based on numerical methods developed for solving ordinary differential equations. An interesting approach is to deform the ray into the original object's coordinate system rather that deforming the object (see *Figure 13*).

These methods have begun to be applied to more complicated objects such as JELL-O[31].

REFERENCES

1. Anderson, D.P., Hidden line elimination in projected grid surfaces *ACM Trans. Graph.* **1**(2), 274–288, April 1982.

2. Barr, A.H., Superquadrics and angle preserving transformations, *IEEE Comput. Graph. Appl.* **1**(1), 11–23, January 1981.

3. Barr, A.H., Global and local deformations of solid primitives. *Comput. Graph.* (Siggraph '84 proceedings) **18**(3), 21–30, July, 1984.

4. Barr, A.H., Ray tracing deformed surfaces. *Comput. Graph.* (Siggraph '86 Proceedings) **20**(4), 287–296, Aug. 1986.

5. Barton E.E. and Buchanon, I., The polygon package. *Comput. Aided Des.* **12**(1), 3–11, January 1980.

6. Baumgart, B.G., Geometric Modeling for Computer Vision. Ph.D. Dissertation, Computer Science Department, Stanford University, 1974.

7. Berlin, E.P., Efficiency considerations in image synthesis. Siggraph '85 Course Notes, July 1985.

8. Bier, E.A., Solidviews, An Interactive Three-Dimensional Illustrator. BS & MS thesis, Dept. of EE & CS, MIT, May 1983.

9. Blinn, J.F. and Newell, M.E., Clipping using homogeneous coordinates. *Comput. Graph.* (Siggraph '78 Proceedings) **12**(3), 245–251, July 1978.

10. Blinn, J.F., A generalization of algebraic surface drawing. *ACM Trans. Graph.* **1**(3), 235–256, July 1982.

11. Bouville, C., Dubois, J.L. and Marchal, I., Generating high quality pictures by ray tracing. In *Eurographics '84*, 161–177 Copenhagen (Sept. 1984); *Comput. Graph. For.* **4**(2), 87–99, June 1985.

12. Bouville, C., Bounding ellipsoids for ray–fractal intersection. *Comput. Graph.* (Siggraph '85 Proceedings) **19**(3), 45–52, July 1985.

13. Bronsvoort, W.F. and Klok, F., Ray Tracing General Sweep-Defined Objects, 84-36, Dept. of Mathematics and Informatics, Delft U. of Tech., Delft, Netherlands, 1984.

14. Casteljau, P. De, Courbes et surfaces a poles, Andres Citroen Automobiles 1959.

15. Catmull, E.E., A Subdivision Algorithm for Computer Display of Curved Surfaces. Ph.D. Dissertation, University of Utah, December 1974.

16. Conte, S.D. and De Boor, D., *Elementary Numerical Analysis*, McGraw Hill, 1972.

17. Coquillart, S. and Gangnet, M., Shaded display of digital maps. *IEEE Comput. Graph. Appl.* 35–42, July 1984.

18. Cyrus, M. and Beck, J., Generalized two and three dimensional clipping. *Comput. Graph.* **3**(1), 23–28, 1978.

19. Dresden, A., *Solid Analytical Geometry and Determinants*, Dover, New York, 1930.

20. Edwards, B.E., Implementation of a Ray-Tracing Algorithm for Rendering Superquadric Solids. Masters thesis, TR-82018, Rensselaer Polytechnic Institute, Troy, NY, Dec. 1982.

21. Faux, I.D. and Pratt, M.J., *Computational Geometry for Design and Manufacture*, Ellis Horwood, 1979.

22. Foley, J.D. and Van Dam A., *Fundamentals of Interactive Computer Graphics*, Addison-Wesley, 1982.

23. Fujimoto, A., Tanaka, T. and Iwata, K., ARTS: Accelerated Ray-Tracing System. *IEEE Comput. Graph. Appl.* 16–26, April 1986.

24. Glassner, A.S., Space subdivision for fast ray tracing. *IEEE Comput. Graph. Appl.* **4**(10) 15–22, Oct. 1984.

25. Goldstein, R. A. and Nagel, R., 3-D visual simulation. *Simulation* **16**(1), 25–31, Jan. 1971.

26. Hakala, D.G., Hillyard, R.C., Malraison, P.J. and Nourse, B.E., Natural quadrics in mechanical design. Seminar: Solid Modeling, Siggraph '81 Course Notes, August 1981.

27. Hall, J.K., PTLOC—FORTRAN subroutine for determining the position of a point relative to a closed boundary. *J. Math. Geol.* **7**(1), 75–79, 1975.
28. Hanrahan, P., Tori: algebraic definitions and display algorithms (unpublished), 1982.
29. Hanrahan, P., Ray tracing algebraic surfaces. *Comput. Graph.* (Siggraph '83 Proceedings) **17**(3), 83–90, July 1983.
30. Heckbert, P.S., Survey of texture mapping. *IEEE Comput. Graph. Appl.* November 1986.
31. Heckbert, P.S., Ray tracing JELL-O brand gelatin. *Comput. Graph.* (Siggraph '87 Proceedings), 1987.
32. Hoffmann, C.M. and Hopcroft, J.E., Automatic surface generation in computer aided design. *The Visual Computer* **1**, 92–100, 1985.
33. Joy, K. I. and Bhetanabhotla, M.N., Ray tracing parametric surface patches utilizing numerical techniques and ray coherence. *Comput. Graph.* (Siggraph '86 Proceedings) **20**(4), 279–285, Aug. 1986.
34. Kajiya, J.T., Ray tracing parametric patches. *Comput. Graph.* (Siggraph '82 Proceedings) **16**(3), 245–254, July 1982.
35. Kajiya, J.T., New techniques for ray tracing procedurally defined objects. *ACM Trans. Graph.* **2**(3), 161–181, July 1983; also appeared in Siggraph '83 Proceedings.
36. Kajiya, J.T. and Von Herzen, B.P., Ray tracing volume densities. *Comput. Graph.* (Siggraph '84 Proceedings) **18**(3), 165–174, July 1984.
37. Kalay, Y., *Comput. Vis. Graph. Image Process.* 1985.
38. Kaplan, M.R., Space-tracing, a constant time ray-tracer. In Siggraph '85 State of the Art in Image Synthesis, Seminar Notes, July 1985.
39. Kay, T.L. and Kajiya, J.T., Ray tracing complex scenes. *Comput. Graph* (Siggraph '86 Proceedings) **20**(4), 269–278, Aug. 1986.
40. Lane, J., Magedson, R. and Rarick, M., An efficient point in polyhedron algorithm. *Comput. Vis. Graph. Image Process.* **26**(1), 118–125, April 1984.
41. Levoy, M., Display of surfaces from volume data. *IEEE Comput. Graph. Appl.*, May 1988.
42. Mantyla, M., CG Tokyo, 1985.
43. Maxwell, E.A., *General Homogeneous Coordinates in Space of Three Dimensions,* Cambridge University Press, Cambridge, England 1951.
44. Mellhorn, K., *Multi-dimensional Searching and Computational Geometry*, Springer-Verlag 1984.
45. Middlevitch, A.E. and Sears, K.H., Blend surfaces for set theoretic volume modeling systems. *Comput. Graph.* (Siggraph '85 Proceedings) **19**(3), 161–170, July 1985.
46. Naylor, B.F. and Thibault, W.C., Application of BSP trees to ray-tracing and CSG evaluations (unpublished) 1986.
47. Newell, M. and Sequin, C., The inside story on self-intersecting polygons. *Lambda* **1**(2), 20–24, 1980.
48. Newman, W.M. and Sproull, R.F., *Principles of Interactive Computer Graphics*, McGraw Hill, 1979.
49. Nishimura, H., Hirai, M., Kawai, T., Kawata, T., Shirakawa, I. and Omura, K., Object modeling by distribution function and a method of image generation (in Japanese). *Proc. Electronics Communication Conference,* **J68-D**(4), 1985.
50. Paul, R.P., *Robot Manipulators*, MIT Press, 1981.
51. Peterson, J.W., Ray tracing general B-splines. *Proc. ACM Mountain Regional Conference*, p. 87, April 1986.

52. Preparata, F.P. and Shamos, M.I., *Computational Geometry: An Introduction*, Springer-Verlag, 1985.

53. Press, W.H., *Numerical Recipes*, Cambridge University Press, Cambridge, England, 1986.

54. Ralston, A. and Rabinowitz, P., *A First Course in Numerical Analysis*, McGraw Hill, 1978.

55. Requicha, A.A.G. and Voelcker, H.B., Boolean operations in solid modeling: boundary evaluations and merging algorithms, *Proc. IEEE* 30–44, January 1985.

56. Robertson, P.K., Fast perspective views of images using one-dimensional operations. *IEEE Comput. Graph. Appl.* 47–56, February 1987.

57. Roth, S.D., Ray casting for modeling solids. *Comput. Graph. Image Process.* **18**(2), 109–144, Feb. 1982.

58. Rubin, S.M. and Whitted, T., A three-dimensional representation for fast rendering of complex scenes. *Comput. Graph.* (Siggraph '80 Proceedings) **14**(3), 110–116, July 1980.

59. Salomon, K.B., An efficient point-in polygon algorithm. *Comput. Geosci.* **4**, 173–178, 1978.

60. Schlusselberg, D.S., Smith, W.K. and Woodward, D.J., Three-dimensional display of medical image volumes, *Proc. NCGA*, March 1986.

61. Sederberg, T.W., Implicit and Parametric Curves and Surfaces for Computer Aided Geometric Design. Ph.D. Dissertation, Purdue University, August 1983.

62. Sederberg, T.W., Anderson, D.C. and Goldman, R.N., Implicit representation of curves and surfaces. *Comput. Vis. Graph. Image Process.* **28**, 72–84, 1984.

63. Sederberg, T.W. and Anderson, D.C., Ray tracing of steiner patches. *Comput. Graph.* (Siggraph '84 Proceedings) **18**(3), 159–164, July 1984.

64. Sederberg, T.W. and Parry, S.R., Free-form deformations of solid geometric models. *Comput. Graph.* **20**(4), 151–160, July, 1986.

65. Steinberg, H.A., A smooth surface based on biquadratic patches. *IEEE Comput. Graph. Appl.* **4**(9), 20–23, Sept. 1984.

66. Sutherland, I. and Hodgman, G.W., Reentrant polygon clipping, *CACM* **17**(1), 32–42, January 1974.

67. Sweeney, M. and Bartels, R.H., Ray tracing free-form B-spline surfaces. *IEEE Comput. Graph. Appl.* **6**(2), 41, Feb. 1986.

68. Tilove, R.B., Set membership classification: a unified approach to geometric intersection problems. *IEEE Trans. Comput.* **C-29**(10), 219–220, October 1980.

69. Toth, D.L., On ray tracing parametric surfaces. *Comput. Graph.* (Siggraph '85 Proceedings) **19**(3) 171–179, July 1985.

70. Tuy, H.K. and Lee Tan Tuy, Direct 2-D display of 3-D objects. *IEEE Comput. Graph. Appl.* **4**(10), 29–34, October 1984.

71. Ullner, M.K., Parallel Machines for Computer Graphics. PhD thesis, California Institute of Technology, 1983.

72. Uspensky, J. V., *Theory of Equations*, McGraw Hill, 1948.

73. Whitted, T., An improved illumination model for shaded display. *CACM* **23**(6), 343–349, June 1980.

74. Wijk, J.J. Van, Ray tracing objects defined by sweeping a sphere. In *Eurographics '84*, pp. 73–82, Copenhagen (Sept. 1984), reprinted in *Comput. Graph.* **9**(3), 283–290, 1985.

75. Wijk, J.J. Van, Ray tracing objects defined by sweeping planar cubic splines. *ACM Trans. Graph.* **3**(3), 223–237, July 1984.

76. Wright, T.J., A two-space solution to the hidden-line problem for plotting functions of two variables. *IEEE Trans. Comput.* **C-20**(1), 28–33, January 1973.

77. Wyvill, G., Mcpheeters, C. and Wyvill, B., Data structures for soft objects. *The Visual Computer* **2**, 227–234, 198.
78. Wyvill, G., Kunil, T.L. and Shirai, Y., Space subdivision for ray tracing CSG. *IEEE Comput. Graph Appl.* 28–34, April 1986.

4 Surface Physics for Ray Tracing

ANDREW S. GLASSNER

1 LIGHT AND ILLUMINATION

1.1 Color

When we want to describe the appearance of some object, we often talk about its color. We might describe a flower as 'pale red,' or its stem as 'bright green.' But just how do we sense these colors? And what do we *mean* by 'red'?

Of course, from one point of view this last question is meaningless. Many people have wondered whether when two people say something is 'red,' they are really both perceiving the 'same' color. Maybe what I call red you would call green if you saw it through my eyes, but we both use the same word for that sensation.

There is a practical point of view which sidesteps these problems. We can speak of colors in some way that we can measure with a piece of hardware, which will be a standard to which we can all refer. This doesn't resolve the above dilemma of whether we're 'really' seeing the 'same' colors, but it lets us pass that issue by and start to study what color is all about.

Thus we're going to approach the issue of color from a physical point of view. We'll first talk about light rays, and how they carry light information, including color. Then we'll see how light interacts with objects, such as through absorption or reflection. Then we'll look at how the human eye and brain responds to incoming light, giving the perception of colors.

1.2 Photons, Frequency, and Wavelength

Nobody completely understands the nature of light. There are two popular models that describe many of the features of light, but neither one is completely correct. On one hand we have the *wave model*, which makes an analogy comparing light to water waves. On the other hand we have the *particle model*, which says that light is made up of many little particles.

The techniques of ray tracing are based mostly on the particle model, which essentially says that a light ray is the straight path of a particle of light. In principle, we could work with the wave model instead, but in some ways it would be more difficult and expensive. And neither model is really complete or correct; under some circumstances light behaves like a wave, but under other circumstances it behaves like a particle. Physicists sometimes say that light seems to exhibit a wave–particle duality. Nevertheless, the particle model alone can go a long way towards understanding and explaining light, and that's what we're going to use in the following discussion.

The basic particle of light is called the *photon* (it is perhaps surprising to note that Einstein won the 1921 Nobel Prize not for relativity, but for his theory of the photon, introduced in a 1905 paper). We can think of the photon as a little billiard ball flying through space. But the photon is not just moving in a straight line; it is also vibrating. Now this 'vibration' is actually a kind of mathematical abstraction. It's useful because much of the mathematics that describe vibrations seem to work in describing the behavior of light. So although there's nothing actually shaking around, just as a photon isn't really a billiard ball, the vibration explanation for color is very useful and powerful, and it gives us a start on understanding color.

It turns out that with every photon we can associate a particular *frequency* of vibration. An alternative way of describing the photon's vibration is with a measure called its *wavelength*. The wavelength and the frequency are very closely related.

Imagine that the photon is vibrating in some fixed pattern (say up and down) as it moves forward in space, as in *Figure 1*. When the photon is at point A, it's just beginning to move downwards in its cycle. The photon moves forward in space, vibrating down and then up as it goes. After some time, it will eventually finish its up-and-down cycle, and begin to move down again. The point where it begins to repeat its cycle is marked B. If the photon

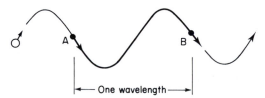

Fig. 1.   As a photon moves through space, it is also vibrating at a constant rate. The distance travelled during the time required to complete one full cycle is called the wavelength of the vibration.

is moving forward at a constant speed, then each time it crosses the same amount of space as the distance from A to B it will also go through one complete cycle of its vibration. This distance is the wavelength of the photon.

If we increase the frequency, the photon will complete its cycle in less time, and so it will cross less space before it begins to repeat. So when the frequency goes up, the wavelength goes down. Similarly, if we slow down the frequency, it will take longer for the photon to repeat its cycle. Since it's moving forward at a constant speed, it will cross more space before it repeats, so when the frequency goes down, the wavelength goes up.

We know from the theory of relativity that the speed of light is a constant in any medium. We can summarize these observations with the equation

$$\lambda = \frac{c}{f} \qquad (1)$$

where λ = wavelength (meters)
f = frequency (cycles second^{-1})
c = the speed of light (in a vacuum, $c \approx 3.00 \times 10^8 \mathrm{m\,s^{-1}}$).

In some situations it will be convenient to speak of the frequency of a photon; in other situations it will be more natural to speak of its wavelength. Keep in mind that both terms describe the same thing in different ways, and that in a given medium we can switch back and forth with equation (1). It is also useful to know that the energy of a photon is directly related to its frequency:

$$E = hf \qquad (2)$$

where E = energy (J)
h = Planck's constant ($h \approx 6.63 \times 10^{-34} \mathrm{J\,s}$).

Now you might wonder what this all gets us. Well, it turns out that there is a direct correlation between the frequency (and thus the energy) of a photon that strikes your eye and the color you see in response. The individual frequencies of different photons are also what give rise to the perceived colors of everyday objects that don't radiate light themselves, but only reflect it.

1.3   Light at Surfaces

In order to generate realistic images we need to understand how light behaves at the surfaces of objects. This is not an easy issue; indeed, many of the subtleties of light interaction are still poorly understood if at all. But there are some simple approximations that we can use to generate surprisingly good images.

We divide the interaction of light and a surface into four classes: *specular reflection*, *diffuse reflection*, *specular transmission*, and *diffuse transmission*. When a given photon hits a surface, it will undergo changes in direction and color as a result of these four effects. The amount of influence of each effect on the photon is mostly dependent on the surface material. But this material may behave differently for light arriving at different frequencies and angles of incidence.

Before we actually study how light behaves at surfaces of different types, we need some background. Specifically, we need to understand the *spectrum* of incident light, and how and why that spectrum changes when light hits a colored surface.

We will first look at the issues of light spectra and reflection in general, and then we'll focus on the four particular effects listed above.

1.4   Color and Spectra

When we look at an ordinary 'white' light bulb, we see 'white light.' Now you might ask yourself where that white light is coming from; for example, have you ever seen a white band in a rainbow? Probably not. White is not a *pure spectral color*; no single vibrating photon can give you the impression of white light. Instead, the impression of white arises when photons of many different colors strike the same region of your eye nearly simultaneously. Your eye blends together all these colors, giving the impression of a single, white light.

So a white light bulb is actually generating photons at many different frequencies, but they're coming so fast and furious that your eye gathers them together and calls it white light. It is interesting and useful to know just how many photons of each frequency are being generated by a given light source. We can set up a measuring instrument to count the average number of photons at each visible wavelength over some period of time, and then plot the results. Such an intensity versus amplitude plot is often called a *frequency spectrum plot*, which is often abbreviated simply as *spectrum*. *Figure 2* shows the spectrum of a light source known as CIE Standard Illuminant D6500, which approximates the spectrum of the sun on a cloudy day.

From now on, we'll often be speaking pretty generally about color, spectra, and photons. The important thing to keep in mind is this: although we'll be illustrating principles with single photons, it is usually photons at all wavelengths that give rise to color phenomena. Thus, when we talk about a photon in some situation, imagine that we're talking about a whole fleet of

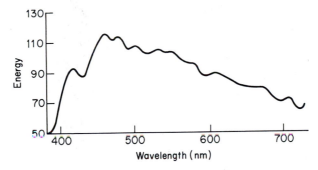

Fig. 2. The spectrum of CIE Standard Illuminant D6500, which approximates sunlight on a cloudy day.

photons, arriving pretty much at the same time and along the same ray, but with different wavelengths. When we speak of the intensity of light at a given wavelength, we're talking about how many photons at that wavelength are riding along that ray.

One convenient way for us to represent all this information will be to associate a spectrum with a ray, as shown in *Figure 3*. In this model, the spectrum summarizes all the photons travelling along that ray, but the convenience of having all that information in one place makes the abstraction useful. A problem with this model is that it cannot model refraction very well.

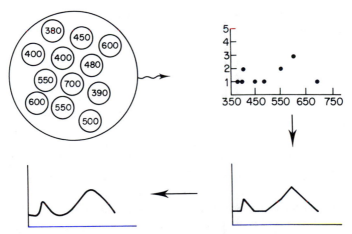

Fig. 3. One way to handle color is to attach a spectrum with each ray, describing the light travelling along that ray. The spectrum is given by points on an intensity vs wavelength plot.

When a light ray passes between two media, it usually changes direction by an amount dependent on wavelength (we'll look at this in more detail later). If we're using a single ray to model all the visible wavelengths simultaneously, then there's no single direction that is going to work correctly.

A better way to go is to assign a particular single wavelength to each ray. If we want to know the amplitude of many wavelengths of light leaving a surface we must use many rays, one for each wavelength in which we have interest.

1.5   Reflection

Imagine a living room with a blue couch, lit by a single white light bulb. Why do we see the couch as blue? This has to do with how the surface of the couch reflects the light that strikes it. We'll talk about the geometry of the reflection in a later section. Here, we'll be more concerned with how an object selectively responds to incoming photons at different wavelengths.

Our goal will be to understand the result of reflection. But we'll look for a moment at the mechanism of reflection; often understanding how something works makes it easier to understand the results.

Suppose that we illuminated a gold bar with the D6500 light of *Figure 2*, as shown in *Figure 4*. One way to describe how gold would react to this incoming light (at a particular angle) is to draw a reflectance spectrum. At a particular angle of incidence, this spectrum indicates the percentage of the incoming light that the gold surface reflects at each wavelength. Thus, to find the color of the light leaving the gold surface, we multiply the amount of incoming light by the percentage reflectance of the gold at each wavelength. Thus, incoming 'sun-colored' light leaves the gold as 'golden-colored light.' How does this happen?

The mechanism takes us back to the idea that a photon is 'vibrating.' If you're at a table with wine glasses, you can slightly wet your finger and run it around the rim of an empty wine glass, making it 'sing.' But other empty wine glasses on the table will usually start to sing as well. This is an example of *sympathetic resonance*. To a certain extent, all physical objects have a frequency at which they will vibrate most easily; this is their *resonant frequency*. If a vibrating object is brought near to another (initially still) object with a similar resonant frequency, the originally unmoving object will begin to vibrate as well.

Consider a vibrating photon striking the surface of some object. The atoms of that object are themselves always vibrating, at a variety of frequencies. When a photon strikes an atom, it has the chance to transfer some or all of its energy. If the photon has exactly enough energy to promote the atom to its next stable energy state, the photon will be absorbed and the atom will sit at

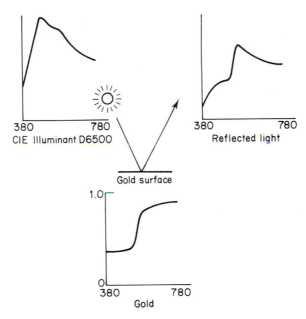

380   780
CIE Illuminant D6500

380   780
Reflected light

Gold surface

1.0

0
380   780
Gold

Fig. 4. When light interacts with a surface, we multiply the incoming spectrum and the appropriate surface spectrum wavelength by wavelength, creating a reflected spectrum.

the higher energy level for a while. If there isn't enough energy for this transfer, the atom will absorb just some of the photon's energy for a moment, but then lose it very soon by radiating that energy away in the form of heat.

But if the photon has just the right frequency to transfer its energy to the atom sympathetically, the atom will absorb the photon's energy (destroying the photon) and oscillate at an increased level. The atom can't keep this up, though, so after a while it drops back down to the energy it had before the photon struck. In the process of shedding this energy a new photon is generated, carrying the energy released by the transition. But recall that that was just the energy that the photon imparted to the atom in the first place. So the photon struck an atom, the atom absorbed the photon and started to vibrate more quickly, and then the atom calmed down and lost this additional vibration, simultaneously emitting a new photon at just about the same frequency as the incoming photon. In effect, the resonant photon appeared to be reflected off the surface. The process is diagrammed in *Figure 5*.

So now we have a rough view of how a blue couch appears blue: non-blue photons are absorbed and converted to heat, but because of the nature of the surface of the couch, blue photons are absorbed and re-radiated. From now

One result of quantum mechanics is that atoms move from one

discrete energy state to another. We can

diagram the allowable energy levels with

horizontal lines, one at each permissible

energy level. Increasing energy rises

from bottom to top. If a photon arrives with insufficient

energy to boost the atom to the next energy level, the

photon is effectively absorbed and converted into heat.

On the other hand, suppose the atom is in energy state E_0

and a photon with energy $E = E_1 - E_0$ arrives. The photon

is absorbed, and the atom is at a higher energy level.

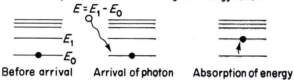

Before arrival   Arrival of photon   Absorption of energy

The atom cannot stay at this excited state indefinitely.

Eventually, it drops back to E_0, and in the process it

emits a new photon of energy $E_1 - E_0$

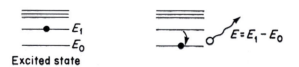

Excited state

At a higher level, it appears that the incoming photon

was reflected from the surface.

Fig. 5.

on, we'll simply say that blue photons are reflected from the surface. This shouldn't all be too much of a surprise: in the summer at roads near the beach, the black tar is usually much hotter than the white paint on it. The black tar is absorbing all the incoming light and turning it into heat, while the white paint is reflecting the incoming light.

1.6   Color and the Eye

Recall that we mentioned that we don't really see 'white' light, but rather our eye averages many incoming photons into white. That's really the way most of what we see takes place; our world has very few *monochromatic* (single frequency) light sources (lasers are a notable exception). It's natural to wonder what spectrum gives rise to a given perceived color.

Physiologists and psychologists have studied this question extensively, and they arrived at a surprising answer. Let's say someone reports seeing orange light. It turns out that there are an infinite number of color spectra that can give rise to that same, perceived color of orange!

This is not to say that we don't understand color and the eye at all. Given a particular perceived color, we know how to make spectra that will give rise to that color. But as we mentioned above, there are an infinite number of these spectra; each of these spectrally different but perceptually equivalent colors are called *metamers*. So there is no one 'correct' spectrum for orange; they all look exactly the same.

This phenomenon is important when we talk about color spectra and photons bouncing around in a 3-D scene. The final spectra at two different pixels may appear absolutely unrelated when we look just at their frequency vs amplitude plots, yet both spectra might produce the same perceived color at the eye.

1.7   Surface Normals

When we study what happens to light at the surfaces of objects, we will often care about geometric property of the surface called the *surface normal*. The surface normal is a vector that indicates a direction perpendicular to the surface at that point. Usually we represent the surface normal as a vector that begins at a point on the surface and points away from the object's 'inside.'

The surface normal to a plane is the same everywhere, as shown in *Figure 6(a)*. The surface normal to a sphere at a given point follows the radius line from the center of the sphere to that point and beyond, as in *Figure 6(b)*. Some other objects and representative normals are shown in *Figure 6(c)*. Except for unusual situations, most objects have a surface normal at every point.

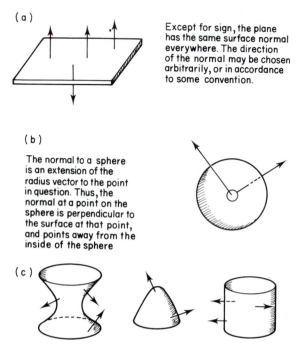

(a)

Except for sign, the plane has the same surface normal everywhere. The direction of the normal may be chosen arbitrarily, or in accordance to some convention.

(b)

The normal to a sphere is an extension of the radius vector to the point in question. Thus, the normal at a point on the sphere is perpendicular to the surface at that point, and points away from the inside of the sphere

(c)

Fig. 6.   Some surfaces and surface normals.

When we work with surface normals in this article, we'll usually represent them with the letter **N**. The normal will be assumed to be a *normalized* vector (that is, **N** has a length of 1.0).

2   FOUR MECHANISMS OF LIGHT TRANSPORT

We mentioned earlier that there are four fundamental mechanisms (or modes) by which light interacts with surfaces (and media). These are called *light transport modes*. In general, the interaction of light has geometric considerations and color considerations. In the next four sections, we will look only at the geometrical issues. We will then follow with a discussion of how to handle color phenomena.

Remember that our goal is to find what light is being emitted by the object in one particular direction—the direction of the ray which originally hit the surface. In backward ray tracing, this is the ray that will carry light away from the surface, eventually back to our eye. We will find it convenient to call this the *incident ray* in the following discussions, and compute other rays as though this ray was carrying light to the surface. But when we are actually computing shading, our program will use the reverse convention; i.e. light is carried to the surface by the reflected and transmitted rays and carried away from the surface and ultimately to our eye by the incident ray.

2.1   Perfect Specular Reflection

Imagine that you're on a basketball court, and you want to send your basketball to a teammate by bouncing it on the ground. You'd probably aim the ball to bounce about halfway between you and your friend. This is because of your experience with balls bouncing off of hard floors.

It turns out that perfect *specular reflection* works in just the same way (this kind of reflection is light that bounces off of the top of a surface of an object, and is not subject to the absorption and re-radiation we studied before). Note that we'll be discussing only *perfect* specular reflection in this section even though there are no perfectly specular surfaces out there. We'll see how to adjust for imperfect specular reflection in the real world later, but this ideal model will prove to be very useful.

As an example, most of what you see in a mirror is specular reflection of the incoming light. The highlights on a shiny surface are also an example of specular reflection.

Light from the light source is striking the top of the object's surface and then bouncing off, so it is barely subject to absorption and re-radiation by the object itself. We'll see later that for some surfaces the light which appears to be specularly reflected is actually getting slightly affected by the coloration of the surface on each bounce.

Figure 7 shows a photon arriving at a hard, flat surface and bouncing off. The angle between the surface normal, marked **N**, and the direction of the incoming (or incident) ray, marked **I**, is called the *angle of incidence*, which we

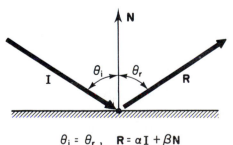

$$\theta_i = \theta_r, \quad \mathbf{R} = \alpha \mathbf{I} + \beta \mathbf{N}$$

Fig. 7.   The geometry of reflection.

denote as θ_i. The angle between the surface normal and the reflected ray, marked $\mathbf{R}$ is called the *angle of reflection*, denoted θ_r. Given $\mathbf{N}$ and $\mathbf{I}$ we wish to find $\mathbf{R}$.

Two physical laws help us find an expression for $\mathbf{R}$. The first is that the incident ray, the surface normal, and the reflected ray all lie in the same plane; thus the reflected ray is a linear combination of the incident ray and the normal. The second principle is that the angle of incidence is equal to the angle of reflection.

We can find $\mathbf{R}$ in many ways; two of the most popular are algebraic and geometrical (we can also use other principles of optics). Many geometric derivations are possible; most are straightforward and make for a good exercise (some examples by Paul Heckbert can be found at the end of Chapter 7). We present an algebraic solution.

We begin by writing our two physical laws mathematically:

$$\mathbf{R} = \alpha\mathbf{I} + \beta\mathbf{N} \tag{3a}$$

$$\theta_i = \theta_r. \tag{3b}$$

We can see from *Figure 7* that $\cos(\theta_i) = -\mathbf{I} \cdot \mathbf{N}$ (observe that we need to reverse the direction of $\mathbf{I}$ to get the acute angle labelled θ_i in the figure). We also see that $\cos(\theta_r) = \mathbf{N} \cdot \mathbf{R}$. So we can rewrite (3b) as:

$$\cos(\theta_i) = \cos(\theta_r) \tag{3c}$$
$$-\mathbf{I} \cdot \mathbf{N} = \mathbf{N} \cdot \mathbf{R}$$
$$= \mathbf{N} \cdot (\alpha\mathbf{I} + \beta\mathbf{N})$$
$$= \alpha(\mathbf{N} \cdot \mathbf{I}) + \beta(\mathbf{N} \cdot \mathbf{N})$$
$$= \alpha(\mathbf{N} \cdot \mathbf{I}) + \beta.$$

The last step is justified by recalling that since $|\mathbf{N}| = 1, \mathbf{N} \cdot \mathbf{N} = 1$. If we arbitrarily set $\alpha = 1$, then

$$\beta = -2(\mathbf{N} \cdot \mathbf{I}). \tag{3d}$$

So our complete formula for the direction of a specularly reflected ray is

$$\mathbf{R} = \mathbf{I} - 2(\mathbf{N} \cdot \mathbf{I})\mathbf{N} \tag{3e}$$

where $\mathbf{I}$ is the incident ray
$\mathbf{N}$ is the surface normal
$\mathbf{R}$ is the reflected ray.

As a check, let us confirm that the vector **R** in (3c) has unit length (recall that for a vector **A**, length (**A**) = |**A**| = $\sqrt{(\mathbf{A} \cdot \mathbf{A})}$ so if **A** · **A** = 1, then |**A**| = 1):

$$
\begin{aligned}
1 &\stackrel{?}{=} \mathbf{R} \cdot \mathbf{R} \\
&= (\alpha\mathbf{I} + \beta\mathbf{N}) \cdot (\alpha\mathbf{I} + \beta\mathbf{N}) \\
&= \alpha^2(\mathbf{I} \cdot \mathbf{I}) + 2\alpha\beta(\mathbf{I} \cdot \mathbf{N}) + \beta^2(\mathbf{N} \cdot \mathbf{N}) \\
&= \alpha^2 + 2\alpha\beta(\mathbf{I} \cdot \mathbf{N}) + \beta^2 \\
&= 1 + 2[-2(\mathbf{N} \cdot \mathbf{I})](\mathbf{I} \cdot \mathbf{N}) + [-2(\mathbf{N} \cdot \mathbf{I})]^2 \\
&= 1 - 4(\mathbf{N} \cdot \mathbf{I})^2 + 4(\mathbf{N} \cdot \mathbf{I})^2 \\
&= 1.
\end{aligned}
\tag{4}
$$

In step 3 we used: $(\mathbf{I} \cdot \mathbf{I}) = (\mathbf{N} \cdot \mathbf{N}) = 1$, and in step 4: $\alpha = 1$, $\beta = -2(\mathbf{N} \cdot \mathbf{I})$.

Make sure that your incident and normal vectors **I** and **N** are normalized (i.e. have length 1) when you use equation (3e) to compute **R**.

2.2 Perfect Diffuse Reflection

The nice, clean situation of specular reflection discussed above usually holds only for hard, shiny surfaces. A rougher surface behaves in quite a different manner; the characteristics of the reflected light don't have such a simple geometry for a rough surface.

Recall our discussion of absorption and re-radiation of light at surfaces. Specularly reflected light is only slightly subject to these phenomena since it bounces off of the top surface of an object. But diffusely reflected light actually interacts with the surface. When a photon is absorbed by an atom of the surface, the photon may be turned into heat or it may eventually be re-radiated. If the photon is re-radiated, there's nothing that determines in which direction the photon ought to proceed. Although any given photon will go in only one direction, many photons over the course of time will tend to go in all possible directions. The upshot is that diffusely reflected light is reflected away from the surface in all directions with equal intensity.

The only geometry that we must take into account is how much of the surface is visible to the light source. We can find this from the angle between the incident light vector and the surface normal. The amount of light reaching the surface is proportional to the cosine of that angle, as shown in *Figure 8*.

This is the *Lambertian reflection* model of perfectly diffuse reflection, and of course it's as idealized a model as perfectly specular reflection.

As far as we're concerned right now, there are no other geometric considerations that we need to study for diffuse reflection; light from all directions can contribute to the light carried out by the incident ray.

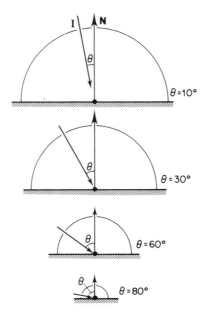

Fig. 8. Diffusely reflected light is reflected in all directions with equal amplitude. That amplitude is proportional to the cosine of the angle between the incident light and the normal.

2.3   Perfect Specular Transmission

In a transparent object, light can arrive from behind the object's surface and pass through, contributing to the light leaving the surface. Such light is called *transmitted light*.

It is not necessary that the media on both sides of the object be the same. For example, we could have a fishbowl filled with water. Light could pass from the air into the glass, then from the glass to the water, than water to glass, and then again from glass to air. Each of these transitions can cause the apparent direction of the ray to bend. For example, consider *Figure 9*, which shows a ruler in a glass of water. The appearance of the bent ruler is due to the bending of the light rays as they pass from the water to the glass, and then the glass to the air.

To properly handle transmitted light, we need to handle the bending of the light as it crosses the boundary (or *interface*) between two media. This bending is called *transmission* or *refraction*. It is important to note that each medium has an *index of refraction*, which actually describes the speed of light in that medium compared to the speed of light in a vacuum. To determine how the light bends

Fig. 9. Refraction causes the ruler to appear bent in a glass of water.

when crossing media, we compare the indices of refraction of the two materials and the angle of the incident light.

Figure 10 shows an incoming light ray (again marked **I**), striking a surface with normal **N**. The incident light makes an angle θ_i (the *angle of incidence*) with the surface normal. The transmitted light **T** makes an angle of θ_t (the *angle of refraction*) with the reflected normal. The incident light, normal, and refracted light again all lie in the same plane. The equation relating the angles of the incident and transmitted light is called *Snell's Law*:

$$\frac{\sin(\theta_1)}{\sin(\theta_2)} = \eta_{21} = \frac{\eta_2}{\eta_1} \tag{5}$$

where η_1 is the index of refraction of medium 1 with respect to vacuum
η_2 is the index of refraction of medium 2 with respect to vacuum
η_{21} is the index of refraction of medium 2 with respect to medium 1.

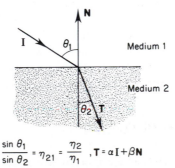

$$\frac{\sin\theta_1}{\sin\theta_2} = \eta_{21} = \frac{\eta_2}{\eta_1} \ , \mathbf{T} = \alpha\mathbf{I} + \beta\mathbf{N}$$

Fig. 10.   The geometry of transmission.

Fig. 11. Sunlight passes through the pinhole, strikes the prism, and is reflected to form a spectrum on a distant screen. Diagram adopted from Newton's Optiks, 1704.

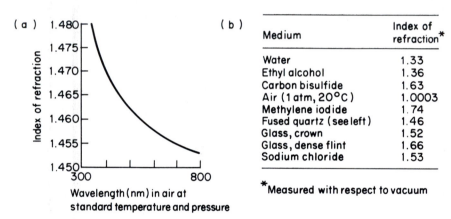

(a) Index of refraction vs. Wavelength (nm) in air at standard temperature and pressure

(b)

Medium	Index of refraction*
Water	1.33
Ethyl alcohol	1.36
Carbon bisulfide	1.63
Air (1 atm, 20°C)	1.0003
Methylene iodide	1.74
Fused quartz (see left)	1.46
Glass, crown	1.52
Glass, dense flint	1.66
Sodium chloride	1.53

*Measured with respect to vacuum

Fig. 12. (a) The index of refraction of fused quartz with respect to vacuum as a function of wavelength. (b) Some indices of refraction.

It turns out that the index of refraction is dependent on the wavelength of the incoming light. This is why a prism separates incoming light into a spectrum: the different wavelengths are refracted by different amounts. This was noticed by Newton in his book on optics; *Figure 11* shows a diagram of a prism refracting sunlight into a spectrum based on one of Newton's diagrams.

Figure 12(a) shows the index of refraction as a function of wavelength for fused quartz. Some useful indices of refraction are listed in *Figure 12(b)*. Although these are all measured with respect to vacuum, the values relative to air are very similar.

2.4   Total Internal Reflection

One phenomenon of light behavior at boundaries between media is called *total internal reflection* (TIR). TIR is a physical phenomenon which occurs when light

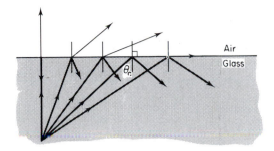

Fig. 13. Below the critical angle, light is both transmitted through and reflected from the interface. At angles greater than or equal to the critical angle, only reflection occurs. This phenomenon is called total internal reflection.

tries to pass from a dense medium to a less-dense medium at too shallow an angle. The result is that the light instead glances off the *interface* between the media, and is in effect specularly reflected instead of transmitted. This effect is the basic mechanism behind optical fibers; they 'trap' the light within the tube of the fiber by making sure that TIR occurs whenever the light tries to get out.

If we wish, we can find a mathematical formula for the *critical angle* beyond which total internal reflection occurs. But in computer graphics we usually just want to detect when TIR occurs—then we use the equations for perfect specular reflection to compute the 'transmitted' ray. *Figure 13* shows light striking an interface between glass and air at various angles; this interface has a critical angle of $41.8°$.

We will see below how to detect when TIR occurs. At that point we forget about our equations for transmitted light, and instead compute the direction for perfect specular reflection.

2.5 Optics for Transmission

We can derive the formula for the transmitted ray direction with the help of *Figure 14*.

Our two physical laws are that the transmitted ray is coplanar with the incident ray and the normal, and Snell's Law from equation (5) above. We will adopt the space-saving notation that $S_\theta = \sin(\theta)$, $C_\theta = \cos(\theta)$, and $T_\theta = \tan(\theta)$. Our physical laws are:

$$\frac{S_t}{S_i} = \eta_{it} \tag{6a}$$

$$\mathbf{T} = \alpha\mathbf{I} + \beta\mathbf{N}. \tag{6b}$$

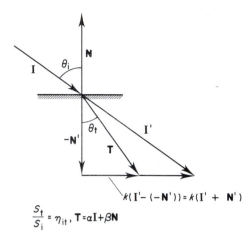

$$\frac{S_t}{S_i} = \eta_{it}, \ \mathbf{T} = \alpha\mathbf{I} + \beta\mathbf{N}$$

Fig 14.   Geometry for computing the transmitted ray.

Note that in (6b) we are computing η_{it}, *not* η_{ti} as you might expect from the form of (5). The relationship is $\eta_{ti} = (1/\eta_{it})$; the term η_{it} will prove to be more useful to us later.

Our goal is to find α and β in (6b). As in the case of specular reflection, we have at least two major methods at our disposal: algebraic and geometric. In the algebraic approach, we solve this pair of equations simultaneously using equation manipulation. In the geometric approach, we analyze the geometry of the situation and write all the relationships we can find; simplification then leads to expressions for the unknowns. Some people find the algebraic solution much easier to follow than the geometric, and of course there are those who prefer the geometry to the algebra. Since both approaches are interesting and non-trivial, we'll give an example of how to solve for α and β with both techniques, starting with the algebraic.

In both approaches we will use the following values (note that we must 'turn around' the incident vector when dotting it with the normal, and similarly 'turn around' the normal when dotting it with the transmitted ray):

$$\cos(\theta_i) = C_i = (\mathbf{N} \cdot -\mathbf{I}) \tag{6c}$$

$$\cos(\theta_t) = C_t = (-\mathbf{N} \cdot \mathbf{T}). \tag{6d}$$

2.6 Algebraic Solution for T

We can square both sides of (6a) and rewrite it:

$$S_i^2 \eta_{it}^2 = S_t^2. \tag{7a}$$

Since $S_\theta^2 + C_\theta^2 = 1$, we replace this with

$$(1 - C_i^2)\, \eta_{it}^2 = (1 - C_t^2). \tag{7b}$$

which we can rewrite:

$$
\begin{aligned}
(1 - C_i^2)\eta_{it}^2 - 1 &= C_t^2 \\
&= [-\mathbf{N} \cdot \mathbf{T}]^2 \\
&= [-\mathbf{N} \cdot (\alpha\mathbf{I} + \beta\mathbf{T})]^2 \\
&= [\alpha(-\mathbf{N} \cdot \mathbf{I}) + \beta(-\mathbf{N} \cdot \mathbf{N})]^2 \\
&= [\alpha C_i - \beta]^2
\end{aligned}
\tag{7c}
$$

The last step is justified by noting that $(\mathbf{N} \cdot \mathbf{N}) = 1$ (since $|\mathbf{N}| = 1$). Equation (7c) is our first condition on α and β. Since we want our new vector **T** to have unit length, we can state our second condition:

$$
\begin{aligned}
1 &= \mathbf{T} \cdot \mathbf{T} \\
&= (\alpha\mathbf{I} + \beta\mathbf{N}) \cdot (\alpha\mathbf{I} + \beta\mathbf{N}) \\
&= \alpha^2(\mathbf{I} \cdot \mathbf{I}) + 2\alpha\beta(\mathbf{I} \cdot \mathbf{N}) + \beta^2(\mathbf{N} \cdot \mathbf{N}) \\
&= \alpha^2 - 2\alpha\beta C_i + \beta^2
\end{aligned}
\tag{7d}
$$

where again we use the fact that $(\mathbf{I} \cdot \mathbf{I}) = (\mathbf{N} \cdot \mathbf{N}) = 1$, and replace $(\mathbf{I} \cdot \mathbf{N})$ by $-C_i$ from (6c). We can write the results of these two derivations in one place:

$$
\begin{aligned}
(1 - C_i^2)\eta_{it}^2 - 1 &= [\alpha C_i - \beta]^2 \\
1 &= \alpha^2 - 2\alpha\beta C_i + \beta^2
\end{aligned}
\tag{7e}
$$

and then solve these two equations simultaneously for α and β. The square roots involved mean that we have four values of α and β that will work. Defining the temporary variables:

$$\omega = \eta_{it} C_i, \quad \nu = \sqrt{(1 + \eta_{it}^2(C_i^2 - 1))} \tag{7f}$$

We can now write

$$
\begin{aligned}
\alpha_1 &= \eta_{it}, & \beta_1 &= \omega - \nu \\
\alpha_2 &= \eta_{it}, & \beta_2 &= \omega + \nu \\
\alpha_3 &= -\eta_{it}, & \beta_3 &= -\omega + \nu \\
\alpha_4 &= -\eta_{it}, & \beta_4 &= -\omega - \nu.
\end{aligned}
\tag{7γ}
$$

The first set of α and β correspond to the **T** vector we seek; the others represent reflections of that vector into the other three quadrants formed by the normal and the surface's tangent.

Thus our final formula for $\mathbf{T}$ is

$$\mathbf{T} = \eta_{it}\mathbf{I} + (\eta_{it}C_i - \sqrt{(1 + \eta_{it}^2(C_i^2 - 1))})\mathbf{N}. \tag{7h}$$

Now it can certainly occur that the expression under the radical for v in (7f) is negative, leading to an imaginary solution. This is our signal that total internal reflection is taking place at this boundary, and that in effect no light is transmitted through.

2.7   Geometric Solution for T

Let's begin by noting from *Figure 14* that the transmitted ray $\mathbf{T}$ may be decomposed into two simpler vectors. One is a scaled version of the reflected normal, which we call $-\mathbf{N}'$. The other is a scaled version of the vector that connects the head of $-\mathbf{N}'$ to the head of $\mathbf{I}'$ (a scaled version of the incident ray $\mathbf{I}$ but with its tail at the origin). Thus this vector is $k(\mathbf{I}' - -\mathbf{N}') = k(\mathbf{I}' + \mathbf{N}')$. So another formula for $\mathbf{T}$ is

$$\begin{aligned} \mathbf{T} &= -\mathbf{N}' + k(\mathbf{I}' + \mathbf{N}') \\ &= k\mathbf{I}' + (k-1)\mathbf{N}'. \end{aligned} \tag{8a}$$

We can now solve for k, $\mathbf{I}'$, and $\mathbf{N}'$ with the help of some trigonometric relations. As with the algebraic solution, we start by squaring both sides of (6a) and rewriting:

$$S_i^2 \eta_{it}^2 = S_t^2. \tag{8b}$$

Since $S_\theta^2 + C_\theta^2 = 1$, we can solve for S_i^2 and C_t:

$$\begin{aligned} S_i^2 &= 1 - C_i^2 \\ C_t &= \sqrt{(1 - S_t^2)} = \sqrt{(1 - \eta_{it}^2 S_i^2)} \\ &= \sqrt{(1 - \eta_{it}^2(1 - C_i^2))} = \sqrt{(1 + \eta_{it}^2(C_i^2 - 1))}. \end{aligned} \tag{8c}$$

We will solve (8a) by finding the vectors $\mathbf{I}'$ and $\mathbf{N}'$, and then the value of k. Since $\mathbf{I}'$ is nothing but a scaled version of $\mathbf{I}$, we can write $\mathbf{I}' = |\mathbf{I}'|\mathbf{I}$. From *Figure 14*, we can see that the projection of $\mathbf{I}'$ onto $\mathbf{N}$ ($|\mathbf{I}'|C_i$) is of the same length as the projection of $\mathbf{T}$ onto $\mathbf{N}$ ($|\mathbf{T}|C_t = C_t$, since $|\mathbf{T}| = 1$). Thus,

$$\mathbf{I}' = |\mathbf{I}'|\mathbf{I} = \frac{C_t}{C_i}\mathbf{I}. \tag{8d}$$

We can follow the same procedure for $\mathbf{N}'$, writing $\mathbf{N}' = |\mathbf{N}'|\mathbf{N}$. The length of $\mathbf{N'}$ is precisely the projection of $\mathbf{T}$ onto $\mathbf{N}$ ($|\mathbf{T}|C_t = C_t$, since $|\mathbf{T}| = 1$). Thus,

$$\mathbf{N'} = |\mathbf{N'}|\mathbf{N} = C_t\mathbf{N}. \tag{8e}$$

Lastly, we solve for k by noting that it scales $(\mathbf{I'} + \mathbf{N'})$ by precisely the ratio of the projections of $\mathbf{T}$ and $\mathbf{I'}$ onto this vector. These projections may be found from the sines of the relevant angles:

$$k = \frac{|\mathbf{T}|S_t}{|\mathbf{I'}|S_i} = \frac{S_t}{\dfrac{C_t}{C_i}S_i} = \frac{S_t C_i}{C_t S_i} = \frac{T_t}{T_i}. \tag{8f}$$

We now have all the information we need to explicitly write the equation of the transmitted ray. We will rewrite (8a) using the values for $\mathbf{I'}$, $\mathbf{N'}$, and k found from (8d), (8e), and (8f):

$$\mathbf{T} = k\mathbf{I'} + (k-1)\mathbf{N'} = \left[\frac{T_t}{T_i}\right]\left(\frac{C_t}{C_i}\mathbf{I}\right) + \left[\frac{T_t}{T_i} - 1\right](C_t\mathbf{N}) \tag{8g}$$

$$= \frac{S_t}{S_i}\mathbf{I} + \left[\frac{T_t}{T_i} - 1\right]C_t\mathbf{N}$$

$$= \eta_{it}\mathbf{I} + \left[\eta_{it}\frac{C_i}{C_t} - 1\right]C_t\mathbf{N}$$

$$= \eta_{it}\mathbf{I} + (\eta_{it}C_i - C_t)\mathbf{N}.$$

Recalling the expression for C_t from (8c), we are led to:

$$\mathbf{T} = \eta_{it}\mathbf{I} + (\eta_{it}C_i - \sqrt{(1 + \eta_{it}^2(C_i^2 - 1))})\mathbf{N}. \tag{8h}$$

When C_t is not a real number, then the light is subject to total internal reflection, as discussed above.

Note that the algebraic solution in (7h) and geometric solution in (8h) are the same!

2.8   Perfect Diffuse Transmission

We saw that in a medium that supported perfect specular transmission, the light passed right through without interference. This is an ideal situation that is never quite realized in practice; fine crystal comes close. At the other extreme is a medium that has many small particles that interfere with the travelling photons. One example of such a material is translucent plastic; it allows light to pass, and colors it along the way, but it is not possible to clearly see anything on the other side of the plastic.

If we could find an ideal example of such a medium, we would say it supported *perfect diffuse transmission*. Certainly the diffuse transmission part is easily satisfied by many materials. A perfectly diffuse transparent medium would scatter light evenly in all directions as it passes through, just as a perfectly diffuse reflective surface scatters light in all directions as it is reflected. Thus, the intensity of diffusely transmitted light would be the same in all directions.

As with the diffuse reflection case, there are no special geometric consider-ations that we must take into account to model diffusely transmitted light; light arriving from all directions (on the side of the material opposite to the side hit by the incident ray) can contribute to light carried out by the incident ray. It is primarily the cosine of the angle between the incident ray and the normal that we care about most, just as with diffuse reflection.

3 PRACTICAL REFLECTION AND TRANSMISSION

3.1 Geometry and Color

Our previous discussion of light transport focused just on the geometry in several idealized circumstances. The most important simplification that we made in discussing reflection was assuming that there was just one perfect direction ($\mathbf{R}$) from which light can arrive to be specularly reflected into the direction of interest. This is not true in general; if a surface has some roughness to it, then light striking nearby points can still be bounced away parallel to the direction we care about. The same situation is true for specular transmission.

We also ignored any coloring of the light during its interaction with the surface. If you look at a shiny copper kettle illuminated by a white light somewhere near your head, the highlight in the kettle looks a lot more copper-colored than white-colored. Something is happening at the surface of the kettle to color the incident light.

If we're going to make realistic-looking images, we need to handle these two important phenomena: rough surfaces and color shifting. The ideal situation would be handle them both in a single model, and happily such a model exists. So rather than look at these two phenomena separately and then try to paste them together, we'll look at them both in the context of a complete *shading model* that does the whole job.

A few points bear mentioning up front. The first is that the nature of the interaction between the incident light and the surface is a function both of the wavelength of the light and the angle of incidence with which it strikes the surface. Secondly, the amount of color you see at a point on a surface can be influenced by where you're standing. This second point is familiar to us all: what I see in a mirror will be different than what you see if we're standing in different places. Thus the same point on an object can reflect differently colored light in different directions; your view direction can make a difference to the color you see.

Much of the literature on shading models considers a simplified case for specular transport, where light is arriving on one ray and departing on another. The vector pointing from the surface in the direction of the arriving light is called the *light vector*; the vector pointing from the surface in the departing direction of interest is called the *viewing vector*. Thus in ray tracing, the ray that hit the surface and caused us to spawn new rays takes the place of the viewing vector. Those new rays (reflected, transmitted, and shadow) in turn take the place of the light vector. Since the light vector can come from a light source, it is not a certainty that it will be specularly reflected into the viewing vector. This will depend on the roughness of the surface and the exact directions of the view and light vector. Of course, when the light vector is the reflection ray we can be pretty sure that it will reflect into the viewing vector—we built it that way!

Another result of this point of view is that shadow rays now become *illumination rays*! When we determine that a light source is visible from a given point, we will proceed to shade that point with the light arriving from that object, and calculate how much light (and of what color) is headed in the direction of the viewing vector.

This business of handling illumination from lights separately from illumination from other objects is prevalent in the shading literature; it's an artifact of convenience, both from the standpoint of exposition and programming. When computers get fast enough we'll probably use shading models sophisticated enough to look everywhere for incoming light and the distinction will disappear, but for now we pay attention to those places where we know we have a good chance of finding incoming light: from the lights themselves, and along reflection and transmission rays.

4 A SHADING MODEL

Our discussion of reflected and transmitted light above looked at the two extremes: perfect mirror-like specular reflection and transmission, and perfect Lambertian (or diffuse) reflection and transmission. The area in between is not simple. In this section we'll look closely only at the issues involved in handling reflected light. The results will be directly applicable to the study of transmitted light. Recall that we'll phrase everything in terms of a viewing vector and a light vector, whose roles may be assumed by a variety of characters when we're ray tracing.

The actual distribution of reflected light from rough surfaces has been studied both with physical measurements and with theoretical models. The approach has been to consider the reflected light as a combination of diffuse and specular components. This simplifies our study of reflected light into a study of the two components.

4.1   Diffuse Reflection $I_{dr}(\lambda)$

The description we gave above for diffuse light reflection is actually pretty complete: the color of the absorbed and re-radiated light is only weakly dependent on the angle of incidence through about $70°$ of the surface normal. And since the same light is radiated in all directions, it doesn't matter from where we're looking. So diffuse reflection is simply a matter of the color of the incoming light, the absorption curve of the object, and the angle between the surface normal and the light vector:

$$I_{dr}(\lambda) = I_{lj}(\lambda)\, F_{dr}(\lambda)(\mathbf{N} \cdot \mathbf{L}) \tag{9}$$

where $I_{dr}(\lambda)$ is the diffusely reflected light
$I_{lj}(\lambda)$ is the spectrum of light source j
$F_{dr}(\lambda)$ is the diffuse reflection curve
$\mathbf{N}$ is the surface normal
$\mathbf{L}$ is the light vector.

If this were part of a complete shading system, we would loop over all light sources and accumulate the light diffusely reflected as a result of each one.

4.2   Specular Reflection $I_{sr}(\lambda)$

In this section we will derive an expression for the color of the specularly reflected light, which we call $I_{sr}(\lambda)$.

How shall we think of a rough surface, when our only understanding at this point is in terms of perfect reflectors? We can think of the surface as actually composed of many tiny, flat reflectors, of *microfacets*. Thus, the surface of a slightly rough object, when viewed up close, looks like a mountain range!

Consider *Figure 15(a)*, which shows a rough surface. Light is arriving from a direction roughly normal to the overall surface, which is also where the eye is located. We would like to follow the path of light from the light source as it

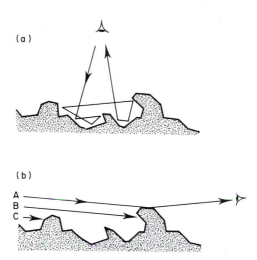

Fig. 15.   (a) Light arriving at near-normal incidence to the overall surface may bounce specularly off of many microfacets before leaving the surface. (b) Light arriving at a grazing angle can be specularly reflected to the eye off of appropriately oriented microfacets. Much of this light (such as rays B and C) are blocked by the surface.

specularly reflects off these microfacets into the eye. This light is specularly reflected from one microfacet to another several times. On each bounce, the light is slightly colored by the material. If it bounces only one or two times, this effect is barely noticeable. But light coming in at this orientation can in fact bounce between the microfacets many times. After enough bounces, the color of the light is strongly affected by the material. So in this orientation, the color of a highlight is the color of the object subject to the spectrum of the incident light.

Figure 15(b) shows light arriving at a grazing angle to the surface. If it is to bounce into the observer's eye, then it can only strike one or two microfacets. Since the light must travel in almost a straight line, any other light would get blocked or redirected along the way. Since the light only strikes a small number of microfacets, it is hardly colored at all. So in this orientation, the color of a highlight is the color of the light source, and is largely irrelevant of the object color.

We can summarize these observations with the following statement: the color and intensity of the specularly reflected light leaving a given point may be dependent on the direction and color of the incoming light, the color of the object, and the distribution of the microfacets on the surface.

The microfacet model is a theoretical model, and it is described by several equations. We'll follow the presentation in [4] and [19]. The math may look complex, but don't let it be overwhelming. Basically researchers have found equations that do a pretty good job in describing the real world, which is not simple. Thus the equations aren't simple either. We're not going to re-derive these results, but we will summarize them and discuss their meaning.

Figure 16(a) shows a typical viewing set-up. A surface is illuminated, and we want to find the light that is reflected back to the observer. The point on the surface is P. The vector in the direction of the observer from P is indicated by **V**. The normal at P is **N**. The vector pointing towards light source j from P is $\mathbf{L}_j$. We also draw a vector exactly between **V** and $\mathbf{L}_j$, called $\mathbf{H}_j$. Thus, **V**, $\mathbf{L}_j$, and $\mathbf{H}_j$ are all in the same plane. We've also marked the angle between **V** and $\mathbf{H}_j$ (which is the same as between $\mathbf{L}_j$ and $\mathbf{H}_j$) as θ, and the angle between $\mathbf{H}_j$ and **N** as α. Keep in mind that all of these vectors are normalized; i.e. they have length 1.0.

Recall that perfect specular reflection takes place when the angle of incidence is equal to the angle of reflection. This is exactly the case for microfacets with a surface normal parallel to $\mathbf{H}_j$, since $\mathbf{H}_j$ makes an equal angle with the viewer and the light source.

So light can come from the light (i.e. along vector $\mathbf{L}_j$) and be specularly reflected to the eye (i.e. into vector **V**), if it hits a microfacet with normal $\mathbf{H}_j$.

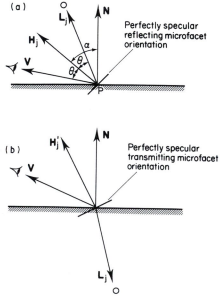

Fig. 16. (a) Geometry for specular reflection of a light source. (b) Geometry for specular transmission of a light source.

The expression for $I_{sr}(\lambda)$ is complex, because here's where we begin getting subtle effects that depend on the material and the viewing geometry. For example, the more the light bounces around, hitting microfacets, the more the color will change because of the interaction with the surface. To account for this we need to have some detailed expressions for how the microfacets are sitting on the surface.

$I_{sr}(\lambda)$ tells us how incident light gets colored by the material before being specularly reflected. The light is reduced in intensity at each wavelength by an amount dependent on that wavelength and the angle of incidence. Thus, $I_{sr}(\lambda)$ tells us the reflectance curve for a material, given incident light at a given angle.

The specular light $I_{sr}(\lambda)$ is

$$I_{sr}(\lambda) = \frac{F(\lambda, \theta)}{\pi} \frac{D(\alpha)G(\mathbf{N}, \mathbf{V}, \mathbf{L})}{(\mathbf{N} \cdot \mathbf{L})(\mathbf{N} \cdot \mathbf{V})} \tag{10}$$

where $I_{sr}(\lambda)$ = the specularly reflected light

   $F(\lambda, \theta)$ describes reflection for a wavelength λ at angle of incidence θ

   $G(\mathbf{N}, \mathbf{V}, \mathbf{L})$ describes microfacet orientation

   $D(\alpha)$ describes how many microfacets are oriented in the direction $\mathbf{H}$

   $\mathbf{N}$ is the surface normal

   $\mathbf{L}$ is the light vector

   $\mathbf{V}$ is the viewing vector.

4.3 The Geometry Term *G*

The equation for G (G stands for geometry) is pretty complex. You can find details for its derivation in [1] and [19]. This is the part of the equation that compensates for the fact that after a reflection off a microfacet, some rays hit another microfacet before they leave the surface. Of course, this can happen time and again.

One of the vectors used in computing G is $\mathbf{H}$; this is the vector which would perfectly reflect the incoming light to the viewer. We'll be needing $\mathbf{H}$ again when we look at the F term later. Since $\mathbf{H}$ would perfectly reflect light from $\mathbf{L}$ into $\mathbf{V}$, $\mathbf{H}$ lies exactly between the two vectors (remember to normalize it!):

$$H = \frac{\mathbf{L} + \mathbf{V}}{|\mathbf{L} + \mathbf{V}|}. \tag{11}$$

The expression for G incorporating shadowing and masking effects is:

$$\gamma = \frac{2(\mathbf{N} \cdot \mathbf{H})}{\mathbf{V} \cdot \mathbf{H}}, \quad G = \min\{1, \gamma(\mathbf{N} \cdot \mathbf{V}), \gamma(\mathbf{N} \cdot \mathbf{L})\}. \tag{12}$$

4.4   The Distribution Term *D*

The term D stands for distribution. It tells us how many microfacets are oriented parallel to a reflection vector $\mathbf{H}$. Recall that these are the microfacets which will reflect light from the source to the observer in a single, perfectly specular bounce. The value of D depends on the value of another variable, m. The value of m describes the 'roughness' of the surface. When m is small (e.g. 0.2), then we're describing a pretty smooth surface. When m is large (e.g. 0.7), then we're dealing with a rather rough surface.

The value of D also depends on α, the angle between $\mathbf{N}$ and $\mathbf{H}$. There are several popular expressions for evaluating D, based on different criteria, such as evaluation speed and physical accuracy. A fast formula for computing D is

$$D(m, c, \alpha) = ce^{-(\alpha/m)^2} \tag{13}$$

where c is an arbitrary constant
            e is Euler's constant.

This is known as the Gaussian model, and is good at matching reality as well as being pretty fast.

If we're willing to spend more time (or build tables, indexed by α, one for each value of m needed in our picture), a more accurate function is the Beckmann distribution function:

$$D(m, \alpha) = \frac{1}{m^2\cos^4(\alpha)} e^{-[(\tan(\alpha))/m]^2} \tag{14}$$

This also has the advantage that there are no arbitrary constants that the user must choose.

Consider that some surfaces may have several scales of roughness, each with a different value of m. For example, we might have a little bit of very rough stuff on the surface, but it's mostly pretty smooth. We can model this by expressing D as a weighted sum of the different distributions factors. If we consider k different values of m ($m_1, m_2, ..., m_k$), then we can write:

$$D = \sum_k w_k D(m_k, \alpha). \tag{15}$$

4.5   The Fresnel Term *F*

Unfortunately, the expression for F isn't quite as straightforward as for D and G. Notice that nowhere in the expressions for D or G did we include the values of θ or λ, the angle and wavelength of the incident light. Yet we know that these values make a difference in the final color; this is where we account for them.

Here is an equation for F which models unpolarized light at a given wavelength:

$$F(g, c) = \frac{1}{2} \frac{(g - c)^2}{(g + c)^2} \left\{ 1 + \frac{[c(g + c) - 1]^2}{[c(g - c) - 1]^2} \right\} \qquad (16)$$

where $c = \cos(\theta) = \mathbf{V} \cdot \mathbf{H}$
$\quad g^2 = \eta_\lambda^2 + c^2 - 1$
$\quad \eta_\lambda$ = index of refraction at this wavelength.

Unfortunately, η_λ depends on wavelength, and the values of this curve are generally not measured. On the other hand, there are some properties of materials which have been studied and cataloged extensively in a variety of reference works [15–17]. One of these properties is the reflectance curve for the material at normal incidence; that is, $F(\lambda, \theta = 0)$ for a variety of values of λ.

We will sometimes want to refer to the entire curve of $F(\lambda, \theta)$ for some fixed value of θ; in such cases we will write $F_\theta(\lambda)$, so $F(\lambda, \theta = 0) = F_0(\lambda)$.

In practice, researchers obtain a sample of some material. They clean the sample, place it perpendicular to a light source, and measure the intensity of the reflected light at many wavelengths. Knowing the intensity of the incident light at these wavelengths enables the creation of a graph that expresses the reflectivity spectrum of the material when illuminated with light parallel to the surface normal of the sample (i.e. at normal incidence).

The advantage of this is that we effectively have solutions to the Fresnel equation above when $\theta = 0$. We can then solve for n at each wavelength, proceeding as follows. We note that at normal incidence, $\theta = 0$, so $c = \cos(\theta) = 1$, so $c^2 = 1$. We can now solve for g: $g^2 = \eta_\lambda^2 + c^2 - 1 = \eta_\lambda^2 + 1 - 1 = \eta_\lambda^2$, so $g = \eta_\lambda$. Plugging these values ($\theta = 0$, $c = 1$, $g = \eta_\lambda$) into the Fresnel equation we get:

$$F_0(\lambda) = \left\{ \frac{\eta_\lambda - 1}{\eta_\lambda + 1} \right\}^2 \qquad (17)$$

We really want η_λ, so we can take the square root of both sides and solve:

$$\eta_\lambda = \frac{1 + \sqrt{(F_0(\lambda))}}{1 - \sqrt{(F_0(\lambda))}} \qquad (18)$$

So now we have a value for η_λ at several values of λ at normal incidence (i.e. when $\theta = 0$). We can find the value of η_λ at each wavelength in which we're interested. Now that we know η_λ, we can solve the Fresnel equation at any other angle of incidence.

The computation of F may be speeded up with a variety of techniques. One might build a table indexed by angle of incidence and wavelength for each material. Another option is to build a much sparser table and interpolate between the entries; this costs less space than a full table but the interpolation will take more time than a simple look-up.

The effect of F on the color of highlights is worth consideration. When light strikes a rough surface with near-normal incidence, the color of the specularly reflected light will be nearly the color of the object. As the light moves away from normal incidence, the specularly reflected light moves towards the color of the light source. This 'color shift' can be expensive to compute. We can make do with a linear interpolation between the colors at normal and perpendicular incidence. This interpolation misses some fine detail in the color transitions.

The plan will be to interpolate from the color we would see at normal incidence to the color we would see at grazing incidence. At normal incidence we'd see the color of the light source multiplied by the reflectance spectrum of the object. At grazing incidence we'd see the color of the light source, basically unaffected by the object's reflectance curve. We'll use linear interpolation to blend these two colors, based on how far the Fresnel function itself has moved between its two extremes at normal and grazing incidence.

Let's establish some notation for the two extremes. At $\theta = 0$, we write $F_0(\lambda)$ to represent that 2-D slice of the Fresnel reflectance curve; the color we would see is the product of the surface's specular reflectance curve $F_0(\lambda)$ and the incoming light's spectrum $I_{lj}(\lambda)$, so our color $C_\theta(\lambda)$ at $\theta = 0$ is $C_0(\lambda) = F_0(\lambda)I_{lj}(\lambda)$.

The corresponding 2-D Fresnel curve at $\theta = \pi/2$ is $F_{\pi/2}(\lambda)$; here we would see the color of the light source itself, so $C_{\pi/2}(\lambda) = I_{lj}(\lambda)$. The Fresnel curve right at some other value of θ is $F_\theta(\lambda)$.

So finally here's the formula for estimating the intensity at wavelength λ and angle of incidence θ. Note that we clamp the value of the Fresnel curve to a minimum of zero in case parts of the middle happen to dip below the endpoints:

$$C_\theta(\lambda) = C_0(\lambda) + [C_{\pi/2}(\lambda) - C_0(\lambda)] \frac{\max(0, F_\theta(\lambda) - F_0(\lambda))}{F_{\pi/2}(\lambda) - F_0(\lambda)} \qquad (19)$$

$$= F_0(\lambda)I_{lj}(\lambda) + [I_{lj}(\lambda) - F_0(\lambda)I_{lj}(\lambda)] \frac{\max(0, F_\theta(\lambda) - F_0(\lambda))}{F_{\pi/2}(\lambda) - F_0(\lambda)}$$

$$= I_{lj}(\lambda) \left\{ F_0(\lambda) + [1 - F_0(\lambda)] \frac{\max(0, F_\theta(\lambda) - F_0(\lambda))}{F_{\pi/2}(\lambda) - F_0(\lambda)} \right\}.$$

So now we have $C_\theta(\lambda)$ written just in terms of the incident light $I_{lj}(\lambda)$, the reflectance curve at $\theta = 0$, $F_0(\lambda)$, and the Fresnel reflectance function at θ, $F_\theta(\lambda)$. The final value of $C_\theta(\lambda)$ that we get out of (19) is the value we use for F in the overall shading model equation (10).

4.6   Summary of the Shading Model

So now we know how to compute both $I_{dr}(\lambda)$ and $I_{sr}(\lambda)$. It requires somewhat lengthy computation, and evaluation of the terms F, G, and D. But the result is that we get light that correctly bounces off complex surfaces, and very realistic shading.

We can use straightforward analogies to the above equations to build another set of formulae which will cover diffuse and specular transparency.

The end result would be seven equations: two reflection and two refraction equations (specular and diffuse for each) for direct illumination from light sources, two to handle specular reflection and refraction from other bodies, and one to lump together diffuse reflection and refraction ('ambient light') from other bodies.

Each of the diffuse equations looks just like (9); each of the specular equations looks just like (10). The only difference is the spectrum and direction of the illuminating light.

In the next section we present a faster, but more simplistic shading model.

5   FASTER SHADING

The preceding discussion presented a shading model of high quality. Unfortunately, it can also be very slow. Table-driven functions and efficient programming can reduce the running time, but only so far. For faster work a simpler shading model is appropriate, and we present one here. It's less accurate and realistic, but it is faster! It's a common technique to debug your images with a faster, cheaper shading model, and then produce the final, high-quality renderings with a more accurate shading equation.

Our fast model is described in [8]. Our discussion will proceed along the same lines as [8] and [18].

The literature describing shading models usually speak in terms of an 'observer' or 'viewer' who is looking at an object. In ray tracing, our 'viewer' is the ray which originally struck this surface. After all, that's the ray that's going to carry the light information back to the viewer (perhaps after passing through or bouncing off other surfaces along the way). For simplicity, we'll usually follow convention and speak of a viewer, but remember that this is really the ray that originally hit the surface, causing the shading to occur, and only for eye rays is it related to the actual view position for the image.

5.1   The Hall Shading Model

The intensity of light leaving a surface in a given direction is a function of the illuminating light, the properties and geometry of the surface itself, and the direction of the viewer. The Hall model divides incoming light into two classes: light arriving directly from light sources and light arriving from other bodies. As we have seen, there are four convenient classes in which to place the light leaving a surface: diffuse reflection, diffuse transmission, specular reflection, and specular transmission. Thus, we have two kinds of incident light and four modes of light transport, giving us a total of eight classes of light–surface interaction to consider.

Figure 18 gives the eight categories of emitted light that we've identified. Each category contains the expression in the Hall model with which it is modeled. Note that there is no expression for diffuse light source transmission, and that diffuse transmission and reflection from other sources are lumped together into an 'ambient' term.

Here is the complete Hall model in one equation for light leaving an object towards an observer:

$$I(\lambda) = k_{sr}\sum_{j} I_{lj}(\lambda)\, F_{sr}(\lambda, \theta_{r,j})(\cos\theta_{r,j})^{n} \tag{20}$$

$$+ k_{st}\sum_{j} I_{lj}(\lambda)\, F_{st}(\lambda, \theta_{t,j})(\cos\theta_{t,j})^{n'}$$

$$+ k_{dr}\sum_{j} I_{lj}(\lambda)\, F_{dr}(\lambda)(\mathbf{N}\cdot\mathbf{L}_{j})$$

$$+ k_{sr}I_{sr}(\lambda)\, F_{sr}(\lambda, \theta_{R})\, T_{r}^{\Delta s r} + k_{st}I_{st}(\lambda)\, F_{st}(\lambda, \theta_{T})\, T_{t}^{\Delta s t} + k_{dr}I_{a}(\lambda)\, F_{dr}(\lambda)$$

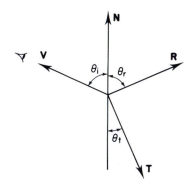

Fig. 17.   Geometry for perfectly specularly reflected (**R**) and transmitted (**T**) light from other bodies.

	Light sources	Other bodies
Specular reflection	$k_{sr} \sum_j I_{l_j}(\lambda) F_{sr}(\lambda, \theta_r)(\mathbf{N} \cdot \mathbf{H}_j)^n$	$k_{sr} I_{sr}(\lambda) F_{sr}(\lambda, \theta_r) T_r^{\Delta sr}$
Specular transmission	$k_{st} \sum_j I_{l_j}(\lambda) F_{st}(\lambda, \theta_t)(\mathbf{N} \cdot \mathbf{H}'_j)^{n'}$	$k_{st} I_{st}(\lambda) F_{st}(\lambda, \theta_t) T_t^{\Delta st}$
Diffuse reflection	$k_{dr} \sum_j I_{l_j}(\lambda) F_{dr}(\lambda)(\mathbf{N} \cdot \mathbf{L}_j)$	$k_a I_a(\lambda) F_a(\lambda)$
Diffuse transmission	—	

Fig. 18.   A summary of the terms in the Hall shading model.

where:

k_{dr} = the diffuse reflectance coefficient

k_{sr} = the specular reflectance coefficient

k_{st} = the specular transmissive coefficient

$I_{sr}(\lambda)$ = the spectrum of the reflected ray

$I_{st}(\lambda)$ = the spectrum of the transmitted ray

$I_{lj}(\lambda)$ = the spectrum of light source j

$F_{dr}(\lambda)$ = the diffuse reflection curve for the surface at wavelength λ

$F_{sr}(\lambda, \theta)$ = the specular reflection curve at wavelength λ and angle θ

$F_{st}(\lambda, \theta)$ = the specular transmission curve at wavelength λ and angle θ

$\theta_{r,j} = \cos^{-1}(\mathbf{N} \cdot \mathbf{H}_j)$

$\theta_{t,j} = \cos^{-1}(\mathbf{N} \cdot \mathbf{H}'_j)$

θ_R = the angle between the normal and the reflected ray

θ_T = the angle between the normal and the transmitted ray

T_r = transmissivity per unit length of the medium containing the reflected ray

T_t = transmissivity per unit length of the medium containing the transmitted ray

Δsr = the distance travelled by the reflected ray

Δst = the distance travelled by the transmitted ray

n = specular reflection highlight coefficient

n' = specular transmission highlight coefficient

$\mathbf{N}$ = the surface normal

$\mathbf{L}_j$ = the vector towards light source j

$\mathbf{V}$ = the direction towards the viewer (or the ray that requires shading)

$\mathbf{H}_j$ = the perfect specular reflection microfacet normal for light source j

$\mathbf{H}'_j$ = the perfect specular transmission microfacet normal for light source j

and $k_{dr} + k_{sr} = 1$
$k_{dt} + k_{st} = 1$
$0 \leqslant k_{dr}, k_{sr}, k_{dt}, k_{st} \leqslant 1$
$0 \leqslant T_r, T_t \leqslant 1.$

Remember that all vectors are assumed to be normalized (i.e. have length 1).

Figures 16 and *17* give the geometry of the equation. We are studying the light leaving point P on the surface and travelling to the viewer. The viewer lies in the direction indicated by vector **V**. We can construct a vector pointing to each light source, to help find the angle of incident light on the surface; such vectors are **L**$_j$ for each light source j.

The vector **H**$_j$ is the same **H** we encountered when studying the color shift of reflected light at a surface. It tells us the normal vector for microfacets that specularly reflect the incoming light source j back to the observer:

$$\mathbf{H}_j = \frac{\mathbf{L} + \mathbf{V}}{|\mathbf{L} + \mathbf{V}|}. \tag{11}$$

The vector **H**$_j^j$ serves the same purpose for transmission, giving the normal of those microfacets which will transmit light directly to the viewer. We can compute **H**$_j^j$ using Snell's law. If media 1 and 2 have indices of refraction η_1 and η_2, then:

$$\mathbf{H}_j^j = \frac{\mathbf{V} - \beta \mathbf{L}_j}{\beta - 1}, \text{ where } \beta = \frac{\eta_2}{\eta_1}. \tag{21}$$

There's a lot of stuff in this shading equation, but we've seen most of the pieces before. The only real surprises come in the approximations. We'll look at each term one by one.

5.2   Diffuse Reflection of Light Sources

$$k_{dr} \sum_j I_{lj}(\lambda) F_{dr}(\lambda)(\mathbf{N} \cdot \mathbf{L}_j)$$

This term describes the amount of light that leaves the surface due to diffuse reflection of light from the light sources. The coefficient k_{dr} describes to what extent this type of reflection occurs for this material. A shiny mirror would have a diffuse reflectance of 0, while a piece of cardboard would have a diffuse reflectance probably above 0.9.

For each light, the dot product computes the cosine of the angle between the direction of that light and the normal to the surface. We use this result to scale the spectrum of the light source, $I_{lj}(\lambda)$. We next multiply the reflected intensity at each frequency by the diffuse reflection curve for this material, $F_{dr}(\lambda)$; this curve is independent of the angle of incidence of the incoming light. After we've summed together the diffuse reflection for each light source, we multiply the composite by k_{dr}, the diffuse reflectivity coefficient of the surface.

5.3 Specular Reflection of Light Sources

$$k_{sr}\sum_{j} I_{lj}(\lambda)F_{sr}(\lambda, \theta_{r,j})(\cos \theta_{r,j})^{n}$$

This term is similar to the diffuse reflection of light sources. We first notice that the Fresnel reflectance is now a function of the angle of incidence, $\theta_{r,j} = \cos^{-1}(\mathbf{N} \cdot \mathbf{H}_j)$. This is the angle between the surface normal and the direction of the microfacet that would cause perfect specular reflection of the light into the direction of the viewer. The particular curve we're using now is the specular reflectance curve.

We also see a dependence on $\cos \theta_{r,j} = (\mathbf{N} \cdot \mathbf{H}_j)$ raised to an exponent, n. This term replaces D and G in the shading model of equation (10). This term was first developed by Phong to exert control on the highlights generated by specular reflection. If n is 1, then we'll get very spread out highlights. But as n rises to 5, 10, or higher, the highlight will get sharper. *Figure 19* shows a cosine curve (which is after all the dot product curve) raised to several different powers. Notice how the gentle cosine curve becomes a sharp bump.

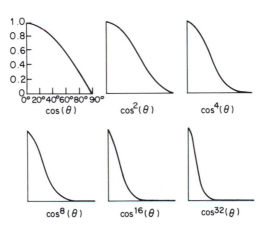

Fig. 19. Exponentiating the cosine of the angle between **N** and **H** or **N** and **H'** gives control over the spread of the reflective or transmissive highlight. Higher powers yield sharper highlights.

Very shiny surfaces will have a large exponent generating very sharp highlights. More matte surfaces have a smaller exponent.

The last difference is that we multiply the result by the specular reflectance coefficient k_{sr}.

Thus for each light, we find its spectrum and scale it on a wavelength-by-wavelength basis as a result of the value from the Fresnel reflectance curve. The whole spectrum is then scaled by the exponentiated dot product, and then scaled again by the overall specularity of the surface.

5.4   Specular Transmission of Light Sources

$$k_{st}\sum_{j} I_{lj}(\lambda)\, F_{st}(\lambda, \theta_{t,j})(\cos\, \theta_{t,j})^{n'}$$

This expression is basically similar to the expression for the specular reflectance of light sources. Recall that $\theta_{t,j} = \cos^{-1}(-\mathbf{N} \cdot \mathbf{H}'_j)$. Here we care about the dot product with $\mathbf{H}'$ instead of $\mathbf{H}$, since we want to transmit the lights, not reflect them. The exponent n' controls the sharpness of the transmitted highlight, just as n controlled the sharpness of the reflected highlight.

The specular transmission curve $F_{st}(\lambda, \theta_t)$ can be derived from principles regarding the conservation of energy. The bottom line is:

$$F_{st}(\lambda, \theta) = 1 - F_{sr}(\lambda, \theta). \tag{22}$$

The result is then scaled by the transmissive coefficient k_{st}.

5.5   Specular Reflection of Light from Other Bodies

$$k_{sr} I_{sr}(\lambda)\, F_{sr}(\lambda, \theta_{\mathbf{R}})\, T_r^{\Delta sr}$$

Not only are light sources reflected to the viewer; so is any other light arriving along the proper angle to be bounced in the direction of the viewer. We sample this light with a reflected ray.

The spectrum of the incoming light (the color of the 'reflected ray' generated when ray tracing) is represented here as $I_{sr}(\lambda)$. Since it is specularly reflected, we multiply it wavelength-by-wavelength by the specular reflectance curve $F_{sr}(\lambda, \theta_{\mathbf{R}})$, computed for the appropriate angle of incidence $\theta_{\mathbf{R}}$, and then scale the result by the specular reflectance coefficient k_{sr}.

We would like to account for the fact that this light is arriving from a distant source, and is diminishing as it travels. The term T_r models how much the light falls off per unit of travel within the media through which it is moving.

The term Δsr is the distance travelled by the ray from the last intersection to this point. Thus, the composite term $T_r^{\Delta sr}$ compensates for the dispersion of the light. As an aside, it sometimes looks better to cheat the geometry here and use $1/(a_r + \Delta sr)$ (where a_r is an arbitrary constant) instead of $T_r^{\Delta sr}$; this has the effect of still diminishing the light as it travels, but the effect is somewhat less drastic.

Note that we don't need to take the dot product of the specularly reflected ray with the surface normal at this point. This is because we know that we generate the perfect specular ray when we are ray tracing, so whatever color comes along this ray is going to be reflected at full strength, modulated by the specular reflectance functions and coefficients.

5.6   Specular Transmission of Light from Other Bodies

$$k_{st} I_{st}(\lambda) F_{st}(\lambda, \theta_T) T_t^{\Delta st}$$

This term is similar to the specular reflection of light from other bodies just discussed. The coefficient is now k_{st} because this is the light coming along the (specularly) transmitted ray. This color of the transmitted ray is $I_{st}(\lambda)$. The reflectance curve is $F_{st}(\lambda, \theta_t)$. Recall that equation (22) tells us this curve in terms of F_{sr}. We also compensate for the distance the light travels with T_t (the reduction in intensity per unit travel) and Δst (the distance travelled), so that $T_t^{\Delta st}$ reduces the intensity of the light the further it needs to travel. As before, we could use $1/(a_t + \Delta st)$ (where a_t is an arbitrary constant) instead of $T_t^{\Delta st}$ for a less drastic reduction of the light intensity.

5.7   Ambient Light

$$k_{dr} I_a(\lambda) F_{dr}(\lambda)$$

This is a catch-all term to approximate the effects of diffusely reflected light from other bodies. A spectrum of 'ambient' light is defined by $I_a(\lambda)$. The light is diffusely reflected and therefore modulated by the diffuse reflectance curve $F_{dr}(\lambda)$. The diffuse reflection coefficient k_{dr} then scales the resulting spectrum.

5.8   An Extension

We can make a couple of extensions to the shading model of (20). Of the four transport modes we've discussed, (20) leaves out diffuse transmission altogether. It's easy enough to add a term for the diffuse transmission of light sources. We need to then add some intelligence to our program: if a light is on the same side of the surface as the viewer, we use diffuse reflection, otherwise diffuse transmission. Note that we need to turn the normal around before computing the dot product for transmitted light.

We also observe that the ambient light can be passed on by all four transport modes, not just diffuse reflection. We can move the ambient light term into the diffuse reflection and transmission curves with no harm. It would be more difficult to add it into the specular terms; we would need some measure of the solid angle that these terms are sampling, and the model is not sophisticated enough to provide that sort of information without some work.

The extended model with these changes is presented in equation (23).

$$I(\lambda) = k_{sr} \sum_j I_{1j}(\lambda) F_{sr}(\lambda, \theta_{r,j})(\cos \theta_{r,j})^n \tag{23}$$

$$+ k_{st} \sum_j I_{1j}(\lambda) F_{st}(\lambda, \theta_{t,j})(\cos \theta_{t,j})^{n'}$$

$$+ k_{dr} F_{dr}(\lambda) \left[I_a(\lambda) + \sum_j I_{1j}(\lambda)(\mathbf{N} \cdot \mathbf{L_j}) \right]$$

$$+ k_{dt} F_{dt}(\lambda) \left[I_a(\lambda) + \sum_j I_{1j}(\lambda)(-\mathbf{N} \cdot \mathbf{L_j}) \right]$$

$$+ k_{sr} I_{sr}(\lambda) F_{sr}(\lambda, \theta_{\mathbf{R}}) T_r^{\Delta sr} + k_{st} I_{st}(\lambda) F_{st}(\lambda, \theta_{\mathbf{T}}) T_t^{\Delta st}$$

where (for other terms see (20)):
  k_{dt} = the diffuse transmission coefficient
  $F_{dt}(\lambda)$ = the diffuse transmission curve for the surface at wavelength λ.

We note that the diffuse transmittance term can be found from:

$$F_{dt}(\lambda, \theta) = 1 - F_{dr}(\lambda, \theta). \tag{24}$$

Notice also that for efficiency we have moved the multiplication of the diffuse components by the diffuse Fresnel terms outside of the summation.

ACKNOWLEDGEMENTS

Thanks to Robert and Raphael Seidl for discussions about shading models, and Doug Turner for conversations about intuitive ray tracing.

REFERENCES

Siggraph '77: *Comput. Graph.* **11**(2), July 1977.
Siggraph '78: *Comput. Graph.* **12**(3), August 1978.
Siggraph '79: *Comput. Graph.* **13**(2), August 1979.
Siggraph '80: *Comput. Graph.* **14**(3), July 1980.
Siggraph '81: *Comput. Graph.* **15**(3), August 1981.
Siggraph '82: *Comput. Graph.* **16**(3), July 1982.
Siggraph '83: *Comput. Graph.* **17**(3), July 1983.
Siggraph '84: *Comput. Graph.* **18**(3), July 1984.
Siggraph '85: *Comput. Graph.* **19**(3), July 1985.
Siggraph '86: *Comput. Graph.* **20**(4), August 1986.

1. Blinn, J.F., Models of light reflection for computer synthesized pictures. Siggraph '77.
2. Blinn, J.F., Light reflection functions for simulation of clouds and dusty surfaces. Siggraph '82.
3. Bui-Tuong, Phong, Illumination for computer generated images. *Communications of the ACM*, v. 18, no. 6, pp. 311–317, 1975.
4. Cook, R.L. and Torrance, K.E., A reflectance model for computer graphics. *ACM Trans. Graph.* **1**, 7–24, 1982.
5. Cook, R.L., Shade Trees. Siggraph '84.
6. Goral, C.M., Torrance K.E., Greenberg, D.P. and Battaile, B., Modeling the interaction of light between diffuse surfaces. Siggraph '84.
7. Gouraud, H., Computer display of curved surfaces. *IEEE Trans. C-20*, 623–628, 1971.
8. Hall, R.A. and Greenberg, D., A testbed for realistic image synthesis. *ACM Trans. Graph.* **3**, 10–20, 1983.
9. Judd, D.B. and Wyszecki, G., *Color in Business, Science, and Industry*, Wiley, New York, 1975.
10. Kajiya, J.T., Anisotropic reflection models. Siggraph '85.
11. Kajiya, J.T., The rendering equation. Siggraph '86.
12. Kay, D.S. and Greenberg, D., Transparency for computer synthesized images. Siggraph '79.
13. Max, N.L., Atmospheric illumination and shadows. Siggraph '86.
14. Moravec, H.P., 3D graphics and the wave theory. Siggraph '81.
15. Purdue University, *Thermophysical Properties of Matter, vol. 7: Thermal Radiative Properties of Metals*, Plenum, New York, 1970.
16. Purdue University, *Thermophysical Properties of Matter, vol. 8: Thermal Radiative Properties of Nonmetallic Solids*, Plenum, New York, 1970.
17. Purdue University, *Thermophysical Properties of Matter, vol. 9 Thermal Radiative Properties of Coatings*, Plenum, New York, 1970.
18. Rogers, D.F., *Procedural Elements for Computer Graphics*, McGraw-Hill, NY, 1985.
19. Torrance, K.E. and Sparrow, E.M., Theory for off-specular reflection from roughened surfaces. *J. Opt. Soc. Am.* **57**, 1105–1114, 1967.
20. Whitted, T., An improved illumination model for shaded display. *Commun. ACM* **23**, 343–349, 1980.

Additional References

Upton, B. and Upton, J., *Photography*, 2nd Edition, Little, Brown, and Company, 1980.

Preparata, F. and Shamos, M., *Computational Geometry: An Introduction*, Springer-Verlag, 1985.

Edwards, C. and Penney, D., *Calculus and Analytic Geometry*, Prentice-Hall, 1982.

Halliday, D. and Resnick, R., *Physics*, 3rd Edition, John Wiley, 1978.

Oppenheim, A. and Schafer, R., *Digital Signal Processing*, Prentice-Hall, 1975.

Press, W., Flannery, B., Teukolsky, S. and Vetterling, W., *Numerical Recipes in C*, Cambridge University Press, 1988.

5 Stochastic Sampling and Distributed Ray Tracing

ROBERT L. COOK

1   INTRODUCTION

Because pixels are discrete, computer graphics is inherently a sampling process. The pixel size determines an upper limit to the frequencies that can be displayed. This limit, one cycle every two pixels, is called the *Nyquist limit*. An attempt to display frequencies greater than the Nyquist limit can produce aliasing artifacts, such as 'jaggies' on the edges of objects [12], jagged highlights [38], strobing and other forms of temporal aliasing [30], and Moiré patterns in textures [12]. These artifacts are tolerated in some real time applications in which speed is more vital than beauty, but they are unacceptable in realistic image synthesis.

Rendering algorithms can be classified as *analytic* or *discrete* according to how they approach the aliasing problem. Analytic algorithms can filter out the high frequencies that cause aliasing before sampling the pixel values. This filtering tends to be complicated and time consuming, but it can eliminate certain types of aliasing very effectively   [3, 12, 14, 15, 25].   Discrete algorithms, such as ray tracing, only consider the image at regularly spaced sample points. Since they ignore everything not at these points, they appear by their nature to preclude filtering the image. Thus they have been plagued by seemingly inherent aliasing artifacts. This is unfortunate, for these algorithms are much simpler, more elegant, and more amenable to hardware implementation than the analytic methods. They are also capable of many features that are difficult to do analytically, such as shadows, reflection, refraction [20,36], constructive solid geometry [32], motion blur, and depth of field [9].

There are two existing discrete approaches to alleviating the aliasing problem: *supersampling* and *adaptive sampling*. Supersampling involves using more than one regularly spaced sample per pixel. It reduces aliasing by raising the Nyquist limit, but it does not eliminate aliasing. No matter how many samples are used, there are still frequencies that will alias. In adaptive sampling, additional rays are traced near edges [36]; the additional rays are traced midway between previously traced rays. Unlike supersampling, this approach can anti-alias edges reliably, but it may require a large number of rays, and it complicates an otherwise simple algorithm.

In this paper, a new discrete approach to anti-aliasing called *stochastic sampling* is presented. Stochastic sampling is a Monte Carlo technique [17] in which the image is sampled at appropriate nonuniformly spaced locations rather than at regularly spaced locations. This approach is inherently different from either supersampling or adaptive sampling, though it can be combined with either of them. Stochastic sampling can eliminate all forms of aliasing, including unruly forms such as highlight aliasing.

With stochastic sampling, aliasing is replaced by noise of the correct average intensity. Frequencies above the Nyquist limit are still inadequately sampled, and they still appear as artifacts in the image. But a highly objectionable artifact (aliasing) is replaced with an artifact that our visual systems tolerate very well (noise).

In addition to providing a solution to the aliasing problem, stochastic sampling also provides new capabilities for discrete algorithms such as ray tracing. The physical equations simulated in the rendering process involve integrals over time, lens area, specular reflection angle, etc. Image synthesis algorithms have usually avoided performing these integrals by resorting to crude approximations that assume instantaneous shutters, pinhole cameras, mirror or diffuse reflections, etc. But these integrals can be easily evaluated by stochastically sampling them, a process called Monte Carlo integration. In a ray tracing algorithm, this involves stochastically distributing the rays in time, lens area, reflection angle, etc. This is called *probabilistic* or *distributed ray tracing* [9]. Distributed ray tracing allows the simulation of fuzzy phenomena, such as motion blur, depth of field, penumbras, gloss, and translucency.

2   UNIFORM POINT SAMPLING

Before discussing stochastic sampling, we first review uniform sampling and the source of aliasing. In a point-sampled picture, frequencies greater than the Nyquist limit are inadequately sampled. If the samples are uniformly spaced, these frequencies can appear as aliases, i.e. they can appear falsely as low frequencies [4, 27, 31].

To see how this happens, consider for the moment one-dimensional sampling; we shall refer to that dimension as time. Let a signal $f(t)$ be sampled at regular intervals of time, i.e. at times nT for integer n, where T is the time period between samples, so that $1/T$ is the sampling frequency. The Nyquist limit is half the sampling frequency, or $0.5/T$. This sampling is equivalent to multiplication by the *shah* function $\text{III}(t/T)$, where

$$\text{III}(x) = \sum_{n=-\infty}^{\infty} \delta(x - n) \tag{1}$$

where δ is the Kronecker delta function. After sampling, information about the original signal $f(t)$ is preserved only at the sample points. The sampling theorem states that if $f(t)$ contains no frequencies above the Nyquist limit, then sampling followed by an ideal reconstruction filter reproduces the original signal $f(t)$ exactly.

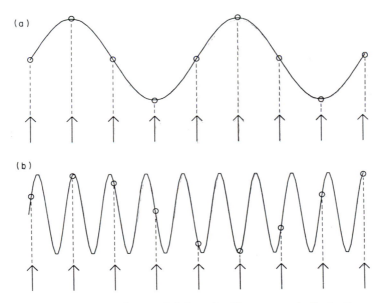

Fig. 1. Point sampling in the spatial domain. The arrows indicate the sample locations, and the circles indicate the sampled values. In (a), the sine wave is within the Nyquist limit, so the sampled values accurately represent the signal. In (b), the sine wave frequency is above the Nyquist limit, and the sampled values incorrectly represent a low-frequency sine wave that is not present in the signal.

This situation is shown in *Figure 1* for a sine wave. In *Figure 1(a)*, the frequency of the sine wave is below the Nyquist limit of the samples, and the sampled values accurately represent the function. But in *Figure 1(b)*, the frequency of the sine wave is above the Nyquist limit of the samples. The sampled values do not accurately represent the sampled sine wave; instead they look like they came from a low-frequency sine wave. The high-frequency sine wave appears incorrectly under the alias of this low-frequency sine wave.

Figure 2 shows this situation in the frequency domain. The Fourier transform of f is denoted by F; the Fourier transform of the shah function $III(t/T)$ is another shah function, $(1/T)III(tT)$. *Figure 2(a)* shows the Fourier transform of the signal in *Figure 1(a)*, a single sine wave whose frequency is below the Nyquist limit. Sampling involves convolving the signal with the sampling grid of *Figure 2(b)* to produce the spectrum shown in *Figure 2(c)*. An

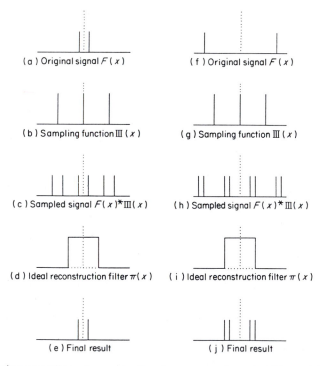

(a) Original signal $F(x)$

(f) Original signal $F(x)$

(b) Sampling function $III(x)$

(g) Sampling function $III(x)$

(c) Sampled signal $F(x)*III(x)$

(h) Sampled signal $F(x)*III(x)$

(d) Ideal reconstruction filter $\pi(x)$

(i) Ideal reconstruction filter $\pi(x)$

(e) Final result

(j) Final result

Fig. 2.   Point sampling shown in the frequency domain. The original signal $F(x)$ is convolved with the sampling grid $III(x)$ and the result is multiplied by an ideal reconstruction filter $\Pi(x)$. The process is shown for a sine wave with a frequency below the Nyquist limit in (a) through (e) and above the Nyquist limit in (f) through (j).

ideal reconstruction filter, shown in *Figure 2(d)*, would extract the original signal, as in *Figure 2(e)*. In *Figures 2(f)–2(j)*, the same process is repeated for the signal in *Figure 1(b)*, a single sine wave whose frequency is above the Nyquist limit. In this case, the sampling process can fold the high-frequency sine wave into low frequencies, as shown in *Figure 2(h)*. These false frequencies, or aliases, cannot be separated from frequencies that are a part of the original signal. The part of the spectrum extracted by the reconstruction filter contains these aliases, as shown in *Figure 2(j)*.

Sampling theory thus predicts that with a regular sampling grid, frequencies greater than the Nyquist limit can alias. The inability to reproduce those frequencies is inherent in the sampling process, but their appearance as aliases is a consequence of the regularity of the sampling grid. If the sample points are not regularly spaced, the energy in those frequencies can appear as noise, an artifact that is much less objectionable than aliasing. In the case of uniform sampling, aliasing is precisely defined; in the case of nonuniform sampling, we use the term aliasing to mean artifacts with distinct frequency components, as opposed to noise.

3   POISSON DISK SAMPLING

An excellent example of a nonuniform distribution of sample locations is found in the human eye. The eye has a limited number of photoreceptors, and, like any other sampling process, it has a Nyquist limit. Yet our eyes are not normally prone to aliasing [37]. In the fovea, the cells are tightly packed in a hexagonal pattern, and aliasing is avoided because the lens acts as a low pass filter. Outside of the fovea, however, the cells are further apart and thus the sampling rate is lower, so we might expect to see aliasing artifacts. In this region, aliasing is avoided by a nonuniform distribution of the cells.

The distribution of cones in the eye has been studied by Yellott [39]. *Figure 3(a)* is a picture of the distribution of cones in an extrafoveal region of the eye of a rhesus monkey, which has a photoreceptor distribution similar to that in the human eye. Yellott took the optical Fourier transform of this distribution, with the result shown in *Figure 3(b)*. This distribution is called a *Poisson disk distribution*, and it is shown schematically in the frequency domain in *Figure 4(b)*. There is a spike at the origin (the d.c. component) and a sea of noise beyond the Nyquist limit. In effect, the samples are randomly placed with the restriction that no two samples are closer together than a certain distance.

Now let us analyze point sampling using a Poisson disk sampling distribution instead of a regular grid. *Figure 4(a)* shows a signal that is a single sine wave whose frequency is below the Nyquist limit. Convolution with the Poisson sampling grid of *Figure 4(b)* produces the spectrum in *Figure 4(c)*. The

(a) (b)

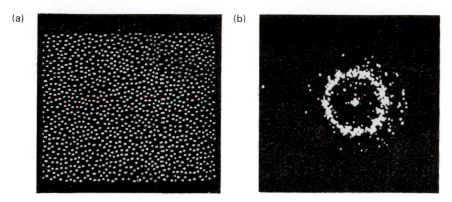

Fig. 3.   (a) Monkey eye photoreceptor distribution. (b) Optical transform of monkey eye.

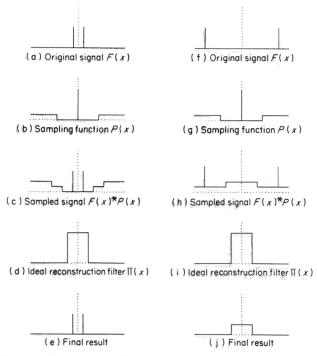

(a) Original signal $F(x)$

(b) Sampling function $P(x)$

(c) Sampled signal $F(x)*P(x)$

(d) Ideal reconstruction filter $\Pi(x)$

(e) Final result

(f) Original signal $F(x)$

(g) Sampling function $P(x)$

(h) Sampled signal $F(x)*P(x)$

(i) Ideal reconstruction filter $\Pi(x)$

(j) Final result

Fig. 4.   Poisson sampling shown in the frequency domain.

ideal reconstruction filter of *Figure 4(d)* would extract the original signal, *Figure 4(e)*. *Figure 4(f)* shows a sine wave whose frequency is above the Nyquist limit. Convolution with the Poisson sampling grid produces the spectrum in *Figure 4(h)*. An ideal reconstruction filter would extract noise, as shown in *Figure 4(j)*. This noise replaces the aliasing of *Figure 1(j)*.

The minimum distance restriction decreases the magnitude of the noise. For example, film grain appears to have a random distribution [34], but without the minimum distance restriction of a Poisson disk distribution. With a purely random distribution, the samples tend to bunch up in some places and leave large gaps in other places. Film does not alias, but it is more prone to noise than the eye.

One possible implementation of Poisson disk sampling to image rendering is straightforward, though expensive. A look-up table is created by generating random sample locations and discarding any locations that are closer than a certain distance to any of the locations already chosen. Locations are generated until the sampling region is full. Filter values are calculated that describe how each sample affects the neighboring pixels, and these filter values must be normalized. The locations and filter values are stored in a table. This method would produce good pictures, but it would also require a large look-up table. An alternative method, jittering a regular grid, is discussed in the next section.

4 JITTERING A REGULAR GRID

4.1 Theory

Jittering, or adding noise to sample locations, is a form of stochastic sampling that can be used to approximate a Poisson disk distribution. There are many types of jitter; among these is additive random jitter, which can eliminate aliasing completely [33]. But the discussion in this paper is limited to one particular type of jitter, the jittering of a regular grid. This type of jitter produces good results and is particularly well suited to image rendering algorithms. The results are not quite as good as those obtained with Poisson disk sampling, in that the images are somewhat noisier and some very small amount of aliasing can remain.

Jitter was analyzed in one dimension ('time') by Balakrishnan [2], who calculated the effect of *time jitter*, in which the nth sample is jittered by an amount ζ_n so that it occurs at time $nT + \zeta_n$, where T is the sampling period (see *Figure 5(a)*). If the ζ_n are uncorrelated, Balakrishnan reports that jittering

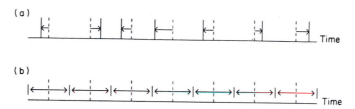

Fig. 5.   (a) Time jitter. Regularly spaced sample times are shown as dashed lines, and the corresponding jittered times are shown as solid lines. Each sample time is jittered by an amount ζ so that the nth sample occurs at time $nT + \zeta_n$ instead of at time nT, where T is the sample period. (b) White noise jitter for $\gamma = 0.5$. Regularly spaced samples, shown as dashed lines, are jittered so that every time has an equal chance of being sampled.

has the following effects:

- High frequencies are attenuated.
- The energy lost to the attenuation appears as uniform noise. The intensity of the noise equals the intensity of the attenuated part of the signal.
- The basic composition of the spectrum otherwise does not change.

Sampling by itself cannot be regarded as a filter, because sampling is not a linearly shift-invariant process. Balakrishnan showed, however, that the combination of jittered sampling plus an ideal reconstruction filter is a linearly shift-invariant process, even though the sampling by itself is not [2], so it is in this context that we can talk about frequency attenuation.

Uncorrelated jitter is jitter in which any two jitter amounts ζ_n and ζ_m are uncorrelated. Balakrishnan analyzed two types of uncorrelated jitter: *Gaussian jitter* and *white noise jitter*. For Gaussian jitter the values of ζ are chosen according to a Gaussian distribution with a variance of σ^2. The gain as a function of frequency ν is then

$$e^{-(2\pi\nu\sigma)^2} \tag{2}$$

This function is plotted with a solid line in *Figure 6* for $\sigma = T/6.5$. With white noise jitter, the values of ζ are uniformly distributed between $-\gamma T$ and γT (see *Figure 5(b)*). The gain in this case is

$$\left[\frac{\sin(2\pi\gamma\nu T)}{2\pi\gamma\nu T}\right]^2, \tag{3}$$

as shown with a dashed line in *Figure 6* for $\gamma = 1/2$.

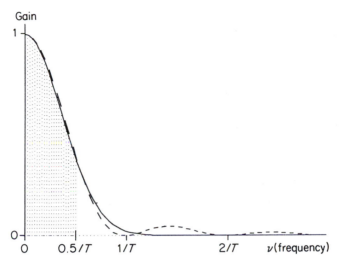

Fig. 6. Attenuation due to jitter. The broken line shows the filter for white noise jitter, the solid line for Gaussian jitter. The shaded area is inside the Nyquist limit.

From this we can see that jittering a regular grid does not eliminate aliasing completely, but it does reduce it substantially. The Nyquist limit of $0.5/T$ is indicated in the figure by the shaded area. Notice that the width of the filter can be scaled by adjusting γ or σ. This gives control of the trade-off between decreased aliasing and increased noise.

For an intuitive explanation of these equations, consider the sine wave shown in *Figure 7(a)*, with samples at regularly spaced intervals λ as shown. These samples are inside the Nyquist limit and therefore sample the sine wave properly. Jittering the location of each sample n by some ζ_n in the range $-\lambda/2 < \zeta_n < \lambda/2$ is similar to adding some noise to the amplitude; note that the basic sine wave frequency is not lost. This noise is less for sine waves with a lower frequency relative to the sampling frequency.

Now consider the sine wave shown in *Figure 7(b)*. Here the sampling rate is not sufficient for the frequency of the sine wave, so regularly spaced samples can alias. The jittered sample, however, can occur at any amplitude. If there are exactly a whole number of cycles in the range $-\lambda/2 < \zeta_n < \lambda/2$, then the amplitude we sample is random, since there is an equal probability of sampling each part of the sine wave. In this case, none of the energy from the sine wave produces aliasing; it all becomes noise. This corresponds to the zero points of the dashed line in *Figure 6*. If the sine wave frequency is not an exact multiple of λ, then some parts of the wave will be more likely to be sampled than others. In this case there is some attenuated aliasing, and some noise

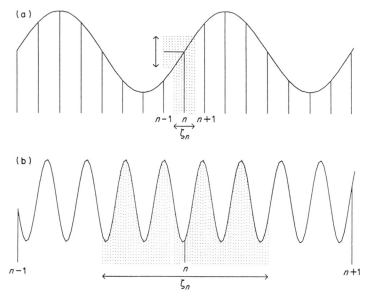

Fig. 7.   (a) The effect of white noise jittering on a sine wave with a frequency below the Nyquist limit. Sample n occurs at a random location in the dotted region. The jitter indicated by the horizontal arrow results in a sampled value that can vary by the amount indicated by the vertical arrow. (b) The effect of white noise jittering on a sine wave with a frequency above the Nyquist limit. The jitter indicated by the horizontal arrow results in a sampled value that is almost pure noise.

because there is some chance of hitting each part of the wave. This attenuation is greater for higher frequencies, because with more cycles of the wave there is less preference for one part of the wave over another. Note also that the average signal level of the noise (the d.c. component or gray level) is equal to the average signal level of the sine wave. The gray level of the signal is preserved.

4.2   Implementation

The extension of jittering to two dimensions is straightforward. Consider a pixel as a regular grid of one or more rectangular *subpixels*, each with one sample point. Each sample point is placed in the middle of a subpixel, and then noise is added to the x and y locations independently so that each sample point occurs at some random location within its subpixel.

Once the visibility at the sample points is known, the sample values are filtered with a reconstruction filter and resampled on a regular grid of pixel locations to obtain the pixel values. How to do this reconstruction properly is an open problem. The easiest reconstruction filter to compute is a box filter. Each pixel value is obtained by simply averaging the sample values in that pixel. Weighted reconstruction filters with wider filter kernels give better variance reduction. In this case, the filter values are a function of the position of each sample point relative to the surrounding pixels. The value of each pixel is the sum of the values of the nearby sample points multiplied by their respective filter values; this total is normalized by dividing by the total of the filter values.

If the random components of the sample locations are small compared to the width of the filter, the effect of the random components on the filter values can usually be ignored. The filter values can then be calculated in advance for the regularly spaced grid locations. These filter values can be prenormalized and stored in a look-up table. Changing filters is simply a matter of changing the look-up table.

5   DISTRIBUTED RAY TRACING

In the previous section, we applied stochastic sampling to the two-dimensional distribution of the sample points used for determining visibility in a z buffer or ray-casting algorithm. But the intensity of a pixel on the screen is an analytic function that may involve several nested integrals: integrals over time, over the pixel region, and over the lens area, as well as an integral of reflectance times illumination over the reflected hemisphere and an integral of transmittance times illumination over the transmitted hemisphere. These integrals can be tremendously complicated.

Image-rendering algorithms have made certain simplifying assumptions in order to avoid the evaluation of these integrals. But the evaluation of these integrals is essential for rendering a whole range of fuzzy phenomena, such as penumbras, blurry reflections, translucency, depth of field, and motion blur. Thus image rendering has usually been limited to sharp shadows, sharp reflections, sharp refractions, pinhole cameras, and instantaneous shutters. Recent exceptions to this are the radiosity method [16] and cone tracing [1].

The rendering integrals can be evaluated with stochastic sampling. If we regard the variables of integration as additional dimensions, we can perform a Monte Carlo evaluation of the integrals by stochastically distributing the sample points (rays) in those additional dimensions. This is called probabilistic ray tracing or distributed ray tracing.

- ■   Distributing reflected rays according to the specular distribution function produces gloss (blurry reflection).

- Distributing transmitted rays produces translucency (blurry transparency).
- Distributing shadow rays through the solid angle of each light source produces penumbras.
- Distributing ray origins over the camera lens area produces depth of field.
- Distributing rays in time produces motion blur.

In this section, we describe some of the situations in which distributed ray tracing is applicable. In the next section, we discuss the application of stochastic sampling to the distribution of the rays.

5.1 Shading

The intensity I of the reflected light at a point on a surface is an integral over the hemisphere above the surface of an illumination function L and a reflection function R [5].

$$I(\phi_r, \theta_r) = \int_{\phi i} \int_{\theta i} L(\phi_i, \theta_i) R(\phi_i, \theta_i, \phi_r, \theta_r) \, d\phi_i \, d\theta_i \qquad (4)$$

where (ϕ_i, θ_i) is the angle of incidence, and
(ϕ_r, θ_r) is the angle of reflection.

The complexity of performing this integration has been avoided by making some simplifying assumptions. The following are some of these simplifications:

- Assume that L is a δ function, i.e. that L is zero except for light source directions and that the light sources can be treated as points. The integral is now replaced by a sum over certain discrete directions. This assumption causes sharp shadows.
- Assume that all of the directions that are not light source directions can be grouped together into an ambient light source. This ambient light is the same in all directions, so that L is independent of ϕ_i and θ_i and may be removed from the integral. The integral of R may then be replaced by an average, or ambient, reflectance.
- Assume that the reflectance function R is a δ function, i.e. that the surface is a mirror and reflects light only from the mirror direction. This assumption causes sharp reflections. A corresponding assumption for transmitted light causes sharp refraction.

The shading function may be too complex to compute analytically, but we can point sample its value by distributing the rays, thus avoiding these simplifying assumptions. Illumination rays are not traced toward a single light direction, but are distributed according to the illumination function L. Reflected rays are not traced in a single mirror direction but are distributed according to the reflectance function R.

Gloss

Reflections are mirror-like in computer graphics, but in real life reflections are often blurred or hazy. The distinctness with which a surface reflects its environment is called *gloss* [18]. Blurred reflections have been discussed by Whitted [36] and by Cook [6]. Any analytic simulation of these reflections must be based on the integral of the reflectance over some solid angle.

Mirror reflections are determined by tracing rays from the surface in the mirror direction. Gloss can be calculated by distributing these secondary rays about the mirror direction. The distribution is weighted according to the same distribution function that determines the highlights.

This method was originally suggested by Whitted [36], and it replaces the usual specular component. Rays that reflect light sources produce highlights.

Translucency

Light transmitted through an object is described by an equation similar to that for reflected light except that the reflectance function R is replaced by a transmittance function T and the integral is performed over the hemisphere behind the surface. The transmitted light can have ambient, diffuse and specular components [18].

Computer graphics has included transparency, in which T is assumed to be a δ function and the images seen through transparent objects are sharp. Translucency differs from transparency in that the images seen through translucent objects are not distinct. The problem of translucency is analogous to the problem of gloss. Gloss requires an integral of the reflected light, and translucency requires a corresponding integral of the transmitted light.

Translucency is calculated by distributing the secondary rays about the main direction of the transmitted light. Just as the distribution of the reflected rays is defined by the specular reflectance function, the distribution of the transmitted rays is defined by a specular transmittance function.

Penumbras

Penumbras occur where a light source is partially obscured. The reflected intensity due to such a light is proportional to the solid angle of the visible portion of the light [7]. The solid angle is part of the Cook and Torrance shading model, but no one has suggested an algorithm for determining this solid angle because of the complexity of the computation involved. The only attempt at penumbras known to the authors seems to solve only a very special case [24].

Shadows can be calculated by tracing rays from the surface to the light sources, and penumbras can be calculated by distributing these secondary rays. The shadow ray can be traced to any point on the light source, not just to a single light source location. The distribution of the shadow rays must be weighted according to the projected area and brightness of different parts of the light source. The number of rays traced to each region should be proportional to the amount of the light's energy that would come from that region if the light was completely unobscured. The proportion of lighted sample points in a region of the surface is then equal to the proportion of the light's intensity that is visible in that region.

5.2 Depth of Field

Cameras and the eye have a finite lens aperture, and hence their images have a finite depth of field. Each point in the scene appears as a circle on the image plane. This circle is called the circle of confusion, and its size depends on the distance to the point and on the lens optics. Depth of field can be an unwanted artifact, but it can also be a desirable effect.

Most computer graphics has been based on a pinhole camera model with every object in sharp focus. Potmesil simulated depth of field with a postprocessing technique. Each object is first rendered in sharp focus (i.e. with a pinhole camera model), and later each sharply rendered object is convolved with a filter the size of the circle of confusion [29]. The program spends most of its time in the focus postprocessor, and this time increases dramatically as the aperture decreases.

Such a postprocessing approach can never be completely correct. This is because visibility is calculated from a single point, the center of the lens. The view of the environment is different from different parts of the lens, and the differences include changes in visibility and shading that cannot be accounted for by a postprocessing approach.

For example, consider an object that is extremely out of focus in front of an object that is in focus. Visible surface calculations done with the pinhole model determine the visibility from the center of the lens. Because the front object is not in focus, parts of the focused object that are not visible from the center of the lens will be visible from other parts of the lens. Information about those parts will not be available for the postprocessor, so the postprocessor cannot possibly get the correct result.

There is another way to approach the depth of field problem. Depth of field occurs because the lens is a finite size. Each point on the lens 'looks' at the same point on the focal plane. The visible surfaces and the shading may be different as seen from different parts of the lens. The depth of field calculations should account for this and be an integral part of the visible surface and shading calculations.

Depth of field can be calculated by starting with the traditional ray from the center of the lens through point p on the focal plane. A point on the surface of the lens is selected and the ray from that point to p is traced. The camera specifications required for this calculation are the focal distance and the diameter of the lens F/n, where F is the focal length of the lens and n is the f stop.

This gives exactly the same circle of confusion as presented by Potmesil [29]. Because it integrates the depth of field calculations with the shading and visible surface calculations, this method gives a more accurate solution to the depth of field problem, with the exception that it does not account for diffraction effects.

Figure 8 shows why this method gives the correct circle of confusion. The lens has a diameter of F/n and is focused at a distance P so that the image plane is at a distance V_P, where

$$V_P = \frac{FP}{P - F} \text{ for } P > F. \tag{5}$$

Points on the plane that is a distance D from the lens will focus at

$$V_D = \frac{FD}{D - F} \text{ for } D > F \tag{6}$$

and have a circle of confusion with diameter C of [29]

$$C = \mid V_D - V_P \mid \frac{F}{n V_D}. \tag{7}$$

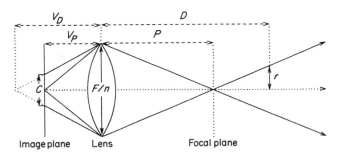

Fig. 8.   Circle of confusion.

For a point I on the image plane; the rays we trace lie inside the cone whose radius at D is

$$r = \frac{1}{2} \frac{F}{n} \frac{|D - P|}{P}.$$ (8)

The image plane distance from a point on this cone to a point on the axis of the cone is r multiplied by the magnification of the lens

$$R = r \left(-\frac{V_P}{D} \right)$$ (9)

It is easily shown that

$$R = \frac{C}{2}$$ (10)

Hence any points on the cone have a circle of confusion that just touches the image point I. Points outside the cone do not affect the image point and points inside the cone do.

The depth of field calculations can also be done in perspective space. It is not obvious at first that this can be done, since the perspective matrix is determined for one eye location, and lens jitter involves changing that location for every ray. As we shall see, however, correct screen space locations for a jittered eye point can be determined in the perspective space of the center of the lens.

We assume that objects are already in *eye space*. In eye space, the center of the lens is at the origin, the line of sight is down the z axis, and the x and y axes are aligned with the x and y axes of screen space. The perspective transformation from eye space to screen space assumes a pinhole camera located at the origin in eye space, and transforms each point (x_e, y_e, z_e) in eye space to a point (x_s, y_s, z_s) in screen space. For depth of field, however, different sample points assume pinhole cameras located at different points on the lens. In eye space, a point on the lens at some location $(r \cdot xl, r \cdot yl, 0)$, where

$$|xl| \leqslant 1, |yl| \leqslant 1$$ (11)

$$r = \frac{F}{2n} = \text{lens radius}.$$ (12)

The values of xl and yl for each sample point are determined by jittering a pattern that assures that the samples are well distributed over the lens;

jittering in distributed ray tracing is described later. This section describes
what to do once *xl* and *yl* have been determined.

A point that is at (x_e, y_e, z_e) in eye space of the center of the lens is at
(x_{el}, y_{el}, z_{el}) in the eye space of the point $(r \cdot xl, r \cdot yl, 0)$ on the lens. In
actuality,

$$z_{el}^2 = z_e^2 + r^2 \cdot (xl^2 + yl^2) \tag{13}$$

but z_e is always large compared to r and the order of the object's z_{el} values is
the same as the relative order of their z values, so we may safely assume that
$z_{el} = z_e$. From the geometry of *Figure 8*, it is easy to show using similar
triangles that

$$x_{el} - x_e = (r \cdot xl - 0) \cdot \left[\frac{D - z_e}{D - 0} \right] \tag{14}$$

$$= r \cdot xl \cdot \left[1 - \frac{z_e}{D} \right] \tag{15}$$

$$y_{el} - y_e = r \cdot yl \cdot \left[1 - \frac{z_e}{D} \right] \tag{16}$$

where D is the distance from the lens to the focal point. For a given lens
location specified by *xl* and *yl*, points are shifted in eye space according to the
above formulas. But what we really need is the shift in screen space.

Given our definition of eye space, we know that the perspective matrix that
transforms from eye space to screen space must be of the form

$$\begin{bmatrix} a & 0 & 0 & 0 \\ 0 & b & 0 & 0 \\ c & d & e & f \\ g & h & i & 0 \end{bmatrix} \tag{17}$$

so that the screen location (x_s, y_s) of the point (x_e, y_e, z_e) is

$$x_s = \frac{a \cdot x_e + c \cdot z_e + g}{f \cdot z_e} \tag{18}$$

$$y_s = \frac{b \cdot x_e + d \cdot z_e + h}{f \cdot z_e} \tag{19}$$

and from a point on the lens, the screen space location (x_{sl}, y_{sl}) is

$$x_{sl} = \frac{a \cdot x_{el} + c \cdot z_e + g}{f \cdot z_e} \tag{20}$$

$$y_{sl} = \frac{b \cdot x_{el} + d \cdot z_e + h}{f \cdot z_e}. \tag{21}$$

We want to calculate (x_{sl}, y_{sl}) given that we already know (x_s, y_s). So we are interested in the difference between the two screen space locations:

$$x_{sl} - x_s = \frac{a \cdot (x_{el} - x_e)}{f \cdot z_e} \tag{22}$$

$$= \frac{a \cdot r \cdot xl}{f} \cdot \left[\frac{1}{z_e} - \frac{1}{D} \right] \tag{23}$$

$$= xl \cdot \left[\frac{ax}{z_e} + bx \right] \tag{24}$$

where

$$ax = \frac{a \cdot r}{f} \tag{25}$$

$$bx = \frac{a \cdot r}{f} \cdot \frac{-1}{D}. \tag{26}$$

Similarly,

$$y_{sl} - y_s = yl \cdot \left[\frac{ay}{z_e} + by \right] \tag{27}$$

where

$$ay = \frac{b \cdot r}{f} \tag{28}$$

$$by = \frac{b \cdot r}{f} \cdot \frac{-1}{D}. \tag{29}$$

Note that only ax, bx, ay, and by depend on the lens parameters. These values can be calculated directly from the elements of the perspective matrix

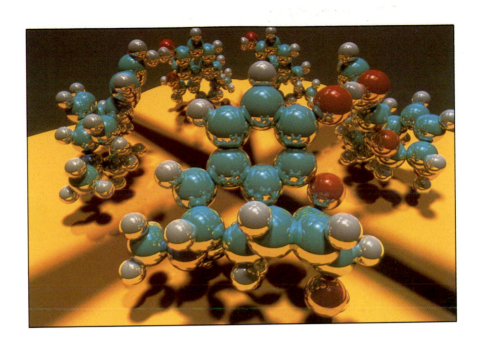

Mirror morphine   This scene is composed entirely of spheres: the 40-sphere morphine molecule is tucked in the corner between two large mirrored balls and the yellow ground ball. The image was calculated at a resolution of 2048 × 2048 with 10 levels of reflections, 3 × 3 supersampling, and analytic penumbra calculations (not probabilistic methods), in 8 days of VAX 11/780 time. For a discussion of shadows and penumbrae, see Section 5.1. (Copyright © Paul Heckbert, NYIT, 1983)

Beam tracing demonstration   This beam traced scene consists of a mirrored cube inside a room with four texture mapped walls and two mirrored walls creating a hall-of-mirrors effect. The beam tracer outputs a decomposition of the screen into non-overlapping, possibly texture-mapped polygons. The 512 × 480 image was beam traced in several seconds and the polygons scan converted in about 2 minutes on a VAX 11/780 beam tracing is discussed in Section 6.9. (Copyright © Paul Heckbert and Pat Hanrahan, NYIT, 1984)

Dino swallowing This frame is a still from the short film "Dino's Lunch". Here we see Dino preparing to swallow the yellow ball as it flies into his mouth. The ball is moving very fast, and thus leaves behind a blurry trail. Motion blur is discussed in Section 1.4.2. (Copyright © Andrew Glassner, UNC-Chapel Hill, 1988)

Dino watching   Another still from "Dino's Lunch". Here we see the ball flying by Dino for the first time. (Copyright © Andrew Glassner, UNC-Chapel Hill, 1988)

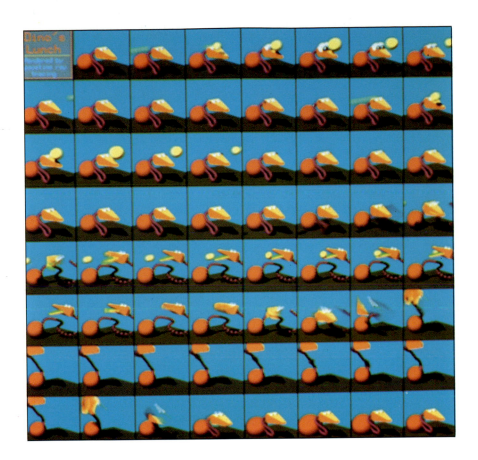

"Dino's Lunch" This image contains 64 frames from the short film "Dino's Lunch". Read them top-to-bottom, left-to-right, to follow the story. The animation was built as a single, static structure in four-dimensional spacetime. Individual rays sampled this structure in both direction and time, to create a motion-blurred animation more efficiently than by rendering each frame individually. The colors in the film are derived from actual materials; for example, Dino's body has the spectral reflectance of purple and red gladiolus petals, and the ground color is that of dirt from Virginia seen on a sunny day. Note that fast-moving objects leave behind blurry trails. Colors and spectra are discussed in Section 4.1; spacetime ray tracing is discussed in Section 6.12. (Copyright © Andrew Glassner, UNC-Chapel Hill, 1988)

Simulated office This was generated using an accelerated ray-tracing algorithm from the image synthesis testbed of Cornell's Program of Computer Graphics (Hank Weghorst and Gary Hooper). This scene was used to test algorithms which used hierarchical bounding volumes for efficiency and used Z-buffering to quickly compute the rays from the eye. The research was part of a NSF grant entitled "Computer Graphics Input and Display Techniques", under the direction of Professor Donald P. Greenberg

Chessboard scene All objects are polygonalized, creating 4944 polygons. Texture maps are used for additional realism. (Copyright © Eric Haines, Cornell University Program of Computer Graphics)

Kitchen countertop Kitchen scene with quadric surfaces (see Section 3.3.1), constructive solid geometry (Section 3.3.3) and texture mapping. The use of non-polygonal surfaces reduces both the database size and the rendering time for the scene. (Copyright © Eric Haines, Cornell University Program of Computer Graphics)

Sphereflake ''Sphereflake'' is a test image from a software package used in testing ray tracing efficiency schemes (Chapter 6). The rendering database itself is created using a short recursive program. A procedural texture map was added to the plane. (Copyright © Eric Haines, 3D/Eye Inc.)

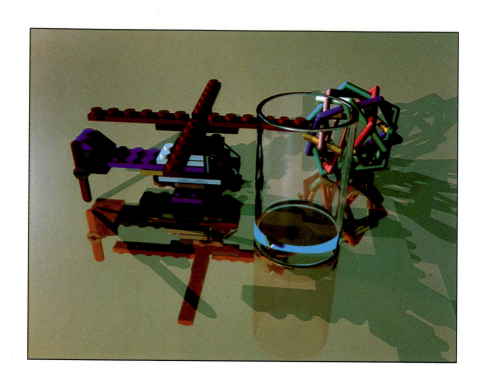

Lego The helicopter was modeled on the solids modeler ME-30. Ray tracing this exact surface description results in a more accurate rendering than rendering a polygonalized version of the database. In addition, time and memory space are minimized. (Copyright © Eric Haines, 3D/Eye Inc. Helicopter model courtesy Hewlett Packard MDDBBN)

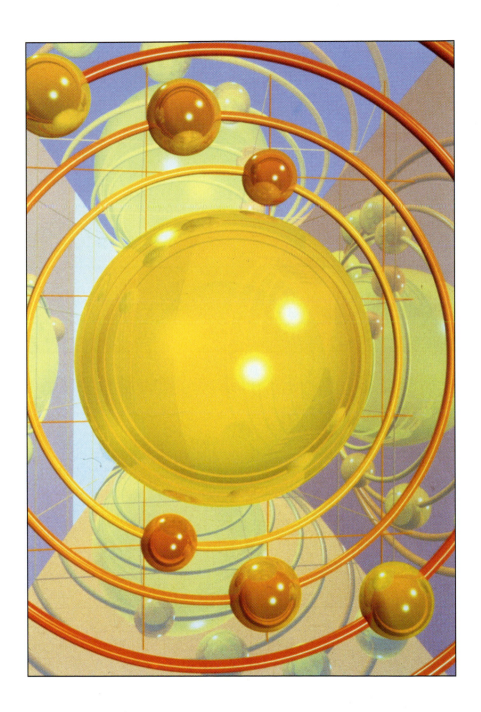

Calendar: July   This image and the two which follow are from a ray-traced calendar. Reflection was used as an analogy for looking backwards in time to review. Transparency indicated looking forward in time to plan.

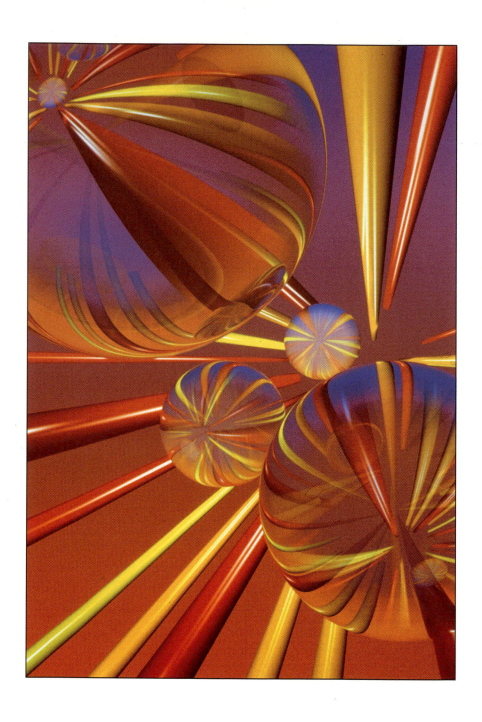

Calendar: August

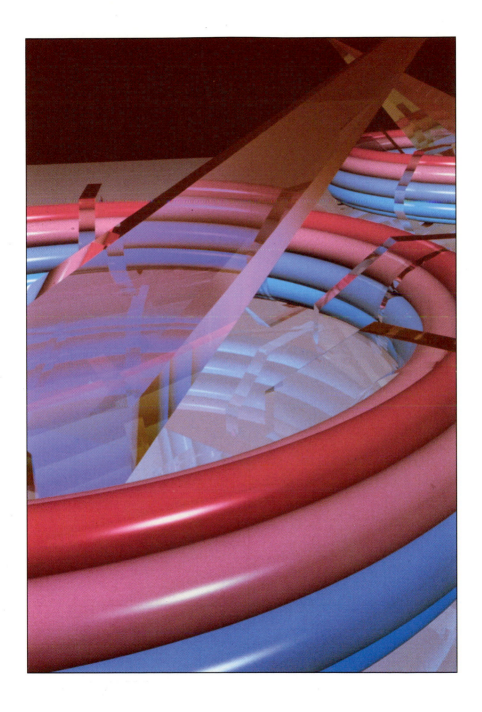

Calendar: November (All calendar images copyright © Smart Art, Inc.; Michael Sciulli, Creative Director; Melissa White, Designer; Apollo Computer AG, Zurich, Switzerland; James Arvo and David Kirk, Ray Tracing Software)

Trellis and ivy   Shown here is a simple trellis with ivy which has been algorithmically grown using "environment-sensitive automata" (see Arvo and Kirk, 1988). The technique constructs botanical forms using particle systems which stochastically navigate through the environment using ray tracing. For ivy, the particles maintain close proximity to surfaces while avoiding collisions. Once modeled, the scene can be rendered in many ways, including ray tracing. (Copyright © James Arvo and David Kirk, 1988)

The six platonic solids Pictured here are the five platonic solids along with an object which has become just as fundamental to the field of computer graphics: the "teapotahedron". This image was ray traced using the ray classification technique described in Section 6.6.4. The columns were given the appearance of marble through solid texturing. (Copyright © James Arvo and David Kirk, 1988)

Arch and ivy   This is another application of "environment-sensitive automata." Here ivy has been algorithmically grown over the surface of a marble arch. (Copyright © James Arvo and David Kirk. 1988)

or alternatively by first finding the screen space coordinates of the points $P_e = (0, 0, 1)$ and $Q_e = (1, 1, 1)$:

$$Px_s = \frac{a \cdot 0 + c \cdot 1 + g}{f \cdot 1} = \frac{c + g}{f} \tag{30}$$

$$Qx_s = \frac{a + c + g}{f} \tag{31}$$

so that

$$Qx_s - Px_s = \frac{a}{f} \tag{32}$$

and similarly

$$Qy_s - Py_s = \frac{b}{f}. \tag{33}$$

It then follows that

$$ax = \frac{r \cdot a}{f} = r \cdot (Qx_s - Px_s) \tag{34}$$

$$ay = \frac{r \cdot b}{f} = r \cdot (Qy_s - Py_s) \tag{35}$$

$$bx = \frac{-ax}{D} \tag{36}$$

$$by = \frac{-ay}{D} \tag{37}$$

Here is a C code fragment that performs this calculation:

```
struct {float x,y,z;} Pe = (0,0,1), Qe = (1,1,1), Ps, Qs;
r = 0.5 * FocalLength / FStop ;
EyeToScreen(&Pe,&Ps) ;
EyeToScreen(&Qe,&Qs) ;
ax = r * (Qs.x − Ps.x) ;
ay = r * (Qs.y − Ps.y) ;
bx = − ax / FocalDistance ;
by = − ay / FocalDistance ;
```

5.3   Motion Blur

Distributing the rays or sample points in time solves the motion blur problem. Before we discuss this method and how it works, let us first look in more detail at the motion blur problem and at previous attempts to solve it.

The motion blur method described by Potmesil [30] is not only very expensive, it also separates the visible surface calculation from the motion blur calculation. This is acceptable in some situations, but in most cases we cannot just calculate a still frame and blur the result. Some object entirely hidden in the still frame might be uncovered for part of the time sampled by the blur. If we are to blur an object across a background, we have to know what the background is.

Even if we know what the background is, there are problems. For example, consider a biplane viewed from above, so that the lower wing is completely obscured by the upper wing. Because the upper wing is moving, the scenery below it would be seen through its blur, but unfortunately the lower wing would show through too. The lower wing should be hidden completely because it moves with the upper wing and is obscured by it over the entire time interval.

This particular problem can be solved by rendering the plane and background as separate elements, but not all pictures can easily be separated into elements. This solution also does not allow for changes in visibility within a single object. This is particularly important for rotating objects.

The situation is further complicated by the change in shading within a frame time. Consider a textured top spinning on a table. If we calculate only one shade per frame, the texture would be blurred properly, but unfortunately the highlights and shadows would be blurred too. On a real top, the highlights and shadows are not blurred at all by the spinning. They are blurred, of course, by any lateral motion of the top along the table or by the motion of a light source or the camera. The highlights should be blurred by the motion of the light and the camera, by the travel of the top along the table, and by the precession of the top, but not by the rotation of the top.

Motion-blurred shadows are also important and are not rendered correctly if we calculate only one shade per frame. Otherwise, for example, the blades of a fan could be motion blurred, but the shadows of those blades would strobe.

All of this is simply to emphasize the tremendous complexity of the motion blur problem. The prospects for an analytic solution are dim. Such a solution would require solving the visible surface problem as a function of time as well as space. It would also involve integrating the texture and shading function of the visible surfaces over time. Point sampling seems to be the only approach that offers any promise of solving the motion blur problem.

One point sampling solution was proposed by Korein and Badler [21]. Their method, however, point samples only in space, not in time. Changes in shading are not motion blurred. The method involves keeping a list of all objects that cross each sample point during the frame time, a list that could be quite long for a fast-moving complex scene. They also impose the unfortunate restriction that both vertices of an edge must move at the same velocity. This creates holes in objects that change perspective severely during one frame, because the vertices move at drastically different rates. Polygons with edges that share these vertices cannot remain adjoining. The algorithm is also limited to linear motion. If the motion is curved or if the vertices are allowed to move independently, the linear intersection equation becomes a higher order equation. The resulting equation is expensive to solve and has multiple roots.

Distributing the sample points in time solves the motion blur problem. The path of motion can be arbitrarily complex. The only requirement is the ability to calculate the position of the object at a specific time. Changes in visibility and shading are correctly accounted for. Shadows (umbras and penumbras), depth of field, reflections and intersections are all correctly motion blurred. By using different distributions of rays, the motion can be blurred with a box filter or a weighted filter or can be strobed.

6   IMPLEMENTATION OF DISTRIBUTED RAY TRACING

The visible surface calculation is straightforward. Since each ray occurs at a single instant of time, the first step is to update the positions of the objects for that instant of time. The next is to construct a ray from the lens to the sample point and find the closest object that the ray intersects. Care must be taken in bounding moving objects. The bound should depend on time so that the number of potentially visible objects does not grow unacceptably with their speed.

Intersecting surfaces are handled trivially because we never have to calculate the line of intersection; we merely have to determine which is in front at a given location and time. At each sample point only one of the surfaces is visible. The intersections can even be motion blurred, a problem that would be terrifying with an analytic method.

The union, intersection, difference problem is easily solved with ray tracing or point sampling [32]. These calculations are also correctly motion blurred.

6.1   Nonspatial Jittering

One way to distribute the rays in the additional dimensions is with uncorrelated random values. For example, one could pick a random time for each ray or a random point on a light source for each shadow ray. This approach produces pictures that are exceedingly noisy, due to the bunching up of samples. We can reduce the noise level by using a Poisson disk distribution, insuring that the samples do not bunch up or leave large gaps that are unsampled. As before, we use jittering to approximate a Poisson disk distribution.

To jitter in a nonspatial dimension, we use randomly created prototype patterns in screen space to associate the sample points with a range of that dimension to sample, then jitter to pick the exact location within each range. In the case of sampling in time to produce motion blur, we divide the frame time into slices and randomly assign a slice of time to each sample point. The exact time within each slice is then determined by jittering.

For example, to assign times in a pixel with a 4 by 4 grid of sample points, one could use a random distribution of the numbers 1 through 16, such as the one shown in *Figure 9(a)*. The sample in the xth column and the yth row would

(a)

7	11	3	14
4	15	13	9
16	1	8	12
6	10	5	2

(b)

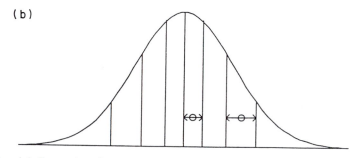

Fig. 9. (a) Example of a prototype time pattern. (b) Importance sampling. Samples are distributed so that each samples a region of equal area under the weighting function. The prototype sample location and jitter range is shown for two of the sampling regions.

have a prototype time

$$t_{xy} = \frac{P_{xy} - 0.5}{16.0} \tag{38}$$

where P_{xy} is the value shown in the xth column and the yth row of the prototype pattern in *Figure 9(a)*. A random jitter of $\pm\,1/32$ is then added to this prototype time to obtain the actual time for a sample. For example, the sample in the upper left subpixel would have a time $6/16 \leqslant t \leqslant 7/16$.

Note that correlation between the spatial locations and the locations in other dimensions can cause aliasing. For example, if the samples on the left side of the pixel are consistently at an earlier time than those on the right side of the pixel, an object moving from right to left might be missed by every sample while an object moving from left to right might be hit by every sample.

6.2   Weighted Distributions

Sometimes we need to weight the samples. For example, we may want to weight the reflected samples according to the specular reflection function, or we may want to use a weighted temporal filter. One approach would be to distribute the samples evenly, and then later weight each ray according to the filter. A better approach is *importance sampling* [17], in which the sample points are distributed so that the chance of a location being sampled is proportional to the value of the filter at that location. This avoids the multiplications necessary for the weighting and also puts the samples where they will do the most good.

In order to use jitter to do importance sampling, we divide the filter in regions of equal area, as shown in *Figure 9(b)*. Each region is sampled by one sample point, with the samples spaced further apart for smaller filter values and closer together for larger filter values. Each sample point is positioned at the center of its region and then jittered to a random location in the region. Note that the size of jitter varies from sample to sample. If the filter shape is known ahead of time, a list of the centers and jitter magnitudes for each region can be precomputed and stored in a look-up table.

For example, for the reflection ray, we create a look-up table based on the specular reflection function. Given the angle between the surface normal and the incident ray, this look-up table gives a range of reflection angles plus a jitter magnitude for determining an exact reflection angle within that range. For any given reflection ray, the index into this table is determined using its ancestral primary ray in screen space to associate it with a randomly generated prototype pattern of table indices.

6.3   Summary of Distributed Ray Tracing

The distributed ray tracing algorithm is illustrated in *Figure 10*. For each primary ray:

- Determine the spatial screen location of the ray by jittering.
- Determine the time for the ray from jittered prototype patterns.
- Move the camera and the objects to their location at that time.
- Determine the focal point by constructing a ray from the eye point (center of the lens) through the screen location of the ray. The focal point is located on this ray so that its distance from the eye point is equal to the focal distance.
- Determine the lens location for the ray by jittering a location selected from a prototype pattern of lens locations.
- The primary ray starts at the lens location and goes through the focal point. Determine the visible point for this ray using standard ray casting or ray tracing techniques.
- Trace a reflection ray. The direction of the reflection ray is determined by jittering a set of directions that are distributed according to the specular reflection function. This is done with a look-up table; the look-up table index is based on a screen space prototype pattern that assigns indices to primary rays and their descendants. The reflection direction is obtained from the look-up table and then jittered. The range of the jitter is also stored in the table.
- Trace a transparency ray if the visible object is transparent. The direction of the transparency ray is determined by jittering a set of

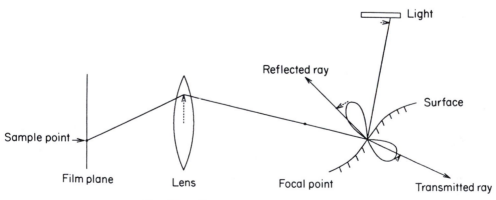

Fig. 10.   Typical distributed ray path.

directions that are distributed according to the specular transmission function.

■ Trace the shadow rays. For each light source, determine the location on the light for the shadow ray, and trace a ray from the visible point to that location on the light. The chance of tracing the ray to a location on the light should be proportional to the intensity and projected area of that location as seen from the visible point on the surface.

6.4 The Effect of Jitter on the Bound Calculations

Many image synthesis algorithms rely on object bounds to limit the number of intersection calculations. An object's bound is often much simpler than the object itself, so that intersecting a ray with the bound is much faster than intersecting the ray with the object or objects in that bound. If the ray misses the bound, it must also miss the objects in that bound, so the more costly object intersection calculations can be avoided. Stochastic sampling may complicate the calculation of these object bounds.

With stochastic sampling, the bound calculations must take into account the effects of jitter. For example, each jittered reflection ray samples the scene at a specific time. To intersect this reflection ray with a particular object, we must first *move* that object to its position at the exact time of the ray before we can perform the intersection calculation. If we can test the ray against the object's bound only after moving the object and its bound into their positions at the time of the ray, we have lost much of the advantage of having a bound in the first place, because moving the object can be as expensive as the intersection calculation itself. We need a bound around the object that is good for the entire frame time, so that if a ray does not intersect that bound, it is guaranteed not to intersect the object, regardless of the time of the ray.

So we want to determine which rays can possibly hit an object without having to consider the specific jitter of each ray. The easiest method for doing this is to modify the object bounds themselves to account for the maximum amount that any ray will possibly be jittered.

For spatial jitter, this change is trivial. After the object has been bounded in screen space in the usual manner, simply expand the bound by the maximum jitter amount in x and in y. Intersections with the bounds can then be done using the regularly spaced, unjittered rays. The rays that potentially intersect the screen space bound are simply those whose unjittered x and y locations are inside the bound. The regularly spaced ray locations make this determination easy, and the calculation is especially trivial if the bound is a box. This is one reason why jittering a regular grid lends itself more easily to image synthesis algorithms than a pure Poisson disk distribution.

For lens jitter (depth of field), the screen space bounds must be expanded an additional amount that depends on the focal length and f stop of the lens, the focal distance, and the z range of the bound. The lens jitter (from the previous section) in x is

$$xl \cdot \left[\frac{ax}{z_e} + bx \right] \tag{39}$$

with $| xl | < 1$, with a similar equation for y. Thus for a particular z_e value, the maximum change in the screen space location is

$$\frac{ax}{z_e} + bx \tag{40}$$

in x and

$$\frac{ay}{z_e} + by \tag{41}$$

in y. Given a bound on z_e, the eye space z, we can calculate the maximum magnitude of this value. It is easy to show that it must occur at one of the two z_e extremes, so we just need to calculate this value for the two extremes and take the maximum. This amount is then added to the screen bound for the object.

For time jitter (motion blur), a bound should be placed around the object over its entire path of motion during the frame. The more complicated the motion, the more complicated is this bound calculation. Linear motion is the easiest, and more complicated motion can often be approximated by piecewise linear motion or with cubic splines. More complicated motion may require a custom bound routine. Here we just describe the bound calculations for linear motion.

The simplest and most obvious way to calculate a bound for linear motion is to bound the object at the instant the frame begins (i.e. when the shutter opens), bound the object at the end of the frame (when the shutter closes), and then bound those two bounds. This method produces a *reliable* bound, in that any ray that misses this bound cannot possibly hit the object. This bound can be computed in screen space for primary rays and in eye space for secondary rays.

If the bound is a bounding box, however, this method may have problems. A bounding box, though reliable, is not always a *tight* bound, and objects can be considered for many more rays than is necessary. For example, consider a pixel-size object that moves 100 pixels in x and 100 pixels in y. With this method it be considered for the rays in $100 \cdot 100 = 10\,000$ pixels, when in actuality it only crosses about 200 or so pixels. This sort of thing can be devastating, in that the program may suddenly become very slow when an object starts moving in the wrong direction.

What's needed, of course, is a better bound, one that either has sloped boundaries in addition to horizontal and vertical ones, or that bounds the object in y and then calculates a bound in x for each scanline. The tighter bound is not difficult to calculate, but it does involve some additional computation. Without motion blur, the tighter bounds are not always worth the extra effort, because they usually only make a significant difference for skinny objects. With motion blur, though, the tighter bound can become important for all objects.

7   EXAMPLES

The jitter used in these examples is white noise jitter with $\gamma = 0.5$. An example of this distribution is shown in *Figure 11(a)*, and the Fourier transform of *Figure 11(a)* is shown in *Figure 11(b)*. Notice how *Figure 11(b)* resembles the Fourier transform of a Poisson disk distribution (shown in *Figure 4(b)*). By contrast, a pure Poisson disk distribution of samples with no minimum distance restriction is shown in *Figure 11(d)*, and the Fourier transform of *Figure 11(d)* is shown in *Figure 11(e)*. The C code in *Figure 11(c)* was used to generate *Figure 11(a)*, and the C code in *Figure 11(f)* was used to generate *Figure 11(d)*.

In *Figures 12* and *13*, a box filter was used for a reconstruction filter to accentuate the noise problems. In all of the other examples, the following Gaussian filter was used:

$$e^{-d^2} - e^{-w^2},\qquad (42)$$

where d is the distance from the center of the sampling region to the center of the pixel, and $w = 1.5$ is the filter width distance, beyond which the filter was set to zero. The effect of jitter on the filter values was ignored.

Consider the comb of triangular slivers illustrated in *Figure 12(a)*. Each triangle is 1.01 pixels wide at the base and 50 pixels high. The triangles are placed in a horizontal row 1.01 pixels apart. If the comb is sampled with a regular grid, aliasing can result as depicted in *Figure 12(b)*. A comb containing 200 such triangular slivers is rendered in *Figures 12(c)–(f)*.

In *Figure 12(c)*, the comb is rendered with a single sample at the center of each pixel. *Figure 12(d)* also has one sample per pixel but the sample location is jittered by $\zeta = \pm 1/2$ pixel in x and y. *Figure 12(c)* is grossly aliased: there are just a few large triangles spaced 100 pixels apart. This aliasing is replaced by

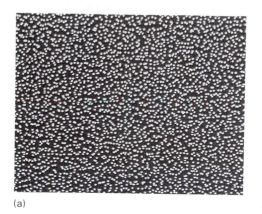

(a)

(b)

(c)

```
/* Draw a jittered sample pattern in a 512 × 512 frame buffer. There is one */
* sample in each sample region of 8 × 8 pixels, for a total of 4096 samples. */
DrawJitterPattern() {
    double Random ();       /* returns a random number in the range 0–1 */
    int x, y;               /* (x, y) is the corner of the sample region */
    int jx, jy;             /* (jx, jy) is the jitter */
    for (y = 0; y < 512; y + = 8) {
        for (x = 0; x < 512; x + = 8) {
            jx = 8 * Random();
            jy = 8 * Random();
            SetPixelToWhite(x + jx, y + jy);
        }
    }
}
```

Fig. 11.   (a) Distribution pattern of jittered samples. (b) Fourier transform of the pattern in (a). (c) C program that generated the pattern in (a). (d)

noise in *Figure 12(d)*. Because there is only one sample per pixel, each pixel can only be white or black, but in any given region, the percentage of white pixels equals the percentage of that region that is covered by the triangles. Note that the white pixels are denser at the bottom, where the triangles are wider.

In *Figure 12(e)*, the same comb is rendered with a regular 4 by 4 grid of samples. In *Figure 12(f)*, the regular 4 by 4 grid is jittered by $\zeta = \pm 1/8$ pixel

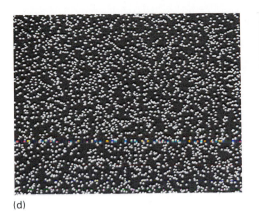

(d)

(e)

(f)

```
/* Draw a random sample pattern with 4096 samples. */
DrawPoissonPattern() {
    double Random ();        /* returns a random number in the range 0-1 */
    int n, sx, sy;           /* (sx, sy) is the sample location */
    for (n = 0; n < 4096; n + +) {
        sx = 512*Random();
        sy = 512*Random();
        SetPixelToWhite(sx, sy);
    }
}
```

Distribution pattern of randomly placed samples. (e) Fourier transform of the pattern in (d). (f) C program that generated the pattern in (d).

in *x* and *y*. Again the regularly spaced samples alias; this time there are a few large overlapping triangles spaced $100/4 = 25$ pixels apart. This aliasing is replaced by noise in the jittered version, *Figure 12(f)*. Notice, though, that the noise is greatly reduced compared to *Figure 12(d)*.

Figure 13 shows a small white square moving across the screen. *Figure 13(a)* was rendered with no jitter and one sample per pixel, so the image is still.

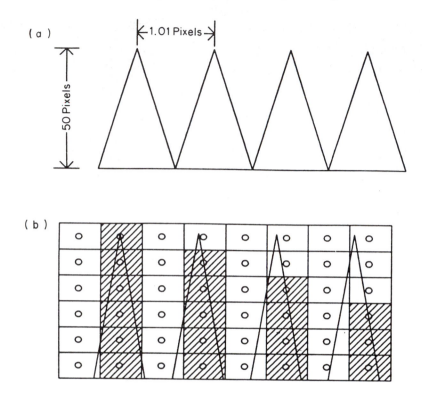

Fig. 12. (a) Schematic diagram of the comb of triangles example. The triangles are 50 pixels high and 1.01 pixels apart. (b) The comb of triangles aliases when rendered with a regular grid of sample points in the manner shown here. Samples are shown as circles, and pixels are shown as rectangles. Pixels

Figure 13(b) was rendered with jitter and one sample per pixel; the image is now blurred but is extremely noisy because, with only one sample, each pixel can be only one of two colors, the color of the square or the color of the background. Notice, though, that in any given region the number of pixels that are white is proportional to the amount of time the square covered that region; thus the percentage of white pixels is constant in the middle and ramps off at the ends. *Figure 13(c)* was rendered with no jitter and 16 samples per pixel, and *Figure 13(d)* with jitter and 16 samples per pixel. Notice the reduction in the noise level with the additional samples.

Figure 14 illustrates motion-blurred intersections. The green beveled cube is stationary, and the red beveled cube is moving in a straight line, perpendicular to one of its faces. Notice that the intersection of the faces is blurred except in the plane of motion, where it is sharp.

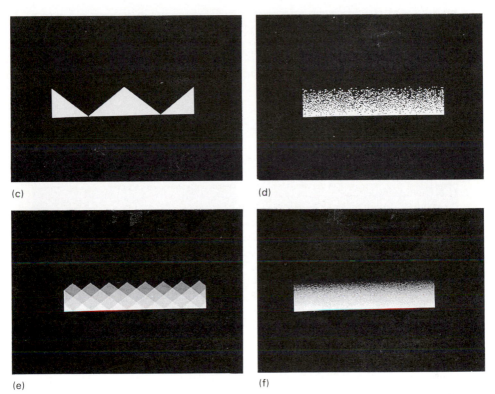

(c)   (d)

(e)   (f)

with samples inside a triangle are shaded. (c) Comb rendered with a regular grid, one sample per pixel. (d) Comb rendered with a jittered grid, one sample per pixel. (e) Comb rendered with a regular grid, 16 samples per pixel. (f) Comb rendered with a jittered grid, 16 samples per pixel.

Figure 15(a) is the ray-traced picture *1984*, with a closeup of the 4 ball shown in *Figure 15(b)*. Notice that the motion is not linear: the 9 ball changes direction abruptly in the middle of the frame, the 8 ball moves only during the middle of the frame, and the 4 ball only starts to move near the end of the frame. The shadow from the stationary 1 ball is sharper where the ball is closer to the table. The penumbras and reflections are motion blurred. The blur is quite extreme, and yet the image looks noisy instead of aliased. This picture was made with 16 samples per pixel.

Figure 16 contains two frames from the short film *The Adventures of André and Wally B.* [28]. These extreme examples of motion blur were rendered with a scan-line algorithm that uses point sampling and a *z* buffer to determine visibility. In these frames, a very simple adaptive method automatically used 16 samples per pixel for most pixels and 64 samples per pixel for pixels that

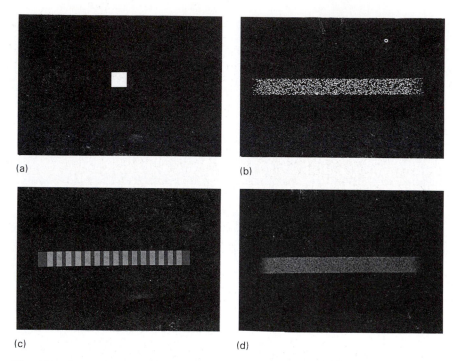

Fig. 13.   Fast-moving polygon. (a) One sample per pixel, no jitter. (b) One sample per pixel, with jitter. (c) Sixteen samples per pixel, no jitter. (d) Sixteen samples per pixel, with jitter.

Fig. 14.   Motion-blurred intersections.

(a)

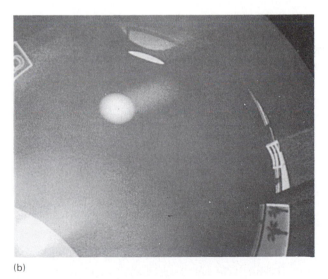

(b)

Fig. 15.   (a) *1984*, By Thomas Porter. (b) Close-up of *1984*.

Fig. 16.   Two examples of motion blur from *The Adventures of André and Wally B.*

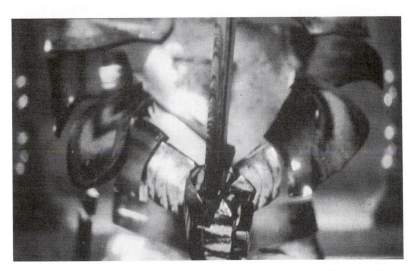

Fig. 17. Example of depth of field from *Young Sherlock Holmes*. Copyright 1985, Paramount Pictures Corp.

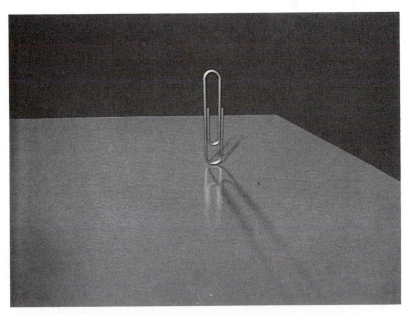

Fig. 18. Example of penumbras and blurry reflection.

contain objects that move more than 8 pixels in x or y within the frame time. This cuts down considerably on the noise level and helps avoid needless computation. Others have since found ways to add more samples adaptively based on an estimate of the variance of the image in each pixel [19, 22].

Figure 17 shows a frame of a computer-synthesized stained glass man from *Young Sherlock Holmes* [26]. The camera is focused on the sword, with the body out of focus. This was also rendered with a scan-line algorithm, but in this case, no adaptive method was used to change the number of samples per pixel; instead there were always 16 samples per pixel. The sequence is also motion blurred.

The paper clip in *Figure 18* shows penumbras and blurry reflection, rendered with 16 samples per pixel.

8 DISCUSSION AND CONCLUSIONS

With correctly chosen nonuniform sample locations, high frequencies appear as noise instead of aliasing. The magnitude of this noise is determined by the sampling frequency. We have found that 16 samples per pixel produces an acceptable noise level in most situations, with more needed only for high-frequency situations such as frames that are extremely motion blurred or out of focus. Stochastic sampling should also work well when integrated with adaptive sampling. This has been the subject of some recent research [19, 22].

The human eye uses a Poisson disk distribution of photoreceptors. A simple and effective approximation to a Poisson disk distribution can be obtained by jittering a regular grid. When this technique is extended to distributed ray tracing, the locations in the nonspatial dimensions can be chosen by jittering randomly generated prototype patterns. Weighted functions can be evaluated using importance sampling.

Stochastic sampling involves some additional computation. Because the samples are not regularly spaced, forward differencing cannot be used to exploit pixel to pixel coherence. Compared to standard ray tracing, distributed ray tracing requires additional calculations to move objects to their correct location for each ray. Moving and out-of-focus objects also require a more sophisticated bounding calculation, and these objects must often be intersected with a larger number of rays.

Aliasing has been a major problem for ray tracing and ray casting algorithms, and this problem is solved by stochastic sampling. The shading calculations, which have traditionally been point sampled, are automatically anti-aliased with stochastic sampling, eliminating problems such as highlight aliasing. Another potential application is texture map sampling.

Extended to distributed ray tracing, stochastic sampling also provides a solution to motion blur, depth of field, penumbras, blurry reflections, and translucency. All of these phenomena are related, and this solution accounts for all of the interrelationships: differences in shading, in penumbras, and in visibility are included for in the depth of field calculations; changes in the depth of field and in visibility are motion blurred; the penumbra and shading calculations are motion blurred.

Others have extended the research described here [8–11]. Jim Kajiya developed the rendering equation, an improved version of the shading equation given in this paper [19]. Others have explored ways to improve the performance and noise characteristics of stochastic sampling [13, 19, 22, 23, 35].

ACKNOWLEDGMENTS

I would especially like to thank Tom Porter, who made the *1984* picture, suggested the extension of the two-dimensional technique to motion blur, and helped test many of the ideas. Alvy Ray Smith found the article on the distribution of cells in the eye. Andy Moorer and Jim Kajiya helped with the theory, and a number of discussions with Loren Carpenter were invaluable. The idea of dithering sample locations originally came from Rodney Stock, who provided inspiration and motivation for this work. Jack Yellott provided the pictures in *Figure 3*. Thanks also to the many people at Lucasfilm who made *The Adventures of André and Wally B.* and the stained glass man sequence from *Young Sherlock Holmes*.

REFERENCES

1. Amanatides, J., Ray tracing with cones. *Comput. Graph.* (Siggraph '84 Proceedings) **18**(3), 129–145, July 1984.
2. Balakrishnan, A.V., On the problem of time jitter in sampling. *IRE Trans. Inform. Theory*, 226–236, April 1962.
3. Blinn, J.F., Computer Display of Curved Surfaces. PhD dissertation, University of Utah, Salt Lake City, 1978. (TR 1060-126, Jet Propulsin Lab., Pasadena.)
4. Bracewell, R.N., *The Fourier Transform and Its Applications*, McGraw-Hill, New York, 1978.
5. Cook, R.L., Whitted, T. and Greeenberg, D.P., *A Comprehensive Model for Image Synthesis*, unpublished report.
6. Cook, R.L., A Reflection Model for Realistic Image Synthesis. Master's thesis, Cornell University, Ithaca, NY, December 1981.
7. Cook, R.L. and Torrance, K.E., A reflection model for computer graphics. *ACM Trans. Graph.* **1**(1), 7–24, January 1982.

8.   Cook, R.L., Antialiased Point Sampling. Technical Memo #94, Lucasfilm Ltd, San Rafael, CA., 3 October, 1983.

9.   Cook, R.L., Porter, T. and Carpenter, L., Distributed ray tracing. *Comput. Graph.* (Siggraph '84 Proceedings) **18**(3), 137–145, July 1984.

10. Cook, R.L., Stochastic sampling in computer graphics. *ACM Trans. Graph.* **5**(1), 51–72, January 1986.

11. Cook, R.L., Practical aspects of distributed ray tracing. In Siggraph '86 Developments in Ray tracing course notes, August 1986.

12. Crow, F.C., The use of grayscale for improved raster display of vectors and characters. *Comput. Graph.* (Siggraph '78 Proceedings) **12**(3), 1–5, August 1978.

13. Dippe, M.A.Z. and Wold, E.H., Antialiasing through stochastic sampling. *Comput. Graph.* **19**(3), 69–78, July 1985.

14. Feibush, E., Levoy, M. and Cook, R. L., Synthetic texturing using digital filtering *Comput. Graph.* **14**(3), 294–301, July 1980.

15. Gardner, G.Y., Simulation of natural scenes using textured quadric surfaces. *Comput. Graph.* (Siggraph '84 Proceedings) **18**(3), 11–20, July 1984.

16. Goral, C.M., Torrance, K.E., Greenberg, D.P. and Battaile, B., Modeling the interaction of light between diffuse surfaces. *Comput. Graph.* **18**(3), 213–222, July 1984.

17. Halton, J.H., A retrospective and prospective survey of the Monte Carlo method. *SIAM Rev.* **12**(1), January 1970.

18. Hunter, R.S., *The Measurement of Appearance*, John Wiley, New York, 1975.

19. Kajiya, J.T., The rendering equation. *Comput. Graph.* **20**(4), 143–150, August 1986.

20. Kay, D.S. and Greenberg D.P., Transparency for computer synthesized images. *Comput. Graph.* **13**(2), 158–164, August 1979.

21. Korein, J. and Badler, N., Temporal anti-aliasing in computer generated animation. *Comput. Graph.* **17**(3), 377–388, July 1983.

22. Lee, M.E., Redner, R.A. and Uselton, S.P., Statistically optimized sampling for distributed ray tracing, *Comput. Graph.* (Siggraph '79 Proceedings) **19**(3), 61–67, July 1985.

23. Mitchell, D., personal communication.

24. Nishita, T., Okamura, I. and Nakamae, E., Shading models for point and linear sources. *ACM Trans. Graph.* **4**(2), 124–146, April 1985.

25. Norton, A., Rockwood, A.P. and Skolmoski, P.T., Clamping: a method of antialiasing textured surfaces by bandwidth limiting in object space. *Comput. Graph.* **16**(3), 1–8, July 1982.

26. Paramount Pictures Corporation, *Young Sherlock Holmes*, stained glass man sequence by Pixar and Lucasfilm Ltd., 1985.

27. Pearson, D. E., *Transmission and Display of Pictorial Information*, Pentech Press, London, 1975.

28. Pixar, *The Adventures of André and Wally B.*, July 1984.

29. Potmesil, M. and Chakravarty, I., Synthetic image generation with a lens and aperture camera model. *ACM Trans. Graph.* **1**(2), 85–108, April 1982.

30. Potmesil, M. and Chakravarty, I., Modeling motion blur in computer-generated images. *Comput. Graph.* **17**(3), 389–399, July 1983.

31. Pratt, W.K., *Digital Image Processing*, Wiley, New York, 1978.

32. Roth, S. D., Ray casting for modeling solids. *Comput. Graph. Image Process.* (18), 109–44, 1982.

33. Shapiro, H.S. and Silverman, R.A., Alias-free sampling of random noise. *SIAM J.* **8**(2), 225–248, June 1960.
34. Society of Photographic Scientists and Engineers, *SPSE Handbook of Photographic Science and Engineering*, Wiley, New York, 1973.
35. Whitted, T., Personal communication.
36. Whitted, T., An improved illumination model for shaded display. *Commun. ACM* **23**, 343–349, 1980.
37. Williams, D.R. and Collier, R., Consequences of spatial sampling by a human photoreceptor mosaic. *Science* **221**, 385–387, 22 July 1983.
38. Williams, L., Pyramidal parametrics. *Comput. Graph.* (Siggraph '83 Proceedings) **17**(3), 1–11, July 1983.
39. Yellott, J.I. Jr., Spectral consequences of photoreceptor sampling in the Rhesus retina. *Science* **221**, 382–385, 22 July 1983.

6 A Survey of Ray Tracing Acceleration Techniques

JAMES ARVO AND DAVID KIRK

1 INTRODUCTION

One of the greatest challenges of ray tracing is efficient execution. Despite its impressive repertoire, ray tracing is often dismissed as being too computationally exorbitant to be useful. Efficiency is therefore a critical issue and has been the focus of much research from the beginning. This has led to creative approaches involving novel data structures [2, 33, 37, 52, 56,], numerical methods [32, 58, 59, 62], computational geometry [13, 44], optics [54], statistical methods [10, 15, 42, 48], and distributed computing [7, 14, 22, 41, 45, 60] among many others. A would-be implementer now has a tremendous assortment of techniques to choose from and many considerations to balance, some of which are listed in *Figure 1*. Nearly all these techniques give rise to useful combinations, further increasing the possibilities.

Though this area is still undergoing rapid development, it is a worthwhile exercise to examine what has been done. As Sutherland *et al.* [57] demonstrated in their characterization of ten hidden-surface algorithms, identifying a taxonomy of current methods can sometimes provide a perspective from which new approaches become apparent. Since several important themes have emerged in the area of efficient ray tracing, the time is ripe for such a taxonomy. Toward this end we attempt to unify some of the terminology and methods which have evolved independently yet build upon similar concepts.

One shortcoming of this survey is the absence of quantitative comparisons. The information contained herein is insufficient to make a clear and absolute

Applicability:

- Does it apply to all rays or just a special class of rays?
- Is it applicable in the context of constructive solid geometry?
- Does it impose a restriction on the class of primitive objects?
- Is it applicable when a temporal dimension is added?

Performance:

- Will it be fast enough to meet the application requirements?
- How well does it scale to very complex environments?
- Does the cost of pre-processing eventually outweigh its benefit?
- How well does it exploit available coherence?

Resources:

- What are the storage limitations of the host machine?
- Can the algorithm make appropriate space/time trade-offs?
- What is the cost of floating point arithmetic relative to integer arithmetic?
- Does the host machine have multiple processors?

Simplicity:

- How difficult is the algorithm to implement?
- How dependent is it on machine architecture?
- Can it extend existing code or does it require a complete rewrite?
- Does it require a priori selection of unintuitive parameters?

Fig. 1.   Some of the considerations which affect the choice of acceleration technique(s).

decision about which algorithm is best for a given application. This deficiency is a reflection of the current state of the art, and is due in part to the difficulty of *a priori* performance analysis. Though there is a movement toward quantitative comparisons through standard benchmarks [26], this is not yet widely practiced. Consequently, we shall concentrate on the underlying concepts and build a framework which highlights differences and similarities. We also discuss pitfalls uncovered by experience and identify several unexplored possibilities.

We begin with background material in Section 2, and proceed in Section 3 to classify acceleration techniques into four broad categories. The first of these categories deals with efficient operations on individual geometrical objects. Sections 4, 5, and 6 cover three families of techniques which fall into the second and largest category of acceleration techniques, those which reduce the cost of 'tracing a ray' in the context of complex environments. In Section 7 we discuss coherence, a concept which appears in many guises and is utilized to some degree by all acceleration techniques. The statistical methods in Section 8 fall into the third category of techniques, those which reduce the total number of rays which need to be processed. Section 9 covers the techniques of the fourth category, those which generalize the concept of a ray in order to more efficiently exploit coherence. Sections 10 and 11 describe special optimizations for CSG (constructive solid geometry) and parallel architectures respectively. Finally, in Section 12 we discuss ways in which many of these techniques can be used in unison. With few exceptions, the techniques of each section are discussed in the order of their chronological development.

2   BACKGROUND

The generality of ray tracing is due to its almost exclusive dependence upon a single operation; calculating the point of intersection between a ray in three-space and an atomic geometrical entity, or *primitive object*. Examples of primitive objects include elementary shapes such as polygons, spheres, and cylinders, as well as more complex shapes such as parametric surfaces [58, 59] and swept surfaces [62]. The task we are primarily concerned with in this survey is that of intersecting rays with a large collection of primitive objects defining an *environment*. For each ray this ultimately reduces to computing the point of intersection closest to the ray origin which results from any of the individual primitive objects in the environment. The cost of this operation typically overshadows everything else, accounting for the vast bulk of the time consumed by ray tracing. An often-quoted statistic reported by Whitted [65] is that better than 95 % of the time can be spent performing this operation for complex environments. Despite dramatic algorithmic improvements, the demand for ever increasing complexity tends to keep this figure realistic or even conservative. Therefore, the search for more efficient techniques continues to be a lively topic of research.

Following common practice, we shall limit our discussion to this 'intersection problem' and assume that a negligible amount of time is spent in all remaining tasks, such as shading calculations and common bookkeeping operations. We note at the outset that the intersection problem has a trivial but usually impractical solution which is commonly referred to as 'standard' (or 'traditional') ray tracing. This solution entails intersecting each ray with the environment by simply testing each and every primitive object and retaining the nearest point of intersection (if one exists). This has a time complexity which is linear in the number of objects. We shall refer to this as *exhaustive* ray tracing in preference to the word 'standard,'which tends to imply widespread application or at least a long history as the method of choice. It is far more appropriate to reserve the term 'standard ray tracing' for the *illumination model* introduced by Whitted [65], which is independent of the mechanism for computing ray–environment intersections. Nevertheless, exhaustive ray tracing is by far the most intuitive solution, and it continues to play a role in the processing of subproblems within more complicated techniques.

3   A BROAD CLASSIFICATION

Faced with the task of accelerating the process of ray tracing, there are three very distinct strategies to consider: (1) reducing the *average cost* of intersecting a ray with the environment, (2) reducing the *total number* of rays intersected with the environment, and (3) replacing individual rays with a more general entity. These appear in *Figure 2* as 'faster intersections,' 'fewer rays,' and 'generalized rays,' respectively. The category of 'faster intersections' further separates into the subcategories of 'faster' and 'fewer' ray–object intersections. The former consists of efficient algorithms for intersecting rays with specific primitive objects, while the latter addresses the larger problem of intersecting a ray with an environment using a minimum of ray–object intersection tests. The distinction between these two subcategories is blurred

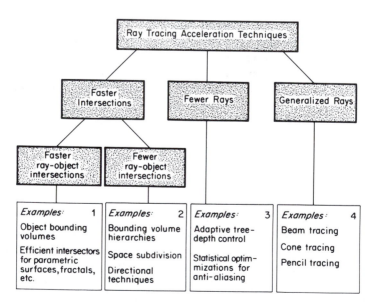

Fig. 2.   A broad classification of acceleration techniques.

somewhat by algorithms which decompose what is normally thought to be a single primitive object into many simpler pieces for the sake of efficiency. An example of this is the approach developed by Sweeney *et al.* for intersecting B-spline surfaces [58]. By subdividing a single surface into easily handled fragments and constructing a bounding volume hierarchy, the algorithm resembles the techniques described in the next section for dealing with collections of autonomous objects.

Other primitive object intersection algorithms are extremely special-purpose, often embodying analytic solutions for the point of intersection with a ray. Though it frequently requires considerable ingenuity to formulate such closed-form expressions, as with algebraic surfaces [28] and Steiner patches [53], these algorithms will not be explored in this survey. Nearly all procedural object approaches have as their basis some technique for efficiently computing the intersection, making the distinction between object definition and acceleration vague as well.

The category labeled 'fewer rays' consists of techniques which allow us to reduce the number of rays which need to be intersected with the environment. This includes first-generation rays as well as those created by reflection, refraction, and shadowing. The first such technique was *adaptive tree-depth control* introduced by Hall *et al.* [27]. Instead of terminating the ray tree at a predefined depth or at nonreflective opaque surfaces, Hall's termination criterion took into consideration the maximum contribution to the pixel color which could result by continuing the recursion. Setting a threshold on this contribution made it possible to eliminate the processing of many rays deep in the ray tree without altering the result perceptibly. This led to considerable savings even for environments with many highly reflective surfaces.

Other techniques for reducing the number of rays are applicable when anti-aliasing through supersampling. By detecting situations in which a relatively small number of samples produce statistically reliable results over some region of the image, many first-generation rays (hence entire ray trees) can be eliminated. Though often thought of as part of the anti-aliasing algorithms, these statistical techniques are, first and foremost, performance optimizations.

The last category, labeled 'generalized rays,' consists of a number of techniques which begin by replacing the familiar concept of a ray with a more general entity which subsumes rays as a special (degenerate) case. For instance, cones of both circular [1] and polygonal [30] cross section have been used successfully. Though the essential concepts of ray tracing remain largely intact, at the heart of these techniques lies the idea of tracing many rays simultaneously. As we shall see in Section 9, this presents many interesting advantages, but limitations as well.

4   BOUNDING VOLUMES AND HIERARCHIES

The most fundamental and ubiquitous tool for ray tracing acceleration is the *bounding volume* (also known as an *extent* or *enclosure*). This is a volume which contains a given object and permits a simpler ray intersection check than the object. Only if a ray intersects the bounding volume does the object itself need to be checked for intersection. Though this actually increases the computation for rays which come near enough to an object to pierce its bounding volume, in a typical environment most rays closely approach only a small fraction of the objects. The result is a significant net gain in efficiency. Whitted [65] initially used spheres as bounding volumes, observing that they are the simplest shapes to test for intersection.

Used in this way, bounding volumes substitute simple intersection checks for more costly ones, but do not decrease their number. From a theoretical standpoint this may reduce the computation by a constant factor, but cannot improve upon the linear time complexity of exhaustive ray tracing. To alleviate this problem, Rubin and Whitted [51] introduced the notion of hierarchical bounding volumes to ray tracing in order to attain a theoretical time complexity which is logarithmic in the number of objects instead of linear. By enclosing a number of bounding volumes within a larger bounding volume it was possible to eliminate many objects from further consideration with a single intersection check. If a ray did not intersect the *parent volume*, there was no need to test it against the bounding volumes or objects contained within. A hierarchy was formed by repeated application of this principle.

This type of 'logarithmic search' was previously employed by Clark [6] to accelerate clipping during display of hierarchically organized data. If a bounding volume was entirely outside the viewing frustrum, its contents could be immediately rejected, whether it enclosed displayable elements or additional bounding volumes. If a bounding volume was entirely inside the viewing frustrum, all of its descendants could be rendered with no further clipping operations. The relationship between this algorithm and that of Rubin and Whitted is quite close. If we consider a ray to be a degenerate viewing frustrum possessing no interior, the algorithms are virtually identical from the standpoint of hierarchy traversal.

The volumes employed by Rubin and Whitted were rectangular parallel-epipeds, more commonly known as *bounding boxes*, which are oriented so as to closely fit their contents and minimize their size. In order to perform the ray–box intersection tests, each ray was first transformed into the coordinate space of the bounding box. This made the subsequent test between the transformed ray and the axis-aligned box very straightforward. The simplicity of this operation motivated the use of bounding boxes for representing the geometry at the terminal nodes of the hierarchy as well. For instance, Rubin

```
procedure BVH__Intersect(in ray, node)
begin
      if node is a leaf then
            Intersect(ray, node.object)
      else if Intersect__P(ray, node.bounding__volume) then
            for each child of node do
                  BVH__Intersect(ray, child);
      end
```

Fig. 3.   A procedure for intersecting a ray with a collection of objects organized in a bounding volume hierarchy. Procedure 'Intersect' and function 'Intersect__P' hide many of the common low-level details.

and Whitted chose to represent polygons by one or more bounding boxes which were degenerate along one axis.

Figure 3 is an outline of procedure 'BVH__Intersect' which intersects a ray with a collection of objects organized in a bounding volume hierarchy. The data structure for this hierarchy is assumed to be a tree (or more generally a directed acyclic graph, or DAG) with an arbitrary branching factor at each internal node. Thus, bounding volumes may enclose any number of other bounding volumes. Each leaf node of the tree is a single primitive object while each interior node consists of a bounding volume and a list of pointers to other nodes in the tree. The procedure 'Intersect' called from within 'BVH__Intersect' is responsible for invoking the appropriate ray–object intersection procedure for the type of primitive object passed to it, and the 'ray' parameter encodes a 3-D origin, a direction vector, and a *distance interval*. Points of intersection which fall outside the distance interval (measured along the ray) are to be ignored. We will assume that 'Intersect' observes this rule because it simplifies this and subsequent examples. In addition, when a new point of intersection is found, 'Intersect' is assumed to shrink the far end of the distance interval to that point and save away whatever additional information will be needed for shading, such as the surface normal. These conventions hide some of the common mechanisms, such as identifying the closest intersection among several candidates, and therefore allow us to concentrate on the more important algorithmic features.

The function 'Intersect__P' (where the 'P' stands for predicate) is very similar to 'Intersect' except that it returns a boolean value indicating whether an intersection was found and it does *not* alter the ray's distance interval. This function is used exclusively to determine if a bounding volume is hit by a ray, whereas the automatic adjustment of the distance interval is only appropriate for true object intersections.

Given 'Intersect' and 'Intersect__P,' the task of intersecting a ray with a given bounding volume hierarchy is quite straightforward. The process begins with the root node of the tree, representing a bounding volume enclosing the entire environment, and an 'unbounded' ray, that is, one whose distance interval is zero to 'infinity.' Each recursive reference of '**BVH__Intersect**' descends another level of the hierarchy, and the recursion terminates with ray–object intersection tests at the leaves. At each level, the ray is tested against all the sibling bounding volumes and we only descend into the ones which are hit by the ray. The others are not processed any further, allowing us to *prune* the branches which they enclose.

An additional benefit of adjusting the ray's distance interval in the way we have described is that it performs a useful optimization [19, 50]. Once a point of intersection has been found with some object, and an upper bound placed on the distance interval, all objects or bounding volumes which intersect the ray completely beyond this bound can be ignored. This provides a second mechanism by which branches can be pruned from the hierarchy during the processing of a ray. An example of this is shown in *Figure 4*. If bounding volume V_1 is processed before V_2, the contents of the latter need not be tested because the point of intersection with object O_1 is closer than any which might occur within V_2. This saves at least one ray–object intersection test and potentially many in cases where V_2 encloses other bounding volumes. If sibling bounding volumes are processed in some fixed order (e.g via a static linked list or array), this technique will take advantage of fortuitous instances in which a nearby intersection is found early on. In Section 4.4 we describe an algorithm introduced by Kay and Kajiya [37] which uses a sorting operation to more consistently benefit from this optimization.

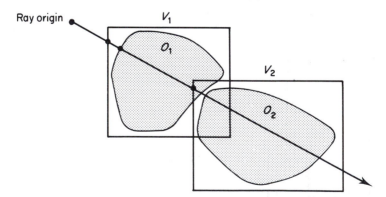

Fig. 4. An optimization which results from shrinking the distance interval associated with a ray whenever an intersection is found. The contents of volume V_2 need not be tested against this ray if the intersection with object O_1 is found first.

4.1   Heuristics for Bounding Volume Optimization

To further improve the efficiency of bounding volumes, Weghorst *et al.* [63] investigated the trade-offs between two competing factors: tightness of fit and cost of intersection. By selecting a sphere, box, or cylinder depending on the characteristics of each object (or cluster of objects) to be enclosed, they were able to increase the efficiency of individual and hierarchically organized bounding volumes. The criterion for this selection began with the observation that the total computational cost associated with an object and its bounding volume is given by

$$\text{Cost} = n * B + m * I \qquad\qquad (1)$$

where n is the number of rays tested against the bounding volume, B is the cost of each test, m is the number of rays which actually hit the bounding volume, and I is the cost of intersecting the object within. Assuming both n and I are fixed, we would like to select a bounding volume which is both inexpensive, making B small, and as tight fitting as possible, minimizing m. One must usually settle for a compromise, however, and making the right trade-off requires estimating both cost and fit. Weghorst *et al.* used the enclosed volume as a measure of fit, observing that it is related to the *projected void area* with respect to any direction; that is, to the difference in the projected areas of the bounding volume and the enclosed object. This difference in area indicates how likely a ray is to hit the bounding volume without hitting the enclosed object. A large void area, resulting from a loose fit, can increase m and cause many unnecessary object intersection checks. Reducing m even at the expense of an increase in B is sometimes warranted. Weghorst *et al.* introduced a simple heuristic to determine when such a trade-off is likely to be advantageous. First, each type of bounding volume was assigned a relative complexity factor to rank the computational cost of the ray intersection tests. In their implementation, spheres were given the lowest complexity rating and cylinders the highest. Then, each volume was 'tried' in turn as a potential bound, and the one producing the smallest *product* of volume and complexity factor was selected. This applies equally well to the bounding volumes of the internal nodes of a hierarchy. Because this heuristic did not take the complexity of the enclosed object into account, however, an interactive program was used to occasionally override the algorithmically selected bounding volume.

Figure 5 shows a number of possible bounding volumes for a complex object, perhaps a surface of revolution. The shaded region represents the projected void area. In most instances this void area is dependent upon the direction along which we form the two-dimensional projection. Assuming for

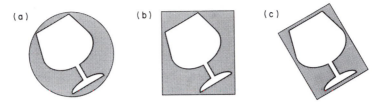

Fig. 5.   A comparison of three different types of bounding volumes for the same primitive object. Each presents a different cost/fit ratio. (a) Bounding sphere. (b) Axis-aligned bounding box. (c) Oriented bounding box.

simplicity that the rays which we are tracing through the environment are effectively randomized by multiple reflections and refractions, the average projected void area (over all directions) becomes the relevant measure of fit. As we shall see in the following section, the surface area of the bounding volume is closely related to this average.

Volumes (b) and (c) in *Figure 5* are axis-aligned and transformed (oriented) bounding boxes, respectively. The latter clearly produces a better fit in this case but carries with it the extra cost of a ray transformation for every ray-bounding volume intersection check. Hence, these are effectively different types of bounding volumes because they present different cost/fit trade-offs. In the case of a complex object, however, the relatively small additional cost of the ray transformation in the bounding volume intersection test may be paid back many times over through a significant reduction in number of ray–object intersection tests. This type of transformation can also be applied to other types of bounding volume; to orient cylinders for example, or to deform spheres into ellipsoids.

Another strategy for achieving a better fit is to use multiple bounding volumes for a single object. For instance, we can enclose the object within the ·

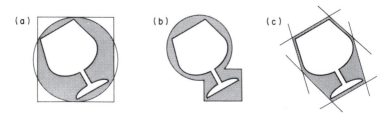

Fig. 6.   The intersection and union of multiple bounding volumes can be used to obtain a better fit. Each approach requires a different ray-intersection algorithm for best performance. (a) Intersection of box and sphere. (b) Union of box and sphere. (c) Intersection of slabs.

intersection of two or more bounding volumes, as in *Figure 6(a)*. A ray must then intersect *all* the volumes before the enclosed object needs to be tested. The cost of this composite bounding volume is the sum of the individual volume costs in the case of a ray which hits them all, but is only the cost of the 'first' volume in the case of a distant miss. Alternatively, the object may be covered by the union of two or more bounding volumes, as in *Figure 6(b)*. Here the object must be tested if *any* of the bounding volumes are hit, making the cost of a complete miss more expensive in this case. Finally, *Figure 6(c)* shows a bounding volume created by the intersection of infinite slabs. This type of bounding volume will be discussed in Section 4.3.

4.2 Predicting the Effectiveness of a Hierarchy

In order to better predict the effectiveness of a bounding volume we need to have information about the distribution of rays which will be tested against it. If every ray were to hit the enclosed object, no bounding volume would be beneficial. That is, every type of bounding volume, no matter how simple, would only increase the average cost of the intersection tests. On the other hand, if no ray even approaches the enclosed object, any bounding volume which is less expensive to test than the object is an advantage. In such a case the cheapest bounding volume is the best, independent of any other factor. In most situations the collection of rays tested against a given bounding volume falls somewhere between these two extremes, and in this mid-ground fit becomes a relevant factor as well as cost.

One way to extract useful information about ray distributions is to consider the effect of one bounding volume upon another instead of examining them in isolation. In particular, we will examine how one bounding volume affects the distribution of rays seen by one or more bounding volumes nested completely within it. This leads to a very natural way of predicting the performance of an entire bounding volume hierarchy. Following the approach of Goldsmith and Salmon [23] we consider the conditional probability of a ray hitting an inner volume, B, given that it has hit a surrounding volume, A. See *Figure 7(a)*. The standard notation for this conditional probability is $Pr(r$ hits $B \mid r$ hits $A)$, where r is a 'random' ray. For simplicity we assume that all rays which hit A are 'equally likely' (i.e. uniformly distributed). Even though the distribution of rays is usually far from uniform in practice, this scenario nevertheless gives a more realistic picture with respect to B than if we had considered it in isolation. The conditional probability expresses the important fact that A 'filters out' most of the rays which would not have hit B.

Under this randomness assumption, a simple calculation shows that $Pr(r$ hits $B \mid r$ hits $A)$ is equal to the ratio of the average projected area of B to the average projected area of A. This is quite convenient because the average

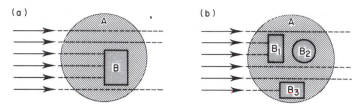

Fig. 7.   (a) We wish to compute the conditional probability of a ray hitting B given that it has hit A. This can be used in cases like (b) to compute the average cost of intersecting a ray with the arbitrary contents of a bounding volume.

projected area of a convex body is equal to one quarter of its surface area [61, p. 110]. Therefore, if both A and B are convex (as most bounding volumes are), we have that

$$Pr(r \text{ hits } B \mid r \text{ hits } A) = \frac{< P(B, \mathbf{d}) >}{< P(A, \mathbf{d}) >} = \frac{S(B)}{S(A)} \tag{2}$$

where $P(V, \mathbf{d})$ is the projected area of V along direction $\mathbf{d}$, $< >$ means the average taken over all directions $\mathbf{d}$, and $S(V)$ is the surface area of volume V. This relationship will be the key to analyzing the expected cost of hierarchically arranged bounding volumes.

There are two relevant costs associated with a bounding volume within a hierarchy: (1) the fixed cost of a ray intersection test with the volume itself, and (2) the average cost of a ray intersection test with its contents given that that ray has hit the volume (*Figure 7(b)*). We shall call these the *external cost* and the *internal cost*, denoted *EC* and *IC*, respectively. These correspond to the constant B and a generalization of the constant I in equation (1). Given equation (2) for conditional probability we can compute the (average) internal cost of a bounding volume, A. There are two components to this cost, and they can be expressed in terms of the costs of the enclosed items. First, there is the fixed cost of testing a ray against all of A's immediate children. This must be done for every ray which hits A. There is also the cost of testing the contents of the children which are actually hit by a given ray (neglecting the distance interval optimization). The former are external costs of the children and the latter are internal costs of the children weighted by the conditional probability that they are hit. This is expressed by equation (3) for a bounding volume, A, enclosing child volumes $B_1, B_2, \ldots B_n$.

$$IC(A) = \sum_{i=1}^{n} \left\{ EC(B_i) + \frac{S(B_i)}{S(A)} * IC(B_i) \right\}. \tag{3}$$

By definition the internal cost of a primitive object is zero, and this implies that we needn't know its surface area. Recursive application of equation (3) results in an average cost of intersecting a ray with a given bounding volume hierarchy expressed in terms of surface areas and external costs. This is valid regardless of the types of primitive objects or bounding volumes used, provided we have a measure of their surface areas and costs of intersection (i.e. their external costs).

We hasten to point out that equation (3), though based on important geometric relationships among bounding volumes, is still a heuristic and not an infallible measure of cost. Many simplifying assumptions have been made in order to arrive at this convenient equation. In addition to the proper nesting, convexity, and randomness assumptions noted earlier, an implicit assumption has been that the external cost of a bounding volume is constant for all rays and independent of whether or not the volume is hit by the ray. We have also neglected the effects of objects occluding one another. For example, in *Figure 7(b)* any of the rays shown which hit an object within B_1 need not be tested against the contents of B_2 due to the distance interval optimization. Occlusion such as this serves to increase efficiency slightly above that which is predicted by equation (3). However, nonuniformity in the distribution of rays can be far more significant and can drastically change the actual cost in either direction from the predicted value.

4.3   Constructing a Hierarchy

Constructing a bounding volume hierarchy involves two types of decisions: which clusters of objects (or bounding volumes) to enclose and what type of bounding volume to enclose them with. In Section 4.1 we described one heuristic for selecting the volume type, and in Section 4.2 we derived an expression for predicting the effectiveness of a given hierarchy. We now turn to the problem of selecting the clusters of objects or bounding volumes when constructing the hierarchy initially. This is a challenging problem because the number of possible hierarchical groupings of objects grows exponentially with the number of objects, making exhaustive search totally impractical. Rubin and Whitted [51] first attacked this problem through the use of a *structure editor*, an interactive program for constructing successive levels of a hierarchy beginning with the unstructured collection of primitive objects. It allowed the user to look for object coherence in the form of closely clustered objects and to select tight-fitting bounding boxes to enclose them. A means of performing this operation automatically was also suggested in [51]. By viewing the environment as a 3-D histogram and identifying the largest peaks, it should be possible to automate what the human operator was attempting to do by visual inspection.

Weghorst *et al.* [63] suggested that modeling hierarchies used in the construction of an environment are often adequate for the task of ray tracing. The model builder typically groups objects which are in close proximity to one another, and this practice tends to reduce the average projected void area of the resulting bounding volume. Goldsmith and Salmon [23] noted, however, that such hierarchies tend to have large branching factors, thereby reducing the benefits of tree pruning during ray intersection testing. To avoid this problem, they developed a method of automatic generation of bounding volume hierarchies which is closely tied to equation (3), and therefore more appropriate for ray tracing. In their approach, the hierarchy is constructed incrementally, inserting the primitive objects into the growing structure one at a time while striving to minimize the resulting increases in the bounding volume surface areas. Each object is inserted by beginning at the root of the tree and selecting the subtree which would incur the smallest increase in surface area if the new object were to become a child of it. This selection process continues until a leaf of the tree is reached. In the case of a tie at any level, all minimal subtrees are searched, and the one which ultimately produces the smallest increase in the estimated cost of the tree is used.

Goldsmith and Salmon observed that the order in which the objects are inserted into the hierarchy is very important because it can greatly influence the eventual form of the tree. The order imposed by the modeler can be used, but other alternatives include sorting along a line and randomizing. Sorting usually proved to be detrimental, while the best trees were discovered by trying a number of different random shuffles. Since the cost of tree generation is very small compared to the time for ray tracing we can afford to examine many alternatives in the search for an efficient hierarchical organization.

4.4   Approximate Convex Hulls

Convexity is a geometrical property which can often be used to great advantage. It is a particularly desirable property for bounding volumes, for example, because it guarantees that any ray will interesect the volume at most twice, and this is virtually a prerequisite for a simple intersection test. The *convex hull* of an object is a uniquely defined convex volume. It is the intersection of all convex volumes which contain the object, and is therefore the smallest such volume. Together, these facts suggest that convex hulls may be exemplary bounding volumes. However, computing and representing the exact convex hull of an object or collection of objects can be difficult. If we elect to use an approximation of the true convex hull, we can eliminate these problems and, moreover, ensure that the resulting volume will be extremely easy to test for intersection.

The best example of this is a method introduced by Kay and Kajiya [37].

The bounding volumes in their approach are many-sided parallelepipeds which can be made to conform arbitrarily closely to the actual convex hulls of the enclosed objects. The algorithm uses the concept of *plane-sets* which are families of parallel planes. Each plane-set is defined by a single unit vector called the *plane-set normal*, and each plane within a family is uniquely determined by its signed distance from the origin (equal to the inner product of the plane-set normal and any point on the plane). Given a plane-set normal and an arbitrary (bounded) object, there are two unique planes of the family which most closely bracket the object. The infinite region between these planes is called a *slab*, and is conveniently represented by a min–max interval associated with the plane-set normal as shown in *Figure 8(a)*. For polyhedral objects, these values can be computed by forming the dot product of the plane-set normal with each of the object's vertices (in world coordinates), then finding the minimum and maximum of these values. For implicit surfaces such as quadrics the values defining the slab can be computed using the method of Lagrange multipliers [37].

The intersection of several different slabs can define a bounded region enclosing the object, as shown in *Figure 8(b)*. In three-space this requires three slabs whose plane-set normals are linearly independent (two suffice in two-space), but we are by no means limited to three. The greater the number of slabs, the more closely we can approximate the actual convex hull of the object. To intersect a ray with such a volume we first compute the interval along the ray, measured from its origin, which lies within each of the slabs. This amounts to computing two ray–plane intersections for each slab. If the intersection of these intervals is empty, the ray misses the volume. Otherwise, the ray hits the volume and the maximum of the minimum interval values is the distance to the point of intersection.

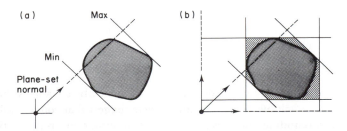

Fig. 8. A plane-set normal defines a family of parallel planes orthogonal to it. Two values associated with a plane-set normal select two of these planes and define a slab. The intersection of several such slabs forms a parallelepiped bounding volume. (a) A single slab bracketing an object. (b) Three slabs defining a bounding volume.

The shape of this type of bounding volume is unaffected by object translation which merely changes the min–max plane constants. Object rotation, on the other hand, affects the quality of approximation. For example, a fairly tight-fitting volume is defined by the three slabs shown in *Figure 6(c)*, but considerably more void area is introduced by a slight rotation of the object relative to the plane-set normals. This suggests that we should select the number and orientation of the plane sets for each individual object in order to obtain very tight-fitting volumes. However, there are tremendous computational advantages to using the same collection of plane-set normals for all the objects of the environment, despite their individual orientations. The most significant advantage is that the task of intersecting a ray with a number of bounding volumes can be greatly accelerated. Common expressions in the ray–plane intersection calculations can be 'factored out' and done once per ray instead of once per bounding volume. When this is done, the calculation requires only two subtracts, two multiplies and a comparison for each slab of a bounding volume [37].

As with other bounding volume techniques, introducing hierarchical nesting is a critical step for efficient execution. To construct a parallelopiped which tightly bounds two or more parallelopipeds (with respect to the same plane-set normals), we compute the new plane constants by finding the minimum and the maximum of all the plane constants associated with each of the plane-set normals. This is directly analogous to constructing nested

```
procedure Hull__Sort__Intersect( in ray, root )
begin
    pre-compute constants for efficient slab intersection;
    initialize heap to contain root bounding volume;
    while heap is not empty do begin
        remove candidate from top of heap;
        if candidate.key > ray.interval.max then return;
        if candidate is a leaf then
            Intersect( ray, candidate.object )
        else for each child of candidate do
            if Intersect__P( ray, child.approx__hull ) then
                add child to heap with key = "estimated distance";
    endwhile
end
```

Fig. 9.   A procedure for intersecting a ray with a collection of objects organized in the hierarchical structure proposed by Kay and Kajiya. In this example 'Intersect__P' makes use of the precomputed constants and also computes the 'estimated distance.'

axis-aligned bounding boxes. In fact, bounding boxes are a special case which results from using the three coordinate axes as the plane-set normals.

Another aspect of the algorithm described in [37] is an efficient method of traversing a bounding volume hierarchy which fully exploits the distance interval optimization described in Section 4. This requires a sorting operation with respect to each ray based on the distances to the points of intersection with the bounding volumes. Kay and Kajiya call these the *estimated distances* because they roughly approximate the distances to the enclosed objects. Using the estimated distance as a key to sort on results in a priority queue for the objects relative to the ray and insures that they are processed in approximately the order that they are encountered by the ray. *Figure 9* is an outline of a procedure which applies this technique to a hierarchy of parallelepipeds formed by intersecting slabs. Here, a *candidate* is any parallelopiped which is intersected by the ray, and each candidate encloses either a single object or a collection of other parallelopipeds. The sorting of the candidates is performed using a heap because, as Kay and Kajiya point out, the efficiency of this operation is quite critical to the performance of the algorithm.

5   3-D SPATIAL SUBDIVISION

The further an object is from the path of a ray, the less work we can afford to do in eliminating it from consideration. As we have seen, bounding volume hierarchies provide a means of recursively narrowing the focus of the search to more promising candidates for intersection. This is a natural divide-and-conquer approach for examining a collection of objects, seeking the member producing the closest intersection. Spatial subdivision begins with a different philosophy. Here we also rely upon simple volumes to identify objects which are good candidates for intersection, but these volumes are constructed by applying a divide-and-conquer technique to the space surrounding the objects instead of considering the objects themselves. Rather than constructing the volumes in a bottom-up fashion by successively enveloping larger collections of objects, we proceed top-down, partitioning a volume bounding the environment into smaller pieces. The smaller volumes thus formed are then assigned collections of objects which are totally or partially contained within them. Therefore a fundamental difference between bounding volume hier-archies and spatial subdivision techniques is that the former *selects volumes based on given sets of objects*, whereas the latter *selects sets of objects based on given volumes*. This leads to a very different approach which places the emphasis on space instead of the objects.

A concept common to all the current techniques of this family is the *voxel*. This is a 'cuboid,' or axis-aligned rectangular prism, and it is the fundamental compartment created by a process of partitioning space. The term itself connotes the extension of 2-D 'picture elements,' or pixels, to 3-D 'volume elements.' A pre-processing step is responsible for constructing nonoverlapping voxels which, taken together, constitute a volume containing the environment. Within these constraints there are different methods of defining the voxels, and these differences lead to the most significant variations within this family. The ramifications of uniform versus nonuniform size are particularly important. Once defined, however, the voxels play the same role in all cases. They are the means of restricting attention to only those objects which are close to the path of a ray.

It the point of intersection between a ray and an object lies within a voxel, both the ray and the object clearly must intersect that voxel. Because the voxels contain the entire environment, every possible point of intersection must lie within some voxel. Therefore, the only objects which we must test for intersection are those which intersect the voxels pierced by the ray. For any given ray, this can potentially eliminate the vast majority of the objects in the environment from consideration. An equally important observation is that a ray imposes a strict ordering on the pierced voxels based on the distance to the point at which the ray first enters each voxel. Because the voxels are nonoverlapping, this ordering guarantees that all intersections occurring within one voxel are closer to the ray origin than those in all subsequent voxels. Consequently, if we process the voxels in the order in which they are encountered along the ray, we needn't consider the contents of any further voxels once we have found a point of intersection (see caveats discussed in Section 5.3). This feature is closely related to the distance interval optimization used in processing bounding volume hierarchies. It can drastically reduce the number of objects which need to be tested and is one of the most attractive features of these techniques.

Spatial subdivision techniques offer an efficient means of identifying the objects which are near the path of a ray while at the same time performing a virtual 'bucket sort' on those objects. In programming terminology, this latter property means that we have moved a portion of the sorting problem from the 'inner loop' of the ray tracing algorithm (as in *Figure 9*) into a pre-processing stage [36]. Naturally, this relies upon the ability to efficiently access the voxels in the order defined by the path of the ray. As we shall see, this operation plays a prominent role in each technique of this family.

5.1   Nonuniform Spatial Subdivision

Nonuniform spatial subdivision techniques are those which discretize space into regions of varying size in order to conform to features of the environment. This variation in size allows more subdivision to be performed in densely populated regions of space and, conversely, it allows large voxels to cover regions which are sparsely populated or entirely void. An *octree* is one possible data structure for creating and organizing such a collection of voxels. Octrees are hierarchical data structures used for efficiently indexing data associated with points in three-space and have been applied to problems such as hidden surface elimination and computation of 3-D digital convex hulls (see [69] and included references). They are constructed by recursively subdividing rectangular volumes into eight subordinate octants until the resulting leaf volumes, or voxels, meet some criterion for simplicity. In most applications the voxels are examined to determine how much of their volume lies within some three-dimensional solid and marked as 'empty,' 'full,' or 'mixed' accordingly.

Glassner [20] introduced an octree variation for use in ray tracing. In this approach each voxel is assigned a list of objects whose surfaces penetrate that volume (*Figure 10*), and these are the intersection candidates for every ray which pierces the voxel. The candidate objects of a given voxel are identified by testing their surfaces against the six faces of the voxel. If a surface intersects one of the faces, the object is immediately added to a candidate list associated with the voxel. For those which do not intersect any of the faces, an additional test for proper containment within this voxel is performed by considering a single point on the object's surface. If the point is inside the voxel, the entire object must be as well (assuming its surface is a connected set), and it is added to the candidate list.

The creation of these candidate lists guides the top-down construction of the octree. A box containing the environment is recursively subdivided until each

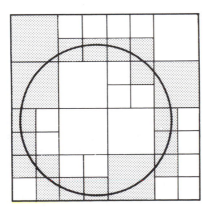

Fig. 10.   A 2-D analogy of a sphere and the octree voxels penetrated by its surface. The sphere must be added to the candidate list associated with each of the shaded voxels.

```
procedure Octree__Intersect( in ray )
begin
   Q = ray.origin;
   repeat { walk through the voxels }
      locate the voxel which contains Q;
      for each object associated with voxel do
         Intersect( ray, object );
      if no intersection has been found then
         Q = a point in the next voxel pierced by ray;
   until an intersection is found or Q is outside
      the bounding box of the environment
end
```

Fig. 11. A procedure for intersecting a ray with a collection of objects organized in an octree. These essential features are present in both Glassner's [20] and Kaplan's [35] approach.

voxel contains fewer than some threshold number of intersection candidates or until a storage limitation is reached. Once the octree is constructed, the algorithm outlined in *Figure 11* is used to perform fast ray–environment intersections. Accessing the voxels which are pierced by a ray is accomplished by two fundamental operations within the main loop of this algorithm: (1) 'locating' a voxel which contains a given point in three-space, and (2) constructing a point which is guaranteed to be in the 'next' voxel. The first of these is intimately related to the particular representation of the octree.

In Glassner's approach, nodes of the octree are linked and accessed by uniquely defined *names* rather than storing explicit pointers to descendent nodes. To construct these names a convention of labeling the eight children with the digits $1 \ldots 8$ is adopted. When a node is subdivided the children derive their names by appending their single digit to the name of the parent. Thus, each node of the tree receives a unique integer name consisting of digits which encode the path to that node from the root (which is named '1'). Given the name of a node, the name of any child is obtained by multiplying by 10 and adding the appropriate digit. To access data associated with a node name, such as the candidate list in the case of leaf nodes, the name is used to retrieve a pointer from a hash table. Glassner observed that simply computing the name modulo the size of the hash table serves as a good hashing function. This mechanism is used to retrieve the candidate list associated with a leaf node (voxel) containing a given point. Beginning at the root node we determine which of the eight octants the point lies within, construct the name of the child corresponding to that octant, and consult the hash table to determine the status of that child. The process is repeated until we reach a leaf node or produce the name of a non-existent node, indicating an empty candidate list.

If a ray hits nothing within a voxel we must proceed to the next voxel pierced by that ray. In Glassner's algorithm, this is accomplished by finding a point within the next voxel and performing the look-up described above. To find such a point we first compute where the ray exits the current voxel using a standard ray–box intersection calculation, then move a small distance into the interior of the neighboring voxel, taking care not to step too far. This can be done using the length of the shortest voxel edge in the entire octree; call it 'minlen.' If the exit point is interior to a face of the current voxel, we move the exit point directly away from this face by a distance of minlen/2. If the ray exits through an edge or a vertex of the current voxel we need to make a similar adjustment for each face containing the exit point. The result is a point which lies within the desired voxel.

Kaplan [35] introduced a very similar approach based on binary space partitioning trees (BSP trees), an alternative method for subdividing space into voxels. A BSP tree partitions space into two pieces at each level by means of a separating place. Though Fuchs's hidden surface algorithm [16] employs BSP trees with arbitrarily oriented partitioning planes, Kaplan's approach restricts these to be axis-orthogonal planes and consequently performs nearly the same voxel subdivision as the octree method. One difference between this and Glassner's approach is that the nodes of the BSP tree are constructed with explicit pointers to their two children. This obviates the need for voxel names and hashing at the expense of a potential increase in storage; a typical space/time trade-off.

Jansen [31] introduced a spatial subdivision algorithm based on BSP trees which differs fundamentally from both of the previous methods in the way it identifies the voxels pierced by the ray. Instead of finding the next voxel by creating a point guaranteed to fall within it and traversing the hierarchical structure from the root, we recursively descend all the branches of the BSP tree which terminate at pierced voxels, making use of each partition node only once per ray. Jansen calls the previous method *sequential traversal* and the new method *recursive traversal*. The recursive traversal algorithm is outlined in *Figure 12*. As the BSP structure is traversed, a ray is recursively 'clipped' by each partitioning plane it pierces. That is, the ray's distance interval is divided into two intervals which correspond to segments of the ray on either side of the plane. The segment closest to the ray origin continues the recursive partitioning process first. If this 'near' segment of the ray is found to intersect an object, the 'far' segment is discarded. Otherwise, the far segment of the ray is also recursively partitioned. Frequently the entire ray interval will be entirely to one side of a partitioning plane. When this happens, one of the segments of the ray ('near' or 'far' in *Figure 12*) will be empty, causing the corresponding recursive call to 'BSP_Intersect' to terminate immediately, pruning one of the branches of the BSP tree.

```
procedure BSP__Intersect( in ray, node )
begin
    if ray.interval is empty or node is nil then return;
    if node is a leaf then { this is a "voxel" node }
        for each object associated with the node do
            Intersect( ray, object );
    else begin { this is a "partition" node }
        near = ray clipped to near side of node.partition;
        BSP__Intersect( near, pointer to near half-space);
        if no intersection has been found then begin
            far = ray clipped to far side of node.partition;
            BSP__Intersect( far, pointer to far half-space);
        endif
    endelse
end
```

Fig. 12. A 'recursive traversal' procedure for intersecting a ray with a collection of objects organized in a BSP tree. Rays are 'clipped' using the distance interval.

Figure 13 shows a 2-D analogy of an environment and the voxels defined by octree subdivision. For simplicity only spheres are depicted here, though the principle is independent of the types of primitive objects used. The subdivision heuristics used to construct this octree were (1) subdivide any voxel with two or more intersection candidates, but (2) subdivide no more than three levels deep. These heuristics are typical of octree approaches, though the values used in this example may not be realistic. Limits placed on the depth

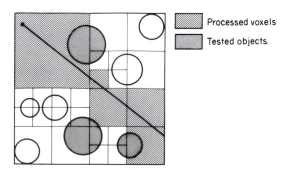

Fig. 13. Non-uniform spatial subdivision via an octree. The ray shown here causes five of the voxels to be examined and three of the eight objects to be tested for intersection. Finer subdivision can decrease the number of ray–object tests at the expense of additional voxel processing overhead.

are usually needed to guard against situations in which the recursion would not terminate based on other criteria. This can occur, for example, when several objects overlap, making them impossible to separate by further subdivision. The processed voxels and tested objects are shaded in this figure for a particular ray. These are independent of the type of traversal algorithm used: sequential or recursive. The ray shown here is a rather bad case, passing through the environment without hitting anything. Nevertheless, only three of the eight objects are tested, and this ratio tends to become more favorable as the complexity of the environment increases. If the ray happens to hit something in a voxel close to the ray origin, fewer voxels need be processed and consequently fewer objects are tested.

5.2 Uniform Spatial Subdivision

Fujimoto *et al.* [17] introduced a different approach to spatial subdivision in which voxels of uniform size are organized in a regular 3-D grid (or lattice). This organization was given the acronym SEADS, for Spatially Enumerated Auxiliary Data Structure. The overall strategy is quite similar to the nonuniform subdivision techniques. Lists of candidate objects are retrieved from voxels which are pierced by a ray and these voxels are processed in the order they are pierced. However, there are two distinguishing features of this approach which are direct consequences of the voxel regularity: (1) the subdivision is totally independent of the structure of the environment, and (2) the voxels pierced by a ray can be accessed very efficiently by incremental calculation. The first is a disadvantage which must be weighed against the obvious benefits of the second. The test cases in [17] are examples where the

```
procedure Grid_Intersect( in ray, node )
begin
    compute i, j, k for the voxel containing ray.origin;
    set up 3DDDA based on ray.direction and ray.origin;
    repeat {walk through the voxels}
        for each object associated with voxel[i,j,k] do
            Intersect( ray, object );
        if no intersection has been found then
            use 3DDDA to compute new i, j, k;
    until an intersection is found or i, j, k is outside
        the limits of the voxel array:
    end
```

Fig. 14. A procedure for intersecting a ray with a collection of objects organized in a uniform grid. The 3DDDA is similar to a line rasterization routine.

speed of voxel access proves to be the dominant factor, indicating that the SEADS approach can sometimes offer significant gains in performance over nonuniform subdivision techniques.

The key to efficient voxel access is that finding the voxels along the path of a ray in a regular lattice is the 3-D analogy of representing a line on a regular array of pixels. To exploit this, Fujimoto *et al.* developed a *three-dimensional digital difference analyzer*, or 3DDDA, to incrementally compute successive voxel indices in the same way that efficient line rasterization algorithms incrementally compute pixel coordinates. One minor difference is that the 3DDDA must step through each voxel which is pierced by the given ray *(Figure 15)*, whereas line rasterization algorithms identify pixels which are merely close to a line in some sense. This requires a departure from the common property of line rasterization algorithms which forces a step to be taken along the dominant axis unconditionally with every iteration. Nevertheless, incremental error terms can still be used to signal discrete steps along the coordinate axes just as in line rasterization. These error terms require careful initialization to correctly handle rays which do not originate from the exact center of a voxel. This is analogous to sub-pixel positioning in line rasterization.

Usually just one of the three indices, i, j, and k, are incremented (or decremented) by the 3DDDA in each iteration of the loop. Exceptions occur when a ray goes through an edge or a corner of a voxel. Because a 3DDDA generates integer coordinate triples, data associated with the voxels is most conveniently stored as a three-dimensional array. In procedure 'Grid__Inter-sect' (*Figure 14*) this array is named 'voxel' and it is assumed to provide access to the intersection candidates, perhaps by storing a pointer to the head of the list. Given the coordinates of any point interior to a voxel, this

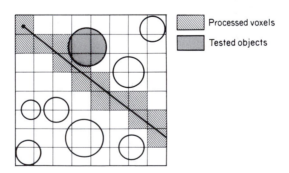

Fig. 15. A 2-D analogy of uniform spatial subdivision. The ray shown here pierces 14 voxels and results in one object being tested for intersection. The uniformity of the grid makes the process of voxel walking similar to representing a line on a rectangular array of pixels.

arrangement allows quick access to its associated data through direct calculation of the voxel indices. This can make the initial construction of the
candidate lists quite efficient and is another benefit of uniform subdivision.

The advantages of this approach cannot always compensate for the lack of
adaptivity, however. Though the voxels which 'digitize' a ray can be made to
approximate the ray with arbitrary precision by increasing the resolution of
the grid, two limitations begin to emerge as we do so. First, it becomes more
costly to pass rays through empty regions of space, and second, the storage for
the corresponding three-dimensional array quickly becomes unmanageable.
Of course the storage problem can be alleviated by only storing the voxels
which have non-empty candidate lists as Glassner did with octrees [20]. This
could be accomplished through a voxel look-up scheme similar to that used by
Wyvill *et al.* [67] to construct polygonal approximations of implicitly defined
surfaces. This is another space/time trade-off because of the overhead which
the hash table look-up adds to the voxel walking process.

Fujimoto *et al.* [17] also made use of the 3DDDA in accessing octree voxels.
Because the 3DDDA is applicable only to uniform subdivision, this restricts
its use to walking 'horizontally' among sibling voxels of the octree. Each
group of eight siblings can be viewed as a small uniform grid and, as such, the
3DDDA provides an efficient means of passing a ray through them. After
stepping through at most four voxels, 'vertical' traversal must be performed
again in order to locate the next block of eight siblings.

5.3   Two Caveats

There are a number of potential pitfalls which one must be careful to avoid
when implementing spatial subdivision techniques. Two in particular stem
from the fact that a single object may intersect several voxels, and these
pertain to both uniform and nonuniform subdivision techniques. The first is
the problem of repeated ray–object intersection tests between the same ray
and object. Multiple tests can result from situations such as that depicted in
Figure 16. As the ray passes through voxels 1 and 2, it finds object A in the
candidate list of each. To avoid testing it twice we can employ a *mailbox* as
described by Arnaldi *et al.* [2]. A mailbox, in this context, is a means of
storing intersection results with individual objects. Each object is assigned a
mailbox and each distinct ray is tagged with a unique number. When an
object is tested for intersection, the results of the test and the ray tag are stored
in the object's mailbox. Before testing every object, the tag stored in its
mailbox is compared against that of the current ray. If they match, the object
has been previously tested against this ray and the results can be retrieved
without being recalculated.

The second caveat is more serious because it can cause erroneous results. A

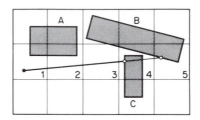

Fig. 16.   We can avoid testing object A in voxel 2 after having tested it in voxel 1 by using a mailbox. We must be careful to terminate the voxel walking process only when the point of intersection is contained within the current voxel. Otherwise, object C could be missed in the situation shown here.

situation in which this problem arises is also depicted in *Figure 16*. Notice that object B will be in the candidate list of voxel 3, and this object is indeed intersected by the ray shown. If this affirmative test causes the voxel walking to terminate at voxel 3, the closer intersection with object C will not be found. This can cause disappearing objects. To remedy this we require that the point of intersection be within the 'current' voxel before terminating the search. That is, we only terminate the voxel walking process if the point of intersection is known to be the closest resulting from any object associated with a voxel up to and including the one which contains that point. By using mailboxes we can save the intersection results computed on behalf of an earlier voxel until it is reached by the voxel walking process.

5.4   A Comparison through Graphs

Thus far we have discussed three fundamentally different methods for organizing data in order to accelerate ray intersection calculations: bounding volume hierarchies, uniform spatial subdivision, and nonuniform spatial subdivision. Each involves a relationship between objects and volumes, and each requires a special algorithm for accessing objects based on which volumes are intersected by a given ray. The differences are easy to see if we depict the object–volume organizations required by these algorithms as graphs, as in *Figure 17*. Here, circles represent bounding volumes, squares represent primitive objects, thick lines represent ray intersection tests, and thin lines represent point containment tests (such as used in descending an octree).

Figure 17(a) is the graph resulting from a bounding volume hierarchy. Because there is exactly one path to each of the leaf nodes, the graph is a tree. The children of a node are processed only if the node is intersected by a ray. Different types of bounding volumes and different orders of testing give rise to some of the variations within this family of algorithms. *Figure 17(b)* is the

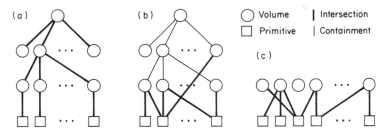

Fig. 17.   A bounding volume hierarchy results in (a) a tree, nonuniform spatial subdivision results in (b) a directed acyclic graph, or DAG, and uniform spatial subdivision results in (c) a bipartite graph.

graph resulting from nonuniform spatial subdivision. The subgraph connected by the thin lines is a tree because there is exactly one path to reach any given leaf volume (voxels in this case). These leaf volumes can be associated with any number of objects, and some objects may belong to more than one leaf volume. This makes the overall graph a DAG (directed acyclic graph). Finally, *Figure 17(c)* is the graph resulting from uniform spatial subdivision. Each object belongs to one or more volumes, and each volume contains zero or more objects. There are no explicit edges connecting the volumes because they are accessed by direct index calculation, not by paths through other volumes. Because each edge has one vertex in the set of objects and the other in the set of volumes, the graph is bipartite.

These graphs clearly do not convey all of the features of the corresponding algorithms, but they do serve to highlight the more fundamental differences. Given this representation it is natural to ask which other graphs represent useful algorithms. As a partial answer to this we refer to Section 12 in which combinations of various acceleration techniques are discussed. The corresponding graphs of these hybrid algorithms contain any or all of the ones shown here as subgraphs.

6   DIRECTIONAL TECHNIQUES

The most recent category to emerge is that of directional techniques. Though every ray tracing approach must take ray direction into account, the directional techniques are those which exploit this information at a level above that of individual rays. To see how this differs from other approaches, consider the use of ray direction within a typical 3-D spatial subdivision scheme. Here the direction is used in selecting the subset of voxels pierced by the ray. This eliminates most of the voxels from consideration and defines an efficient order for processing those which remain. However, this selection and ordering of voxels must be performed on a ray-by-ray basis because direction is not taken into account during the construction of the voxels. In contrast, directional techniques explicitly incorporate directional information into data structures which allow more of the overhead to be moved from the 'inner loop' into a less costly stage. Operations such as backface culling and candidate sorting can be done on behalf of many rays instead of individual rays. A common penalty which accompanies these advantages is a very large storage requirement.

There are currently three members in the family of directional techniques: the 'Light Buffer' [25], the 'Ray Coherence' algorithm [47], and 'Ray Classification' [3]. An important mechanism employed by all the members of this family is direction subdivision. Before describing how this is used in each of the algorithms, we introduce some useful terminology and machinery.

6.1 The Direction Cube

A concept which has appeared independently in all three of the algorithms discussed in this section is something which we shall call the *direction cube*. A direction cube plays a similar role to that of the 'hemi-cube' used in the radiosity method [8]. It is a means of discretizing directions into a finite number of square or rectangular *direction cells* and is analogous to spatial subdivision methods which discretize bounded regions of space into a finite number of voxels. More precisely, a direction cube is an axis-aligned cube centered at the world coordinate origin. The six faces of this cube correspond to six *dominant axes* which we label $+X$, $-X$, $+Y$, $-Y$, $+Z$ and $-Z$ (see *Figure 18(a)*). Each of these faces subtends a solid angle of $2\pi/3$ steradians from a vantage point of the coordinate origin.

The direction cube allows us to translate 3-D directions into the language of 2-D rectangular coordinates. To account for 4π steradians (i.e. all possible directions) we define these 2-D rectangular coordinates, designated u and v, on six independent squares corresponding to the faces of the direction cube. For any given ray, we can then construct an alternative representation for its direction by imagining it translated to the coordinate origin, determining which face of the direction cube it intersects (i.e. finding the dominant axis of the ray) and then computing the u–v coordinates of the point of intersection (*Figure 18(a)*). Scaling the U and V axes so that the cube edges are of length two guarantees that all points of intersection will have coordinates between -1 and 1. This convention makes calculations particularly efficient. *Figure 19* shows a procedure for performing this mapping by defining U and V axes on each face as synonyms for two of the world coordinate axes, X, Y, or Z. The exact correspondence chosen in each case is immaterial, so this procedure

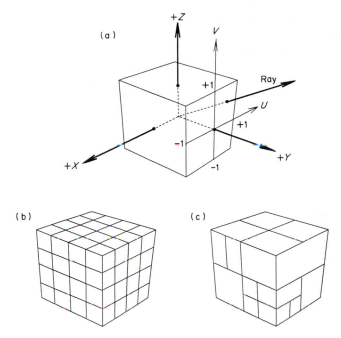

Fig. 18.   The direction cube is used to translate 3-D directions 2-D rectangular coordinates. This provides a means of applying subdivision techniques in the context of directions. (a) Three of the dominant axes associated with a direction cube. (b) Uniform subdivision. (c) Adaptive subdivision.

simply selects U and V to be the two axes, in lexicographic order, which are parallel to the face.

This translation to 2-D rectangular coordinates allows us to easily and efficiently apply subdivision techniques in the context of directions. Just as in spatial subdivision, we can choose to subdivide the squares uniformly or nonuniformly, and in the latter case, standard techniques such as BSP trees or quadtrees are applicable. Examples of uniform and nonuniform direction subdivision are depicted in *Figures 18(b)* and *18(c)*, respectively. Each direction cell resulting from subdivision defines an infinite skewed pyramid with its apex at the coordinate origin and its edges through the cell corners. We shall refer to these as *direction pyramids*. A direction pyramid is the volume of space accessible to rays which begin at the coordinate origin and pass through the given direction cell. Notice that even in the case of uniform subdivision the direction cells do not all subtend equal solid angles. This poses no problem, however, because it is the efficiency of the translation from directions to 2-D coordinates which is important to the algorithms in the following sections, not the exact shapes of the direction pyramids.

```
procedure Direction_to_UV( in direction; out axis, u, v )
begin
    ax = | direction.x |
    ay = | direction.y |
    az = | direction.z |
    if ax > ay and ax > az then begin { X is dominant }
        if direction.x > 0 then axis = pos_X else axis = neg_X
        u = direction.y / ax
        v = direction.z / ax
    endif
    else if ay > az then begin { Y is dominant }
        if direction.y > 0 then axis = pos_Y else axis = neg_Y
        u = direction.x / ay
        v = direction.z / ay
    endif
    else begin { Z is dominant }
        if direction.z > 0 then axis = pos_Z else axis = neg_Z
        u = direction.x / az
        v = direction.y / az
    endelse
end
```

Fig. 19. A procedure for mapping 3-D direction vectors into points in one of six 2-D rectangular coordinate systems indexed by the six dominant axes.

Given a subdivided direction cube, it is a simple matter to determine which direction cell is pierced by any ray. We begin by determining the ray's dominant axis and $u-v$ coordinates, as discussed above. Then, in the case of uniform subdivision, the row and column indices of the direction cell containing this 2-D point are found by direct calculation. In the case of nonuniform subdivision more work is required, such as traversing a hierarchical partitioning structure for that face. These cases are the exact analogs of problems encountered in uniform and nonuniform spatial subdivision techniques. Furthermore, the role played by the direction cells is similar to that of voxels. Both are used to access lists of candidate objects, indexed by direction neighborhoods in one case and by spatial neighborhoods in the other. In both cases the purpose of locating the appropriate neighborhood is to retrieve the associated candidate list.

We now turn to applications of this directional information. The key to understanding the connection between the three algorithms in this section is to observe that they each begin by associating direction cubes with specific collections of rays. The most straightforward application is to consider only rays which originate from a finite number of isolated points. Special points which are particularly appropriate are point light sources (which we can think of as emitting the rays used in shadow testing) and the eye point. The 'Light Buffer' algorithm [25] was developed to take advantage of the former case. Other collections of rays which can be associated with direction cubes are those which originate from the surfaces of individual objects. The 'Ray Coherence' algorithm [47] takes this approach. Finally, we can associate direction cubes with collections of rays which originate from 3-D voxels. The 'Ray Classification' [3] algorithm is closely related to this concept, although as we shall see it partially removes the distinction between direction cells and voxels.

6.2   The Light Buffer

The Light Buffer, introduced by Haines and Greenberg [25], is a directional technique which accelerates the calculation of shadows with respect to point light sources. One of the facts exploited by this algorithm is that points can be determined to be in shadow without finding the closest occluding object. Since any opaque occluding object will suffice, shadowing operations are inherently easier that normal ray–environment intersections. Furthermore, constraining light sources to be single points allows a particularly effective application of the direction cube to these operations.

The search for an occluding object can be narrowed to a small set of objects by making use of the direction from the light source to the point in question. The light buffer algorithm accomplishes this by associating a uniformly subdivided direction cube with each light source, and a *complete* list of candidate objects with each of the direction cells. That is, each candidate list contains every object which can be 'seen' through the corresponding direction cell. These candidate lists are retrieved by finding the direction cell pierced by each light ray which is (conceptually) cast from the light source. The objects in this list are the only ones which can block the ray and thereby cast a shadow.

The light buffers are constructed as a pre-processing step, before ray tracing begins. The candidate lists are created by projecting each object of the environment onto the six faces of each direction cube, adding them to the candidate lists of those direction cells which are partially or totally covered by the projection. For polygonal objects this is performed efficiently by applying a modified scan-line algorithm to the projected edges. Nonpolygonal objects can be enclosed in polyhedral hulls for the purpose of creating the candidate lists, although the actual shadow intersection testing must use the object itself. Once all the lists are created, they are sorted into ascending order according to depth.

There are several observations which can lead to simplified candidate lists.

First, all polygons which face away from the light and are part of opaque solids may be culled. Also, any list which consists of exactly one polygon can be deleted, because a polygon cannot occlude itself unless it is facing away from the light. Finally, if the projection of an object completely covers a direction cell, the candidate list can be terminated by a *full-occlusion record* at the object depth, and all candidates at a greater depth can be eliminated. The direction pyramid from this depth onward is completely in shadow with respect to that light source. In order to exploit this optimization for objects with curved surfaces, we can detect totally covered direction cells by using enclosed polygonal meshes instead of bounding hulls.

To determine if a point on a given surface is in shadow, we first check the orientation of the surface with respect to the light source. If it is facing away, the polygon is known to be in shadow. Otherwise, we retrieve the list of potential occluding objects from the light buffer using the direction of the light ray. The objects in the list are then tested for intersection, in order of increasing depth, until an occlusion is found or until we reach an object whose depth is beyond the point we are testing. In the former case the point is in shadow, and in the latter case it is illuminated. If the list is marked with a full occlusion record and the point we are testing is at a greater depth, we can immediately conclude that the point is in shadow without performing any intersection tests. Note that this optimization is one of the benefits of the special treatment of light rays. It is irrelevant whether the object causing full occlusion is the first one hit by the light ray.

6.3   The Ray Coherence Algorithm

In this and the following section we describe algorithms which extend the use of directional information to the acceleration of general intersection calculations. Ohta and Maekawa [47] achieved this through application of what they have termed the 'ray coherence theorem.' This is a mathematical tool for placing a bound on the directions of rays which originate at one object and then hit another, making it possible to broaden the application of direction cubes from single points to bounded objects. In its simplest form, the ray coherence theorem applies to objects which are bounded by nonintersecting spheres, as in *Figure 20*.

Any ray which originates within sphere S_1 and terminates within sphere S_2 defines an acute angle, θ, with the line through the sphere centers. Inequality (4) is a bound on this angle in terms of the sphere radii and the distance between their centers.

$$\cos \theta > \sqrt{\left(1 - \frac{r_1 + r_2}{|| O_1 - O_2 ||}\right)}. \tag{4}$$

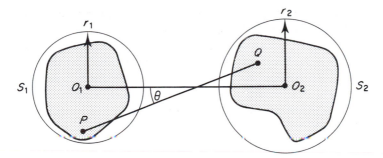

Fig. 20. A bound on the angle between lines O_1O_2 and PQ can be computed in terms of the distance between the centers of the two bounding spheres and their radii. This can be used to bound the directions of the rays which originate at one object and intersect the other.

Ohta and Maekawa also used a version of this theorem which is applicable when the objects are bounded by convex polyhedra instead of spheres. The resulting direction bound is phrased in terms of a 2-D convex hull on the surface of a sphere. In either case, approximations of these direction bounds are stored by means of uniformly subdivided direction cubes associated with each entity in the environment from which rays can originate. This includes the eye point, light sources, and reflective or refractive objects. Each of these direction cubes is constructed and used in nearly the same manner as a light buffer. A pre-processing operation creates depth-sorted lists of intersection candidates for each direction cell of each direction cube. These candidate lists determine the objects which need to be tested for intersection with any ray based on its direction and the entity whence it originated. The direction cube therefore accelerates the process of finding the 'next' object hit, providing an efficient way of progressing from object to object as the path of a ray is traced. This essentially reduces to a light buffer in the case of shadow tests with respect to point light sources.

Departures from the light buffer algorithm occur in both the construction and intersection testing of the candidate lists. During candidate list construction, objects are associated with individual direction cells by means of a relationship such as (4) rather than by projecting the objects (or their bounding volumes) on to a single point. This is equivalent to sweeping the center of projection over the object from which the rays originate and identifying all the direction cells which are touched by the projections. The difference in testing a candidate list for intersection is that nonshadowing rays require that the closest point of intersection be found. Objects in the list are tested *in order* until the list is exhausted or the minimum distance, given by d in

for *each entity,* A, *from which rays can originate* **do begin**
    for *each object* B **do begin**
        d = *lower bound on distance between* A *and* B;
        S = *direction bound for rays from* A *which hit* B;
        for *each direction cell of* A *which intersects* S **do begin**
            insert B *into the cell's sorted candidate list*
            according to the distance d;
        endfor
    endfor
endfor

Fig. 21.   The pre-processing algorithm of the 'ray coherence' algorithm. The sorting operation can be performed by insertion, as shown here, or after all the candidate lists have been formed.

Figure 21, is greater than the distance to a known point of intersection. This is the distance interval optimization yet again.

An outline of the pre-processing algorithm which creates the candidate lists is shown in *Figure 21*. It is assumed that bounding volumes are all spheres or all convex polyhedra. The direction bound, *S*, will be a unit vector and an angle (or cosine) defining a cone in the case of bounding spheres and a spherical convex hull in the case of bounding polyhedra.

6.4   Ray Classification

The ray classification algorithm, described by Arvo and Kirk [3], does not use explicit direction cubes except in the special case of first-generation rays. The data structure used to accelerate the intersection process for other rays is. closely tied to the concept of a direction cube, however. Ray classification is based upon the observation that rays in three-space have five degrees of freedom and correspond to the points of $R^3 \times S^2$, where S^2 is the unit sphere in three-space. The algorithm proceeds by partitioning the five-dimensional space of rays into small neighborhoods, encoded as 5-D hypercubes, and associating a complete list of candidate objects with each. A hypercube represents a collection of rays with similar origins and similar directions, and its associated candidate list contains all objects which are hit by any of these rays (neglecting occlusion). To intersect a ray with the environment, we locate the hypercube which contains the 5-D equivalent of the ray and test only the objects in the associated candidate list.

Rays with a given dominant direction can be conveniently encoded as 5-tuples, (x, y, z, u, v), where the first three elements specify the origin of the ray, and the last two are the *UV* direction coordinates obtained from a face of the direction cube. Any ray in three-space can be specified by such a 5-tuple and an element of the set $\{ +X, -X, +Y, -Y, +Z, -Z \}$. If B is a 3-D box which contains the environment, then a set containing all rays which are relevant to this environment can be represented by six 'copies' of the space $B \times [-1, 1] \times [-1, 1]$. These *bounding hypercubes*, corresponding to the six dominant axes, are a basis for combined spatial and directional subdivision using a hyper-octree, a 5-D analog of an octree. The 5-D hypercubes at the leaves of the hyper-octree are assigned lists of candidate objects in direct analogy with the voxels of a 3-D spatial subdivision scheme. We find the candidate list for a given ray by converting the ray into a 5 tuple and, beginning at the root of the hyper-octree corresponding to the ray's dominant axis, traversing the tree until we find the leaf node containing that 5-tuple. The most recently accessed hypercubes can be cached in order to avoid this hierarchy traversal in most cases.

To construct the candidate lists, we observe that a 5-D hypercube represents a collection of rays which originate from a 3-D voxel and possess directions given by a single direction cell. This collection of rays sweeps out an unbounded 3-D polyhedral volume called a *beam*. See *Figure 22*. The candidate list of a hypercube must contain all objects which intersect this beam. As the nodes of the hyper-octree are subdivided, a child's candidate list can be obtained from the parent list by removing those objects which fall outside of its narrower beam. By bounding objects with convex polyhedra, the operation of comparing objects with a beam reduces to detecting polyhedral

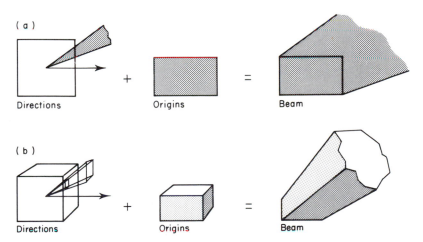

Fig. 22.   Beams in (a) 2-space and in (b) 3-space. A beam can be defined as the set sum of the direction pyramid and the voxel. That is, every point of the beam can be expressed as the vector sum of a point within the pyramid volume and a point within the voxel.

intersections. This can be solved by linear programming, for example, however Arvo and Kirk found this to be too costly. An effective alternative is to bound objects by spheres and beams by cones. The cone–sphere intersection test is only a rough approximation, but it is very fast. It is also possible to use object hierarchies for efficient creation of candidate lists. The techniques described by Dadoun and Kirkpatrick [13] for the acceleration of 'beam tracing' may be useful here.

As with the other directional techniques, the candidate lists are sorted by depth in order to most effectively apply the distance interval optimization. A difference in the ray classification approach is that only the candidate lists associated with the original bounding hypercubes need be sorted. These lists contain all the objects in the environment and the sorting is with respect to minimum object extents along the six dominant directions. All subsequent lists are derived from these by deleting entries, so the sorted order can be passed down with no additional work.

Because the hyper-octrees and associated candidate lists can potentially become very large, there are a number of important space-saving measures which can be applied. By far the most critical of these is restricting subdivision to occur only in regions of 5-space which are actually populated by rays of interest. The best way of achieving this is to subdivide only on demand, as rays are being traced. Building the entire data structure by lazy evaluation saves a vast amount of storage because the rays which are actually used occupy a very sparse subset of the rays represented by the bounding hypercubes.

Another means of saving space is to store only partial candidate lists. We can truncate a candidate list at a given distance from the beam origin and discard all of the objects which lie entirely beyond this distance. In order to complete the tracing of a ray which is not intercepted by any of the remaining objects, we 'push' the ray origin up to the truncation plane and begin anew with this ray. Carried to an extreme, this discarding of information makes the ray classification algorithm resemble non-uniform 3-D spatial subdivision with sequential traversal (see Section 5.1).

Figure 23 shows the organization of the ray classification algorithm. The notation $C(H)$ means the candidate list associated with hypercube H, and $C(H) \cap Beam(H)$ means the subset of this candidate list which intersects the beam defined by H. Another aspect of lazy evaluation is that we do not form the candidate list of any hypercube until it is actually needed. When we subdivide a hypercube into 32 children (by splitting along each of 5 axes), only one of the children receives a newly created candidate list. The others simply *inherit* (a pointer to) the parent's list. Only when these other children are visited by a ray will their candidate lists be intersected with their beams.

```
        procedure RC__Intersect( ray )
        begin
```

classification
of the ray

```
        {  p = the 5-tuple corresponding to ray;
           axis = dominant axis of ray;
           H = the leaf hypercube of hyper-octree[ axis ] containing p;
```

lazy
subdivision
& candidate
list creation

```
           if C(H) is "inherited" then C(H) = C(H) ∩ Beam(H);
           while C(H) is too large and H is not too small do begin
              partition H along each of the 5 axes;
              Let all the new children "inherit" C(H);
              H = the child hypercube which contains p;
              C(H) = C(H) ∩ Beam(H); { reclassify candidates }
           endwhile;
```

candidate
processing

```
           for each candidate in C(H) do begin { stepping in
              ascending order }
              d = projection of ray.interval.max onto axis;
              if d < candidate.min then return; { past distance interval }
              Intersect( ray, candidate );
           endfor
        end
```

Fig. 23.   An outline of the ray classification algorithm. The construction of the 5-D hierarchy is an integral part of the algorithm because it occurs as a side effect of tracing rays. Subdivision continues until the candidate list is sufficiently small, or *H* becomes too small.

6.5   Comparing the Directional Techniques

Figure 24 shows a number of important similarities and differences among the directional techniques. Only features in which there is some variation are shown. Most of the differences are a direct result of nonuniform versus uniform direction subdivision. For instance, nonuniform subdivision leads naturally toward lazy evaluation and also requires more parameters and heuristics to control it. Conversely, uniform subdivision requires few parameters and leads to very efficient look-up, but also encourages construction as a pre-processing step. Note that these are not necessarily immutable properties but merely a reflection of the initial descriptions of these algorithms. Improvements and generalizations are no doubt possible in each case.

	Light buffer	Ray coherence	Ray classification
Directions crossed with	Points (representing light sources)	Objects (including light sources)	Space (bounding environment)
Applies to	shadowing rays	all rays	all rays
When data structure is built	preprocessing	preprocessing	lazily during ray tracing
Construction of candidate list	modified scan-line algorithm	'coherence theorem' applied to pairs of objects	object classification using hierarchy of beams
Direction subdivision	uniform	uniform	nonuniform
Parameters	direction cube resolution	direction cube resolution	max tree depth, max candidates, truncation size, etc.
Candidate list look-up	direct calculation given ray direction and light source	direct calculation given ray direction and object of origin	traversal of 2-D or 5-D hierarchy and caching

Fig. 24.   Comparisons within the family of directional techniques.

7   EXPLOITING COHERENCE

Why is it that we can expect to design algorithms which perform better than exhaustive ray tracing? The answer lies in properties of the environment which are often tacitly assumed. These are properties which insure that the environment is well behaved in some sense, and are usually expressed in terms of some form of *coherence*.

Sutherland *et al.* [57] identified many types of coherence which can be exploited by hidden surface algorithms. There are four types which are commonly exploited in the context of ray tracing. Of these, *object coherence* is the most fundamental. It expresses the fact that objects tend to consist of pieces which are connected, smooth, and bounded, and that distinct objects tend to be largely disjoint in space. Objects are not typically intermingled clouds of randomly scattered fragments. *Image* (or *scene*) *coherence* is the view-dependent version of object coherence. It expresses the fact that object coherence carries over to 2-D projections of the environment. That is, we have at least the same degree of connectedness, smoothness, etc. in the image plane as existed among the original 3-D objects. *Ray coherence* means that similar rays are likely to intersect the same object in the environment. Thus, two rays which have nearly the same origin and nearly the same direction are likely to trace out similar paths through the environment, hitting the same objects in nearly the same places. This is clearly related to connectedness and smoothness properties of the objects, and is therefore another manifestation of object coherence. *Frame coherence* is essentially image coherence with an added temporal dimension. It means that the projection of an environment tends to change continuously over time. In other words, two successive 'frames' of an animation are likely to be similar if the difference in time is small. This again depends upon object coherence, but with the added property that objects (including the eye and light sources) tend not to move chaotically with time.

Spatial subdivision techniques rely heavily upon coherence, though this dependence is rarely stated explicitly. The fact that small voxels tend to intersect relatively few objects in the environment (i.e. that objects tend to be 'locally separable') is directly attributable to object coherence. This property is precisely what makes spatial subdivision work. If the candidate lists associated with voxels could not be made significantly simpler (on average) than the original environment, spatial subdivision would gain nothing over exhaustive ray tracing. In addition, other aspects of object coherence tend to lessen the impact of 'difficult' voxels. If the objects associated with a voxel are not separable by further subdivision, they will tend to intercept most rays which pierce the voxel. As a result, the penalty of large candidate lists is at least partially counterbalanced by a greater likelihood of terminating the voxel walking. Kaplan [36] observed that this compensating effect can keep the cost of ray tracing relatively insensitive to the number of objects in the environment. Though the complexity of individual voxels may increase, fewer voxels are processed per ray on average.

Ray coherence is more difficult to exploit directly than object coherence, though several approaches do so successfully. Among these are the generalized ray techniques which will be described in Section 9. These rely upon the fact that bundles of similar rays interact with the environment in a fairly uniform way, making it significantly more efficient to process them as a group than individually. As with individual rays, we can expect a narrow cone or beam to miss most of the objects in the environment. This fact allows much of the work involved in ray–environment intersection testing to be shared among many rays.

Perhaps the most direct use of ray coherence in the setting of standard ray tracing was attempted by Speer *et al.* [56]. In this approach the entire ray tree resulting from a first-generation ray is retained in order to serve as a guide for the construction of one or more subsequent ray trees. Ray coherence implies that similar first-generation rays are likely to produce similar ray trees. The problem addressed by Speer *et al.* was that of quickly identifying situations in which a ray tree will have exactly the same structure as the previous one, intersecting the same objects in the same order. If this were known *a priori*, the new tree could be constructed very efficiently from the old one, performing exactly one ray–object intersection calculation for each ray.

In the absence of such *a priori* knowledge, Speer's approach examines each ray of the new tree to determine which of them 'behaves coherently.' That is, to identify the rays which (1) hit the same object as the corresponding ray of the previous tree, and (2) do not hit any new intervening objects. The first can be verified by a direct ray–object intersection calculation. In order to quickly verify the second, each ray of the retained tree is given a cylindrical *safety zone* which is as large as possible without intersecting any objects aside from those at which the ray originates and terminates. *Figure 25(a)* shows the safety zones for a ray tree consisting of two rays. If the corresponding rays of the next tree intersect the same objects and do not pierce any of these cylinders, then no other objects need be checked. This is the case of the dashed ray in *Figure 25(a)*. If any cylinder is pierced, a more costly method is needed to find the appropriate point of intersection, and the retained ray tree must be updated with new objects and safety zones. Test results reported in [56] indicated that a large percentage of the rays can be handled in a 'coherent' manner. Unfortunately, the cost of testing and maintaining the cylindrical safety zones were found to negate the benefits of this coherence.

Hanrahan [29] achieved better success with a related method. This method also retains an entire ray tree but differs from Speer's approach in that it does not attempt to guarantee unobstructed passage from one object to the next. Instead, all objects which can possibly prevent a ray from reaching the previously hit object are identified using cones circumscribed around pairs of objects (*Figure 25(b)*) and are associated with the retained ray tree. This retained tree is used as a cache, indicating which objects are likely to be hit by each ray of a new ray tree, and also providing enough information to determine when the 'hint' fails. A cache miss occurs when the ray either misses the previously hit object or hits one of the potential blockers. When a cache miss occurs, the tree is updated and new potentially blocking objects are identified. Though the number of potential blockers may be large, requiring an equal number of ray–object intersection tests, a greater number of coherent rays are tracked and no ray–cylinder intersection checks are needed.

The directional techniques of Section 6 all exploit ray coherence in a natural way. Each algorithm constructs candidate lists which are associated with neighborhoods of similar rays, though these neighborhoods are defined

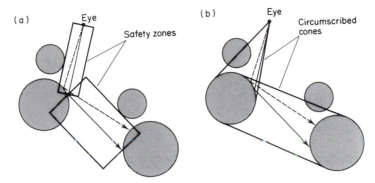

Fig. 25. Two methods of using a previous ray tree to accelerate subsequent intersection tests. In (a) cylindrical safety zones are used to determine when a new object may be hit. In (b), objects which intersect the circumscribed cones are potential blockers which cause cache misses.

differently in each case. One such collection of candidates can be efficiently shared among all the rays of a neighborhood by virtue of the fact that similar rays tend to interact with the environment similarly.

8 STATISTICAL OPTIMIZATIONS

Statistical methods have begun to play an important role in ray tracing. Cook *et al.* [10] described a stochastic sampling technique which provided a means of anti-aliasing as well as simulating effects such as motion blur, penumbrae, depth of field, and dull reflections. Kajiya's rendering equation [34] extended these ideas to simulate effects such as caustics and diffuse interreflection of light between objects. In most implementations, the color to be displayed at a single pixel can be viewed as a weighted integral of the *image function* over a neighborhood of the pixel, where the weight may be a filter for anti-aliasing [42]. Stochastic sampling serves to compute reliable estimates of these integrals via Monte Carlo integration. Naturally there is always a degree of uncertainty in such estimates, although we can produce results of arbitrarily high precision by computing the mean of a large number of samples.

To reduce the expense we wish to draw only enough samples to produce an estimate of the desired accuracy. For example, we may wish to draw the minimum number of samples which will place the estimate within 1% of the true solution with 95% confidence. For maximal efficiency we need to establish a relationship between the number of samples and the quality of the estimate without resorting to rules of thumb such as '*n* is usually enough.' If we knew the variance of the image function over each pixel *a priori*, we could pre-compute the appropriate number of samples which need to be drawn from each. Unfortunately, this type of information is very hard to produce, especially when the number of dimensions being sampled is large due to effects such as motion blur and depth of field [9]. A more practical solution is to rely upon the samples which are drawn not only to estimate the integral of the image function, but also the variance of the estimator. If the variation among the initial samples is sufficiently small, no further samples need to be drawn.

After obtaining each sample we can compute a new estimate of the true variance over the pixel. Such an estimator is itself a random variable, and its distribution is related to the chi-square distribution if we assume that the original samples are normally distributed. Lee *et al.* [42] used this fact to devise a convenient stopping criterion for the stochastic sampling process. Two parameters, T and β are used to control the quality of the image. The tolerance, T, specifies the acceptable variance of the computed pixel values, and β is the probability of stopping too early. That is, β is the probability of incorrectly inferring that the true variance is sufficiently low that the samples drawn thus far will provide a good estimate. The parameters T and β determine threshold values which are pre-computed and stored in a table. When the Nth sample is drawn, the estimated variance is incrementally updated and compared with the Nth entry in the table. If the computed value is less than the table entry, the sampling stops and the mean of the N samples is used as the pixel value. A very similar approach based on the Student t-test was described by Purgathofer[48].

9   GENERALIZED RAYS

The difficulty of anti-aliasing and exploiting coherence in ray tracing stems from its use of infinitesimally thin rays. Though the simple form of these rays leads to easy representation, efficient intersection calculations, and great generality, some of these benefits can be traded in exchange for others. One way to do this is to dispense with individual rays and, instead, operate simultaneously on entire families of rays which are bundled as beams [30], cones [1], or pencils [54]. Each of these *generalized rays* requires some type of sacrifice. For instance, we may need to impose constraints on the environment, such as restricting the types of primitive objects, or we may need to abandon the notion of 'exact' intersection calculations, accepting an approximation instead. The advantages gained in return can include faster execution, effective anti-aliasing, and even additional optical effects.

Amanatides [1] generalized rays to right circular cones which are represented by an apex, center line, and spread angle. For the purpose of anti-aliasing, the intersection calculation not only needs to detect when a cone and an object intersect, but how much of the cone is blocked by the object. A sorted list of the closest few objects which intersect the cone is required so that the partial coverages can be properly combined. For reflection and refraction, the new center line is computed using standard ray tracing techniques. The calculation of the new virtual origin and spread angle required knowledge of the surface curvature. The method of cone tracing also extends the repertoire of ray tracing to include penumbrae (from area light sources) and dull reflections. Due to the difficulty of the cone intersection and partial coverage calculation for most objects, the environment is restricted to spheres, planes, and polygons.

Kirk [38] extended the cone technique by accelerating the processing of partial intersections. The projected area of cone–sphere and cone–plane intersections can be pre-calculated for a wide range of cases and stored in a table. Using a table look-up instead of a direct calculation produces an approximate but fast partial coverage calculation. The cone area at the intersection can also be used to properly anti-alias procedural textures. The cone radius at the intersection determines the aperture size of the smallest feature which should be represented in the texture.

Heckbert and Hanrahan [30] introduced a different ray generalization in their *beam tracing* algorithm. In this approach rays are replaced by beams which are cones with arbitrary polygonal cross section. That is, a beam consists of a collection of rays which originate at a common apex and pass through some planar polygon. Note that this is different from the definition of a beam in the context of the ray classification algorithm discussed in Section 6.4. There the rays are restricted to pass through a rectangular polygon and the origins are not restricted to a single point.

The restriction placed on the environment by this algorithm is that all objects must be constructed with planar polygonal facets. This preserves the basic characteristics of beams under various interactions with the environment. For instance, the portion of a beam which continues past a partially occluding object still has polygonal cross section (*Figure 26*), as do beams which are reflected from any surface (*Figure 27*). Refraction is the one phenomenon which does not preserve the nature of beams. Because of nonlinearity, a refracted beam may no longer be a cone. One remedy is to approximate the effect of refraction with a linear transformation. This is another compromise which must be made in order to obtain the benefits of beam tracing.

Many aspects of the beam tracing algorithm are very similar to those of standard ray tracing. A *beam tree* is constructed by recursive reflection and transmission of beams, though the process of applying these operations to

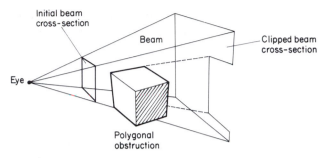

Fig. 26.   A polygonal obstruction is clipped out of the cross section of a beam. This operation can quickly lead to cross sections which are non-simple polygons (e.g. disconnected with holes).

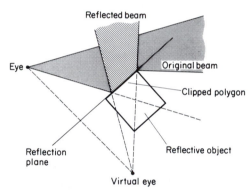

Fig. 27.   A top view of the arrangement in Fig. 26. When a reflective face is encountered by a beam, the reflected beam is formed by reflecting the original apex through the plane of the polygon, and clipping the polygon against the beam.

beams is more complex than the corresponding operations used in constructing a standard ray tree. When reflective surfaces are encountered, a 'virtual eye' point is computed by reflecting the apex of the beam through the plane of the polygon. The reflected beam has the virtual eye as its apex and its cross section is obtained by (effectively) intersecting the reflective polygon with the beam. See *Figure 27*. An important property of beams is that they can be partially occluded, whereas rays either hit an object or not. When a beam is partially occluded we 'clip out' the silhouette of the obstruction from the beam cross section and continue processing the remainder. See *Figure 26*. This clipping of the beam is a generalization of the distance interval optimization for rays. It makes it possible to avoid processing far away objects which are occluded by near ones. Heckbert and Hanrahan [30] therefore performed a sorting operation on the polygons intersected by the beam before processing them.

The beam clipping at the heart of the beam tracer requires operations on polygons similar to those described by Weiler and Atherton [64]. We must be able to subtract one polygon from another, or find their intersection, and express the result as another polygon. These operations can quickly lead to nonconvex or fragmented polygons containing holes. Because of the recursive nature of the beam tracing algorithm, the output of one such operation may become the input to another. This requires robust methods which can operate on arbitrarily complex polygons.

Beam tracing can be broken down into three basic subproblems: intersection, sorting, and clipping. Dadoun and Kirkpatrick [13] showed that all three of these can be accelerated by introducing a *hierarchical scene representation*. This data structure employs both nested convex hulls and partitioning planes, combining aspects of bounding volume hierarchies with spatial subdivision. To construct it, the environment is first recursively subdivided, top-down, using a BSP tree. As in Fuch's hidden surface algorithm [16], the partitioning planes may be selected to contain given polygons in the environment. All remaining polygons are grouped according to the two half-spaces defined by the plane, which requires splitting polygons which straddle the plane. After the BSP decomposition, we build a binary tree of nested convex hulls, bottom-up, beginning at the leaves of the BSP tree. The convex hulls at intermediate levels of the tree are constructed from the convex hulls of the two linearly separated child nodes. This operation is linear in the number of hull points, making this part of the pre-processing phase very fast. As Dadoun and Kirkpatrick [13] point out, the hierarchy thus constructed allows us to exploit convexity even in highly nonconvex environments. It can greatly accelerate beam intersection testing by rejecting objects in clusters rather than individually, which is exactly analogous to the bounding volume hierarchy techniques of Section 4.

The hierarchical scene representation is a binary tree of convex hulls separated by planar partitions. Given a beam origin, the partitions provide an efficient means of assigning a priority to the groups of enclosed objects in exactly the same way that polygons are prioritized in the BSP hidden surface algorithm [16]. This moves much of the sorting operation into the initial construction of this data structure. The recursive traversal algorithm shown in *Figure 12* is based upon the same principle and requires little modification to be applicable in this context. The result is similar to that achieved by the algorithm of Kay and Kajiya shown in *Figure 9*. Hierarchically nested convex hulls are examined in the order in which they are encountered by the beam.

To further accelerate the beam–hull intersection testing, Dadoun and Kirkpatrick [13] augment the beam and each convex hull of the hierarchy with an *outer sequence* [12]. This is a nested sequence of successively large and simpler convex polyhedra which are formed by removing bounding half-spaces. Given two polyhedra with n and m hull points, respectively, if both are augmented by an outer sequence the intersection test can be done in $O(\log(m) + \log(n))$ time [12].

A pencil is another type of generalized ray. It is comprised of rays which are in the vicinity of a special ray called the *axial ray*. Each of these nearby *paraxial* rays can be represented as a 4-D vector encoding its deviation from the axial ray. Shinya *et al.* [54] used techniques from paraxial approximation theory to determine how these pencils interact with surfaces encountered in an environment, viewing it as an optical system. By restricting attention to small deviations from the axial ray, the pencil transformations could be assumed to be linear, and therefore representable as 4×4 *system matrices*. Propagation of rays grouped as pencils could then be carried out by combining the system matrices corresponding to the individual surfaces. The approximation is only valid for sufficiently smooth surfaces, however, so it can only be applied to pencils which do not encounter edges or surface discontinuities. Shinya *et al.* traced individual rays in the areas which posed these problems.

10 OPTIMIZATIONS FOR CSG

Using the method of CSG (Constructive Solid Geometry), solid objects are represented by combining primitive solids with the boolean set operators *intersection* (&), *union* (+), and *difference* (−). One way to generate shaded images from a CSG model is to generate a boundary surface representation from the model and then render those surfaces using some hidden-surface algorithm. In contrast, ray tracing can generate images of CSG models by intersecting rays directly with the CSG tree. A straightforward method for intersecting rays with CSG trees is to 'classify' each ray against the CSG tree, determining the intervals along the ray which intersect the solid. Roth [50] described this process as a recursive walk down the tree structure, intersecting the ray with each primitive in the tree, and combining the resultant intervals on the way back up the tree.

This algorithm can be accelerated by the use of object bounding volumes. Roth [50] discussed the application of 2-D box and 3-D sphere bounding volumes in this manner and reported a factor-of-two speed-up. The 2-D box aids in the first-generation rays only, but the sphere may be used for other rays as well. In addition, the ray distance interval optimization described in Section 4 can be used to eliminate some CSG subtrees from consideration.

Gervautz [19] used both of these techniques and also applied 3-D bounding boxes within the tree to reduce the number of ray/primitive intersection checks.

It is possible to reduce the number of intersections by using known characteristics of the CSG operators. In the case of union (+), the tree can be rearranged without affecting the root object. Gervautz [19] pointed out that this can be advantageous in terms of reducing the size of aggregate bounding volumes. One can also take advantage of potential subtree elimination with the ' – ' and '&' operators [50]. For instance, in the combination 'A–B,' if the ray does not intersect 'A,' there is no value in checking the 'B' subtree for intersection with the ray, since it cannot affect the outcome.

Since the process of ray–CSG tree intersection is recursive, it is advantageous to reduce the overhead typically associated with recursion, such as procedure calls and dynamic memory allocation [50]. Unfortunately, the organization of the task is such that the classification and combination of intervals must be performed independently for each ray, regardless of any coherence which exists. Also, the entire set of 1-D ray intervals must be computed since it is not known *a priori* which will be the closest. The classification, which is essentially a depth sorting operation, must be performed on all of the intervals. Atherton [4] proposed using a hybrid scan-line/ray tracing algorithm to solve this problem. The primitives in the CSG tree are decomposed into polygonal approximations, and a Y–X–Z scan-line algorithm is applied. Spans are maintained which represent simplifications of the original CSG tree. At each pixel, the CSG problem is only solved for the first intersection.

Bronsvoort *et al.* [5] described an alternative way to utilize the coherence properties of scan-line algorithms. The ray-bounding volume check described by Roth [50] is replaced by a point/scan-line interval test. At each scan line, only part of the CSG tree may contribute to the image. It is possible, therefore, to maintain an *active subtree* of the CSG tree which is analogous to the active polygon list in a typical scan-line algorithm. This greatly reduces the complexity of the ray–CSG tree intersection which must be performed. Maintaining a list of intervals instead of a hierarchy of bounding boxes is more efficient because the intervals represent a tighter bound. The performance improvement is lessened due to the extra cost of computing and sorting the intervals. A greater gain is realized by the simplification of the CSG tree which can be performed.

Gervautz [19] also created 'temporary' active subtrees to accelerate the ray tracing process. The subtrees for first-generation rays are created by projecting the bounding volumes of primitive objects onto the view plane and maintaining a quadtree structure. Each pixel in the quadtree can be associated with those objects which penetrate it. In order to accelerate the tracing of shadowing rays, another quadtree can be generated for a projection plane from a point light source. For other rays (reflection and transparent), an octree was used. The CSG object tree must be quite complicated before the savings in ray tracing time are negated by the cost of constructing the subtrees, particularly in the octree case.

Youssef [71] described a variation of CSG in which the objects are restricted to interval representations in some coordinate space. Examples of such objects are boxes in Cartesian coordinates, spheres in spherical coordinates, and cylinders in cylindrical coordinates. Aggregate objects are constructed by combining the coordinate spaces using the union (+) or subtraction (–) operators. Intersection (&) is not provided. The process of ray tracing is carried out by tracing rays through the *coordinate volumes* in which the objects are represented. This approach is most effective when representing many regularly spaced similar objects, such as bricks in a wall.

Wyvill *et al.* [68] also considered the use of an octree to subdivide space. Within each voxel of the octree, the space can be classified with respect to the solid represented by the CSG tree (or DAG). The possible classifications are: (1) full (completely contained within some solid); (2) empty (completely outside all solids); (3) contains boundaries between empty space and one primitive object; (4) contains boundaries between full space and one subtracted primitive object; (5) volume is below some minimum size threshold.

Cases (1)–(4) are straightforward to ray trace directly, but case (5) is more complex. In their early paper [66], Wyvill and Kunii labeled these voxels as 'nasty cells' and either ignored them or colored them black. In [68] each of the voxels in case (5) is represented as a pruned CSG subtree which contains only those primitives which are present in that voxel. The subtrees are constructed as part of the process of generating the octree. The full CSG tree is traversed, subdividing each primitive into its component octree voxels. The different octree structures are then combined according to the CSG operators linking them together. The CSG tree simplification is implicit in this process in which only relevant primitives ever appear in a given voxel. In the process of ray tracing, the octree structure is traversed and only those subtrees which are encountered are intersected with the rays. This simplification of a CSG tree into smaller subtrees is a theme which recurs in almost all of the approaches for ray tracing acceleration in the context of CSG.

Fujimoto *et al.* [18] described a similar approach, but used the SEADS approach described in Section 5.2. The task of filling this data structure was performed by a pre-processor termed B-COM, for 'boolean compiler.' The B-COM classified voxels as being either *homo* or *hetero*. The homo case corresponds to cases (1) and (2) from [68], and the hetero case corresponds to cases (3), (4) and (5). In the process of tracing rays, all homo voxels can be ignored and rays need only be intersected with the contents of hetero voxels which the ray pierces. Fujimoto's results indicate that SEADS outperforms the octree method if the pre-processing time is ignored.

Arnaldi *et al.* [2] also described a voxel structure within which simplified CSG subtrees can be used to accelerate ray intersection calculations. The structure is hierarchical but not regular. The image plane is divided into parallelepiped cells which closely surround projections of the primitive objects. These cells are constructed around the bounding boxes of the primitives and intermediate nodes. Some minimization of the bounding boxes at the intermediate intersection (&) nodes is possible by computing the intersections of the bounding boxes. A Binary Space Partitioning (BSP) algorithm is used to perform the subdivision and classification of bounding boxes with respect to the voxels.

After the 2-D partitioning has been performed, each resulting frustrum is subdivided in depth to generate a stack of frustra. This presents some difficulty in determining which voxel is a neighbor when a ray passes from one column of voxels to another. To accelerate the voxel walking, a set of pointers is maintained to express the connectivity. The adjacency is expensive to compute, but the cost can be reduced by calculating it as subdivision proceeds and updating it continuously. Tracing first-generation rays is efficient because each ray traverses a single column. Other rays are much more costly due to the added expense of calculating the neighbor across columns.

The main optimization which underlies all of the approaches for accelerating ray tracing of CSG is to subdivide space and pre-process or compile the CSG structure into the spatial hierarchy. Subtrees of the main CSG tree can be generated for individual spatial hierarchy nodes by intersecting the volume of the node (or voxel) with the CSG tree. This process allows the ray tracer to take advantage of the coherence present due to the locality of primitives.

11 PARALLELIZATION AND VECTORIZATION

Acceleration of ray tracing can also be achieved by performing some of the operations concurrently. Several approaches to this have been attempted, including: (1) vectorization; (2) execution on a collection of general-purpose computers; (3) execution on a general-purpose multicomputer; and (4) custom special-purpose hardware.

In addition, a number of parallel algorithms have been developed which are broadly applicable. We will discuss the different classes independently, progressing in roughly chronological order. Approach (2), execution on a collection of general-purpose computers, has not really been directly addressed in any research, although it clearly has a place in this taxonomy. Although we will not explicitly discuss this case, it is interesting to note that many of the special-purpose architectures are described in terms of simulated performance on one or more general-purpose computers.

11.1 Vectorization

Max [43] organized a restricted procedural ray tracer for the vectorizing compiler on a Cray-1 supercomputer. The procedural model rendered ocean waves and islands. The waves are represented as a height field constructed from superimposed traveling sine waves. The islands are also represented as height fields composed of elliptical paraboloids with superimposed cosine terms to give rolling hills. First-generation rays are traced against the water and islands, as are up to two reflections from the water. No shadow rays are traced, although island surfaces which face away from the light source (sun) are considered to be in shadow. This relatively uniform organization allows the ray tracing to be vectorized more efficiently.

The ocean height field points which are relevant for a given scan line are bounded by an ellipse. Using this bound, only a subset of the possible points must be generated. The set of points is passed through a depth-buffer to determine the visible points. The first-generation rays are processed as a vector, and the resulting shading calculations are also vectorized. Similarly, those rays which are reflected are gathered into smaller vectors to be processed as a unit.

Plunket and Bailey [49] described a more general implementation of ray tracing on a CDC Cyber 205. The task is organized to trace a list of rays sequentially against all of the surfaces in the scene. The list accumulates until it is large enough to be traced, and each ray is considered concurrently and totally independently. In other words, there is no advantage taken of coherence between rays. A simple implementation of vectorized ray tracing was described as follows.

While there are still unfinished pixels:

(1) Add first-generation, reflection, and shadowing rays to the queue until it is full.
(2) Intersect the entire queue of rays with each surface in the scene using vector code.
(3) Determine the visible surface for each ray using CSG evaluation techniques.
(4) Spawn additional rays for modeling special effects and add these to the queue.
(5) Determine the intensity of pixels which have complete visible surface calculations.

This algorithm is necessarily more complex than the scalar version since more than one pixel is being processed at the same time. An additional problem is that given that CSG operations are going to be performed based on the intersection distances, the results of processing the queue must include enough information to resolve the CSG tree. The storage space required for results is proportional to the product of the number of rays and the number of objects. This conflicts with the desire to make the vector queue as long as possible to most effectively use the vector capabilities. A compromise is to process rays in groups of 500.

The process of traversing the CSG tree is also vectorized because the time spent in this operation becomes significant once the intersection calculations are vectorized. Vectorizing the tree traversal requires that the tree be traversed in the same order for all rays and therefore precludes the subtree simplifications of many other CSG algorithms. Though more arithmetic operations are required in the vectorized organization, there is a net gain in performance due to the absolute speed of the vector processing.

11.2   Special-purpose Hardware

An example of special purpose ray tracing hardware is the LINKS-1 multicomputer [46]. This is a rare specimen among special-purpose rendering architectures because it has actually been built and is in operation generating ray traced images. LINKS-1 is similar to the vectorized approaches in that each ray is traced concurrently and independently. The LINKS-1 architecture consists of 64 *node computers* interconnected with a single controlling root computer. The root computer can dynamically reconfigure the organization of the node computers, using them in parallel, as a pipeline, or in any combination. Communication between node computers is achieved through an *intercomputer memory swapping unit*, which is a device for transferring large amounts of data between node computers.

Each node computer consists of a Zilog Z8001 control processor (CU), an Intel 8086/8087 arithmetic processor (APU), 1 Mbyte of local memory, and is attached to two intercomputer memory swapping units (IMSU). The APU operates as a slave of the CU. Each node computer N(i) is connected to its nearest neighbor N($i + 1$) by an IMSU. It is also connected to the root computer via another IMSU. These connections allow rapid swapping of data between processors.

The process of ray tracing on the LINKS-1 is described as a pipelined sequence of object sorting, ray tracing, and shading. The node computers can be configured as a set of parallel pipelines to render a sequence of images. It is assumed that each pipeline retains the entire world database, and rays are distributed among different pipelines. Timings for execution of such a configuration provided parallel utilization of up to 65%, largely because of the ray tracing component of the pipe which is kept busy. However, the first and third stages of the pipe (object sorting and shading, respectively) are often kept waiting.

While the LINKS architecture duplicates the entire database and distributes rays, Kobayashi *et al.* [41] proposed a parallel machine in which the database is distributed over a set of intersection processors (IPs). Each IP receives only a portion of the world which corresponds to spatial subdivision and rays are passed from one processor to another as they are propagated through space. A host computer generates the initial viewing rays and distributes them to the appropriate IP based on the ray direction. Each IP checks its rays for intersection with its objects and passes on the rays which do not intersect anything. Each IP is also responsible for calculation of the next IP. Rays which do intersect an object are passed to a network of shading processors (SP) which resolve the ray tree and generate final pixel colors.

The space bounding the environment is subdivided using an octree. To ease the problem of stepping between voxels of varying size, a quadtree is maintained on each voxel face to keep track of the neighbors. The octree is first generated based on the distribution of objects, and then the *face-neighbor quadtree* is constructed. This method was termed an *adaptive division graph*. The resulting space was mapped onto a 6-D hypercube computer, allowing nearest-neighbor communication for face-adjacent voxels of identical size. Due to the sixfold connectivity of a hypercube, neighbors at different levels of the octree are also close in terms of the number of message hops. Timing results were presented for a 512×512 image, ignoring the time for constructing the subdivided space. The ray tracing time for environments containing between 1 and 4096 objects was found to be almost constant. The performance for the adaptive division graph appeared to be better than both regular grid subdivision and a normal octree without the quadtree face-neighbor structure.

Dippé and Swenson [15] also described an adaptive subdivision algorithm and a parallel architecture for ray tracing. The world was initially subdivided into a regular grid in three dimensions, which was mapped on to a hypothetical 3-D array of processors. Viewing rays are generated by the processor responsible for the region containing the eye, and are propagated to other processors based on their paths. The load at each processor, defined as the product of the number of rays to and the number of objects, was used as a metric for redistribution of objects and rays. The redistribution was achieved by relaxing the requirements of regularity and reshaping the voxels. Several different geometries for the voxels were discussed, including orthogonal parallelepipeds, general cubes, and tetrahedra.

The orthogonal case was dismissed because it does not allow for local redistribution. A local redistribution request forces other regions to shift regardless of the utility of shifting them. Tetrahedra were also dismissed since they can too easily become inappropriately shaped for bounding objects. The case of general cubes was used for most of the discussion. General cubes or loosely termed hexahedra are regions with six (possibly non-planar) faces, six neighbors, and eight vertices. Loads are transferred between regions when a processor determines that its load is greater than its neighbors by more than a fixed threshold. The shift was accomplished by moving one vertex and then reshuffling the objects and rays based on the new region shape.

A proposed implementation of this mechanism would have a 3-D array of autonomous computers, which communicate by passing messages. Computers on the edge would be connected to frame buffers, disks and other peripherals. A preliminary analysis of the performance of the algorithm suggests an upper bound of $O(S^{2/3})$, where S is the number of processors. A problem which arises when load is transferred by moving a vertex is that eight regions are affected. In order to do well with this redistribution, we must efficiently determine which vertex to move by how much and in what direction. This is a nontrivial problem. Also, in order to redistribute objects, we must intersect them with the boundaries of these general cubes, and intersect rays with them.

Nemoto and Omachi [45] attempted to address some of these problems. They simulated a similar 3-D processor grid using a simpler redistribution algorithm. The basis of the approach was to subdivide space using a regular grid structure (Fujimoto *et al.* [18]) and distribute the voxels to different processors. Each processor generates a portion of the viewing rays and passes them to the appropriate processor for intersection checking. Rays are propagated efficiently between processors using a variant of Fujimoto's 3DDDA. The redistribution was performed only along one axis. It was determined which axis had the most variation in number of objects and the boundaries of the voxels were allowed to 'slide' along this 'driving axis.' Redistribution occurred when the load, defined as running time/idle time was determined to be above a given threshold compared to the neighbors along the driving axis. The object intersection with the new boundaries was a simple plane intersection check, and ray propagation was only slightly complicated from the normal 3DDDA case. After the 3DDDA step, an adjustment might have to be made along the driving axis to find the correct voxel.

This method achieved far greater efficiency in tracing rays and speed of load balancing at the cost of less effective load balancing. A software simulation of this algorithm operating on a 1, 8, 64, and 512 processor version of this architecture showed reasonable performance improvements when redistribution was used, as compared to a normal 3-D grid spatial subdivision. The measurements indicated very near linear performance increases for multiple processors, when the scene complexity was high.

Cleary *et al.* [7] independently analyzed the performance of ray tracing with 2-D and 3-D space subdivisions on multiprocessor systems. No attempt was made at load balancing, but a detailed performance analysis was offered. The analysis was performed for an empty scene, assuming that the intersection times for real scenes would scale down with larger numbers of processors. The upper bound for the speedup of a 3-D network was given as $N^{2/3}$, and for a 2-D network varied from N to $N^{1/2}$ as the number of processors increased. The conclusion was that given a small number of processors, a 2-D spatial subdivision may be more efficient. Simulation was performed for a number of processors varying from 1 to 10 000, and a number of objects varying from 1 to 8.

Ullner [60] examined the mathematics involved in the actual task of intersecting rays with objects, specifically convex quadrilaterals. A ray tracing peripheral was described which used special purpose hardware to intersect the environment of polygons with each ray. This task was decomposed into three stages: fetching each polygon, computing the distance to the point of intersection (if one exists), and comparing these distances to find the nearest one. These three stages can be pipelined and each stage can be further pipelined and parallelized. Exhaustive ray tracing was performed using one or more of these peripherals. The performance of one of these theoretical devices was quite impressive (for 1983), being able to compute a new ray–polygon intersection every $1/3$ microsecond once the pipe was full. This is comparable to the speed of a CRAY-1 supercomputer. It would thus be able to exhaustively ray trace an anti-aliased 512×512 image containing 1000 polygons in approximately 10 minutes.

Ullner also observed that a 3-D regular grid subdivision could be applied, producing commensurate performance improvements. This additional intelligence of walking voxels and retrieving only a subset of polygons is beyond the scope of the original hardware and requires an additional processor. This processor uses the voxel data structure to determine which polygons may potentially intersect the ray, and passes them to the pipeline containing the ray. Using a test scene of 1000 polygons, Ullner's simulation achieved optimal results with a grid of approximately $11 \times 11 \times 11$ voxels. Other test scenes produced similar results.

Another parallel hardware approach suggested by Ullner involved massive use of VLSI circuits. A relatively slow (5 ms/intersection) ray–polygon intersection processor could be implemented on a chip. A large scale machine could be constructed by stringing together a large number of such chips in a pipeline.

A more practical solution, also described by Ullner, is to use a 2-D grid of special purpose intersection processors to implement the 3-D regular grid subdivision described above. In order to balance the load more evenly between these processors, it was suggested that the voxels can be shifted so that a given processor is responsible for a stairstep pattern of voxels, instead of a slab.

11.3   General-purpose Multicomputers

Goldsmith and Salmon [22] described an actual implementation of a ray tracer on a hypercube. A hypercube is a multicomputer with 2^N processors connected with the topology of an N-dimensional hypercube. Messages are passed between processors via these connections and it may require several hops to get from one processor to another. An important property of the hypercube topology is that no more than N hops are ever required to pass a message from one processor to another. Thus, in a hypercube of dimension 5, there are 32 processors, each of which is directly connected to 5 other processors, and the most widely separated processors are a 'distance' of 5 hops apart. Frequently the message passing speed is much slower than the processing speed, so it is important to minimize interprocess communication. In Goldsmith's approach, first-generation rays are treated as being completely independent and are distributed among the processors of the hypercube with no interaction between rays. Therefore, rays traced on one processor do not affect the outcome of rays traced on any other processor.

Two basic methods are described in [22]. One involves replicating the entire database and distributing rays, while the other involves partitioning the database among the processors and distributing the rays. In the first method, assuming that the entire database is replicated in each processor, one must decide on the optimal distribution of rays between processors. A scattered decomposition is preferred because it balances the load of sparse and difficult pixels among the processors. A disadvantage is that in anti-aliasing, the nearest neighbors are important and are not readily available in the scattered decomposition. Therefore, it is reasonable to switch from a scattered to a regular decomposition after the intersections have been computed.

In the second method, a bounding volume hierarchy is distributed among multiple processors. Each processor maintains the top few levels of the hierarchy, but the lower (larger) structures are distributed among the processors. Each processor maintains the following data structures: (1) its subset of the pixel array; (2) the top of the bounding volume hierarchy (known to all processors); (3) one or more subtrees of the hierarchy (private to this processor); (4) the database for the background (known to all processors).

This method is reasonable assuming that the communication time does not overwhelm the actual computation. Because of the hypercube connection scheme, the time to communicate between two processors is proportional to the number of bits which differ between the processor numbers. Therefore, the average time can be reduced by duplicating subtrees into processors whose ids are 1's complements of each other. If each subtree connection chooses the nearest neighbor of the two, the average communication time is cut in half.

Another potential optimization described by Goldsmith and Salmon [22] is that the load between processors can be adaptively balanced by processors which complete early and request additional work. However, this increases communication requirements and could actually degrade performance. This approach was not implemented, so there are no results to indicate its effectiveness.

12   COMBINING OPTIMIZATIONS

The spatial subdivision methods described in Section 5 simply change one large problem into many small problems which are typically handled by exhaustive ray tracing. This needn't be the case. Bounding volumes may still be appropriate within voxels, as well as virtually any other optimization technique. Because there may be a large number of these reduced problems, and more than one may be encountered per ray, the start-up overhead and space requirements of the techniques applied to them must be minimal. A number of recent contributions have addressed the idea of combining several acceleration techniques to gain some of the benefits of each. By constructing a hierarchy comprised of several different techniques, the performance can be superior to that of any individual technique.

Snyder and Barr [55] compared the performance of uniform 3-D spatial subdivision, octree-based nonuniform subdivision, bounding volume hierarchies, and lists of primitive objects. They observed that for large numbers of homogeneously distributed objects of similar scale, a regular grid outperforms octree methods due to the efficiency of voxel walking. In the event that the primitive objects are not all of the same scale or are unevenly distributed, the regular divisions become costly. A compromise involves defining an object abstraction which allows primitive objects, regular 3-D grids, and lists to be handled similarly. This is achieved by defining a C-language structure for these objects in which a representation of any one of these constructs may be stored. Each of the elements of the environment hierarchy may be one of these objects. In this way the environment can be constructed from a hierarchy of regular 3-D grids, lists and primitive objects. Through instancing, this allowed Snyder and Barr to render environments containing billions of objects.

Scherson and Caspary [52] described a similar mechanism. By analyzing the complexity of ray tracing several environments, they were able to identify some general situations in which octrees are likely to outperform bounding volume hierarchies, and other cases in which the reverse is true. They concluded that octrees performed well in cases where the the first intersection was likely to be found near the perimeter of the environment, before many voxels had been processed. The costs associated with fragmentation (objects appearing in more than one voxel) and voxel walking diminished effectiveness if most of the intersections were found deep within the environment. In the latter case, bounding volume hierarchies were found to be superior. Scherson and Caspary found that a compromise between these methods was effective. They created a hybrid structure in which the top levels of the hierarchy are formed by octree spatial subdivision while the lower levels consist of bounding volume hierarchies. The method described by Kay and Kajiya [37] was used in the latter case.

Glassner [21] developed a different approach which combines advantages of both bounding volume hierarchies and nonuniform spatial subdivision. Glassner observed that bounding volumes can offer tight bounds but usually produce hierarchies in which the volumes overlap, thereby decreasing overall efficiency. On the other hand, nonuniform spatial subdivision produces hierarchies in which the volumes are disjoint, though they do not provide tight object bounds. By using nonuniform space subdivision to guide the construction of a bounding volume hierarchy, volumes can be selected which are both tight fitting and disjoint. This is done by top-down construction of an octree followed by a bottom-up construction of bounding volumes based on the plane-set approach of Kay and Kajiya [37]. Each bounding volume is chosen to tightly enclose only the portions of the objects which are within each voxel. The bounding volumes are therefore guaranteed to be disjoint because they are contained within disjoint voxels. This is quite similar to the approach described by Dadoun and Kirkpatrick [13] for constructing a hierarchical scene representation. Glassner also generalized this technique to four dimensions representing space-time in order to accelerate the creation of animated sequences complete with motion blur. Instead of ray tracing objects which are moving in 3-D space, the technique processes static objects in 4-D space-time.

A very general mechanism for combining optimizations was described by Kirk and Arvo [39]. In their approach, acceleration techniques are encapsulated in such a way that they present essentially the same interface as procedurally defined primitive objects. That is, an acceleration technique becomes an *aggregate object* which is responsible for computing ray intersections with a collection of subordinate objects, or children. The children may include other aggregate objects as well as primitive objects. By adhering to a uniform procedural interface among all primitive and aggregate objects, it is possible to create *meta hierarchies* consisting of any number of diverse algorithms including octrees, uniform grids, bounding volume hierarchies, and directional techniques. Though the nesting of different techniques through this mechanism carries additional costs which might be avoided by special-purpose implementations, Kirk and Arvo found that its flexibility allowed easy experimentation and proved to be effective in constructing and rendering environments containing millions of objects.

13 FUTURE DIRECTIONS

As mentioned at the outset, there is currently a lack of meaningful quantitative comparisons among acceleration techniques. A fertile area for future research is to provide quantitative techniques for performing such analysis. This will require more sophisticated statistical tools which can accurately predict average case behavior in very complex environments. Such tools may also provide an important ingredient for more intelligent algorithms which are 'self-tuning' and can adjust to the local complexity of the environment. This may prove to be the next logical step beyond automatic construction of bounding volume hierarchies. Goldsmith and Salmon's [23] work has provided an excellent start in terms of characterizing how well a given hierarchy will perform. They also achieved good results without resorting to an exhaustive search of all of the possibilities. Perhaps methods such as simulated annealing [40] can be applied in more complex settings to achieve similar results.

New areas of research such as directional techniques have only begun to be investigated. Thus far these techniques have improved performance only at the cost of greatly increased storage requirements. More investigation is needed to determine if this is an inherent shortcoming or merely a drawback of the particular implementations which have been explored. Storage reduction may be achievable through hybrid algorithms which combine features of directional techniques with bounding volume hierarchies or spatial subdivision techniques.

The rendering equation [34] poses new problems for acceleration. Since the role of ray tracing in the solution of the rendering equation involves random walks, many of the acceleration techniques will fail to take advantage of environment coherence. Efficient solution will require new variance reduction techniques which can characterize the energy balance in the environment and increase the statistical efficiency of the random paths which are traced. Conversely, the use of techniques which rely heavily on ray coherence can be extended to have a wider application to acceleration. Generalized rays such as cones [1, 38], beams [13, 30] and pencils [54] can be used to characterize sets of rays before application of other techniques.

Another opportunity exists in the area of parallelization and concurrent execution of ray tracing. The only approaches which have made efficient use of multiple processors to date have distributed first-generation rays to different processors, each supplied with a complete copy of the environment. This is unreasonable for extremely complex environments and wasteful of coherence information which could further accelerate the process. Algorithms which utilize multiple processors yet minimize both storage and communication requirements need to be developed.

ACKNOWLEDGMENTS

We wish to thank Christian Bremser, John Francis, Semyon Nisenzon, Ken Severson, Cary Scofield, and in particular Douglas Voorhies for their assistance in preparing this paper.

REFERENCES

1. Amanatides, J., Ray tracing with cones. *Comput. Graph.* **18**(3), 129–135, July 1984.
2. Arnalldi, B., Priol, T. and Bouatouch, K., A new space subdivision method for ray tracing CSG modelled scenes. *The Visual Computer*, Springer-Verlag, Vol. 3, pp. 98–108, 1987.
3. Arvo, J. and Kirk, D., Fast ray tracing by ray classification. *Comput. Graph.* **21**(4), 55–64, July 1987.
4. Atherton, P., A scan-line hidden surface removal procedure for constructive solid geometry. *Comput. Graph.* **17**(3), 73–82, July 1983.
5. Bronsvoort, W.F., van Wijk, J.J. and Jansen, F.W., Two methods for improving the efficiency of ray casting in solid modeling. *Comput. Aided Design* **16**, 51–55, 1984.
6. Clark, J.H., Hierarchical geometric models for visible surface algorithms. *Commun. ACM* **19**(10), 547–554, October 1976.
7. Clearly, J.G., Wyvill, B.M., Birtwistle, G.M. and Vatti, R., Multiprocessor ray tracing. *Comput. Graph. For.* **5**, 3–12, 1985.
8. Cohen, M.F., and Greenberg, D.P., The hemi-cube: a radiosity solution for complex environments. *Comput. Graph.* **19**(3), 31–41, July 1985.
9. Cook, R.L., Porter, T. and Carpenter, L., Distributed ray tracing. *Comput. Graph.* **18**(3), 137–145, July 1984.
10. Cook, R.L., Stochastic sampling in computer graphics. *ACM Trans. Graph* **5**(1), January 1986.
11. Coquillart, S., An improvement of the ray-tracing algorithm. *Proceedings Eurographics '85* (ed. C.E. Vandoni), Elsevier (North-Holland), pp. 77–88, 1985.
12. Dobkin, D.P. and Kirkpatrick, D.G., Fast detection of polyhedral intersection. *Theor. Comput. Sci.* **17**, 241–253, 1983.
13. Dadoun, N. and Kirkpatrick, D.G., The geometry of beam tracing. *Proc. of the Symposium on Computational Geometry*, pp. 55–61, June 1985.
14. Dippe, M. and Swensen, J., An adaptive subdivision algorithm and parallel

architecture for realistic image synthesis. *Comput. Graph.* **18**(3), 149–158, July 1984.

15. Dippe, M. and Wold, E.H., Antialiasing through stochastic sampling. *Comput. Graph.* **19**(3), 69–78, July 1985.

16. Fuchs, H., On visible surface generation by a priori tree structures. *Comput. Graph.* **14**(3), 124–133, July 1980.

17. Fujimoto, A., Tanaka, T. and Iwata, K., ARTS: Accelerated Ray-Tracing System. *IEEE Comput. Graph. Appl.* **6**(4), 16–26, April 1986.

18. Fujimoto, A., Perrott, C.G. and Iwata, K., Environment for fast elaboration of constructive solid geometry. *Adv. Comput. Graph.* (Proc. of Computer Graphics Tokyo '86), 20–32, April, 1986.

19. Gervautz, M., Three improvements of the ray tracing algorithm for CSG trees. *Computers and Graphics* **10**(4), 333–339, 1986.

20. Glassner, A.S., Space subdivision for fast ray tracing. *IEEE Comput. Graph. Appl.* **4**(10), 15–22, October 1984.

21. Glassner, A.S., Spacetime ray tracing for animation. *IEEE Comput. Graph. Appl.* **8**(3), 60–70, March 1988.

22. Goldsmith, J. and Salmon, J., A ray tracing system for the hypercube. Caltech Concurrent Computing Project Memorandum HM154, California Institute of Technology, 1985.

23. Goldsmith, J. and Salmon, J., Automatic creation of object hierarchies for ray tracing. *IEEE Comput. Graph. Appl.* **7**(5), 14–20, May 1987.

24. Goldstein, R.A. and Nagel, R., 3-D visual simulation. *Simulation* **16**(1), 25–31, January 1971.

25. Haines, E.A. and Greenberg, D.P., The light buffer: a shadow testing accelerator. *IEEE Comput. Graph. Appl.* **6**(9), 6–16, September 1986.

26. Haines, E., A proposal for standard graphics environments. *IEEE Comput. Graph. Appl.* **7**(11) 3–5, November 1987.

27. Hall, R.A. and Greenberg, D.P., A testbed for realistic image synthesis. *IEEE Comput. Graph. Appl.* **3**(10), 10–20, November 1983.

28. Hanrahan, P., Ray tracing algebraic surfaces. *Comput. Graph.* **17**(3), 83–89, July 1983.

29. Hanrahan, P., Using caching and breadth-first search to speed up ray-tracing, *Proc. of Graphics Interface '86*, Vancouver, B.C., 56–61, May 1986.

30. Heckbert, P.S. and Hanrahan, P., Beam tracing polygonal objects. *Comput. Graph.* **18**(3), 119–127, July 1984.

31. Jansen, F.W., Data structures for ray tracing. In *Data Structures for Raster Graphics*, *Proceedings Workshop* (eds L.R.A. Kessener, F.J. Peters, M.L.P. Lierop) pp. 57–73, Eurographics Seminars, Springer Verlag, 1986.

32. Joy, K.I. and Bhetanabhotla, M.N., Ray tracing parametric surface patches utilizing numerical techniques and ray coherence. *Comput. Graph.* **20**(4), 279–285, August 1986.

33. Kajiya, J.T., New techniques for ray tracing procedurally defined objects. *Comput. Graph.* **17**(3), 91–102, July 1983.

34. Kajiya, J.T., The rendering equation. *Comput. Graph.* **20**(4), 143–150, August 1986.

35. Kaplan, M.R., Space tracing a constant time ray tracer. State of the Art in Image Synthesis (Siggraph '85 Course Notes), Vol. 11, July 1985.

36. Kaplan, M.R., The use of spatial coherence in ray tracing. In *Techniques for Computer Graphics* (eds David F. Rogers and Rae A. Earnshaw), Springer-Verlag, New York, 1987.

37. Kay, T.L., and Kajiya, J., Ray tracing complex scenes. *Comput. Graph.* **20**(4), 269–278, August 1986.

38. Kirk, D.B., The simulation of natural features using cone tracing. *The Visual Computer*, Springer-Verlag, Vol. 3, No. 2, pp. 63–71, 1987.

39. Kirk, D. and Arvo, J., The ray tracing kernel. *Proc. of Ausgraph '88*, Melbourne, Australia, pp. 75–82, July 1988.

40. Kirkpatrick, S., Gelatt, Jr., C.D., and Vecchi, M.P., Optimization by simulated annealling. *Science* **220**, 671–680, 13 May 1983.

41. Kobayashi, H., Nakamura, T. and Shigei, Y., Parallel processing of an object space for image synthesis using ray tracing. *The Visual Computer*, Springer-Verlag, Vol. 3, No. 1, pp. 13–22, 1987.

42. Lee, M., Redner, R.A. and Uselton, S.P., Statistically optimized sampling for distributed ray tracing. *Comput. Graph.* **19**(3), 61–67, July 1985.

43. Max, N.L., Vectorized procedural models for natural terrain: waves and islands in the sunset. *Comput. Graph.* **15**(3), 317–324, August 1981.

44. Muller, H., Imge generation by space sweep. *Comput. Graph. For.* **5**, 189–196, 1986.

45. Nemoto, K. and Omachi, T., An adaptive subdivision by sliding boundary surfaces. *Proc. of Graphics Interface '86*, Vancouver, B.C., pp. 43–48, May 1986.

46. Nishimura, H., Ohno, H., Kawata, T., Shirakawa, I. and Omura, K., LINKS-1: a parallel pipelined multimicrocomputer system for image creation. *Proc. of the 10th Symposium on Computer Architecture*, SIGARCH, pp. 387–394, 1983.

47. Ohta, M. and Maekawa, M., Ray coherence theorem and constant time ray tracing algorithm. *Computer Graphics 1987* (Proc. of CG International '87) (ed. T.L. Kunni), pp. 303–314.

48. Purgathofer, W., A statistical method for adaptive stochastic sampling, *Proc. Eurographics '86* (ed. A.A.G. Requicha), Elsevier (North-Holland), pp. 145–152. 1986.

49. Plunkett, D.J. and Bailey, M.J., The vectorization of a ray-tracing algorithm for improved execution speed. *IEEE Comput Graph. Appl.* **5**(8), 52–60, August 1985.

50. Roth, S.D., Ray casting for modeling solids. *Comput. Graph. Image Process.* **18** 109–144, 1982.

51. Rubin, S. and Whitted, T., A three-dimensional representation for fast rendering of complex scenes. *Comput. Graph.* **14**(3), 110–116, July 1980.

52. Scherson, I.D. and Caspary, E., Data structures and the time complexity of ray tracing. *The Visual Computer*, Springer-Verlag, Vol. 3, pp. 201–213, 1987.

53. Sederberg, T.W. and Anderson, D.C., Ray tracing of Steiner patches. *Comput. Graph.* **18**(3), 159–164, July 1984.

54. Shinya, M., Takahashi, T. and Naito, S., Principles and applications of pencil tracing. *Comput. Graph.* **21**(4), 45–54, July 1987.

55. Synder, J.M. and Barr, A.H., Ray tracing complex models containing surface tessellations. *Comput. Graph.* **21**(4), 119–126, July 1987.

56. Speer, L.R., DeRose, T.D.,and Barsky, B.A., A theoretical and empirical analysis of coherent ray tracing. *Computer-Generated Images* (Proc. of Graphics Interface '85), 27–31 May 1986, pp. 11–25.

57. Sutherland, I.E., Sproull, R.F. and Schumacker, R.A., A characterization of ten hidden-surface algorithms. *Comput. Surv.* **6**(1), 1–55, March 1974.

58. Sweeney, M.A.J. and Bartels, R.H., Ray tracing free-form B-spline surfaces. *IEEE Comput. Graph. Appl.* **6**(2), 41–49, February 1986.

59. Toth, D.L., On ray tracing parametric surfaces. *Comput. Graph.* **19**(3), 171–179, July 1985.

60. Ullner, M.K., Parallel machines for computer graphics. Ph.D. Dissertation, California Institute of Technology, Pasadena, California, 1983, 5112:TR:83.

61. van de Hulst, H.C., *Light Scattering by Small Particles*, Dover Publications, New York, 1981.

62. van Wijk, J.J., Ray tracing objects defined by sweeping planar cubic splines. *ACM Trans. Graph.* **3**, 223–237, (3), July 1984.

63. Weghorst, H., Hooper, G. and Greenberg, D., Improved computational methods for ray tracing. *ACM Trans. Graph.* **3**(1), 52–69, January 1984.

64. Weiler, K. and Atherton, P., Hidden surface removal using polygon area sorting. *Comput. Graph.* **11**(2), 214–222, July 1977.

65. Whitted, T., An improved illumination model for shaded display. *Commun. ACM* **23**(6), 343–349, June 1980.

66. Wyvill, G. and Kunii, T.L., A functional model for constructive solid geometry. *The Visual Computer*, Vol. 1, No. 1, pp. 3–14, July 1985.

67. Wyvill, G., McPheeters, C. and Wyvill, B., Soft objects. *Advanced Computer Graphics* (Proc. of Computer Graphics Tokyo '86), pp. 113–128, April 1986.

68. Wyvill. G., Kunii, T.L. and Shiral, Y., Space division for ray tracing in CSG. *IEEE Comput., Graph. Appl.* **6**(4), 28–34, April 1986.

69. Yau, Mann-May and Srihari, S.N., A hierarchical data structure for multi-dimensional digital images. *Commun. ACM* **26**(7), 504–515, July 1983.

70. Youssef, S., Vectorized Simulation and Ray Tracing. Supercomputer Computations Research Institute, October 1987, FSU-SCRI-87-63.

71. Youssef, S., A new algorithm for object oriented ray tracing. *Comput. Vis. Graph. Image Process.* **34**, 125–137, 1986.

7 Writing a Ray Tracer

PAUL S. HECKBERT

1 INTRODUCTION

Writing a ray tracer is much like any other large software development project: a good fraction of the work involves researching algorithms and designing the structure of the software. Once the design is determined and the algorithms, data structures, and modules have been chosen, coding the program is fairly straightforward. We assume the reader is already familiar with ray tracing algorithms, so this document focuses on software design.

2 OPTIONS FOR A RAY TRACER

The first step of design is deciding on goals. As shown in the outline below, a number of options are possible in a ray tracer. Some features listed require only minor modifications to a standard ray tracer but others require major redesign of the data structures, algorithms, and interfaces.

The options are grouped into four categories: geometry, optics, optimization, and systems. Within each category the options are ordered roughly by difficulty and the major implementation implications of each option are listed.

2.1 Geometry

- Extensible set of primitives
  Adding a new class of primitives should be easy ⇒ *use object oriented programming*.
- Simple operations on primitives
  Implement the following operations for each primitive class.
  - read
    Read a primitive specification from a model file. Parameterized, hierarchical models are convenient ⇒ *develop a modeling language*.

■ intersect
Find the first intersection of a ray with an object—the fundamental operation of ray tracing. For some primitives, intersection calculation is best done by transforming the ray into its local coordinate system ⇒ *store a transformation matrix with each object.*

■ normal
Find normal vector at a surface point.

■ bound
Tight bounding volumes around each object are desirable for optimization ⇒ *do not use unbounded primitives such as infinite planes and cylinders.*

■ Complex operations on primitives
The following modeling operators can be specified in the model file. They need not be implemented for each primitive class, however.

■ transform
Translation, scaling, and rotation are convenient modeling operations ⇒ *read transformation commands in modeling language and store a 4 × 4 matrix with each object.*

■ deform
Warping of objects beyond the usual linear transformations is a powerful modeling operator ⇒ *either rays become bent or objects are subdivided and transformed; both schemes increase ray–object intersection time.*

■ CSG (constructive solid geometry)
Difference and intersection operators ease modeling ⇒ *the intersection routine must return a list of all intersection points* [105], *not just the first. This slows every ray–object intersection calculation (see 'optimize CSG union case' below).* ⇒ *Use of CSG requires all (or most) primitives to be closed solids.*

■ Primitive types
Some common primitive types:

■ polygon
⇒ *Implement line–plane intersection, 2-D-point-in-polygon testing, polygon data structure.*

■ polyhedron
⇒ *To optimize ray–polyhedron intersection use a polyhedron data structure with topological information, e.g. winged-edge.*

■ quadric surface
second degree implicit surfaces

■ sphere
⇒ *Trivial.*

■ cylinder, cone, ...
⇒ *If CSG is used and objects are bounded then caps are needed on cylinders, cones, and other infinite quadrics.*

■ torus
Can have four intersection points with ray ⇒ *quartic root finder needed.*
■ blob
⇒ *numerical root finder needed* [14].
■ parametric patch
⇒ *If implicitization methods are used, a high-degree 1-D polynomial root finder is needed* [70]. *If the parametric method is used, a 2-D Newton's method root finder is needed* [117]. *Preprocessing is recommended to create a hierarchy of bounding volumes* [114].
■ fractal
⇒ *A method to bound each perturbation is needed* [83].

2.2 Optics

A number of optical effects can be simulated in a ray tracing algorithm. Some of the techniques listed below are applicable to almost any rendering algorithm, however.

■ Camera
The primary or pixel rays.
   ■ orthographic projection
   Parallel rays (viewpoint at infinity).
   ■ perspective projection
   All rays pass through a viewpoint within the scene.
   ■ other (fisheye, Omnimax, etc.)
   Use a procedural camera to generate a ray given an (x, y) screen location.
■ Shadows
The first step in global shading models. ⇒ *Send shadow rays toward each light and test for occluding objects. These secondary rays random access the entire scene.*
■ Specular reflection
⇒ *Trace a ray in the specular reflection direction by stacking or recursing. These secondary rays random access the entire scene.*
■ Transmission (refraction)
⇒ *Trace a ray in the transmitted direction by stacking or recursing. These secondary rays random access the entire scene.*
⇒ *Store an index of refraction with each solid object. Choose precedence rules: which object's material properties are used inside intersecting transparent objects?*
■ Fog
Attenuate intensities exponentially with distance to simulate absorption. ⇒ *Store a translucency parameter and body color with each solid object.*

- Light falloff
  Light intensity from a point source is proportional to $1/\text{distance}^2$. This fall-off is an effect often ignored in computer graphics. ⇒ *This has major ramifications in animation: an automatic gain control system is needed to set picture brightness. Either the global gain for an image must be precomputed by guessing what the brightest pixel in an image will be or the gain must be set after post-processing the entire image.*
- Fresnel reflection law
  Gives the coefficients of specular reflection and refraction as functions of incident angle and index of refraction.
- Programmable shading
  ⇒ *Develop a language for shading formulas* [34]. *Write an interpreter or compiler for it. In the extreme, this language would allow explicit control over the spawning of new rays.*
- Texture mapping
  ⇒ *Compute surface parameters u and v and pass these on to the shader as texture map coordinates.*
- Procedural texture
  An extension to programmable shading. ⇒ *Develop band-limited texture primitives.*
- Probabilistic ray tracing
  To compute the color returned along a ray, a number of spatial, angular, temporal, and spectral distributions must be integrated. These can be integrated numerically by firing rays within some probability distribution.
  - numerical integration techniques
    Numerical integration techniques are used since analytic integration is not possible in general.
    - point sampling
      Approximates all probability distributions with the δ function.
    - uniform supersampling
      Samples at fixed spacing are used. In the case of supersampling a pixel, n^2 samples are typically used.
    - stochastic sampling (Monte Carlo integration)
      Random sample points are chosen, often jittered from a uniform grid rather than totally random [35,36]. ⇒ *Incremental techniques cannot be used when sample spacing is nonuniform.*
    - adaptive sampling
      Both uniform and stochastic sampling can be done adaptively, subdividing more finely in areas of high variance. ⇒ *Rays must be buffered to avoid redundant tracing.* Subdivision can be based on various criteria:

■ intensity and ray tree difference
Do the intensities at four corners of a pixel differ a lot [126]?
Does the ray tree intersect different objects from pixel to
pixel? ⇒ *To compare ray trees, hash the ray tree into an integer
'signature' at each pixel.*

■ variance estimate
Subdivide each pixel until variance of a subpixel is below a
threshold or size is too small [45,83].

■ distributions needing integration
The following effects have some domain over which integration may
be performed [34–36]. the parameters of that domain can be
position, direction, time, wavelength, or other variables. Many of
these distributions can be integrated simply by spawning the right set
of rays.

■ pixel area (edge anti-aliasing)
⇒ *Trace rays throughout pixel area.*

■ texture area (texture anti-aliasing)
Texture filtering is fairly independent of ray tracing. ⇒ *Sample
texture throughout texture area. Either texture area information for each ray is
needed* [1–3] *or adaptive techniques must be used* [45].

■ lens area (depth of field)
⇒ *Trace rays throughout lens area. Additional camera parameters are needed
to specify focal distance and depth of field.*

■ specular reflection angle (gloss, highlight anti-aliasing)
⇒ *Trace rays throughout solid angle of specular reflection. Solid angle
information and surface curvature measures are needed for good highlight
anti-aliasing* [1–3].

■ specular transmission angle (surface translucency)
⇒ *Trace rays throughout solid angle of specular transmission.*

■ exposure time (motion blur)
⇒ *Trace rays throughout exposure time. Object positions must be undated for
each time snapshot. This implies that the model has access to its animation
database.*

■ light angle (penumbras)
Soft shadows give important visual cues and enhance realism.
⇒ *Trace rays throughout solid angle of light to determine fractional occlusion.
Lights must have a solid angle if infinite, or be geometric objects in the scene if
local.*

■ diffuse reflection angle (indirect lighting, radiosity)
Illumination in indoor scenes is often dominated by indirect diffuse
reflection (radiosity). Radiosity can be simulated as a pre-process
which calculates the incident illumination on each surface

or ⇒ *trace rays throughout the visible hemisphere to calculate diffuse illumination on the fly. This distribution is so broad that many rays must be traced. The numerical integration is very susceptible to small, intense lights.*

■ spectral integration

Reflectance is wavelength-dependent [B,62]. ⇒ *Store colors as spectral distributions sampled at more than 3 frequencies and convert to rgb for output.*

■ spectral refraction angle (dispersion)

Index of refraction is a function of wavelength, so different wavelengths of light are refracted at different angles. ⇒ *Trace rays at different wavelengths and combine the results to compute an rgb color* [116].

■ atmosphere (fog, material translucency)

⇒ *Integrate absorption and scattering along ray. Compute atmospheric density from a volume of data or a space function* [73].

■ Relativistic effects

⇒ *Photons (and hence rays) don't travel instantaneously. Moving along a ray takes you back in time.*

■ Light ray tracing

Trace rays along photon paths (backward relative to pixel rays) [66] and accumulate incident illumination as a texture on each surface. ⇒ *Lots of preprocessing and memory are required to store a texture for each object. Every surface must be parameterized.*

2.3   Optimization

After adding all of the above options, your program will need optimization.

■ Algorithmic optimizations

Most optimization methods for ray tracing involve reducing the number of rays generated or reducing the number of objects against which each ray must be tested.

■ reduce the number of rays

The following methods for reducing the number of rays have been proposed:

■ adaptive supersampling and subsampling

Supersampling for anti-aliasing is most important near high contrast edges [126]. If supersampling resolution is proportional to intensity variance then the sampling resolution can be reduced in flat shaded areas, even becoming sparser than the pixel spacing (subsampling) [105].

■ ray insignificance test

If the weight for a ray's color drops below a threshold then its effect can be considered negligible and recursion can be aborted [62]. ⇒ *Weights must be passed down the ray tree. Some shading must be done on the fly.*

- importance sampling
  Numerical integration is most efficiently done by sampling more densely in heavily weighted areas [74]. ⇒ *Reduce the ray tree branching factor by firing only one of shadow, reflected, and transmitted rays at each interface, with probability proportional to weight.*
- Reduce number of objects tested against each ray
  - use a fast hidden surface algorithm for primary rays
    Z-buffer or scanline algorithms can be used to quickly determine the objects intersected by primary rays [123]. In scenes with little reflection and transmission the primary rays form a large fraction of the total. ⇒ *Write a conventional renderer.*
  - bounding volumes
    Testing for intersection with a hierarchy of nested bounding volumes can quickly cull out most ray–object intersection tests. ⇒ *Pre-process the model to create the hierarchy of bounding volumes, develop software to fit bounds tightly. This may involve implementing a 3-D convex hull algorithm.* Common bounding volumes are:
    - sphere
      ⇒ *Has simplest intersection test, but nesting is trickier than box.*
    - box
      A rectangular parallelepiped parallel to world space axes. ⇒ *Intersection test is more difficult than sphere's, but nesting is simpler.*
  - spatial subdivision
    World space can be subdivided into cubical cells through which a ray steps. Each cell contains a list of the surfaces which intersect it. ⇒ *Pre-process the model to initialize the cell lists. Write cell stepping code. Cell lists can use a lot of memory.* There are two competing subdivision schemes:
    - uniform
      Stepping is easy in a uniform grid; a 3-D variant of Bresenham's algorithm is used [49]. ⇒ *A uniform grid uses substantially more memory than an octree in some cases. A tight box around the scene is needed.*
    - octree
      An octree adapts better to the local density of objects than a uniform grid. ⇒ *An octree uses less memory than a uniform grid for non-homogeneous scenes, but stepping is slower.*
  - coherence
    Intersected objects can be cached for quick look-up. ⇒ *Caching works best in simple scenes with high ray-to-ray coherence* [65, 110].

- shadow rays
  Rays shot toward each light account for a large fraction of the total rays in most scenes.
    - stop at light
      ⇒ *Stop tracing as soon as you find an object between the shadow ray origin and the light source.*
    - light buffer
      By rendering the scene from the point of view of each light source, one can create a list of potential light blockers of any point [59].
      ⇒ *Write a special renderer to create the light buffers.*
- Make each intersection test cheaper
    - optimize CSG union case
      If a CSG subtree uses the union operator only, then intersection calculations needn't keep a list of all intersected points, just the first.
      ⇒ *Preprocess the CSG tree to create union-only subtrees.*
    - don't shade shadow rays
      We care only if the ray intersects anything, not about the intersection's position or color. ⇒ *Make separate trace and intersect modules; the former shades but the latter does not.*
    - don't compute normal until needed
      ⇒ *don't compute normal in intersection routine.*
- Conventional optimization techniques
  These techniques are not limited to ray tracing [A].
    - change hardware
      ⇒ *Port program to a faster machine or a parallel processor. This can reduce software portability.*
    - change programming languages
      Use a language with better floating point support or a lower level language such as assembler or microcode. ⇒ *This can reduce portability.*
    - change data structures or data types
      Optimize commonly used data structures (such as ray and color) for your machine. Integer arithmetic may help speed some computations.
      ⇒ *Precision problems, reduced portability.*
    - isolate hot spots
      Profile program to locate hot spots (the most commonly executed code). ⇒ *Optimize only the hot spots, not the entire program. Fast, single precision math routines may be worth investigating. In-line code instead of subroutine calls can help (in C, use macros in place of subroutines).*

2.4   System

Systems issues must be addressed to create a production tool.

- Modularity
  Add features in a modular fashion so they can be switched in and out.
  ⇒ *Make module interfaces simple and clean.*
- Debugging and testing
  ⇒ *Develop a set of test scenes and options which exercise all features of the program.*
- Interaction
  Since ray tracers are typically used in batch mode with multi-hour turnaround, any interactive tools which speed the design of composition, shading, and lighting will be great time savers.
  - option selection
    ⇒ *Put all options which the user might want to change (e.g. image resolution, maximum tree depth, and various tolerances) under user control. Develop consistent schemes for option selection, model specification, picture output, and error handling. Develop a true language for model specification, not just a crude ascii file format.*
  - previewing
    Since ray tracing is so slow, you'll probably want to use another display algorithm for interactive previewing. ⇒ *Develop software compatible with your ray tracer's modeling language for line drawing or other fast display. For 'interactive ray tracing' use a tablet or mouse and trace rays only where the user points* [12].
  - quick shading
    Quick schemes for adjusting colors and lighting are desirable. ⇒ *Save the ray tree at each pixel and shade image as a post-process* [126]. *This requires a lot of memory or disk space. Trace routine must return a ray tree, not just a color.*
- Animation
  ⇒ *Develop an animation system integrated with your modeling language.*
- Distributed computing
  Since ray tracers tend to take hours per frame, it's tempting to spread the compute among all available computers. ⇒ *This can require porting your program to other languages and operating systems. Develop distributed computing and network communication tools.*

3   DESIGN

Novice programmers often neglect the design phase, instead diving into coding without giving thought to the evolution of a piece of software over time. The result is haphazard, poorly modularized code which is difficult to maintain and modify. A few minutes of planning short-term and long-term goals at the beginning is time well spent.

The remainder of this paper illustrates the design and implementation process for a ray tracer with the following features:

- standard Whitted reflection, transmission, and shadows
- extensible primitives
- CSG
- anti-aliasing.

Code samples are given in the C programming language.

3.1   Modules

Clear definition of modules and the interfaces between them is one of the most important design steps. *Figure 1* is a block diagram of modules for our CSG

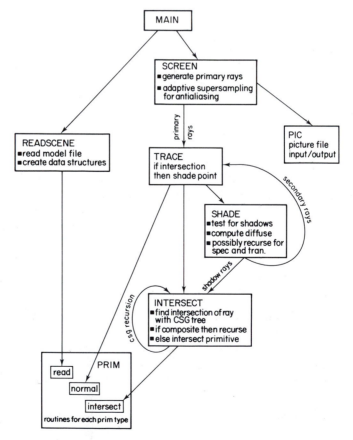

Fig. 1.   CSG ray tracer modules.

ray tracer. Ignoring the primitive-related routines for a moment, the modularization is fairly standard, with perhaps a few exceptions:

(1) All shading operations have been pulled out of the *TRACE* module, where they are often put, to facilitate experimentation with various shaders.

(2) The *INTERSECT* module is recursive because of CSG. For composite solids it recurses on the left and right branches of a CSG tree.

In addition to these major modules, we will also need some utility routines for standard vector and matrix operations and a library of routines to read our modeling language.

3.2 Object Oriented Programming

Our goal of extensible primitives can be met in various ways. Probably the most obvious method in C for handling a variety of primitives is to put a large `switch` statement in the *INTERSECT* module with one case for each primitive type. Unfortunately, this would require recompiling *INTERSECT* each time a new primitive is added.

A better approach is *object oriented programming*. Rather than group the software by procedure, we group it by data structure. Thus, instead of collecting all the intersection methods into one file and all the normal vector formulas into another, we split the problem the other way, collecting procedures for each primitive type into a file of its own. There will be one file containing sphere-related routines, another file for polygon-related routines, etc. This has the advantage that primitive-dependent information can be hidden in data structures local to each file and the procedure interfaces can be very simple and generic. Adding new primitives to the system becomes easy with this scheme.

Since the details of each primitive's data structure will be local to that sub-module, all operations on the primitive must be supported by generic procedures, the most important of which are:

read   Read a primitive specification from a model file and create an instance of that primitive.

intersect Find intersection points of a ray with a primitive. Since we're supporting CSG, a list of all intersection points must be returned.

normal   Return a normal vector given a point on the surface.

3.3 Data Types

First, we'll need some basic data types:

```
typedef double Flt;        /* floating point data type */
typedef Flt Vec[3];        /* a 3 vector */
typedef Vec Point;         /* xyz point data type */
typedef Vec Color;         /* rgb color data type */
```

We will use `Flt` as our floating point data type throughout. During debugging we will leave `Flt` as a `double` (double precision real) but we may want to switch to `float` later if our compiler supports single precision calculations well. We define the `Vec,Point`, and `Color` data types identically so that we can use the same vector routines to manipulate all three types. As a convention, we use capital letters for `Point` and `Vec` data types to help distinguish them from scalars and colors. Before proceeding with other data types, we can define a few of the basic vector routines we'll be needing.

```
Vec A, B, C; Flt a,b;
```

`Flt VecLen(A)`	vector length: returns $\|\vec{A}\|$.
`Flt VecDot(A, B)`	dot product: returns $\vec{A} \cdot \vec{B}$.
`VecCopy(A, B)`	vector copy: $\vec{B} = \vec{A}$.
`VecAdd(A, B, C)`	addition: $\vec{C} = \vec{A} + \vec{B}$.
`VecSub(A, B, C)`	subtraction: $\vec{C} = \vec{A} - \vec{B}$.
`VecComb(a, A, b, B, C)`	linear combination: $\vec{C} = a\vec{A} + b\vec{B}$.
`VecAddS(a, A, B, C)`	add scalar multiple: $\vec{C} = a\vec{A} + \vec{B}$.
`Flt VecUnit(A, B)`	vector unitize (normalize): $\vec{B} = \vec{A}/\|\vec{A}\|$, returns $\|\vec{A}\|$.

To optimize these we could implement them as macros.
We'll also want a ray data type to represent the vector $\vec{P} + t\vec{D}$ for $t > 0$:

```
typedef struct Ray {     /* A RAY */
   Point P;              /* position (origin) */
   Point D;              /* direction (unitized) */
} Ray;
```

Note that we'll assume that D is unit in all rays. A `point` on `ray` with parameter `t` can be calculated with

```
#define RayPoint(ray, t, point)
        VecAddS(t, (ray)->D, (ray)->P, point)
```

A clean implementation of the above vector routines provides a sound foundation for the higher level routines.

Next we will need some data types for geometric solids. We've decided to support CSG, so the model will consist of a binary tree of solids [105], each solid being a composite (`Comp`) or primitive (`Prim`). Restricting the CSG tree to have branching factor of two is not limiting; it is easy to construct a binary tree from a general tree and the CSG intersection routine will be simpler if we make this restriction.

Composite solids form the inner nodes of the CSG tree and primitives form the leaves. To allow the tree to be built out of a mixture of these nodes we will use a trick: start the two structures the same and include a composite/primitive flag at the beginning. Routines can check the flag of the node to determine which type it is, and cast a `Prim` pointer to a `Comp` pointer or vice versa if necessary. Note that this sort of runtime type checking is easier in some other languages.

The composite solid structure is quite simple, consisting merely of an operation code:

```
'&'        intersection
'|'        union
'-'        difference
```

and pointers to its two subsolids, which can be either composite or primitive.

```
typedef struct Comp {      /* A COMPOSITE SOLID */
    int compflag;          /* =1 */

    int op;                /* operation: intersection, union or difference */
    struct Comp *left;     /* pointer to left sub-solid */
    struct Comp *right;    /* pointer to right sub-solid */
} Comp;
```

Another of our design goals is extensible primitives, so our primitive structure `Prim` should be very generic. We'll collect all primitive-dependent information in its own little structure and put a pointer to it (cast to a character pointer) in `Prim`. This primitive-dependent information varies from type to type; for example, the info for a sphere is a center point and radius, while a polygon is defined by a list of vertices and perhaps a plane equation. For speed and code simplicity, we can store pointers to the generic routines for a primitive type in `Prim` as well. `Prim` should also include a transform matrix between world space and that primitive's local (object) space. This is helpful for some primitive types (cylinders and cones, for instance) which can perform intersections more quickly by transforming the ray into their object space instead of transforming the object into world space. The final item in the `Prim` structure is a pointer to its surface description.

```
typedef struct Prim {      /* A PRIMITIVE SOLID */
    int compflag;          /* =0 */

    char *info;            /* ptr to prim-dependent info (must be cast) */
```

```
    struct PrimProcs *procs;    /* generic procedures for this primitive type */
    Matrix mat;                 /* world to object transform (optional) */
    struct Surf *surf;          /* surface description */
} Prim;
```

The above composite and primitive structures are fairly minimal. Likely additions to each would be a bounding volume pointer and solid name or id. Note how we've isolated **PrimProcs** and **Surf**; the **Prim** structure contains only pointers to them, not copies. This is done both for modularity—primitive types should be independent of surface types—and for storage economy. We need only one **PrimProcs** structure for each type of primitives and one **Surf** structure for each type of surface. It would be wasteful to make a copy of this information for each instance of a primitive.

PrimProcs is a collection of pointers to the generic procedures for a given primitive type. The structure is shown below:

```
typedef struct PrimProcs {   /* GENERIC PROCEDURES ON PRIMITIVES */
    char *(*name) ();          /* primitive type name */
    int (*print) ();           /* print */
    Prim *(*read) ();          /* read from model file */
    int (*intersect) ();       /* intersect with ray */
    int (*normal) ();          /* compute normal vector */
} PrimProcs;
```

If we have designed **Prim** and **Primprocs** well then they should require no modification as new primitives are added to the system.

The **Surf** structure will contain all the optical parameters associated with a surface type. Since we are doing CSG, this entails material (body) attributes as well as surface attributes. We will describe a very simplistic implementation which assumes constants for the diffuse, specular, and transparency coefficients.

```
typedef struct Surf {        /* A SURFACE TYPE */
    Flt kdiff;                 /* diffuse reflection coefficient */
    Flt kspec;                 /* specular reflection coefficient */
    Flt ktran;                 /* transmission coefficient */
    Color color;               /* surface and body color */
    Flt refrindex;             /* index of refraction */
} Surf;
```

A more accurate optical model would include a translucency coefficient for solid body color and employ Fresnel's formulas to compute the reflection and transmission coefficients as a function of incidence angle and wavelength. We leave the definition of lights and camera as an exercise for the reader.

The last data type we'll need is an intersection point. This structure is a grab bag of information returned by the primitive intersection routines. The following must be included in this structure or derivable from it: ray parameter t, intersection point, surface normal, primitive hit, type of surface intersected, and exiting and entering solid materials (to compute relative index or refraction).

```
typedef struct Isect {    /* AN INTERSECTION POINT*/
    Flt t;                /* line parameter at intersection (as in P+tD) */
    Prim *prim;           /* primitive we hit */
    int enter;            /* entering=1, exiting=0 */
    Surf *medium;         /* primitive whose material we're in when < t */
} Isect;
```

3.4 Global Variables

We will need a few global variables and constants:

```
Comp *modelroot;         /* the root of the CSG tree, contains entire scene */

int maxlevel = 5;        /* maximum ray tree depth */
Flt minweight = .01;     /* significance threshold for ray weights */
Flt rayeps = 1e-7;       /* roundoff error tolerance */
```

In practice there will be more globals than this. Any parameters which are the same for all rays are potential globals. We try to keep global variables to a minimum, however, as they encourage violation of modularity.

3.5 Interfaces

Given these data structures, we can now define the interfaces between modules. Refer to the block diagram.

MAIN parses arguments and calls the *READSCENE* module to read a model file and create data structures:

```
Comp *SceneRead(file)
char *file;
/* read model file and return CSG tree for entire scene */
```

and calls *SCREEN* to generate and trace primary rays and write a picture file. *SCREEN* needs to know the scene, camera, and display parameters and the name of an output file.

```
Screen(scene, view, display, picfile)
Comp *scene; Camera *view; Display *display; char *picfile;
/* generate rays according to view and display to ray trace scene,
                                      output to picfile */
```

Camera would be a structure containing information such as viewpoint, look-at point, up vector, angle of view, and image aspect ratio (the preceding can be encapsulated in a 4 × 4 matrix if you like) and **Display** would contain image resolution, pixel aspect ratio, and window of interest.

SCREEN generates primary rays according to the view and display, calls the *TRACE* module to do the actual ray tracing, and writes a picture file using the *PIC* module. We'll define the *PIC* interface quite generally so it can be used for both picture files and frame buffers. Buffering writes by scan line is a good idea for either output style. The *PIC* interface routines are:

```
Pic *PicOpen(file, mode)
char *file, *mode;
/* open named file and return structure pointer, much like fopen */
```

```
PicWriteLine(pic, y, buf)
Pic *pic; int y; Pixel *buf;
/* write scanline buf to picture file at line y */
/* Pixel might be "struct { unsigned char r, g, b;}", for example */
```

```
PicClose(pic)
Pic *pic;
/* close picture file */
```

Additional routines are needed to set the picture resolution, pixel depth, and other parameters. *SCREEN* must also set the global mode! root and then call *TRACE* on all primary rays. In addition to the input ray and the output color, we'll pass a level number and a ray weight to help determine recursion termination.

```
Trace(level, weight, ray, color)
int level; Flt weight; Ray *ray; Color *color;
/* trace ray at given level and weight and return color */
```

TRACE is quite simple, merely calling the *INTERSECT* module to see if the ray intersects any objects, and if so, calling *SHADE* to compute the returned color, else calling a background shader routine. *SHADE* requires three primary arguments (a point, a normal, and a returned color) for standard shading, plus the incident ray direction and surface information to support specular reflection and refraction.

```
Shade(P, N, I, hit, color)
Point P, N, I; Isect *hit; Color color;
/* return color at point P with normal N, incident direction I,
                                    and intersection list hit */
```

Both *TRACE* and *SHADE* call *INTERSECT*, which computes a list of intersection points of a ray with a CSG tree:

```
Intersect(ray, solid, hit)
Ray *ray; Comp *solod; Isect *hit;
/* compute intersection list hit of ray with CSG tree solid */
```

The generic procedures in the *PRIM* module have the following interface:

```
char *PrimName(prim)
Prim *prim
/* print type name of primitive */

PrimPrint(prim)
Prim *prim;
/* print prim->info (for debugging) */

Prim *PrimRead(fp)
FILE *fp;
/* read a primitive from input stream fp and return a primitive pointer */
/* note that this interface might change depending on the modeling format */

PrimIntersect(ray, prim, hit)
Ray *ray; Prim *prim; Isect *hit;
/* intersect ray with prim, return intersection list hit */

PrimNormal(prim P, N)
Prim *prim; Point P, N;
/* compute normal N of prim at surface point P */
```

In the above routines, *Prim* is the primitive type name, e.g. **Sphere Polygon Quadric**, etc. There is one set of these routines for each primitive type. These procedures are always called through the function pointers in PrimProcs.

3.6 Procedures

With the data structures and interfaces defined, we can now start writing procedures. We will begin with the generic procedures for each primitive: name, print, read, intersect, and normal. We illustrate them for the sphere primitive.

/ all coordinates in world space (other primitives might use object space) */*

```
typedef struct {              /* SPHERE (pointed to by prim->info) */
    Point CEN;                /* center of sphere */
    Flt rad, rad2;            /* radius and radius^2 */
} Sph;

PrimProcs SphProcs =
    {SphName, SphPrint, SphRead, SphIntersect, SphNormal};

char *SphName(prim)
Prim *prim;
{
    return "sphere";
}

SphPrint(prim)
Prim *prim;
{
    Sph *s;

    s = (Sph *)prim->info;
    printf("sphere: center(%g, %g, %g) radius %g\n",
        s->CEN[0], s->CEN[1], s->CEN[2], s->rad);
}
/*
 * SphIntersect: intersect ray with sphere prim and put intersections in hit list.
 * The intersection of ray X=P+tD with sphere |C−X|²=r²
 * solves t²−2t(D•V)+(V•V−r²)=0 at t=D•V±√(D•V)²−V•V+r²,
```

```
 * where V=C-P, assuming |D|=1
 */
SphIntersect(ray, prim, hit)
Ray *ray;
Prim *prim;
Isect *hit;
{
    int nroots;
    Flt b, disc, t1, t2;
    Point V;
    Sph *s;

    s = (Sph *)prim->info;
    VecSub(s->CEN, ray->P, V);
    b = VecDot(V, ray->D);
    disc = b*b-VecDot(V, V)+s->rad2;
    if (disc<=0.) return 0;                 /* doesn't hit */
    disc = sqrt(disc);
    t2 = b+disc;                            /* 2nd root */
    if (t2<=rayeps) return 0;               /* behind ray origin */
    t1 = b-disc;                            /* 1st root */
    /* add intersection points to hit list */
    if (t1>rayeps) {
        IsectAdd(hit, t1, prim, 1, 0);              /* entering sphere */
        hit++;
        nroots = 2;
    }
    else nroots = 1;
    IsectAdd(hit, t2, prim, 0, prim->surf);    /* exiting sphere */
    return nroots;                          /* return number of roots */
}

/*
 * SphNormal: compute normal N given prim and point P.
 */
SphNormal(prim, P, N)
Prim *prim;
Point P, N;
{
    Sph *s;

    s = (Sph *)prim->info;
    VecSub(P, s->CEN, N);
    VecUnit(N, N);
}
```

Note that the Sph structure need not (and should not) be known outside the above source file.

We will only rough out the **Screen** routine, as it varies significantly depending on the supersampling scheme used. Let's say we use adaptive, non-recursive supersampling. Rays will be traced at the corner of each pixel and only those pixels whose four corner colors differ by more than some threshold will be supersampled. Some sort of caching scheme should be used to avoid tracing each corner ray four times.

```
Screen(scene, view, display, picfile)
Comp *scene;
Camera *view;
Display *display;
char *picfile;
{
    Pixel buf[XMAX];

    modelroot = scene;
    pic = PicOpen(picfile, "w");
    for y=ymin to ymax {
        for x=xmin to xmax {
            compute world space primary ray which passes through
                screen point (x+.5,y+.5)
            Trace(0, 1., ray, color);
            save color in cache
            if pixel's four corner colors at (x±.5,y±.5) differ by more than a threshold
                then supersample with an n×n grid and average the n² colors
                else average the four corner colors
            buf[x] = avgcolor
        }
        PicWriteLine(pic, y, buf);
    }
    PicClose(pic);
}
```

The **Trace, Shade**, and **Intersect** routines form the heart of the ray tracer:

```
/*
 * Trace: Trace a ray (in world space) through the scene and return its color.
 * Find first intersection for t>0 and shade it.
 */
```

```
Trace(level, weight, ray, col)
int level;
Flt weight;
Ray *ray;
Color col;
{
    Prim *prim;
    Point P, N;
    Isect hit[ISECTMAX];

    /* intersect ray with everything in scene */
    if (Intersect(ray, modelroot, hit)) {
        /* find prim, point P, and normal N at first intersection */
        prim = hit[0].prim;
        RayPoint(ray, hit[0].t, P);
        (*prim->procs->normal) (&hit[0], P, N);
        if (VecDot(ray->D, N) > 0.)       /* flip normal if necessary */
            VecNegate(N, N);

        /* shade that surface point */
        Shade(level, weight, P, N, ray->D, hit, col);
    }
    else {
        /* if no intersections return background color */
        ShadeBackground(ray, col);
    }
}

/*
 * Shade: shade a surface point (recursively if necessary)
 * Stop recursing when level>maxlevel or when weight<minweight
 *       weight is cumulative weight for this ray's color in final pixel value
 *       P is point on surface, N is normal, I is incident ray
 *       hit is intersection list containing misc. info
 *       col (returned) is color of light returning along ray
 */
Shade(level, weight, P, N, I, hit, col)
int level;
Flt weight;
Point P, N, I;
```

```
Isect *hit;
Color col;
{
    Ray tray;
    Color tcol;
    Surf *surf;
```

    /* *compute diffuse* */
    col=0
    for all lights
        L=direction vector from P to light
        if N•L>0 and **Shadow***(ray from P toward light, distance to light)>0*
            then col += (N•L)*lightcol

    /* *if we're not too deep then recurse* */
```
    if (level+1<maxlevel) {
        VecCopy(P, tray.P);         /* start point for new rays */
```

```
        surf = hit[0].prim->surf;
        /* recurse on specular reflection ray if significant */
        if (surf->kspec*weight > minweight) {
            SpecularDirection(I, N, tray.D);
            Trace(level+1, surf->kspec*weight, &tray, tcol);
            VecAddS(surf->kspec, tcol, col, col);
        }
```

```
        /* recurse on transmission ray if significant */
        if (surf->ktran*weight > minweight) {
            /* hit[0].medium and hit[1].medium
            are exiting and entering media */
            if (TransmissionDirection(hit[0].medium,
                hit[1].medium, I, N, tray.D)) {
                    Trace(level+1, surf->ktran*weight,
                        &tray, tcol);
                    VecAddS(surf->ktran, tcol, col, col);
            }
        }
    }
}
```
/*
 * *Shadow: determine fraction of unblocked light in ray direction for*
 * *a light at* t=tmax.
 * *For penumbras, this routine would return a fraction.*

```
    */
Flt Shadow(ray, tmax);
Ray *ray;
Flt tmax;
{
    int nhit;
    Isect hit[ISECTMAX];

    nhit = Intersect(ray, modelroot, hit);
    if (nhit==0 || hit[0].t > tmax-rayeps) return 1.;
    else return 0.;
}
```

Below is code for **SpecularDirection** and **TransmissionDirection**, the routines which compute secondary ray directions. See the attached 'Derivation of Refraction Formulas' for a discussion of these formulas. The following formulas generate unit output vectors if given unit input vectors.

```
/*
 * SpecularDirection: compute specular direction R from incident direction I
 * and normal N.
 * All vectors unit.
 */
SpecularDirection(I, N, R)
Point I, N, R;
{
    VecAddS(-2.*VecDot(I, N), N, I, R);
}
```

```
/*
 * TransmissionDirection: compute transmission direction T from incident
 * direction I, normal N, going from medium m1 to m2, with refraction governed
 * by the relative index of refraction according to Snell's law: η₁sinθ₁=η₂sinθ₂
 * If there is total internal reflection, return 0, else set T and return 1.
 * All vectors unit. Formula from [Heckbert-Hanrahan84].
 */
TransmissionDirection(m1, m2, I, N, T)
Surf *m1, *m2;
Point I, N, T;
{
```

```
    Flt n1, n2, eta, c1, cs2;

    n1 = m1 ? m1->refrindex : 1.;
    n2 = m2 ? m2->refrindex : 1.;
    eta = n1/n2;                        /* relative index of refraction */

    c1 = -VecDot(I, N);                 /* cosθ₁ */
    cs2 = 1.-eta*eta*(1.-c1*c1);        /* cos²θ₂ */
    if (cs2<0.) return 0;               /* total internal reflection */
    VecComb(eta, I, eta*c1-sqrt(cs2), N, T);
    return 1;
}
```

The intersect routine intersects a ray with a CSG tree. If the root of the tree is composite then it recurses on the left and right halves and merges the resultant lists by calling **IntersectMerge** [105], else it calls the primitive's intersection routine.

```
/*
 * Intersect: Intersect a ray with the solid, which can be either composite
 * or primitive.
 * Put a sorted list of intersections in hit and return the number of intersections.
 * Note that shade expects this routine to set hit[1].medium always.
 * Recursive because of CSG.
 */
Intersect(ray, solid, hit)
Ray *ray;
Comp *solid;
Isect *hit;
{
    int nl, nr;                    /* #intersections on left and right */
    Isect lhit[ISECTMAX], rhit[ISECTMAX];
                                   /* intersection lists on left and right */

    if (solid->compflag) {               /* composite solid */
        /* recursive on left */
        nl = Intersect(ray, solid->left, lhit)
        if (nl==0 && solid->op!='|') {
            /* optimization: if l is null then l&r and l-r are null, so skip r */
            return 0;
```

```
        }
    else {
        /* recurse on right */
        nr = Intersect(ray, solid->right, rhit);

        /* merge left and right lists */
        return IntersectMerge(solid->op, nl, lhit,
                              nr, rhit, hit);
    }
  }
  else                               /* primitive solid */
    return (*((Prim *)solid)->procs->intersect) (ray,
                              (Prim *)solid, hit);
}
```

This code may look over-modularized now, but as new options are added (bounding volumes, probabilistic ray tracing, etc.) these routines will grow. It is better to modularize the software cleanly at first and then make a simplifying pass later than to restrict the generality by premature optimization.

3.7 Testing

Collecting statistics throughout the ray tracer aids debugging and optimization. You may want to print the following statistics at the end of each run:

- average number of rays per pixel
- average ray tree branching factor
- average number of objects tested against each ray
- percentages of rays which are (a) primary rays, (b) secondary rays, or (c) shadow rays
- for bounding volume testing: percentages of bounding box tests which (a) miss bound, (b) hit bound but miss object, or (c) hit both
- for spatial subdivision testing: average number of voxels stepped through by each ray
- CPU time per ray.

Debugging a model is often a slow and tedious process with a ray tracer. Each interaction of adjustments to shapes, camera, lighting, or surfaces can take hours if done naively. Short of optimizing the program, a number of simple shortcuts can be used to speed rendering:

- render at low resolution (e.g. 64 × 64) or render only the window of interest to reduce the number of pixels computed

- turn the maximum ray tree depth (`maxlevel`) down and minimum ray weight (`minweight`) up to reduce the ray tree depth
- turn pixel supersampling down or off to reduce the number of rays per pixel
- turn off some lights to reduce the number of shadow rays
- turn off expensive shading options such as textures, motion blur, and diffuse reflection
- disable (comment out) irrelevant parts of the model to reduce the number of objects tested against each ray, in effect switching to a lower level of detail representation.

4 EXERCISES FOR THE READER

Change the modules, data structures, and algorithms in the ray tracer outlined above to:

- trace primary rays only; no secondary or shadow rays
- remove CSG; allow union of solids only
- add more geometric primitives: polygons, quadrics, bicubic patches, surfaces of revolution, tori, ...
- add fog to the shader
- add bounding volumes
- add spatial subdivision
- add probabilistic ray tracing for penumbras, motion blur, and other effects
- do spectral integration (sample the spectrum at more than 3 frequencies)
- save the ray tree at each pixel to allow post-process shading
- port to a SIMD parallel processor (e.g. array processor, CRAY, Connection Machine)
- port to a MIMD parallel processor (e.g. Transputers, cluster of Suns).

5 DERIVATION OF REFRACTION FORMULAS

We derive three alternative formulas for the refracted ray direction in ray tracing in order to prove their equivalence and to demonstrate the process of translating physical laws into optimized computational formulas.

It is common knowledge that light rays refract when they strike an interface between two different transparent media, such as air–water, air–glass, or glass–water. In 1621, Dutch mathematician Willebrord Snell discovered a formula quantifying this observation: the ratio of the sines of the incident and refracted angles equals the ratio of the indices of refraction of the two materials. Snell's law is:

$$\eta_1 \sin(\theta_1) = \eta_2 \sin(\theta_2)$$

where θ_1 is the angle of incidence, θ_2 is the angle of refraction (both measured from the perpendicular to the interface) and η_1 and η_2 are the two indices of refraction on the incident and refracted sides of the interface, respectively

Light passing through a material slows relative to its speed in a vacuum by a factor equal to the index of refraction of that material. In fact, Snell's law is a simple consequence of this speed variation and Fermat's *Principle of Least Time*, which states that light takes the fastest path to get from one point to another [D].

For computation we need to recast Snell's law in terms of (x, y, z) direction vectors. This can be done in several different ways. In the derivations below we make extensive use of angles and trigonometry, but, thankfully, it is possible to eliminate all of these terms from the final formulas, so θ_1 and θ_2 need never be computed. As a convention, vectors are upper case and scalars are lower case.

5.1 Whitted's Method

We first derive the refraction formulas which appeared in Whitted's original paper [126]. Referring to *Figure 2*, we are given the incident ray direction $\mathbf{I}$ and surface normal $\mathbf{N}$, and we need to calculate the transmitted (refracted) ray direction $\mathbf{T}'$. Whitted assumes that $\mathbf{N}$ is unit, but not $\mathbf{I}$. First, we scale the incident ray $\mathbf{I}$ so that its projection on $\mathbf{N}$ is equal to $\mathbf{N}$. Recall from geometry that the component of $\mathbf{I}$ parallel to $\mathbf{N}$ is $\mathbf{I}_{par} = \mathbf{N}(\mathbf{I} \cdot \mathbf{N})/(\mathbf{N} \cdot \mathbf{N})$. But $\mathbf{N}$ is a unit vector, so $\mathbf{I}_{par} = \mathbf{N}(\mathbf{I} \cdot \mathbf{N})$. As shown in *Figure 3*, by similar triangles we have

$$\frac{-\mathbf{I}}{-\mathbf{I}'} = \frac{-\mathbf{I}_{par}}{\mathbf{N}} = \mathbf{I} \cdot \mathbf{N}$$

so $\mathbf{I}' = \mathbf{I}/(-\mathbf{I} \cdot \mathbf{N})$. The vector $\mathbf{I}' + \mathbf{N}$ is thus parallel to the surface (a surface tangent), so we can write the refracted ray as $\mathbf{T}' = \alpha(\mathbf{I}' + \mathbf{N}) - \mathbf{N}$ for some α. Note that this refracted ray is not necessarily a unit vector. We must now express α in terms of $\mathbf{I}$, $\mathbf{N}$, and $\mathbf{I}'$. As shown in *Figure 3*, $|\mathbf{I}'| = \sec\theta_1$,

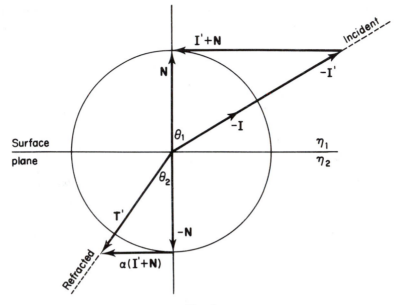

Fig. 2.

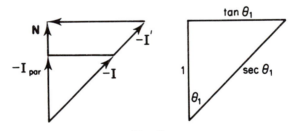

Fig. 3.

$|\mathbf{I}' + \mathbf{N}| = \tan \theta_1$, and $\alpha |\mathbf{I}' + \mathbf{N}| = \tan \theta_2$, so

$$\alpha = \frac{\tan \theta_2}{\tan \theta_1} = \frac{\sin \theta_2 \cos \theta_1}{\sin \theta_1 \cos \theta_2} = \frac{(\eta_1/\eta_2) \cos \theta_1}{\sqrt{(1 - \sin^2 \theta_2)}} =$$

$$\frac{(\eta_1/\eta_2) \cos \theta_1}{\sqrt{(1 - \eta_1^2/\eta_2^2 \sin^2 \theta_1)}} = \frac{1}{\sqrt{(n^2 \sec^2 \theta_1 - \tan^2 \theta_1)}}$$

where $n = \eta_2/\eta_1$, employing Snell's law to eliminate the ratio of sines. We can now eliminate the trigonometric terms:

$$\alpha = (n^2 |\mathbf{I}'|^2 - |\mathbf{I}' + \mathbf{N}|^2)^{-1/2}.$$

Total internal reflection occurs when α is imaginary (square root of a negative number). This happens when rays travel from a dense material to a sparser one $(n < 1)$ and the incident angle is above a critical angle: $\theta_1 > \theta_c = \sin^{-1} n$.

In Whitted's article, he used slightly different notation than the above: $\mathbf{V}$ for $\mathbf{I}$, $\mathbf{V}'$ for $\mathbf{I}'$, $\mathbf{P}$ for $\mathbf{T}'$, k_n for n, and k_f for α.

5.2   Heckbert's Method

The second formula comes from [66]. Referring to *Figure 4*, the basic idea is to decompose $\mathbf{I}$ into its components parallel and perpendicular to $\mathbf{N}$ and then synthesize the transmitted ray $\mathbf{T}$ from these components. In this formula we assume that $\mathbf{I}$ is unit in addition to $\mathbf{N}$, and we'll guarantee that $\mathbf{T}$ will be unit. Since $\mathbf{I}$ is unit, $c_1 = \cos \theta_1 = -\mathbf{I} \cdot \mathbf{N}$. The parallel and perpendicular components of $\mathbf{I}$ can then be written: $\mathbf{I}_{par} = -c_1 \mathbf{N}$ and $\mathbf{I}_{perp} = \mathbf{I} + c_1 \mathbf{N}$. As a bonus, we can easily compute the unit reflected ray direction as shown by the

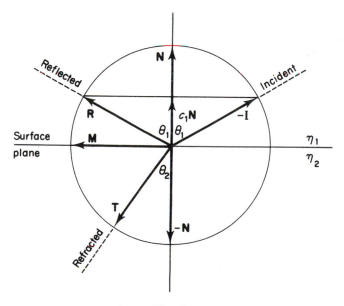

Fig. 4.

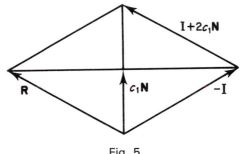

Fig. 5.

parallelogram in *Figure 5*:

$$\mathbf{R} = \mathbf{I} + 2c_1\mathbf{N}.$$

The refracted ray can be expressed as $\mathbf{T} = \sin\theta_2\mathbf{M} - \cos\theta_2\mathbf{N}$ where $\mathbf{M}$ is a unit surface tangent vector in the plane of $\mathbf{I}$ and $\mathbf{N}$:

$$\mathbf{M} = \frac{\mathbf{I}_{perp}}{|\mathbf{I}_{perp}|} = \frac{\mathbf{I} + c_1\mathbf{N}}{\sin\theta_1}.$$

Therefore,

$$\mathbf{T} = \frac{\sin\theta_2}{\sin\theta_1}(\mathbf{I} + c_1\mathbf{N}) - \cos\theta_2\mathbf{N}.$$

But by Snell's law, the relative index of refraction η is: $\eta = \sin\theta_2/\sin\theta_1 = \eta_1/\eta_2 = 1/n$, so

$$\mathbf{T} = \eta\mathbf{I} + (\eta c_1 - c_2)\mathbf{N}.$$

where $c_2 = \cos\theta_2$. We can easily express $\cos\theta_2$ in terms of known quantities:

$$c_2 = \cos\theta_2 = \sqrt{(1 - \sin^2\theta_2)} = \sqrt{(1 - \eta^2\sin^2\theta_1)} = \sqrt{(1 - \eta^2(1 - c_1^2))}.$$

Total internal reflection occurs when c_2 is imaginary (square root of a negative number).

5.3   Other Method

The third formulation is a slight variation on Heckbert's simply replacing η

with $1/n$:

$$\mathbf{T} = \eta \mathbf{I} + (\eta c_1 - \sqrt{(1 - \eta^2(1 - c_1^2))})\mathbf{N} =$$

$$\frac{\mathbf{I}}{n} + \frac{(c_1 - n\sqrt{(1 - (1 - c_1^2)/n^2)})}{n}\,\mathbf{N} = \frac{\mathbf{I} + (c_1 - \sqrt{(n^2 - 1 + c_1^2)}\mathbf{N})}{n}.$$

5.4 Comparison of Methods

The formulas are all equivalent, of course, so the only advantage of one over another comes from computational speed and perhaps numerical precision. We count the number of arithmetic operations (square roots, divisions, multiplications, and additions/subtractions) required by each method below:

Whitted's method

$\sqrt{}$	$/$	$\times$	$+$	
	1			$n = \eta_2/\eta_1$
	3	3	2	$\mathbf{I}' = \mathbf{I}/(-\mathbf{I} \cdot \mathbf{N})$
			3	$\mathbf{J} = \mathbf{I}' + \mathbf{N}$
1	1	8	5	$\alpha = 1/\sqrt{(n^2(\mathbf{I}' \cdot \mathbf{I}') - (\mathbf{J} \cdot \mathbf{J}))}$
		3	3	$\mathbf{T}' = \alpha\mathbf{J} - \mathbf{N}$
1	3	3	2	$\mathbf{T} = \mathbf{T}'/|\mathbf{T}'|$
2	**8**	**17**	**15**	Total

Note: **I** is not required to be unit in Whitted's method.

Heckbert's method

$\sqrt{}$	$/$	$\times$	$+$	
	1			$\eta = \eta_1/\eta_2$
		3	2	$c_1 = -\mathbf{I} \cdot \mathbf{N}$
1		3	2	$c_2 = \sqrt{(1 - \eta^2(1 - c_1^2))}$
		7	4	$\mathbf{T} = \eta\mathbf{I} + (\eta c_1 - c_2)\mathbf{N}$
1	**1**	**13**	**8**	Total

Note: Heckbert's method uses $\eta = 1/n$, not n.

Other method

$\sqrt{}$	$/$	$\times$	$+$	
	1			$n = \eta_2/\eta_1$
		3	2	$c_1 = -\mathbf{I} \cdot \mathbf{N}$
1		2	3	$\beta = c_1 - \sqrt{(n^2 - 1 + c_1^2)}$
	3	3	3	$\mathbf{T} = (\mathbf{I} + \beta\mathbf{N})/n$
1	4	8	8	Total

Either the second or third method will be fastest depending on the relative speed of division on a particular machine.

REFERENCES

The references cited are listed in chapter 8, with the following exceptions:

A. Bentley, J. L., Writing Efficient Programs. Prentice-Hall, Englewood Cliffs, NJ, 1982.
B. Cook, R. L. and Torrance K. E., A reflectance model for computer graphics. *ACM Trans. Graph.* **1**(1), 7–24, Jan. 1982.
C. Nishita, T. and Nakamae, E., Half-tone representation of 3-D objects illuminated by area sources or polyhedron sources. COMPSAC '83, *Proc. IEEE 7th Intl. Comp. Soft. and Applications Conf.*, Nov. 1983, pp. 237–242.
D. Feynman, R. P., Leighton, P., and Sands, M., *The Feynman Lectures on Physics*, Addison-Wesley, Reading, Mass., 1963, p. 26-3.

8 A Ray Tracing Bibliography

Collected and annotated by

PAUL S. HECKBERT and ERIC HAINES

1. Amanatides, J. and Foumier, A., Ray casting using divide and conquer in screen space. Int. Conf. on Engineering and Computer Graphics, Beijing, China, Aug. 1984, similar to Siggraph '84 paper but more emphasis on recursive screen subdivision, extents [screen subdivision, bounding volume].
2. Amanatides, J., Ray tracing with cones. *Comput. Graph.* (Siggraph '84 Proceedings), **18**(3), 129–135, July 1984. Ray tracing spheres and polygons with circular conical rays [cone tracing, anti-aliasing].
3. Amanatides, J., Ray tracing with cones. *Proceedings of Graphics Interface '84*, May 1984, 97–98. Brief summary of his Siggraph paper [cone tracing].
4. Amanatides, J., A fast voxel traversal algorithm for ray tracing. *Eurographics '87*, North-Holland, Amsterdam. Uniform grid space subdivision.
5. Appel, A., Some techniques for shading machine renderings of solids. *AFIPS 1968 Spring Joint Computer Conf.*, **32**, 37–45, 1968. First ray tracing paper, light ray tracing, b&w pictures on Calcomp plotter.
6. Arnaldi, B., Priol, T., and Bouatouch, K., A new space subdivision method for ray tracing CSG modelled scenes. *Vis. Comput.* **3**, 98–108, 1987 [CSG].
7. Arvo, J., Backward ray tracing. Siggraph '86 Developments in Ray Tracing seminar notes, Aug. 1986. Light ray tracing.
8. Arvo, J. and Kirk, D., Fast ray tracing by ray classification. *Comput. Graph.* (Siggraph '87 Proceedings), **21**(4), 55–64, July 1987 [octree], five dimensional space subdivision.
9. Atherton, P. R., A scanline hidden surface removal procedure for constructive solid geometry. *Comput. Graph.* (Siggraph '83 Proceedings), **17**(3), 73–82, July 1983 [CSG].
10. Barr, A. H., Decal projections. Siggraph '84 Mathematics of Computer Graphics seminar notes, July 1984 [texture mapping].
11. Barr, A. H., Ray tracing deformed surfaces. *Comput. Graph.* (Siggraph '86 Proceedings), **20**(4), 287–296, Aug. 1986.
12. Bier, E. A., Solidviews, an interactive three-dimensional illustrator. BS & MS thesis, Dept. of EE&CS, MIT, May 1983. Use of Roth's CSG ray tracer as part of an interactive system [CSG].

13. Blinn, J. F. and Newell, M. E., Texture and reflection in computer generated images. *CACM* **19**(10), 542–547, Oct. 1976. Early paper on texture mapping, discusses spherical sky textures [texture mapping, reflection].

14. Blinn, J. F., A generalization of algebraic surface drawing. *ACM Trans. Graph.* **1**(3), 235–256, July 1982. Ray tracing 'blobby' models: finding roots of sums of gaussians [blob, root finding].

15. Bouatouch, K., A new algorithm of space tracing using a CSG model. *Eurographics '87*, North-Holland, Amsterdam.

16. Bouville, C., Brusq, R., Dubois, J. L. and Marchal, L., Image synthesis by ray-casting (in French). *Acta Electron. (France)* **26**(3/4), 249–259, 1984.

17. Bouville, C., Dubois, J. L., and Marchal, L., Generating high quality pictures by ray tracing. *Eurographics '84*, Copenhagen, Sept. 1984, pp. 161–177 (also *Comput. Graph. For.* **4**(2), 87–99, June 1985).

18. Bouville, C., Bounding ellipsoids for ray–fractal intersection. *Comput. Graph.* (Siggraph '85 Proceedings) **19**(3), 45–52, July 1985 [bounding volume].

19. Bouville, C., Image synthesis through ray tracing. *Banc-Titre*, France, 50 pp., Mar. 1985 [hardware].

20. Bronsvoort, W. F. and Klok, F., Ray tracing general sweep-defined objects. 84-36, Dept. of Mathematics and Informatics, Delft U. of Tech., Delft, Netherlands, 1984.

21. Bronsvoort, W. F., Jansen, F. W. and van Wijk, J. J., The use of ray casting in solid modeling. *Informatie* (Netherlands), **26**, 50–59, Jan. 1984 [CSG].

22. Bronsvoort, W. F., van Wijk, J. J. and Jansen, F. W., Two methods for improving the efficiency of ray casting in solid modeling. *Computer-Aided Design* **16**(1), 110–116, Jan. 1984 [CSG], enhancements to Roth: scanline interval enclosures, CSG tree optimization, and recursive screen subdivision.

23. Bronsvoort, W. F. and Klok, F., Ray tracing generalized cylinders. *ACM Trans. Graph.* (note corrigendum in ACM TOG July 1987 issue, Vol. 6, No. 3, pp. 238–239), **4**(4), 291–303, Oct. 1985.

24. Brooks, J., Extension and adjuncts to the BRL-COMGEOM Program (for Ballistic Research Laboratories), Aug. 1974, NTIS AD/A-000 897, MAGI: intersection of ray and ellipsoid, ray tracing in the punch card era [CSG, quadric].

25. Brooks, J., Murarka, R., Onuoha, D., Rahn, F. and Steinberg, H. A., An extension of the combinatorial geometry technique for modeling vegetation and terrain features, (for Ballistic Research Laboratories), June 1974, NTIS AD-782 883, MAGI: hierarchical bounding boxes, adaptive subsampling, pine tree models [CSG, bounding volume, botanical tree].

26. Brown, C., Special purpose computer hardware for mechanical design systems, *Proc. 1981 Nat. Comput. Graph. Assoc. Conf.*, 403–414.

27. Bukow, H. M. T., Bailey, M. J. and Stevenson, W. H., Simulation of reflectance sensors using image synthesis techniques, *Comput. Mech. Eng.* **3**(4), 69–74, Jan. 1985 [CAM], simulating assembly line optical sensors.

28. Chang, A. G., Parallel architectural support for ray tracing graphics techniques, Masters thesis, EECS Dept, UC Berkeley.

29. Chattopadhyay, S. and Fujimoto, A., Bi-directional ray tracing, *Comput. Graph. 1987*, Tosiyasu Kunii ed., Springer Verlag, Tokyo, 335–343, 1987.

30. Chung, W. L., A new method of view synthesis for solid modelling, *CAD84*, Butterworth & Co, Guildford, Surrey, UK, 470–480, Apr. 1984 [CSG].

31. Cleary, J. G., Wyvill, B., Vatti, R. and Birtwistle, G. M., Design and analysis of

a parallel ray tracing computer, *Proceedings Graphics Interface '83*, 33–34, May 1983, (also Proceedings XI Association of Simula Users Conference, 1983), [hardware], short note describing their project.

32. Cleary, J. G., Wyvill, B., Birtwistle, G. M. and Vatti, R., Multiprocessor ray tracing, Technical Report No. 83/128/17, Dept. of CS, U of Calgary, Oct. 1983, [hardware], analysis of square and cubical processor arrays for ray tracing.

33. Cleary, J. G. and Wyvill, G., An analysis of an algorithm for fast ray tracing using uniform space subdivision, Research Report 87/264/12, U. of Calgary, Dept. of CS, 1987.

34. Cook, R. L., Porter, T. and Carpenter, L., Distributed ray tracing, *Comput. Graph.* (Siggraph '84 proceedings), **18**(3), 137–145, July 1984, Monte Carlo distribution of rays to get gloss, translucency, penumbras, depth of field, motion blur [probabilistic ray tracing, monte carlo, motion blur, stochastic sampling].

35. Cook, R. L., Stochastic sampling in computer graphics, *ACM Trans. Graph.*, **5**(1), 51–72, Jan. 1986.

36. Cook, R. L., Practical aspects of distributed ray tracing, Siggraph '86 developments in ray tracing seminar notes, Aug. 1986 [probabilistic ray tracing].

37. Coquillart, S., An improvement of the ray tracing algorithm, *Eurographics '85*, 77–88, Sept. 1985, North-Holland, Amsterdam.

38. Cordonnier, E., Bouville, C., Marchal, I. and Dubois, J. L., Creating CSH modelled pictures for ray casting display, *Eurographics '85*, Sept. 1985, North-Holland, Amsterdam.

39. Dadoun, N., Kirkpatrick, D. G. and Walsh, J. P., The geometry of beam tracing, *Proc. of the Symp. on Comput. Geometry*, 55–61, June 1985, the use of BSP trees and hierarchical bounding volumes for fast beam intersection testing.

40. Davis, J. R., Nagel, R. and Guber, W., A model making and display technique for 3-D pictures, *Proceedings of the 7th Annual Meeting of UAIDE*, San Francisco, 47–72, Oct. 1968 [CSG], synthavision genesis: CSG, primitives, optimization by region adjacency lists and adaptive subdivision for line drawings.

41. Davis, J. E., Bailey, M. J. and Anderson, D. C., Realistic image generation and the modeling of mechanical solids, *Computers in Mechanical Engineering*, **1**(1), Aug. 1982, intro to CAD, solid modeling, and Whitted ray tracing, pre-Roth.

42. Davis, J. E., Recursive ray tracing for the realistic display of solid models, MSME thesis, dept of ME, Purdue U., May 1982 [CAD].

43. Deguchi, H., Nishimura, H., Yoshimura, H., Kawata, T., Shirakawa, I. and Omura, K., A parallel processing scheme for three-dimensional image creation, *Conf. Proc. Int. Symp. on Circuit and Systems (ISCAS '84)*, 1285–1288, 1984 [hardware], LINKS-1 hardware.

44. Deguchi, H., Nishimura, H., Tatsumi, T., Kawata, T., Shirakawa, I. and Omura, K., Performance evaluation of parallel processing in computer graphics system LINKS-1, submitted to Siggraph '85, 1985 [hardware].

45. Dippe, M. A. Z. and Wold, E. H., Antialiasing through stochastic sampling, *Comput. Graph.* (Siggraph '85 proceedings), **19**(3), 69–78, July 1985 [probabilistic ray tracing, stochastic sampling].

46. Dippe, M. E. and Swensen, J., An adaptive subdivision algorithm and parallel architecture for realistic image synthesis, *Comput. Graph.* (Siggraph '84 proceedings), **18**(3), 149–158, July 1984, 3-D network of processors, algorithm for adaptive load distribution [hardware].

47. Edwards, B. E., Implementation of a ray tracing algorithm for rendering superquadric solids, Masters thesis, TR-82018, Rensselaer Polytechnic Insti-

tute, Troy, NY, Dec. 1982, ray traced unions and differences of superquadrics [superquadric].

48. Fitzhorn, P. A., Realistic image synthesis: A time complexity analysis of ray tracing, Masters thesis, Dept. of CS, Colorado State U., Fort Collins, CO, Spring 1982.

49. Fujimoto, A. and Iwata, K., Accelerated ray tracing, *Comput. Graph.: Visual Technology and Art* (Proceedings of Computer Graphics Tokyo '85), Tosiyasu Kunii ed., Springer Verlag, Tokyo, 41–65, 1985 [octree].

50. Fujimoto, A., Tanaka, T. and Iwata, K., ARTS: accelerated ray-tracing system, *IEEE Comput. Graph. and Appl.*, 16–26, Apr. 1986 [octree].

51. Gjoystdal, H., Reinhardsen, J. E. and Astebol, K., Computer representation of complex 3-D geological structures using a new 'solid modeling' technique, *Geophy. Prospect.* (*Netherlands*), **33**(8), 1195–1211, Dec. 1985 [dynamic ray tracing].

52. Glassner, A. S., Space subdivision for fast ray tracing, *IEEE Comput. Graph. and Appl.* **4**(10), 15–22, Oct. 1984, use of octrees to speed intersection testing [bounding volume, octree].

53. Glassner, A. S., Spacetime ray tracing for animation, *IEEE Comput. Graph. and Appl.* **8**(2), 60–70, March 1988.

54. Goldsmith, J. and Salmon, J., A ray tracing system for the hypercube, Caltech, 1984 [parallel processing].

55. Goldsmith, J. and Salmon, J., Automatic creation of object hierarchies for ray tracing, *IEEE Comput. Graph. and Appl.* 1987 [ray tracing, bounding volume].

56. Goldstein, R. A., A system for computer animation of 3-D objects, Proceedings of the 10th Annual UAIDE Meeting, 1971.

57. Goldstein, R. A. and Nagel, R., 3-D visual simulation, *Simulation,* **16**(1), 25–31, Jan. 1971, introduction to CSG, ray tracing, director's language [CSG].

58. Graham, E., Graphic scene simulations, *Amiga World*, 18 pp., May/June 1987, C source for sphere ray tracer (runs on Amiga).

59. Haines, E. A. and Greenberg, D. P., The light buffer: A ray tracer shadow testing accelerator, *IEEE Comput. Graph. and Appl.* **6**(9), 6–16, Sept. 1986 [shading, ray tracing, shadows].

60. Haines, E., A proposal for standard graphics environments, *IEEE Comput. Graph. and Appl.* **7**(11), 3–5, Nov. 1987 [benchmark], renderer bench-marking environments and how to obtain them.

61. Hall, R. A., A methodology for realistic image synthesis, Masters thesis, Cornell U., 1983 [shading, color].

62. Hall, R. A. and Greenberg, D. P., A testbed for realistic image synthesis, *IEEE Comput. Graph. and Appl.* **3**(8), 10–20, Nov. 1983, concerns shading and color more than ray tracing, but nice pictures! [shading, color].

63. Hanrahan, P., Ray tracing algebraic surfaces, *Comput. Graph.* (Siggraph '83 proceedings), **17**(3), 83–90, July 1983, numerical techniques for finding roots of polynomials [root finding, algebraic surface].

64. Hanrahan, P. and Heckbert, P. S., Introduction to beam tracing, *Intl. Conf. on Engineering and Comput. Graph*, Beijing, China, 286–289, Aug. 1984, early version of their Siggraph paper.

65. Hanrahan, P., Using caching and breadth-first search to speed up ray tracing, *Graphics Interface '86*, 56–61, May 1986 [seed fill, coherence].

66. Heckbert, P. S. and Hanrahan, P., Beam tracing polygonal objects, *Comput. Graph.* (Siggraph '84 proceedings), **18**(3), 119–127, July 1984, Weiler-Atherton algorithm applied to ray tracing [polygon].

67. Heckbert, P. A., Ray tracing JELL-O (R) brand gelatin, *Comput. Graph.* (Siggraph '87 proceedings), **21**(4), 73–74, July 1987.

68. Jansen, F., Data Structures for Ray tracing, Kessener L. R. A. Peters, F. J. and van Lierop M. L. P. eds, *Data Structures for Raster Graphics*, (Eurographic Seminar), New York, Springer-Verlag, 57–73, 1986, {data structures, CSG}, overview of published algorithms for ray tracing using spatial subdivision.

69. Joy, K. I. and Bhetanobhoktla, M. N., Ray tracing parametric surface patches utilizing numerical techniques and ray coherence, *Comput. Graph.* (Siggraph '86 Proceedings), **20**(4), 279–285, Aug. 1986.

70. Kajiya, J. T., Ray tracing parametric patches, *Comput. Graph.* (Siggraph '82 proceedings) **16**(3), 245–254, July 1982, ray tracing bivariate polynomial patches, [patches].

71. Kajiya, J. T., New techniques for ray tracing procedurally defined objects, *ACM Trans. on Graph.* **2** (3) 161–181, July 1983, (also appeared in Siggraph '83 proceedings), ray tracing fractals, prisms, and surfaces of revolution, [fractal].

72. Kajiya, J. T., Siggraph '83 tutorial on ray tracing, Siggraph '83 State of the Art in Image Synthesis seminar notes, July 1983, good survey of ray tracing.

73. Kajiya, J. T. and Von Herzen, B. P., Ray tracing volume densities, *Comput. Graph.* (Siggraph '84 proceedings), **18**(3), 165–174, July 1984, ray tracing and meterological simulation of clouds, [cloud].

74. Kajiya, J. T., The Rendering Equation, *Comput. Graph.* (Siggraph '86 Proceedings), **20**(4) 143–150, Aug. 1986, [shading, diffuse reflection, radiosity].

75. Kaplan, M. R., Space-tracing, a constant time ray tracer,. Siggraph '85 State of the Art in Image Synthesis seminar notes, July 1985, like Glassner.

76. Kay, D. S. and Greenberg, D. P., Transparency for computer synthesized images', *Comput. Graph.* (Siggraph '79 proceedings), **13**(2) 158–164, Aug. 1979, 2.5-D ray tracing: refraction by warping background image, contains better refraction formula than Whitted.

77. Kay, D. S., Transparency, refraction, and ray tracing for computer synthesized images, Masters thesis, Cornell U., Jan. 1979.

78. Kay, T. L. and Kajiya, J. T., Ray tracing complex scenes, *Comput. Graph.* (Siggraph '86 Proceedings), **20**(4) 269–278, Aug. 1986, [bounding volume].

79. Kedem, G. and Ellis, J. L., The Raycasting Machine, *Proc. IEEE Intl. Conf. on Computer Design*: VLSI in Computers (ICCD '84), (Port Chestner, NY 8–11 Oct. 1984), IEEE Computer Society Press, Silver Spring, MD, 533–538, 1984.

80. Kirk, D. B., The simulation of natural features using cone tracing, *Advanced Computer Graphics* (Proc. of CG Tokyo '86), Tosiyasu Kunii ed., 129–144, Springer Verlag, Tokyo, 1986, [antialiasing].

81. Kitaoka, S., Kit: An experimental solid modelling system, MS thesis, University of Utah, April 1985, Roth-style ray tracer with the addition of several new surfaces including patches, sweeps, etc. Produced 'Scene with Corkscrew' on Siggraph '85 back cover, [solid modeling, primitive shapes].

82. Kitaoka, S., KIT: An experimental solid modeling system, *The Visual Computer*, **2**(1), 9, Jan 1986, Roth-style ray tracer with the addition of several new surfaces including patches, sweeps etc., [solid modeling, primitive shapes].

83. Lee, M. E., Redner, R. A. and Uselton, S. P., Statistically optimized sampling for distributed ray tracing, *Comput. Graph.* (Siggraph '85 Proceedings), **19**(3) 61–67, July 1985, [probabilistic ray tracing, stochastic sampling].

84. Levner, G., Tassinari, P. and Marini, D., A simple method for ray tracing bicubic surfaces, *Comput. Graph. 1987*, Tosiyasu Kunii ed., 285–302, Springer Verlag, Tokyo, 1987.

85. Martin, R. R., Recent advances in graphical techniques, *1985 European Conference on Solid Modeling*, (London, 9–10 Sept. 1985), Oyez Sci. and Tech. Services, London, 1985, [texture mapping].

86. Max, N. L., Vectorized procedural models for natural terrain: waves and islands in the sunset, *Comput. Graph.* (Siggraph '81 Proceedings), 15(3), 317–324, Aug. 1981, ray tracing on a CRAY + many tricks, [orientation code, colormap animation, hardware, wave].

87. Max, N. L., An anti-aliased wave reflection algorithm, Siggraph '82 Advanced Image Synthesis seminar notes, July 1982, improved ray tracing of waves, [wave].

88. Miller, G. S. and Hoffman, C. R., Illumination and reflection maps: simulated objects in simulated and real environments, Siggraph '84 Advanced Computer Graphics Animation seminar notes, July 1984, reflection maps: how to make and use them [illumination map].

89. Montcel, B. and du Tezenas, A. N., An Illumination Model for Ray-Tracing, *Eurographics '85*, Sept. 1985.

90. Moravec, H. P., 3D graphics and the wave theory, *Comput. Graph.* (Siggagraph '81 Proceedings), 15(3), 289–296, Aug. 1981, illumination by wave fronts, rather than light rays [wave theory].

91. Marakami, K. and Hitoshi Matsumoto, Ray tracing with octree data structure, Proc. 28th Information Processing Conf., 1983.

92. Nemoto, K. and Omachi, T., An adaptive subdivision by sliding boundary surfaces for fast ray tracing, *Graphics Interface '86*, 43–48, May 1986, [adaptive subdivision algorithm on a parallel architecture].

93. Nishimura, H., Ohno, H., Kawata, T., Shirakawa, I. and Omura, K., Links-1: a parallel pipelined multimicrocomputer system for image creation, Conference Proceedings of the 10th Annual International Symposium on Computer Architecture, SIGARCH, 1983, 387–394, a parallel hardware architecture being used for ray traced animation; the paper does not discuss ray tracing or their software, [hardware].

94. Ohta, M. and Maekawa, M., Ray coherence theorem and constant time ray tracing algorithm, *Comput. Graph. 1987*, Tosiyasu Kunii ed., Springer Verlag, Tokyo, 303–314, 1987.

95. Peachey, D. R., PORTRAY—An image synthesis system for realistic computer graphics, TR 84-18, Dept of Computational Science, U. of Saskatchewan, Saskatoon, Saskatchewan, Canada, 1984, [modeling, shading], excellent survey of image synthesis, system issues.

96. Peachey, D. R., PORTRAY—an image synthesis system, *Graphics Interface '86*, 37–42, May 1986, [modeling, shading], image formats, condensed version of U of Sask tech report.

97. Peng, Q. S., A fast ray tracing algorithm using space indexing techniques, *Eurographics '87*, North-Holland, Amsterdam.

98. Peterson, J. W., Ray tracing general B-splines, Proceedings of the ACM Mountain Regional Conference April, 1986, 87 pp., [B-splines, surfaces], extensions to Sweeney's patch algorithm to handle a wider range of surfaces.

99. Plunkett, D. J. and Bailey, M. J., The vectorization of a ray-tracing algorithm for improved execution speed, *IEEE Comput. Graph. and Appl.* 5(3) 52–60, Aug. 1985.

100. Potmesil, M., Generating three-dimensional surface models of solid objects from

multiple projections, PhD thesis, IPL-TR-033, Oct. 1982, Image Processing Laboratory, RPI, Troy, NY, contains brief description of his ray tracer, camera model and motion blur as post-processes, appendix on ray-patch intersection methods, [computer vision, patch, quadtree].

101. Pulleyblank, R. and Kapenga, J., The feasibility of a VLSI chip for ray tracing bicubic patches, *IEEE Comput. Graph. and Appl.* **7**(3), 33–44, March 1987, [bicubic, patch].

102. Purgathofer, W., A statistical method for adaptive stochastic sampling, *Eurographics '86*, North-Holland, Amsterdam, 145–152, 1986, [probablistic ray tracing].

103. Reddy, D. R. and Rubin, S. M., Representation of three dimensional objects, CMU-CS-78-113, Dept. of CS, Carnegie-Mellon U., Apr. 1978, [bounding volume].

104. Rogers, D. F., *Procedural Elements for Computer Graphics*, McGraw-Hill, New York, 1985, [hidden surface], the only book on image synthesis, good summary of ray tracing.

105. Roth, S. D., Ray casting for modeling solids, *Comput. Graph. and Image Processing*, **18**(2), 109–144, Feb. 1982, the other classic ray tracing paper [CSG, hidden line].

106. Rubin, S. M. and Whitted, T., A 3-dimensional representation for fast rendering of complex scenes, *Comput. Graph.* (Siggraph '80 Proceedings), **14**(3), 110–116, July 1980, hierarchical bounding boxes, used to speed up ray tracing & other algs, [bounding volume].

107. Sederberg, T. W. and Anderson, D. C., Ray tracing of steiner patches, *Comput. Graph.* (Siggraph '84 Proceedings), **18**(3), 159–164, July 1984, implicitization of Steiner patch, solution of resulting quartic, [patch, root finding].

108. Shinya, M., Takahashi, T. and Naito, S., Principles and applications of pencil tracing, *Comput. Graph.* (Siggraph '87 Proceedings), **21**(4), 45–54, July 1987.

109. Snyder, J. M. and Barr, A. H., Ray tracing complex models containing surface tessellations, *Comput. Graph.* (Siggraph '87 Proceedings) **21**(4), 119–128, July 1987, [parametric surface, tessellation, 3D grid].

110. Speer, L. R., DeRose, T. D. and Barsky, B. A., A theoretical and empirical analysis of coherent ray-tracing, *Graphics Interface '85*, May 1985, [coherence], they conclude that their cylinder-piercing optimization doesn't work.

111. Steinberg, H. A., A smooth surface based on biquadratic patches, *IEEE Comp. Graph. Appl.* **4**(9), 20–23, Sept. 1984, ray tracing biquadratic and bicubic Coons patches, [patch].

112. Steinberg, H. A., Ray tracing and CSG applications, Siggraph '85 Introduction to Solid Modeling seminar notes, July 1985, [CSG],

113. Sweeney, M. A. J., The Waterloo ray tracing package, CS-85-35 (Master's thesis), Dept of CS, U. of Waterloo, Oct. 1985.

114. Sweeney, M. and Bartels, R. H., Ray tracing free-form B-spline surfaces, *IEEE Comp. Graph. Appl.*, **6**(2), 41, Feb. 1986.

115. Tamminen, M., Karonen, O. and Mantyla, M., Ray-casting and block model conversion using a spatial index, *Computer Aided Design*, **16**, 203–208, July 1984.

116. Thomas, S., Dispersive refraction in ray tracing, *The Visual Computer*, **2**(1), 3–8, Jan. 1986, prismatic effects.

117. Toth, D. L., On ray tracing parametric surfaces, *Comput. Graph.* (Siggraph '85 Proceedings), **19**(3), 171–179, July 1985.

118. Ullner, M. K., Parallel machines for computer graphics, PhD thesis, California Institute of Technology, 1983, hardware for ray tracing, [hardware].

119. Vatti, B. R., Multiprocessor ray-tracing, MS thesis, Dept. of CS, U of Calgary, May 1985, [parallel processing, space subdivision], multiprocessor algorithm and uniprocessor simulation results, regular space subdivision to reduce object/ray intersections.

120. Verbeck, Channing P., Extended geometrics and directional intensity variation for light sources, *Banc-Titre*, France, 53–54, Mar. 1985, [shading, ray tracing, numerical integration].

121. Wallace, J. R., Cohen, M. F. and Greenberg, D. P., A two-pass solution to the rendering equation: a synthesis of ray tracing and radiosity methods, *Comput. Graph.* (Siggraph '87 Proceedings), **21**(4), 311–320, July 1987, [radiosity, probabilistic ray tracing, z-buffer].

122. Warren, V., Geometric hashing for rendering complex scenes, MS thesis, University of Utah, May 1986, Divides the scene into a volume of regular small cubes, and traces the rays between cubes, [geometric hashing].

123. Weghorst, H., Hooper, G. and Greenberg, D. P., Improved computational methods for ray tracing, *ACM Trans. on Graphics*, **3**(1), 52–69, Jan. 1984, discussion of bounding volumes, hierarchical structures and the 'item buffer', [bounding volume].

124. Whelan, D. S., A multiprocessor architecture for real-time computer animation, Computer Science TR 5200, Caltech, 1985, [hardware].

125. Whitted, T., Processing requirements for hidden surface elimination and realistic shading, *IEEE Digest of Papers, COMPCON*, 245–250, Spring '82, discussion of various visible surface and illumination methods, including ray tracing [efficiency].

126. Whitted, T., An improved illumination model for shaded display, *CACM*, **23**(6), 343–349, June 1980, the classic ray tracing paper.

127. Whitted, T., The Hacker's guide to making pretty pictures, Siggraph '85 Image Rendering Tricks seminar notes, July 1985, general tricks for image synthesis, includes C sourced for simple ray tracer.

128. Wijk, J. van, J. and Jansen, F. W., Realism in raster graphics, *Comput. Graph.*, **8**(2), 217–219, [image synthesis].

129. Wijk, J. van, J., Ray tracing objects defined by sweeping planar cubic splines, *ACM Trans. Graphics*, **3**(3) 223–237, July 1984, ray tracing prisms, cones, and surfaces of revolution.

130. Wijk, J. van, J., Ray tracing objects defined by sweeping a sphere, *Eurographics '84*, Copehagen, 73–82, Sept. 1984, (reprinted in *Computers and Graphics*, **9**(3), 283–290, 1985).

131. Wyvill, G., Ward, A. and Brown, T., Sketches by ray tracing, Research Report 1/1/87, Dept. of CS, U. of Otago, New Zealand, [hidden line], line drawing.

132. Wyvill, G., Kunii, T. L. and Shirai, Y., Space division for ray tracing in CSG, *IEEE Comp. Graph. and Appl.*, 28–34, Apr. 1986, [CSG].

133. Yamamoto, T., The three dimensional computer Graphics, CQ Publishing, 1983, a Japanese book on ray tracing! No English, but some BASIC(!) listings of ray tracing programs.

134. Yasuda, T., Yokoi, S., Toriwaki, J. I., Tsurouoka, S. and Miyake, Y., An improved ray tracing algorithm for rendering transparent objects (in Japanese), *Trans. Inf. Process. Soc. of Japan*, **25**(6), 953–959, 1984.

135. Yokoi, S., Yasuda, T. and Toriwaki, J., Simplified ray tracing algorithms for rendering transparent objects. Technical Report, Information Engineering Dept., Nagoya University, Japan.
136. Youssef, S., A new algorithm for object oriented ray tracing, *Computer Vision, Graphics and Image Processing* **34**, 125–137, 1986.

ADDITIONAL BIBLIOGRAPHY

Badt, Jr. S., Two algorithms for taking advantage of temporal coherence in ray tracing. *Vis. Comput.*, **4**(3), 123–132, September 1988.

Bouatouch, K., Theoretical developments on polygonal approximation of parametric surfaces for ray tracing. *Comput. Graph. For.*, **7**(4), 257–264, December 1988.

Bouatouch, K. and Priol, T., Parallel space tracing: An experience on an iPSC hypercube, In *New Trends in Computer Graphics*, (eds N. Magnenat-Thalmann and D. Thalmann), 170–187, 1988.

Buckalew, C. and Fussell, D., Illumination networks: Fast realistic rendering with general reflectance functions. *Comput. Graph.* (Siggraph '89 Proceedings), **23**(3), 89–98, July 1989.

Caspary, E. and Scherson, I. D., A self-balanced parallel ray tracing algorithm, *Parallel Processing for Computer Vision and Display*, (eds P. M. Dew, T. R. Heywood and R. A. Earnshaw), Addison Wesley, Mass., 408–419, 1989, [parallelism].

Crow, F. C., Demos, G., Hardy, J., McLaughlin, J. and Sims, K., 3D Image synthesis on the connection machine, In *Parallel Processing for Computer Vision and Display*, (eds, P. M. Dew, T. R. Heywood and R. A. Earnshaw). Addison Wesley, Mass., 254–269, 1989, [parallelism].

Devillers, O., Puech, C. and Sillion, F., Efficiency of space subdivision structures for ray tracing, *Technical Report 88-2*, Laboratoire d'Informatique de l'Ecole Normale Superieure, Paris, France, 1988.

Devillers, O., The macro-regions: an efficient space subdivision structure for ray tracing, *Technical Report 88-13*, Laboratoire d'Informatique de l'Ecole Normale Superieure, Paris, France, 1988, [using grid subdivision, save time by finding empty blocks of grid cubes].

Forgue, M.-C., Ray-tracing parallelization on a SIMD/SPMD machine, (PhD), Laboratoire de Signaux et Systems (LASSY), Universite de Nice, Nice, France, September 1988.

Gaudet, S., Hobson, R., Chilka, P. and Calvert, T., Multiprocessor experiments for high-speed ray tracing, *ACM Trans. Graph.*, **7**(3), 151–179, July 1988.

Gervautz, M., Three improvements of the ray tracing algorithm for CSG trees, *Comp. Graph.*, **10**(4), 333–339, 1986, [image synthesis].

Green, S. A., Paddon, D. J. and Lewis, E., A parallel algorithm and tree-based computer architecture for ray traced computer graphics. *TR-89-02*, University of Bristol Computer Science Department, 1989, [parallelism].

Green, S. A. and Paddon, D. J., A parallel algorithm and tree-based computer architecture for ray traced computer graphics, In *Parallel Processing for Computer Vision and Display*, (eds P. M. Dew, T. R. Heywood and R. A. Earnshaw), Addison Wesley, Mass., 431–442, 1989, [parallelism].

Green, S. A. and Paddon, D. J., Exploiting coherence for multiprocessor ray tracing, *IEEE Comput. Graph. and Appl.*, **9**(6), 12–26, 1989, [parallelism].

Hall, R., *Illumination and Color in Computer Generated Imagery*, Springer-Verlag, New York, 1989.

Hart, J. C., Sandin, D. J. and Kauffman, L. H., Ray tracing deterministic 3-D fractals, *Comput. Graph.* (Siggraph '89 Proceedings), **23**(3), 289–296, July 1989, [fractal].

Jevans, D. and Wyvill, B., Ray tracing implicit surfaces, *Technical Report 88/292/04*, University of Calgary, 1988, [voxel and octree hybrid efficiency structure].

Jevans, D. A. J., Optimistic multi-processor ray tracing, In *New Advances in Computer Graphics*, (eds R. A. Earnshaw and B. Wyvill), Springer Verlag, New York, 507–522, 1989.

Jevans, D. and Wyvill, B., Adaptive voxel subdivision for ray tracing, *Proc. Graph. Interface '89*, 164–172, June 1989.

Kajiya, J. T. and Kay, T. L., Rendering fur with three dimensional textures, *Comput. Graph.* (Siggraph '89 Proceedings), **23**(3), 271–280, July 1989, (textel rendering), [teddy bear].

Kalra, D. and Barr, A. H., Guaranteed ray intersections with implicit surfaces, *Comput. Graph.* (Siggraph '89 Proceedings), **23**(3), 297–306, July 1989, (Automatic interval finding for implicit surface intersection), [root finding].

Kaplan, M. R., The use of spatial coherence in ray tracing, In *Techniques for Computer Graphics*, (eds David E. Rogers and Rae A. Earnshaw) Springer Verlag, New York, 173–193, 1987, [octree].

Kobayashi, H., Nakamura, T. and Shigei, Y., Parallel processing of an object space for image synthesis using ray tracing, *Vis. Comput.*, **3**(1), 13–22, February 1987.

Kobayashi, H., Nishimura, S., Kubota, H., Nakamura, T. and Shigei, Y., Load balancing strategies for a parallel ray-tracing system based on constant subdivision, *Vis. Comput.*, **4**(4), 197–209, October 1988.

Kobayashi, H., Horiguchi, S., Kubota, H. and Nakamura, T., Effective parallel processing for synthesizing continuous images, In *New Advances in Computer Graphics* (eds Ray A. Earnshaw and B. Wyvill), Springer Verlag, New York, 343–352, 1989.

Kobayashi, H., Nakamura, T. and Shigei, Y., A strategy for mapping parallel ray-tracing into a hypercube multiprocessor system, In *New Trends in Computer Graphics* (eds N. Magnenat-Thalmann and D. Thalmann), 160–169, 1988.

Kuchkuda, R., An introduction to ray tracing, In *Theoretical Foundations of Computer Graphics and CAD*, (ed. R. A. Earnshaw), Springer-Verlag, Berlin, 1039–1060, 1988.

Leister, W., Maus, Th., Muller, H., Neidecker, B. and Stosser, A., "Occursus cum novo" – Computer animation by ray tracing in a network, In *New Trends in Computer Graphics*, (eds, N. Magnenat-Thalmann and D. Thalmann), 89–92, 1988.

MacDonald, D., Space subdivision algorithms for ray tracing, (Masters Thesis), University of Waterloo, 1988.

MacDonald, J. D. and Booth, K. S., Heuristics for ray tracing using space subdivision, *Proc. Graph. Interface '89*, 152–163, June 1989.

Magnenat-Thalmann, N. and Thalmann, D., *Image Synthesis*, Springer-Verlag, Tokyo, 1987, (includes summaries of ideas from many articles in this bibliography).

Marsh, S. C., Fine grain parallel architectures and the creation of high-quality images, In *Theoretical Foundations of Computer Graphics and CAD*, (ed. R. A. Earnshaw), Springer-Verlag, Berlin, 727–754, 1988.

Muller, H., Ray-tracing complex scenes by grids, *Technical Report 22*, Universitat Karlsruhe,, Fakultat fur Informatik, December 1985.

Musgrave, F. K., Kolb, C. E. and Mace, R. S., The synthesis and rendering of eroded fractal terrains, *Comput. Graph.* (Siggraph '89 Proceedings), **23**(30, 41–50, July 1989, (info on efficiently ray tracing height fields), [fractal, height fields].

Painter, J. and Sloan, K., Antialiased ray tracing by adaptive progressive refinement, *Comput. Graph.* (Siggraph '89 Proceedings), **23**(3), 281–288, July 1989, (adaptive stochastic sampling), [antialiasing, filtering].

Pearce, A., An implementation of ray tracing using multiprocessor and spatial subdivision, (Master's thesis), University of Calgary, Dept. of Computer Science, 1987.

Peng, Q. S., A fast ray tracing algorithm using space indexing techniques, *Eurographics '87*, North-Holland, Amsterdam, August 1987.

Perlin, K. and Hoffert, E. M., Hypertexture, *Comput. Graph.* (Siggraph '89 Proceedings), **23**(3), 253–262, July 1989, (volume-related texturing via a "ray marching" algorithm).

Potmesil, M. and Hoffert, E. M., The pixel machine: A parallel image computer, *Comput. Graph.* (Sigraph '89 Proceedings), **23**(3), 69–78, July 1989, (architecture of a machine which can ray trace quickly), [parallel].

Priol, T. and Bouatouch, K., Static load balancing for a parallel ray tracing on a MIMD hypercube, *Vis. Comput.*, **5**(1/2), 109–119, March 1989.

Salmon, J. and Goldsmith, J., A hypercube ray-tracer, *Proceedings of the Third Conference on Hypercube Computers and Applications*, 1988.

Scherson, I. D. and Caspary, E., Data structures and the time complexity of ray tracing, *Vis. Comput.*, **3**(4), 201–213, December 1987.

Scherson, I. D. and Caspary, E., Multiprocessing for ray tracing: a hierarchical self-balancing approach, *Vis. Comput.*, **4**(4), 188–196, October 1988.

Schmitt, A., Mueller, H. and Leister, W., Ray tracing algorithms – theory and practice, In *Theoretical Foundations of Computer Graphics and CAD* (ed. R. A. Earnshaw), Springer-Verlag, Berlin, 997–1030, 1988.

Sequin, C. H. and Smyrl, E. K., Parameterized ray tracing, *Comput. Graph.* (Siggraph '89 Proceedings), **23**(3), 307–314, July 1989, (store ray tree data to allow quick material changes).

Shinya, M., Saito, T. and Takahashi, T., Rendering techniques for transparent objects, *Proc. Graph. Interface '89*, 173–182, June 1989.

Sillion, F. and Puech, C., A general two-pass method integrating specular and diffuse reflection, *Comput. Graph.* (Siggraph '89 Proceedings), **23**(3), 335–344, July 1989, [radiosity].

Stettner, A. and Greenberg, D. P., Computer graphics visualization for acoustic simulation, *Comput. Graph.* (Siggraph '89 Proceedings), **23**(3), 195–206, July 1989, (using ray tracing for acoustics), [acoustics, simulation, scientific visualization, monte carlo].

Wallace, J. R., Elmquist, K. A. and Haines, E. A., A ray tracing algorithm for progressive radiosity, *Comput. Graph.* (Siggraph '89 Proceedings), **23**(3), 315–324, July 1989, (calculating form-factors via ray tracing to avoid hemicube problems), [radiosity].

Ward, G. J., Rubinstein, F. M. and Clear, R. D., A ray tracing solution for diffuse interreflection, *Comput. Graph.* (Siggraph '88 Proceedings), **22**(4), 85–92, August 1988, [radiosity].

Williams, N. S., Buxton, B. F. and Buxton, H., Distributed ray tracing using a SIMD processor array, In *Theoretical Foundations of Computer Graphics and CAD*, (ed. R. A. Earnshaw), Springer-Verlag, Berlin, 703–725, 1988.

Woo, A., Shadow determination accelerators for ray tracing, (Master's thesis), University of Toronto, Ontario, 1989.

Yokio, S., Kurashige, K. and Toriwaki, J.-I., Rendering gems with asterism or chatoyancy, *Vis. Comput.* **2**(5), 307–312, 1986.

Yuan, Y., Kunii, T. L., Inamato, N. and Sun, L., Gemstone fire: Adaptive dispersive ray tracing of polyhedrons, *Vis. Comput.*, **4**(5), 259–270, November 1988.

Zeitler, K. D., Algorithms for ray tracing, (Master's thesis), University of Waterloo, Ontario, 1988, [parallelism].

9 A Ray Tracing Glossary

ANDREW S. GLASSNER

acceleration The use of efficiency techniques to speed up the process of generating a ray-traced image.

adaptive sampling Using a quality estimate to control the sampling density of some parameter.

adaptive tree-depth control Each ray ultimately makes some contribution to the color of an eye ray. Higher generation rays generally contribute less. Adaptive tree-depth control is a mechanism which causes the system to stop tracing any ray whose contribution is below some threshold.

algebraic surface A surface defined by the points in space where a given 3-D algebraic equation has constant value (usually 0). Algebraic surfaces are a class of implicit surface.

aliasing When a signal is undersampled, high-frequency components of the original signal can appear as lower frequency components in the sampled version. These high frequencies assume the alias (or false identity) of the low frequencies, because after sampling these very different phenomena cannot be distinguished. Some common computer graphics artifacts due to aliasing are jagged lines, missing objects and jerky motion.

ambient light An imaginary light that is presumed to strike every point on every object with equal color and intensity. It is used to approximate the large-scale effects of diffuse inter-reflections, a phenomenon not usually well modeled by ray tracing programs. This approximation may be left out of the shading model when using a technique that takes into account the diffuse reflection of light between surfaces.

anti-aliasing The act of taking special precautions to limit or eliminate aliasing artifacts. Also used to refer to these precautions, as in 'a new anti-aliasing technique.'

anti-aliasing, analytic Using mathematical techniques to directly find (within the tolerance of machine arithmetic) exact solutions for the information needed to perform anti-aliasing. For example, finding the visible area of a polygon within a

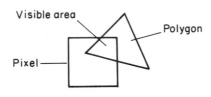

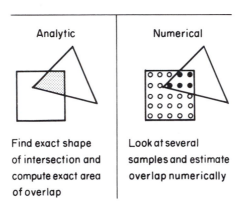

Fig. 1.   Anti-aliasing.

pixel by finding the exact shape of the intersection between the polygon and the pixel, and then calculating its exact area (*Figure 1*).

anti-aliasing, numerical   Using numerical techniques to find estimates for the information needed to perform anti-aliasing. For example, estimating the visible area of a polygon within a pixel by examining many points within the pixel, and calculating the ratio of those hitting the polygon to those missing it (*Figure 1*).

angle of incidence   The acute angle between an incident ray and the surface normal at the point of intersection with a surface (θ_i in   *Figure 2*).

angle of reflection   The acute angle between a reflected ray and the surface normal at the point on the surface from which it was reflected (θ_r in   *Figure 2*).

angle of refraction   The acute angle between a transmitted (refracted) ray and the line colinear with the surface normal at the point on the surface from which it began (θ_t in   *Figure 2*).

aperture   The size of the lens opening through which light passes. The relative aperture is measured as the focal length of the lens divided by the diameter of the opening; this is expressed as an *f*-number: e.g. *f*/8, *f*/11.

backward ray tracing   Following light rays in the direction opposite to that in which they travel. Backward ray tracing is computationally attractive because one may

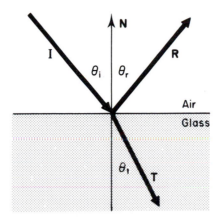

I = Incident ray
R = Reflected ray
T = Transmitted ray
N = Surface normal

Fig. 2.   Reflection and refraction.

direct attention on only those rays that are known to be important for a particular image. This is the most popular mode of ray tracing in use today.

beam tracing   By using a polygonal cone as a primitive imaging element, one may take advantage of the coherence between rays with a common origin. In some situations, beam tracing can provide very accurate estimates of the incident light, useful for high-quality shading and anti-aliasing techniques. Under certain circumstances, the computational savings from using a single plane to represent many rays can outweigh the additional cost per plane.

bidirectional reflectance   A function which relates incoming intensity in a given direction to outgoing intensity in another direction, within a small solid angle.

binary space partition (BSP) tree   A data structure for space subdivision.

bleeding   The effect of diffuse inter-reflections between objects. One object is said to 'bleed' color to another, such as a red carpet 'bleeding' a pink tinge to nearby white walls.

blue noise   A set of samples with a frequency distribution close to that of a Poisson distribution.

bounce light   Synonym for bleeding.

bounding volume   This term (sometimes abbreviated as bound) usually refers to a mathematically simple surface that encloses one or more objects. Bounding volumes are usually designed so that it is less expensive to intersect a ray with the bounding volume than with its contents. Bounding volumes are often arranged in a hierarchy, each level typically enclosing several smaller objects (or bounding volumes). Rays that do not intersect a bounding volume need not examine the objects within; rays that do penetrate a bounding volume typically must consider each enclosed object. Hierarchies of bounding volumes are a popular acceleration technique.

candidate list   A list of objects which have a high probability of intersection with a given ray.

caustic   An optical term referring to light focused by reflection from or refraction through a curved object. For example, when a magnifying glass is used to burn a piece of paper, the intense point of focused light at the paper's surface (and the body of light rays that create it) forms a caustic. Ray tracing algorithms typically have difficulty correctly detecting and handling this phenomenon.

child   A node in a hierarchy which is the direct descendant of another node, called the parent.

chromatic aberration   A lens characteristic that bends rays of different colors at different angles and therefore focuses them on different planes.

circle of confusion   The tiny circle of light formed by a lens as it projects the image of a single point of a subject. The smaller the diameters of all the circles of confusion in an image, the sharper the image will be.

classification   An efficiency technique which assigns a given ray to one of a finite number of classes. Every ray in each of these classes shares some common attributes (direction, frequency, starting point, etc.) within some tolerance. Any pre-computed information for a given class may be used to accelerate processing for each ray assigned to that class.

coherence   When information can be shared across different computations, we say this is a use of coherence. For example, if we save information about one ray to help us process another, our algorithm is making use of ray coherence. If we use information from one frame of an animation to help us create the next frame, we are using frame coherence. Seeking out new forms of coherence and ways to capitalize on them is a central theme in the study of efficient ray tracing.

complete candidate list   A candidate list guaranteed to include the nearest object intersected by a ray (if one exists).

cone tracing   An image synthesis technique that replaces light rays with cones. Rather than sending several independent rays outward from a surface to sample the incident light, a smaller number of circular cones are generated; each has its apex at the same point, but spreads out symmetrically to its axis. In some situations, cone tracing can provide very accurate estimates of the incident light, useful for high-quality shading and anti-aliasing techniques. Under certain circumstances, the computational savings from using a single cone to represent many rays can outweigh the additional cost per cone.

constructive solid geometry (CSG) A modeling technique where primitive objects are combined into a tree using the operators union, subtraction, and difference in order to form more complex shapes.

contrast The difference between the brightest and darkest values in some set of samples.

contribution factor The percentage contribution of a given ray to the eye ray at the top of its ray tree.

convex A region of space with the property that for any two points in the region, the straight line connecting those points is entirely within the region.

convex hull The smallest convex shape (or its polygonal or polyhedral approximation) that contains some set of points or objects.

critical angle That angle for a given pair of media where light is refracted into the plane of the interface. Light arriving with an angle of incidence equal to or greater than the critical angle thus undergoes total internal reflection.

depth of field The area between the nearest and farthest points from the camera that are acceptably sharp in the focused image.

diffraction A deviation from rectilinear propagation arising when a light wave is obstructed by some object with features whose size are on the order of the wavelength of visible light. Diffraction is a difficult phenomenon for ray tracing programs.

diffuse inter-reflections When an object reflects or transmits light diffusely, this scattered light may fall upon another object. Ray tracing algorithms typically have difficulty correctly handling this form of light transport.

diffuse reflection A mode of light transport, in which incident light on an object's surface is absorbed and re-radiated. The radiated light is distributed uniformly from the point of incidence on the same side of the surface as the incident light. The reflected light has a spectrum equal to the product of the spectrum of the incident light and the absorption spectrum of the surface (*Figure 3(a).*)

diffuse transmission A mode of light transport, in which incident light on an object's surface is absorbed and re-radiated. The radiated light is distributed uniformly from the point of incidence on the side of the surface opposite to the side on which the light arrives. The radiated light has a spectrum equal to the product of the spectrum of the incident light and the absorption spectrum of the surface. Since the light passes through the material, the intensity of the radiated light is reduced by a factor related to the distance travelled in the medium (*Figure 3(b).*)

digital signal processing A field of engineering mathematics which studies the relationship between continuous (or analog) signals and their digital counterparts, as well as techniques for analyzing and processing digital signals. Computer graphics techniques often find their theoretical basis (or lack of it) from techniques in this field.

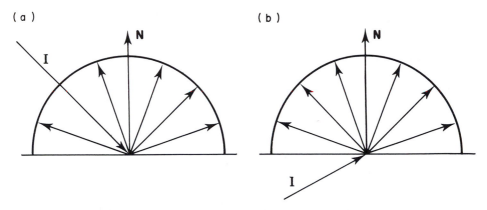

Fig. 3.   (a) Diffuse reflection. (b) Diffuse transmission.

direction cube   An axis-aligned cube with subdivided faces, used for directional queries.

directional data structure   A data structure that helps classify rays based on their direction.

distributed ray tracing   A multidimensional form of stochastic ray tracing.

emittance   The light emitted by a surface.

enclosure   A surface that surrounds another surface.

environment bound   A simple, convex object that surrounds the environment. When a ray strikes the environment bound it will never again enter the environment. It is common to assign the environment bound the color desired for the scene background, or to assign it a texture representing the distant sky.

environment map   A projection of the environment onto a 2-D surface, as seen from some 3-D point of view. Useful as a texture to simulate reflection of far-away objects.

environment   The collection of all objects of interest in a 3-D scene, and the volume of space enclosing them. The environment may or may not include the camera and light sources, depending on the rendering system and the model.

exhaustive testing   The process of testing a ray with every object when seeking the first intersected object. This is a very simple but expensive way to perform ray tracing.

explicit surface   A surface in space given by some set of parameters which directly create the surface as they are swept through their ranges. An explicit description can directly generate all the points on a surface.

extent   The minima and maxima of an object's surface along the three primary spatial directions.

external cost   The average cost of intersecting a ray with a node in a bounding volume hierarchy.

eye ray   A ray beginning at the eyepoint and passing through the screen. This ray occupies the root of the ray tree, and contributes directly to the color of some pixel in the image.

eyepoint   The 3-D position of the viewer's virtual eye.

f-number   A number that equals the focal length of a lens divided by the diameter of the aperture at a given stop. Theoretically, all lenses at the same *f*-number produce images of equal brightness.

film plane   Synonym for focal plane.

focal length   The distance from the lens to the focal plane when the lens is focused on infinity. The longer the focal length, the greater the magnification of the image.

focal plane   The plane or surface on which a focused lens forms a sharp image.

focus   (1) The position at which rays of light from a lens converge to form a sharp image. (2) To adjust the distance between lens and image to make the image as sharp as possible.

forward ray tracing   Following light rays in the same direction in which they travel. Forward ray tracing thus starts with light rays at the light source and follows them until they become sufficiently weak or are guaranteed to have no further effect on the image. Forward ray tracing is computationally unattractive because it expends virtually all of one's resources on rays that will be unimportant for the particular image being generated.

fractal   A set which is self-similar under magnification.

frame buffer   A two-dimensional memory usually used for storing images. Each entry in the memory is large enough to hold a color value for a single pixel.

frequency aliasing   An aliasing effect due to undersampling of the visible light spectrum. Because light is insufficiently sampled as it passes through and reflects off of surfaces, the final color in the image is incorrect. This is a common problem in systems that only trace rays with wavelengths corresponding to the display device primaries (typically hues of red, green, and blue).

frequency   The speed of a regular oscillation in cycles per second.

Fresnel reflection law   The reflectance of a perfectly smooth surface in terms of the index of refraction, the extinction coefficient, the wavelength of the incident light, and the angle of incidence.

frustum   A frustum is a pyramid minus its top. Typically a frustum is used as a viewing volume in computer graphics: the viewing plane is the top of the frustum; the eye is at the apex (*Figure 4*).

gaze direction   The direction in which the viewer of a virtual environment is looking. Usually the viewing plane is perpendicular to and centered about this vector.

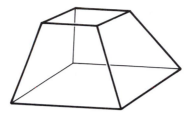

Fig. 4.   A frustum.

generalized cylinder   The surface generated when a (possibly changing) 2-D contour is swept along a 3-D trajectory.

generalized ray   The primitive imaging element used in some image synthesis algorithms structurally similar to ray tracing. A generalized ray is usually more geometrically sophisticated than a ray. Beams and cones are examples of generalized rays.

generation   The level in the ray tree for a given ray. The eye ray is a zero-generation ray; the first reflected ray is first generation, and so on.

geometrical optics   A branch of optics that studies light with the assumption that all objects in the environment are much larger than the wavelengths of visible light; this allows one to ignore diffraction effects. Ray tracing is a standard tool in this field.

hierarchy   A system of organizing a multitude of elements into a tree or directed acyclic graph. The hierarchy entry associated with a particular element is called a node. If two nodes are in a hierarchy such that one is above the other, the higher one is called the parent; the lower is called the child. Nodes with no children are called leaves. Nodes with no parents are called roots.

highlight   That portion of radiated light from a surface that was propagated by specular reflection and transmission.

hypercube   A multi-dimensional cube. In n-space it has $2n$ faces and 2^n vertices.

hyperfocal distance   The distance to the nearest plane of the depth of field (the nearest object in focus) when the lens is focused on infinity. Also the distance to the plane of sharpest focus when infinity is at the farthest plane of the depth of field. Focusing on the hyperfocal distance extends the depth of field from half the hyperfocal distance to infinity.

illumination   The complete description of all light striking a particular point on a particular surface.

illumination model   Synonym for shading model.

illumination ray   A hypothetical ray that carries light from a light source to an object. An illumination ray is pointed in the direction opposite to its associated shadow ray.

image plane   The plane or surface on which a focused lens forms a sharp image.

implicit surface   A surface defined by those points that satisfy $f(x, y, z) = c$ for some constant c. If f happens to be an algebraic function, then this is an algebraic surface. Implicit surfaces provide for easy inside/outside testing.

index of refraction   The ratio of the angle of incidence to the angle of refraction for light entering a given medium from a vacuum.

inside/outside function   An equation which accepts as arguments a 3-D point and an object of interest, and produces a scalar value. If the scalar is less than 0, the point is within the object; if the scalar is greater than 0, the point is outside. The surface itself is composed of all points that evaluate to 0. The analysis of some classes of objects may allow the creation of specialized inside/outside functions that are particularly efficient. These functions may even be expressed in algorithmic form (e.g. polygon inside/outside testing).

inside/outside test   The act of evaluating the inside/outside function for a given point.

interface   The suface defined by the meeting of two different media. If the media have different indices of refraction then light will bend as it passes through the interface.

internal cost   The average cost of intersecting a ray with the contents of a bounding volume, given that the ray is known to have hit that volume.

intersection   In ray tracing algorithms, this term usually refers to a point that is both on a surface and on a particular ray.

inverse mapping   Given a point on a surface, this is the task of finding the parameters of the explicit representation of the surface that generate that point.

inverse-square law   A law of physics stating that the intensity of illumination is inversely proportional to the square of the distance between light and subject.

jaggy   A colloquial term for the stairstep appearance of a tilted edge that has not been correctly anti-aliased.

jittering   A mechanism for efficiently generating a series of samples that approximate a Poisson distribution. Jittered samples may be used for numerical anti-aliasing.

Jordan Curve Theorem   The Jordan Curve Theorem states that a simple closed curve partitions the plane into two disjoint regions, a bounded interior and an unbounded exterior, which are separated by the curve. This theorem may be used to implement an efficient polygon inside/outside test.

Lambert's law   Lambert's law is the fundamental description of diffuse light transport. It states that diffusely reflected and transmitted light is scattered in all radiated directions with equal intensity, and that this intensity is proportional to the intensity of the incident light, the reflectance of the surface, and the cosine of the angle between the incident light and the surface normal.

lazy evaluation   A programming technique which may be used to help manage potentially large or expensive data structures. The program assumes such structures exist, but only calculates necessary parts on demand. These structures may be used as part of a ray tracing acceleration technique.

leaf   A node in a hierarchy that has no descendent (child) nodes.

light buffer   A shadow-testing acceleration scheme where each point light source is surrounded by a direction cube, which contains a list of the objects visible through each cell. The direction of an illumination ray is first looked up in the light buffer associated with that light source as a means of fast shadow testing.

light transport   A mechanism for the transfer of light through a medium or from one surface to another.

lighting model   Synonym for shading model.

metamer   One of an infinite number of spectra that give rise to the same perceived color.

microfacet   A single planar facet of a rough surface, with an average orientation given by the microfacet distribution equation.

monochromatic light   Light that contains photons of only a single frequency.

motion blur   The blurry path left on a time-averaged image by a fast-moving object. Animation that includes correct motion blur often looks more fluid and smooth than the same animation without motion blur.

node   An entry in a hierarchy.

normal   Shorthand for surface normal.

normalization   The process of scaling a vector so that it has length 1.0. A vector $\mathbf{V}$ may be normalized into $\mathbf{V}'$ by $\mathbf{V}' = \mathbf{V}/|\mathbf{V}| = \mathbf{V}/\sqrt{(\mathbf{V} \cdot \mathbf{V})}$.

Nyquist limit   The highest frequency in a signal that may be reliably sampled. The theoretical limit is at half the sampling rate.

object buffer   A ray tracing acceleration technique where the image is first rendered using traditional techniques into a frame buffer. Rather than record colors, each entry in the buffer is assigned the object number of the nearest intersected object. For each pixel, this object is then known to be the first object intersected by the ray passing through the center of the pixel.

octree   A 3-dimensional data structure which subdivides space into axis-aligned boxes of varying size. The result is a tree with 8 branches at each node. The contents of the boxes vary between applications of the data structure. When used to accelerate ray tracing, each node usually contains a list of objects within its box.

When a ray enters a box corresponding to a leaf node it attempts to intersect each object; if none are hit the ray proceeds to the next leaf node on its path.

optics A branch of physics that studies light.

parallel processing Using several computers simultaneously to solve a problem more quickly than with one. Ray tracing is very amenable to parallel processing since each ray may be treated essentially independently. Techniques that use ray coherence are more difficult to frame in a parallel-processing context.

parameterization Finding a set of equations that assign unique coordinates (or parameters) to each point on a surface. These coordinates and equations are typically used for intersection calculations or texture mapping.

parent A node in a hierarchy that has one or more (child) nodes beneath it.

patch A bounded piece of surface. Usually patches have a small number of distinguishable sides, and may be characterized by the degree of the equation with which they are described (linear, quadric, cubic, etc.). Typically patches are parameterized in two coordinates called u and v. A popular form of patch is cubic along both coordinates; it is called bicubic. When ray tracing, patches are often subdivided until they are locally flat.

path tracing Following the path of a single photon backwards from the eye, rather than branching out several rays at each intersection.

penumbra The soft edge on a shadow, caused by a light source with finite shape (as opposed to a point light source).

Phong illumination An illumination model. The original Phong model has been extended so that it now handles diffuse reflection, diffuse transmission, specular reflection, and specular transmission.

photon An imaginary particle of light. A photon's energy is related to its speed of vibration, which is also related to the color with which it is perceived within the eye.

pinhole camera A simple camera model consisting of a box with a piece of film on the inside of one wall, and a pinhole in the center of the opposite wall.

pinhole The tiny opening in the front of a pinhole camera.

pixel The smallest addressable region in a frame buffer.

Poisson disk distribution A frequency distribution that has a spike at the origin, and a flat sea of noise beyond the Nyquist limit. In the spatial domain, this corresponds to a random set of points, with the constraint that no two points are closer than a fixed distance.

polygon A region of a plane bounded by a set of linear edges. In practice, any shape you can cut out of a piece of stiff cardboard. A polygon may include holes.

polyhedron A 3-D structure constructed of polygons.

pop   When a moving object is detected in some frames but not in others, it will blink on and off over time. This phenomenon is also called 'popping.'

primitive object   In ray tracing techniques, this is any object that can be intersected directly with a ray.

prism   The shape formed by extruding some 2-D contour along a linear path not in the plane of the contour.

procedural texture   A function that accepts as input a ray/object intersection point or texture coordinates, and produces texture values in response. The function may simply look the texture value in a table index by the coordinates, or it may involve complex calculation.

propagated light   Light that arrives at a surface and then is subsequently sent outward again by some mechanism.

quadric surface   The set of points that satisfy a general second-degree equation in 3 variables. Important special cases include the sphere, ellipsoid, linear cone, elliptic paraboloid (blunt cone), and hyperbolic paraboloid (saddle).

quartic surface   The set of points that satisfy a general fourth-degree equation in 3 variables. The torus is the most common quartic.

radiated light   The sum total of light leaving a point on a surface, also called the point's radiosity.

radiosity   A technique for balancing the distribution of light energy in an environment. One of radiosity's main strengths is the accurate modeling of diffuse inter-reflections between objects. Once the balancing has been performed, image generation from a particular viewpoint only requires hidden surface removal. Radiosity has been extended to include specular reflections, and has been merged with ray tracing algorithms.

ray   An infinite line bounded at one end. We describe a ray with an origin (a point in space) and a direction (a 3-D vector).

ray tracing   An image synthesis technique using geometrical optics and rays to evaluate recursive shading and visibility.

ray tree   The complete description of all rays traced to determine the color of a particular eye ray.

ray—object intersection.   The act of finding any or all points that simultaneously lie on a particular ray and a particular object.

recursion   See recursion.

recursive shading   A technique for estimating the parameters in a shading model, where the incident light at a surface is determined by generating new rays to detect the sources of that light.

reflected ray   A ray generated at a surface to aid in shading calculations. A reflected ray samples the incident light that is then reflected in the direction of interest.

reflection   A general term for light that strikes a surface and then leaves again from the same side.

rendering equation   A formal statement of light balancing in an environment. Most image synthesis algorithms may be viewed as solutions to an equation written as an approximation of the rendering equation.

root   (**1**) A value or set of values that satisfy a particular equation; in ray tracing, a root typically lies on a surface of interest. (**2**) The node in a hierarchy that has no parent node.

root-finding   Any procedure that seeks to find the roots of an equation.

root-polishing   Improving an estimated root by using a high-precision iterative technique, starting with the original estimate.

sampling density   The quantity of samples used to find the average value of a distribution. Typically a higher sampling density yields a more accurate estimate, but at higher cost.

shading model   The particular equation used when performing shading.

shading   The general technique of determining the incident and radiated light at a surface. In ray tracing, usually three steps are involved: finding the incident light, evaluating the interaction of this light and the surface, and determining the light finally radiated from the surface into a given direction.

shadow ray   A ray sent from a surface towards a light source to determine if the surface is directly illuminated by the light. The same ray in the opposite direction carries light from the light source; this is called the illumination ray.

shadow   That region of space or an object's surface which is not directly illuminated by a given light source.

slab   A region of space bounced by two parallel planes. For a given plane normal, a slab may be described by only two numbers. Collections of slabs can approach the convex hull, and make a computationally attractive bounding volume.

Snell's law   One of the fundamental laws of refraction; it states that $n_i \sin \theta_i = n_t \sin \theta_t$, where n_i and n_t are the indices of refraction for the incident and transmitted media, and θ_i and θ_t are the angles of incidence and refraction with respect to the surface normal at the point of intersection.

solid texture   A 3-D texture function. Useful for modeling objects that are to appear 'carved' out of some material, such as wood or stone.

space subdivision   A data structure that considers an environment to be a collection of disjoint regions of space. Space subdivision structures are used in ray tracing as an acceleration strategy. Popular variations include uniform subdivision and adaptive subdivision.

spectrum   The forms of radiant electromagnetic energy arranged by size from thousand millionths of a millimeter (gamma rays) to several kilometers (radio waves). The visible spectrum is the part that the human eye sees as light: wavelengths of about 380 to 730 nanometers produce the sensation of the colors violet, indigo, blue, green, yellow, orange, and red.

specular reflection   A mode of light transport, in which incident light on an object's surface is reflected off the outer layers of the surface. The directional distribution of the reflected light is dependent on the surface roughness, but occurs on the same side of the surface that the light hit. The reflected light has a spectrum dependent on the spectrum of the incident light, the surface color, and the angle of incidence (*Figure 5(a)*).

specular transmission   A mode of light transport, in which incident light on an object's surface is transmitted through the surface. The directional distribution of the transmitted light is dependent on the surface roughness and thickness, but occurs on the opposite side of the surface that the light hit. The transmitted light has a spectrum dependent on the spectrum of the incident light, the surface color, the surface thickness, and the angle of incidence (*Figure 5(b)*.)

specularity   A measure of a surface's 'shinyness.' High specularity means 'very shiny.'

sphere   The surface formed by the collection of all points at the same distance from a given point.

steradian   A unit of measure for solid angles. The unit sphere measures 4π steradians.

stochastic ray tracing   An image-synthesis technique which uses pseudo-random, discrete sampling to estimate continuous phenomena. With the correct distribution

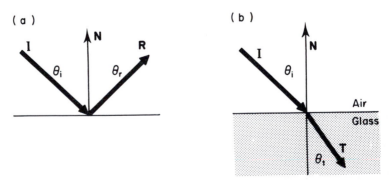

Fig. 5. (a)   Specular   reflection: $\theta_i = \theta_r$.   (b)   Specular   transmission: $\eta_i \sin(\theta_i) = \eta_t \sin(\theta_t)$

of samples, aliasing errors will appear in the image as uncorrelated noise, instead of the regular features seen in images with uniform sampling. The human visual system is much more forgiving of this noise, so the resulting image looks better than an equivalent image generated with uniform sampling. Stochastic ray tracing provides a single, elegant algorithm for alleviating many sampling problems.

strobing When viewing a piece of animation that has not been motion blurred, fast-moving objects may appear to jump, or have two different images appear superimposed as a double image. These effects are due to discrepancies between where the brain expects the object to appear and where the eye perceives it, and are known as strobing.

subdivision The act of reducing a complex structure into several smaller structures, each of which is usually simpler in some relevant way.

supersampling The process of taking additional samples of a signal usually under the control of some quality-estimation function.

surface normal A vector (usually of unit length) perpendicular to some point on a surface. The normal usually points outward from the surface. For rough surfaces, the normal may be defined to point in the average perpendicular direction.

surface of revolution The surface formed by taking a 2-D contour and sweeping it around a given axis. Examples include a cylinder, a vase, and anything produced on a lathe.

temporal aliasing The phenomena that result when motion blur is not accounted for in an image. Typical examples are popping edges, strobing, and doubled-up images of fast-moving objects.

texel The fundamental unit of texture space.

texture map A stored table of texture.

texture mapping The act of applying detail to a surface without explicitly modeling it as part of the surface geometry. Typically one assigns some parameterization to a surface, and uses the parameters at a particular point to access a texture map (or procedural texture). Values retrieved from the texture may determine or modify any surface characteristic, including color, reflectivity, transparency, or even surface normal.

torus A 3-D shape generated by revolving a circle in the xz plane around the z-axis. Intuitively, a ring doughnut.

total internal reflection (TIR) When light passes from a dense medium into a sparser medium, its angle of incidence must be considered. If the angle of incidence is less than the critical angle (whose value is a function of the two media), the light will pass through into the sparser medium, refracted into a direction farther away from the normal than the incident ray. If the incident angle is greater than the critical angle, the light undergoes total internal reflection: it is reflected off of the interface back into the denser medium (*Figure 6*).

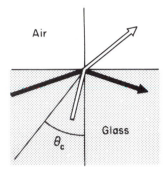

Air

Glass

θ_c

Fig. 6.   Total internal reflection. Light rays arriving at greater than the critical angle are bounced back into the denser medium.

transmission   A general term for light that strikes a surface and then leaves again from the opposite side.

transmitted ray   A ray generated at a surface to aid in shading calculations. A transmitted ray samples the incident light that is transmitted by the surface in the direction of interest.

tree depth   The maximum number of generations in a ray tree.

tree   The form of hierarchy typically used in ray tracing acceleration schemes. Each node in a tree has only a single parent. A tree typically has only a single root.

uniform sampling   A distribution of samples for numerically estimating some signal, where all samples are equally spaced in all dimensions.

vectorization   The process of restructuring an algorithm to run efficiently on a vector computer.

viewing plane   The virtual focus plane in the computer graphics analogy of a pinhole camera.

voxel   An axis-aligned box; typically an element in a space subdivision structure.

wave optics   A physical model which assumes a wave model of light; it includes geometrical optics as an important limiting case. This model has not proven popular in image synthesis due to its computational cost.

wavelength   The distance travelled by a photon during the time it takes to complete a single oscillation.

white noise   A set of samples with a flat frequency distribution.

winding number   The number of times the boundary of a polygon goes around a particular point. This value may be used to implement an efficient polygon inside/outside test.

world bound   Synonym for environment bound.

world map   Synonym for environment map.

ACKNOWLEDGMENT

Thanks are due to Jim Arvo, Eric Haines, and Doug Turner.

Index